SPANISH STILL LIFE

SPANISH STILL LIFE

IN THE GOLDEN AGE

1600–1650

by

WILLIAM B. JORDAN

with assistance from
and an essay by

SARAH SCHROTH

KIMBELL ART MUSEUM
Fort Worth
1985

This catalogue is published on the occasion of an exhibition of Spanish still-life painting shown at the Kimbell Art Museum, Fort Worth, May 11–August 4, 1985, and at The Toledo Museum of Art, Toledo, Ohio, September 8–November 3, 1985.

Spanish Still Life in the Golden Age: 1600–1650 is an exhibition organized by the Kimbell Art Museum, Fort Worth, in association with The Toledo Museum of Art. It is supported by a federal indemnity from the Federal Council on the Arts and Humanities.

Copyright 1985 by the Kimbell Art Museum. All rights reserved.
Library of Congress Catalogue Card Number: 85–50356

LIBRARY OF CONGRESS CATALOGING IN PUBLICATION DATA

Jordan, William B., 1940–
    Spanish still life in the golden age, 1600–1650.

    "This catalogue is published on the occasion of an exhibition...shown at the Kimbell Art Museum, Fort Worth, May 11–August 4, 1985, and at the Toledo Museum of Art, Toledo, Ohio, September 8–November 3, 1985"–
T.p. verso.
    Bibliography: p.
    Includes index.
    1. Still-life painting, Spanish–Exhibitions.
2. Still-life painting–17th century–Spain–Exhibitions.
I. Schroth, Sarah. II. Kimbell Art Museum. III. Toledo Museum of Art. IV. Title.

ND1393.S73J67 1985 758'.4'094607401645315 85–50356
ISBN 0-912804-19-X
ISBN 0-912804-20-3 (pbk.)

Catalogue produced by Perpetua Press, Los Angeles:
Edited by Letitia O'Connor, with Aleida Rodríguez
Designed by Dana Levy
Production art by Marybeth Mackenzie and Leslie Carlson
Typeset in Bembo by Continental Typographics, Chatsworth, CA
Printed by Nissha Printing Company, Kyoto

Printed in Japan

Cover illustration: Juan van der Hamen y León, 1596–1631
Still Life with Sweets and Pottery (detail), 1627
National Gallery of Art, Washington, D.C.
Plate No 17

Frontispiece: Diego Velázquez, 1599–1660
Christ in the House of Martha and Mary (detail)
The National Gallery of London
Plate 7

ISBN: 0–912804–19–X (Cloth) ISBN: 0–912804–20–3 (Paper)

CONTENTS

LENDERS TO THE EXHIBITION

AUSTRIA   Rohrau: Schloss Rohrau, Graf Harrach'sche Familiensammlung (Plates 37, 38)
Vienna: Kunsthistorisches Museum, Gemäldegalerie (Plate 40)

FINLAND   Mänttä: The Gösta Serlachius Fine Arts Foundation (Plate 43)

FRANCE   Paris: Musée du Louvre (Plate 28)
Strasbourg: Musée des Beaux-Arts (Plate 29)

GREAT BRITAIN   London: H. M. Queen Elizabeth II (Plate 23)
London: The National Gallery (Plate 7)
London: The Wellington Museum (Apsley House) (Plate 8)

THE NETHERLANDS   Amsterdam: The Rijksmuseum (Plate 45)

NORWAY   Bergen: The Hilmar Reksten Foundation (Plate 9)

PORTUGAL   Lisbon: Museu Nacional d'Arte Antiga (Plate 42)

SPAIN   Barcelona: Museo de Arte de Cataluña (Plate 44)
Barcelona: Private collection (Plate 31)
Granada: Museo de Bellas Artes (Plates 5, 12)
Madrid: José Luis Várez Fisa Collection (Plates 2, 10)
Madrid: Bank of Spain Collection (Plate 19)
Madrid: Museo del Prado (Plates 22, 25, 26, 27)
Madrid: Private collections (Plates 1, 11, 18)
Segovia: Lafora Collection (Plate 30)
Zaragoza: Museo de Zaragoza (Plate 41)
Spain: Plácido Arango Collection (Plates 15, 32)
Spain: Private collection (Plate 39)

THE UNITED STATES OF AMERICA   Atlanta: High Museum of Art (Plate 6)
Chicago: The Art Institute of Chicago (Plates 4, 46)
Cleveland: Cleveland Museum of Art (Plate 14)
Houston: The Museum of Fine Arts (Plate 16)
New Haven: Yale University Art Gallery (Plate 36)
New York: Lila and Herman Shickman Collection (Plate 21)
San Diego: San Diego Museum of Art (Plate 3)
Washington, D. C.: Dumbarton Oaks (Plates 34, 35)
Washington, D. C.: National Gallery of Art (Plate 17)
Williamstown: Williams College Museum of Art (Plate 20)

FOREWORD

Spanish Still Life in the Golden Age: 1600–1650 is the first international exhibition on the subject held in the United States. Its inauguration coincides with the fiftieth anniversary of the opening in Madrid of the historic exhibition *Floreros y bodegones en la pintura española,* which surveyed the entire history of the still life in Spain from the sixteenth century to the nineteenth century. That exhibition, which presented to the European public for the first time the little-known still-life painters of Spain, contributed to scholarly interest throughout the continent in the various national schools of still-life painting. The presentation in Paris in 1952 of the great anthological exhibition *La nature morte de l'antiquité à nos jours* cemented the fascination of the twentieth-century public with this neglected genre that displays such affinities with the modern aesthetic. In the years since, a series of important exhibitions and books has treated the still-life painters of Holland, Flanders, France and Italy, yet no book has yet appeared in the English language on the still life in Spain.

In the autumn of 1983, the Museo del Prado mounted an ambitious exhibition of Spanish still lifes covering a period of more than two centuries (1600–1828), concentrating primarily on works from Spanish collections. The current exhibition complements the recent one in Madrid in two significant ways: it focuses attention on the creative issues and stylistic cohesion of the generative phase of the still life and, by enlarging its source of loans to include collections throughout Europe and North America, it represents a select group of artists by their best-known works. In many cases remarkable depth is achieved. For example, all five of the generally accepted still lifes by Juan Sánchez Cotán are shown together for the first time. Eleven paintings by Juan van der Hamen y León, by far the most prolific of the artists, establish the surpassing importance of this painter. The enigmatic Juan Fernández "El Labrador" is represented by three certain works. Antonio de Pereda, one of the finest still-life painters of the seventeenth century, by whom not a single authentic still life has ever been shown in the United States, is represented by four of his best works. A significant advance is made in understanding the art of Juan de Zurbarán, son of the great Sevillian master. A rare signed work from a Finnish collection, never before recognized, is exhibited together with paintings from Barcelona and Chicago which may now be attributed to this painter. All considered, the bringing together of these forty-six paintings accomplishes what an international exhibition does best. In seeking to clarify our understanding of all fifteen painters, it gives the most detailed view to date of the quality and achievement of Spanish still-life painters in the early seventeenth century.

As the first study of the Spanish still life in English, the catalogue of the exhibition fills a large gap in the bibliography. The catalogue deals with the question of the origins of still-life painting in Spain, its various types and their place in seventeenth-century collections, the meaning or symbolic content of some still lifes, the place of the still life in contemporary theoretical literature as well as in the actual practice of most painters, and the history of scholarship in the field. The catalogue entries are interspersed with extensive monographic essays on each painter, which should ensure that the life and usefulness of the book will transcend the exhibition and that it will remain a valuable reference work.

The Board of Directors of the Kimbell Art Foundation, which owns and operates the Kimbell Art Museum, owes a special debt of gratitude to Dr. William B. Jordan, Deputy Director, for organizing the exhibition and preparing the exemplary catalogue. Without his scholarship and connoisseurship, it would not have been possible to mount this exhibition. The Board is no less grateful to the Toledo Museum of Art and its director, Roger Mandle, for agreeing to share the exhibition and thus ensure the wider appreciation of the subject in this country. A final word of thanks is owed to the scholars and other individuals who have contributed in various ways to the success of the undertaking. Of these, we particularly wish to acknowledge the help and assistance of Dr. Alfonso E. Pérez Sánchez, Director of the Museo del Prado, who has supported the project from its inception and provided invaluable help and advice on a wide range of scholarly and practical matters. We also deeply appreciate the assistance of the curators and owners of the works included in the selection. Their cooperation in lending has been unusually generous in the case of this exhibition. The entire thrust of the project is predicated on being able to juxtapose, often for the first time ever, actual paintings that are related to one another. In that sense, thanks to the lenders, the exhibition should accomplish what no book can ever do.

EDMUND P. PILLSBURY
Director, Kimbell Art Museum

AUTHOR'S PREFACE

On May 11, 1935, the Sociedad Española de Amigos del Arte inaugurated in Madrid the monumental exhibition *Floreros y bodegones en la pintura española,* a pioneering undertaking which introduced a twentieth-century museum audience to the complete range of still-life painting in Spain from the early seventeenth to the nineteenth century. Organized by Julio Cavestany, Marquis of Moret, the exhibition contained 179 paintings from public and private collections. In keeping with a long-standing tradition of the Sociedad de Amigos del Arte, the exhibition was commemorated by the publication of a deluxe, scholarly catalogue, which, due to the intervention of the Spanish Civil War, did not appear until 1940. This extraordinary volume, with its dense compendium of biographies and documentary appendices, has remained to this day one of the most indispensable scholarly tools in the bibliography of Spanish art. It ignited the curiosity of scholars and lovers of art throughout the world and stimulated a long series of monographic investigations. Today, many of the paintings exhibited in Madrid in 1935 are no longer in Spanish collections. Others, unknown then, have since been discovered, adding unexpected dimensions to our knowledge and understanding of the field.

In November 1983, an exhibition of similar scope and magnitude, *Pintura de bodegones y floreros de 1600 a Goya,* was organized for the Museo del Prado by its director, Dr. Alfonso E. Pérez Sánchez. Its 190 paintings, drawn mostly from Spanish collections, included many unpublished works, and its catalogue, written with exemplary style, incorporated the published research since Cavestany and brought valuable insights into the personalities and styles of individual painters, as well as the overall development of still-life painting in Spain. This eminently readable book, like Cavestany's, will not be supplanted in its usefulness and importance.

The present exhibition, undertaken as a complement to those, focuses more sharply on the early years of still-life painting in Spain—from its origins just prior to 1600 to the generation that fully elaborated it before 1650. This phase in the history of the still life was intimately related to the origins and development of naturalism in Spain, and the exhibition explores the contributions of fifteen artists to that development. Left out of consideration here is the rich development of the still life in the second half of the seventeenth century, including the development of the specialty of flower painting, which is a complex problem that requires a special study of its own.

The personal origin of this study dates back more than twenty years to my graduate work at the Institute of Fine Arts, New York University. First among the debts that I must acknowledge is the gratitude I feel to the man who awakened in me an interest in this subject, Dr. José López-Rey, whose guidance and intellectual generosity will not be forgotten, and whose brief but important essay on the subject (Newark 1964) has had a lasting impact.

Over the years, I have profitted from the exchange of ideas on the Spanish still life with Alfonso Pérez Sánchez, and this exhibition could not have taken place without his support and generous assistance. Most importantly, as director of the Museo del Prado, he supported and obtained the approval of his museum's *Patronato* for the inclusion here of four outstanding paintings from the museum's collection, without which the exhibition would have been deficient. Members of his staff—Dr. Manuela B. Mena Marqués, deputy director, and curators Dr. Juan J. Luna and Rocío Arnaez—have also rendered valuable assistance in countless ways over a period of many years.

Research institutions in Spain have always opened their doors to foreign scholars, and individuals in those institutions have gone out of their way to be of assistance in gathering information. I would particularly like to thank Professor Diego Angulo Iñiguez, Director Emeritus, and Dr. Elisa Bermejo, Director, of the Instituto Diego Velázquez in Madrid; and Dr. José Gudiol, Director Emeritus, and Dr. Santiago Alcolea Blanch, Director, of the Instituto Amatller de Arte Hispánico in Barcelona. Monserrat Blanch de Alcolea of the Archivo Mas in Barcelona has also provided invaluable aid in furnishing many of the photographs that are reproduced in this catalogue. Other Spanish scholars have also been particularly helpful in solving specific research problems. Among these, I wish to acknowledge my appreciation of Dr. Enrique Valdivieso and Dr. J. M. Serrera of the Universidad de Sevilla.

In connection with specific loans from Spain, I would like to express my gratitude to officials of the other lending institutions: Francisco González de la Oliva, Director of the Museo de Bellas Artes, Granada; Miguel Beltrán, Director of the Museo de Zaragoza; Dr. Juan Ainaud de Lasarte, Director, and Carmen Farré, Curator, Museo de Arte de Cataluña; Ramón Andrada Pfeiffer, Consejero Delegado Gerente, and Paloma Acuña, the Patrimonio Nacional; Mariano Rubio, Gobernador, Banco de España. The numerous private collectors in Spain who have lent to the exhibition or who, over the course of the past two decades, have permitted me the privilege of studying the still lifes in their collections have made possible the most important part of this study, the direct assessment of the works of art upon which it is based.

Often a scholar owes much to the assistance of picture dealers who are able to direct him to works they have sold or of whose existence they are aware in private collections. In this regard, I wish to acknowledge the contributions in Madrid of Richard de Willermin, Francisco Piñanes de Tena, Manuel González and Edmund Peel. In Barcelona, the same aid was provided by Xavier Vila and José I. Saldaña Suanzes. In New York, I was assisted by Clyde Newhouse, Stanley Moss, Ian Kennedy and Dr. Otto Naumann.

In the United Kingdom, I owe a debt of thanks to Sir Roy Strong, Director of the Victoria and Albert Museum, and to S. S. Jervis, Deputy Keeper at Apsley House, for their generous support with the loan of Velázquez's TWO YOUNG MEN AT TABLE. At the National Gallery, Sir Michael Levey, Director, and Michael Helston, Curator, are responsible for graciously approving and obtaining the permission of the trustees for the loan of Velázquez's CHRIST IN THE HOUSE OF MARTHA AND MARY. Sir Oliver Millar, Keeper of the Queen's Pictures, facilitated the loan of Her Majesty's STILL LIFE WITH QUINCES AND ACORNS by El Labrador. Over the years, my research in England has also been aided by the generous favors from Sir Ellis Waterhouse, Enriqueta Harris Frankfort, Eric Young and Peter Cherry. I express my thanks to each of them.

In France, I wish to thank Hubert Landais, Director of the Museums of France, and Pierre Rosenberg, Chief Curator of Paintings at the Louvre, for their support. From the staff of the Louvre, I am also indebted to Jeannine Baticle and Claudie Ressort for their many kindnesses over the years. Gilberte Martin-Méry, Chief Curator of the Musée des Beaux-Arts, Bordeaux, also provided needed assistance with research on paintings in French collections.

For their help with important loans from the rest of Europe, I wish to acknowledge the contributions of the following individuals: Dr. Wolfgang Prohaska, Curator of the Kunsthistorisches Museum, Vienna; Countess Stephanie Harrach and Dr. Robert Keyszelitz of the Graf Harrach'sche Familiensammlung; Maritta Pitkanen, Director of The Gösta Serlachius Museum of Fine Arts, Mänttä, Finland; Grace Reksten, Trustee of The Hilmar Reksten Foundation, Bergen, Norway; Maria Alice Beaumont, Director of the Museu d'Arte Antiga, Lisbon; Dr. S. H. Levie, Director General of the Rijksmuseum, Amsterdam.

In Italy, valuable assistance was provided by Dr. Pierluigi Leone de Castris, Museo Nazionale di Capodimonte, and Pietro Lorenzelli, Bergamo.

United States collections are particularly rich in important examples of Spanish still-life painting. The following individuals and institutions have joined us in this project, for which we are especially appreciative: Dr. Gudmund Vigtel, Director, the High Museum of Art, Atlanta; James N. Wood, Director, Dr. Richard Brettell, Curator of European Painting and Sculpture, and Susan Wise, Associate Curator, The Art Institute of Chicago; Dr. Evan Turner, Director, and Ann Tzeutschler Lurie, Curator of Paintings, the Cleveland Museum of Art; Dr. Peter Marzio, Director, and David Warren, Associate Director, The Museum of Fine Arts, Houston; Alan Shestack, Director, Yale University Art Gallery; Lila and Herman Shickman, New York; Dr. Steven L. Brezzo, Director, and Martin E. Petersen, Curator, the San Diego Museum of Art; Dr. Giles Constable, Director, Dumbarton Oaks, Washington, D. C.; J. Carter Brown, Director, and Dr. Sydney J. Freedberg, Chief Curator, the National Gallery of Art, Washington, D. C.; Charles Parkhurst, Co-Director, Williams College Museum of Art.

A number of scholars and friends in the United States have assisted with specific problems and have, thus, contributed in some way to this catalogue. I wish to thank Dr. Richard Kagan, The Johns Hopkins University; Dr. Marcus Burke, State University of New York—Purchase; Dr. George Kubler, Yale University; Dr. Duncan Kinkead; Dr. Priscilla E. Muller, Curator, The Hispanic Society of America; Irene Martín, Assistant Chief Curator, Dallas Museum of Art, Dallas; Dr. John Spike, New York; Dr. Barry Wind, The University of Wisconsin—Milwaukee; William Hutton, Senior Curator, the Toledo Museum of Art; Dodge Thompson, Chief of Exhibitions, the National Gallery of Art; Cathy Stover, former Archivist of the Pennsylvania Academy of Fine Arts. Most especially, I wish to thank my good friend and fellow hispanist, Dr. Jonathan Brown, of the Institute of Fine Arts, New York University, for reading my manuscript and responding with helpful comments and criticisms which have contributed beyond measure to the improvement of my text.

Throughout the process of planning the exhibition and producing the catalogue, I was encouraged by the support of Roger Mandle, Director of the Toledo Museum of Art, our collaborator on this exhibition. The coordination of loans from Spain and the innumerable tasks related to that were ably handled by Marta Medina of Madrid, whose experience and skilled assistance were decisive in the realization of the project. I wish to express my appreciation of her excellent work. The designing, editing and production of this catalogue were carried out with characteristic professionalism and style by Dana Levy and Letitia Burns O'Connor of Perpetua Press in Los Angeles. It has been a great pleasure to work with them and to see the handsome product of their labors.

To my colleagues at the Kimbell Art Museum, I wish to express my thanks for their enthusiastic and able support in every phase of the research and realization of the exhibition and the catalogue. Dr. Edmund Pillsbury, in his commitment to the project, has allowed me the opportunity to focus my energies on a subject that has concerned me for many years. Other staff members, whose contributions are too numerous to specify, include: Karen King, Curatorial Secretary; Jeannette Downing, Librarian, and Chia-Chun Shih, Assistant Cataloguer; Margaret Booher, Registrar; Peggy Buchanan, Assistant Registrar; Wendy Gottlieb, Public Relations Coordinator; Adrian Martinez, Exhibition Designer; and John Denman, Photographer.

Finally, I wish to thank my collaborator on the exhibition, Sarah Schroth, Kimbell Art Museum Curatorial Fellow and a Ph.D. candidate at the Institute of Fine Arts, New York University. She provided invaluable assistance in many ways, but particularly in the collecting and analysis of bibliographic material without which the writing of the catalogue would have been more difficult and the result less complete. Her own contribution to the catalogue, an essay on the early history of collecting still-life painting in Spain, truly breaks new ground by giving us for the first time some notion of who the first collectors of the still life in Spain were, what kinds of pictures they collected, and when and where they did it. Her conclusions form an integral part of this book.

WILLIAM B. JORDAN

STILL LIFE AND THE ORIGINS OF NATURALISM IN SPAIN

William B. Jordan

A European Perspective: A Changing World

From Caravaggio and Sánchez Cotán, to Chardin and Goya, to Cézanne and Picasso, successive generations of great painters have wrestled with the most serious pictorial issues in their attempts to depict a simple arrangement of fruit, flowers or familiar objects. The decorative potential of such subject matter has been exploited since antiquity, and its symbolic role has developed since the Middle Ages, but the depiction of natural and artificial objects was transformed toward the end of the sixteenth century. From then on, no longer conceived as merely decorative or symbolic, the depiction of such things became the focus of a new relationship between the painter's eye, his brush and his mind. This essentially "modern" approach to art, as Roberto Longhi called it, has sometimes cut close to the quick of creativity.[1] Indeed, the cubist painters in the twentieth century, led to the still life by Cézanne, made it a vehicle for exploring the very boundaries of art (fig. 1). Their concern with purely formal values was the ultimate extension of an attitude that, more than three hundred years before them, led another generation of radical young artists to paint the first such pictures without narrative content—works in which the perception of nature, the endurance of art and the power of the artist were the principal subjects.

The emergence throughout Europe of the modern still life toward the end of the sixteenth century was a phenomenon related to rapidly evolving conditions of a European society at the threshold of the modern age in politics, science, philosophy and art. Exactly where the first still lifes were painted has been much debated and will probably continue to be, because the conditions that led artists to focus their attention on material things were so widespread that similar results were reached from various starting points. Certain things are clear, however: that this was an

Fig. 1   Pablo Picasso. GUITAR, SHEET MUSIC
AND WINE GLASS. 47.9 × 36.5 cm. Collage and
charcoal. Marion Koogler McNay Art
Museum, San Antonio.

international movement and that communication among the protagonists—artists and patrons—in the major European cultural centers existed during the formative phase of the new genre's creation. Spain, with its political domination of Europe still largely intact and its aristocratic emissaries scattered about the globe, was very much involved in this exchange of information and ideas: its artists and intellectuals were among the first to express the new view of nature and art.

Toward the middle of the sixteenth century, a new secular spirit in art began to develop, particularly among the Bassanos in Venice and at the courts of northern Europe. Painters frequently depicted allegories of the Five Senses, the Four Elements, the Four Seasons or the Twelve Months—compositions in which plants and animals functioned associatively and which called upon a painter's ability to describe accurately what his senses perceived. This fixation of the mind's eye on natural objects paralleled in some European countries, especially England and Spain, the development of a rich metaphorical literature in which the association of objects and concepts added subtlety and expressiveness to modern language. In Spain, the development of such language among the mystic poets—Fray Luis de Granada, Santa Teresa de Jesús and others—has sometimes been mistaken for a causative factor in the development of the still life, rather than as a parallel but directly unrelated form of expression.

At the same time that the still life was in its formative stage in Spain, similar innovations in literary forms and philosophic outlook reached their full realization. Nowhere was the modern novel, for example, more brilliantly inaugurated than in Spain, with the publication in 1605 of part one of Cervantes's *Don Quixote de la Mancha*. By the late sixteenth and early seventeenth centuries, not only were writers like Cervantes beginning to satirize the literary forms of the Renaissance, but also some thinkers were discarding the epistemological systems, based largely on the writings of Aristotle, that had dominated thought since antiquity, thus laying the foundations of modern empirical inquiry. The writing of a Toledan physician, Juan Huarte de San Juan, whose *Examen de ingenios para las ciencias* was published in 1575 and by 1600 had been reprinted and translated ten times, was an early and influential force in the new empirical infrastructure. Huarte asserted the impossibility of knowing the truth through the study of ancient categories and advocated instead pursuing general truths about the nature of man through the study of individuals.[2] This new outlook on the nature of knowledge reflects a shift in perspective that, in painting, was expressed in the stylistic approach of naturalism. Without the preoccupation of artists with testing their ability to imitate the natural appearances of individual things, the still life would not have developed as it did.

One of the first and certainly the most dramatic manifestation of the shift in focus from universal to particular was the invention in Amsterdam, around 1550, of an ambitious compositional type which modern scholarship has called the inverted still life. First painted by Pieter Aertsen (1508–1575) and his nephew Joachim Beuckelaer (c. 1530–c. 1573), these were fundamentally religious paintings. But they were religious paintings in which the artist inverted the relative emphasis of things, relegating the religious scene to a tiny portion of the background while bringing elaborate still-life elements to the fore, where his extraordinary technique

Fig. 2 Joachim Beuckelaer. CHRIST ON THE ROAD TO EMMAUS. 169 × 110 cm. Mauritshuis, The Hague.

could be displayed in the description of a dazzling array of foodstuffs and utensils. Aertsen's CHRIST IN THE HOUSE OF MARTHA AND MARY in Vienna (fig. III.2) and Beuckelaer's CHRIST ON THE ROAD TO EMMAUS in The Hague (fig. 2), exemplify the works of these two artists who specialized in religious subjects that lent themselves to such virtuosic displays. In Beuckelaer's work, the artist's spectacular skill is dramatized by the strong contrast of light and shade that plays upon the textures of delicate feathers, crinkly cabbage leaves, folded linen napkins and countless other material things that lay in preparation for the meal during which Christ's miraculous triumph over the flesh will be revealed to his disciples. The spirituality of the painting is ironically underscored by its emphatic materialism.

This inverted emphasis was an outgrowth of Erasmian humanism and was supported by the great scholar's belief in trying to make complex concepts understandable through the means of familiar things.[3] In the humanistic environment in which Aertsen and Beuckelaer painted, their works were also compared to the literary descriptions of the fabled low-life subjects of the ancient Greek painter Peiraikos.[4] Ancient precedent was not invoked merely to justify the artists' innovations, but also to highlight their achievements in a spirit of competition with works that existed only as descriptions in ancient texts. While the effectiveness of such paintings as subtle expressions of faith is undeniable, it cannot be doubted that they were also conceived as tours de force showing the artists' skill at imitating nature.

Aertsen and Beuckelaer also purged such paintings of their religious content and pioneered the creation of purely secular market scenes (fig. 3) which showed

Fig. 3 Joachim Beuckelaer. THE BUTCHERSHOP. 144.5 × 199 cm. Signed, 1566. Museo di Capodimonte, Naples

Fig. 4 Vincenzo Campi. CHRIST IN THE HOUSE OF MARTHA AND MARY. 186 × 130 cm. Galleria Estense, Modena.

men and women going about the business of their daily lives amidst extensive displays of food. Such works were quickly imitated and collected across Europe. By at least the 1570s, paintings of this type had reached northern Italy, where they exerted an enormous influence on the Cremonese painter Vincenzo Campi (c. 1530–1591).[5] Campi followed the format of the inverted still life in works like his CHRIST IN THE HOUSE OF MARTHA AND MARY (fig. 4), but he also painted many pictures without religious content (fig. 32), contributing to the secularization of art that gained momentum as the century drew toward its end. Campi's brother Antonio wrote in his *Cremona fidelissima . . .* (1585) that many of these paintings were sent to Spain. Indeed, as Schroth is able to document for the first time in the essay that follows, the aristocratic collections in Madrid at the turn of the seventeenth century abounded in paintings of this type—both Italian and Flemish. The immediate impact on Spanish artists of these new secular subjects expressed in compositions featuring both objects and human figures has not been widely acknowledged.

Information contained in the testament written in 1599 by the court painter Juan Pantoja de la Cruz (1553–1608),[6] the foremost court portraitist after Sánchez Coello (fig. 5) and painter to kings Philip II and Philip III, illuminates the profound secularization of taste in art which Spanish aristocrats shared with their European counterparts in the 1590s. Pantoja mentions in this document that he had just finished painting four large allegories of the Four Elements for Francisco Tejada, an important collector who in the late 1620s became the first patron of the young Antonio de Pereda (see Chapter XIV). Unknown today, these works conform perfectly to the type of paintings being collected at the time by other aristocrats in Madrid. Pantoja's further statement that Agustín Álvarez de Toledo, a member of the Council of the Indies, still owed him in 1599 part of the money due for three "*bodegones de Italia* which I made in the year ninety-two" reflects the dispersal of new art forms across Europe. Surely a reference to the kind of paintings made by

Campi, the document is the earliest mention of such pictures painted by Spaniards. The term *bodegones de Italia* suggests that the genre that eventually became common in Spain was at first perceived as a foreign import and confirms that the creation of such works was part of an international tendency to expand and secularize the subject matter of art.

In the same way that ancient precedent was useful and inspiring to artists who first chose to paint scenes of daily life, it played a positive role in the origins of the modern still life. Small easel paintings which we would call still lifes had, of course, been painted in Greek antiquity.[7] Although no such pictures survive, the accounts of ancient artists by Pliny the Elder (d. 79 A.D.) are replete with descriptions of them and with anecdotes about their painters. The names of Peiraikos, Zeuxis, Parrhasios and Apollodoros came readily to the lips of sixteenth-century persons learned in matters of painting. The still life did not have to be reinvented in modern times, since it existed as a vaguely defined form in the collective imagination of educated painters. Yet, having lain dormant for centuries, it was revived only when man's view of his world and the place of art in it suggested that this discarded genre from antiquity might be of some value in the modern world.

When, because of the growing secular imperative and the empirical spirit of the age, painters in the late sixteenth century wanted to isolate certain objects in compositions by themselves, the existence of these ancient antetypes was perhaps the single most important factor in the rapid proliferation of the independent still life. These imagined antetypes allowed painters in widely separated places to pursue the still life from their own perspectives, resulting in great diversity of styles. Some of the early masterpieces of the genre from Italy, the Low Countries and Spain demonstrate how differently artists from these places set about doing the same thing.

The one surviving still life by Michelangelo da Caravaggio (1571–1610), the famous Basket of Fruit in the Ambrosiana in Milan (fig. 6), is the first still life of the subject by a great artist whose reputation is founded mainly on his figural works. Generally dated around 1600 or slightly before, the Basket of Fruit was consciously conceived in the manner of an antique trompe l'oeil[8] but was executed with a degree of naturalism without parallel in the surviving frescoes from antiquity or the panels of the Italian Renaissance. The individual characteristics of each piece of fruit and leaf—including the evident process of decay and the glistening dewdrops—are rendered with breathtaking clarity, yet Caravaggio's handling of his medium is fluid and dextrous. Despite its emphasis on the ephemerality of the subject, the painting has a monumentality and an internal equanimity of design that is utterly classical. Caravaggio's religious paintings revitalized rather than rejected the classical tradition, and his still life may be the most profoundly classical in the history of art. Perhaps the artist was motivated in painting it by a brimming sense of the superiority of his own talent to that of the painters of antiquity.

Before Caravaggio, a few lesser artists in Lombardy had made a specialty of pictures of fruit and flowers, though none of their works has been firmly documented before 1600. Lombard artists Ambrogio Figino (1548–1608) (fig. 16) and Carlo Antonio Procaccini (1555–c.1605) practiced the genre. According to Filippo

Fig. 5 Pantoja de la Cruz. Queen Margarita of Austria. 204×122 cm. Signed, 1606. Museo del Prado, Madrid.

Fig. 6 Caravaggio. BASKET OF FRUIT, detail 31 × 47 cm. Pinacoteca Ambrosiana, Milan.

Fig. 7 Fede Galizia. STILL LIFE WITH PEACHES IN A PORCELAIN BOWL. 30 × 41.5 cm. Silvano Lodi Collection, Campione d'Italia.

Baldinucci (1681–1728), many of Procaccini's pictures of fruit and flowers were sent to Spain, but none is known today. It is possible that such pictures were important to the origins of still-life painting in Spain. Typical of Lombard still lifes are the works of Fede Galizia (1578–1630) and Panfilo Nuvolone (active 1581–1631), some of which were also sent to Spain in the seventeenth century. Fede Galizia's STILL LIFE WITH PEACHES IN A PORCELAIN BOWL (fig. 7) shares the simple, symmetrical composition, dark background and polished facture that characterize her work, the earliest dated example of which was painted in 1602. Caravaggio doubtless knew these and other precedents in his native Lombardy, but, in comparison to the grandeur of his BASKET OF FRUIT, they seem slight indeed.

A very different tradition of painting still lifes developed in northern Europe at the same time. Specialists have named one such northern type "the breakfast-piece." The earliest known dated painting of this sort was signed in 1601 by the Dutchman Nicolaes Gillis (1575–after 1632).[9] He and his colleague Floris van Dijck (1575–1651) had fully developed the genre about a decade later, when the outstanding STILL LIFE WITH CHEESE AND FRUIT (fig. 8) was signed and dated in 1610 by Floris van Dijck. No more or less interested than Caravaggio in capturing the details of observed reality, the Dutch artist's vision is, nonetheless, completely different. Disinclined toward the internal *disegno* that gives Caravaggio's BASKET OF FRUIT its overriding monumentality, van Dijck sought instead to emphasize the intimacy of sensory experience through microscopic observation of detail and the random disarray affected in his composition. Rightly said to be descended from the realistic vision of Jan van Eyck, just as Caravaggio's naturalism is a descendant of the Italian Renaissance, these pictures departed significantly from tradition in their

implicit assertion that the mere observation and imitation of reality was in itself an acceptable aim of art.

The earliest still lifes from Spain are exactly contemporaneous with those of Italy and the Low Countries. The astonishing work by Juan Sánchez Cotán (1560–1627) in the San Diego Museum of Art (fig. 9, Plate 3) was recorded in the artist's studio in 1603. With the same degree of intensity that Caravaggio, Fede Galizia and Floris van Dijck brought to their subjects, Sánchez Cotán scrutinizes the quince, cabbage, melon and cucumber. As they did, he wishes to tell us everything he can about these objects, and he entices us to focus on them through the arresting hyperbolic curve of his elegant and ingenious composition. In the relationship of the objects to the dark background and the rather cold light, Sánchez Cotán may owe something to the Lombard tradition but, if so, what he added is beyond comparison. While the Dutch painter seems bound by what he saw, the Spaniard seems freed by his imagination to pursue extremes of artifice found nowhere else in Europe. Created in the cosmopolitan atmosphere of El Greco's Toledo, and as unlike his works as any paintings could be, the still lifes of Sánchez Cotán seem at first to relate to nothing, but as we examine the frayed fabric of antecedents and coincidences, a meaningful context begins to emerge for the origins of the still life in Spain.

Francisco Pacheco on the Origins of Still-Life Painting in Spain

THE MOST INFORMATIVE SOURCE on the early history of the still life in Spain is Francisco Pacheco (1564–1644), the learned painter and teacher of Velázquez whose *Arte*

Fig. 9 Juan Sánchez Cotán. QUINCE, CABBAGE,
MELON AND CUCUMBER. 69.21 × 85.09 cm.
Signed. San Diego Museum of Art.

de la pintura (1649) was finished by 1638 after more than thirty years of work. Pacheco's book, which deals with all aspects of the art of painting—theory, practice and iconography—reflects his basically conservative stand on the hierarchy of genres. That is to say, like most of his contemporaries, he considered paintings of fruit and flowers to be innately inferior to other kinds of subjects. Nevertheless, his text reveals curiosity about them and an interest in the practice—indeed he even tried it himself. Pacheco was only slightly younger than Sánchez Cotán, and he lived through the entire period of the invention and early development of still-life painting. His brief references to it tell us a good deal about the reaction of a sophisticated painter of his generation to the new subject matter:

> The painting of spring flowers from life can be very entertaining, and some have even reached eminence in this field, particularly the famous Florencio of Flanders.... Neither was antiquity lacking in this amusing genre, for the founder of this type of painting was Pausias Siconius. In his youth he fell in love with Glisera, a maker of garlands, and in imitation of her he brought to art an innumerable variety of flowers; and he painted his lady seated composing a garland [fig. 10]. This painting was called *stephanopoli,* because Glisera made her living selling garlands. And Lucius Lúculo bought a copy of this panel in Athens for two talents. In our own time there is no want of painters who are fond of the entertainment afforded by this

genre, which can be easily learned and gives delight by its variety. Among those who have done it with power and skill can be counted Juan van der Hamen, archer to Philip IV [see Chapter VI].

Oil painting is most suitable for this genre, because you can retouch over and over again and refine the colors so that they truly imitate natural flowers. You must also master the painting of vases of glass, clay, silver and gold, and the little baskets in which flowers are usually placed, and the use of lighting and the arrangement of all these things. And occasionally good painters can amuse themselves this way, although it does not lead to artistic glory....[10]

Despite his conservative view that a painting is only worthy of true esteem if it deals with a noble theme, Pacheco cannot conceal the pleasure afforded by this "entertaining" genre, "which can be easily learned and gives delight by its variety." This is far from the statement attributed to Caravaggio by Vincenzo Giustiniani before 1620: "Caravaggio said that it was as difficult for him to make a good painting of flowers as one of figures."[11] Pacheco, in his ambivalence about the worthiness of flower painting, takes comfort in the ancient precedent related by Pliny, reminding us of its invention by Pausias. Caravaggio, feeling at once freed from and by the past, states the modern view—that painting is painting, regardless of the subject.[12] The painter who, according to Pacheco, "reached eminence in this field, Florencio of Flanders," has sometimes been misidentified, or not identified at all. He must be Jan Breughel the Elder (1568–1625), one of whose nicknames, "Flower" Breughel, has been latinized by the Spaniard. Breughel's delicate paintings (fig. 11) were well known in Italy in the 1590s and were probably found in Spanish collections not long thereafter. Although Pacheco says that there was no want of painters in his time who practiced flower painting, no signed, independent flowerpiece by a Spaniard has yet been discovered that predates the 1630s. From documents, as well as from Pacheco's account, we can be sure that they were painted, however—not only by Van der Hamen, but also by Sánchez Cotán, Loarte and others. Pacheco continues his account by describing the art of painting fruit:

The painting of fruit follows the same path, although it demands greater skill and poses greater problems of imitation because it sometimes figures in serious history painting. Blas de Prado painted it very well, and when he went to Morocco on the King's orders, he took some paintings of fruit [lienzos de frutas] with him, which I saw, that were very well done. His disciple Padre Juan Sánchez [Cotán], before professing religion in the Charterhouse of Granada, was very well known for his work in this genre.[13]

The still lifes of Sánchez Cotán (Plates 1–5) have survived and are still well known. Pacheco refers to Cotán's career prior to 1603 when he left Toledo to take religious vows. From Pacheco we also learn that Sánchez Cotán's master was Blas de Prado (c. 1545–1599). Although no signed still life by Prado has survived, his position as the earliest documented painter of still lifes in Spain and his role as teacher to Sánchez Cotán, make a deeper study of this artist a high priority.[14]

Blas de Prado was born in the province of Toledo. We know nothing about his education nor if he, like many Spanish artists in the sixteenth century, traveled to Italy. But his art reveals a thorough familiarity with and preference for Italian mod-

Fig. 10 Peter Paul Rubens and Osias Beert. PAUSIAS AND GLYCERA. 204 × 194 cm. The John and Mable Ringling Museum of Art, Sarasota.

Fig. 11 Jan Breughel. FLOWERPIECE. 44 × 35 cm. Silvano Lodi Collection, Campione d'Italia.

Fig. 12　Blas de Prado. HOLY FAMILY WITH
SAINT JOHN THE EVANGELIST, ST. ILDEFONSUS
AND MAESTRO ALONSO DE VILLEGAS. 209 × 165
cm. Signed, 1589. Museo del Prado, Madrid.

els that is evident in THE HOLY FAMILY WITH SAINT JOHN THE EVANGELIST, SAINT
ILDEFONSUS AND MAESTRO ALONSO DE VILLEGAS (fig. 12), which he painted in 1589.
The donor who commissioned this picture was an ecclesiastic and one of the best-
known literary figures in Toledo, author of the famous *Flos Sanctorum* (1578–94).
His portrait at the lower right of the composition is executed with a sure realism
that contrasts sharply the idealized religious figures in the painting. Prado seems to
have been successful as a portraitist, but his portraits, like those of nearly all of his
contemporaries who worked in that field, have been eclipsed by the fame of his
great contemporary, Alonso Sánchez Coello (1531/32–1588).

According to Palomino (1724), Prado's skill and reputation as a portraitist led
to the well-known event in his biography that was first related by Pacheco: that he
was sent to Morocco. Pacheco reports that Prado traveled at the behest of Philip II,
but a document recently discovered by J. M. Serrera (in press) shows that he made
the trip while on the payroll of the powerful Duke of Medina Sidonia, Captain
General of the Ocean, responsible for the coastlines of Andalucía.[15] Pacheco does
not say what the purpose of Prado's journey was, but Palomino suggests that it was
to portray the royal family of Morocco. The newly found document says simply
that he was going "to Bevería [Barbary] ... to serve the *Xarife*." Pacheco saw
Prado's paintings of fruit during his stopover in Seville in May of 1593, around the
same time that the Lombard painters Ambrogio Figino and Carlo Antonio
Procaccini are reported to have been painting still lifes in Milan, some of which
were sent to Spain. Prado was sufficiently proud of his *lienzos de frutas* to bring them
along on his trip and to show them to Pacheco. Perhaps he sensed that his work was
in the vanguard of a developing tradition. We do not know how long Prado was
away from Spain, but he died in Madrid before February 1600.[16]

In 1983 Pérez Sánchez very tentatively advanced the hypothesis that a pair of
small paintings representing glass compotes of plums and pears (figs. 13, 14) might
be by Blas de Prado. Despite obvious compositional parallels to the Lombard still
lifes of Fede Galizia and Panfilo Nuvolone, these paintings have a painterliness and
warmth of color that definitely associate them with the Spanish School in the final
years of the sixteenth century. The delicate observation but rather broad execution
of the glass compotes recall the manner in which portraitists of the school of
Sánchez Coello rendered the elaborate costumes and jewels of their sitters. While it
cannot be proven at this time, the hypothesis that Blas de Prado painted these works
is plausible and deserves to be kept in mind.

What appears to be a painting by the same hand, of similarly small dimensions,
depicts a metal plate of pears (fig. 15). Its simple composition and rather high point
of view resemble the only signed still life by Ambrogio Figino (fig. 16), which has
been dated to around 1595.[17] As in COMPOTE OF PLUMS and COMPOTE OF PEARS, the
sensuous handling of the paint and warm coloration differentiate the painting from
the polished Lombard manner. A delicate sensibility is evident in the observation of
the reflections in the flange of the plate and in the highlights on the fruit and plate
executed in pure white, as they are in the small pair. Until a signed still life by Blas
de Prado is discovered, which would resolve the matter of their authorship, these
three small convases at least give us some idea of the cultural interchanges that must

have occurred between Castile and Lombardy at the turn of the seventeenth century.

The only painters that Pacheco mentions by name as practitioners of the still life are Blas de Prado and Sánchez Cotán, who established the genre in Toledo, and Juan van der Hamen, who later developed it at the court of Madrid.[18] Although he distinguishes between the painting of fruit and flowers on canvases by themselves, and painting them as accessories in figural compositions or as pure decoration, Pacheco obviously considers it all to be the same thing—imitating nature. Further in his discussion of painting fruits, he notes the practice in other media, saying "Antonio Mohedano painted them very well, as is shown by the festoons that he did in fresco in the cloister of San Francisco...."[19] These frescoes have not survived. Mohedano (c. 1563–1626) was a cultivated man—a poet as well as a painter—who apprenticed in the Córdoban studio of Pablo de Céspedes (1538–1608). Céspedes, one of the best-educated and most refined painters of his century in Spain, is quoted at length by Pacheco on the subject of grotesque painting and probably taught Mohedano his craft. Although Mohedano's activity as a painter was not out of the ordinary, he made a specialty of painting, in tempera and oil, grotesque decorations on fabric hangings *(sargas)*, which took the place of tapestries as room furnishings. In the passage quoted above, Pacheco obviously refers to Mohedano's ability as a painter in this decorative vein, which he also practiced in fresco. It has sometimes been assumed that he learned the art of grotesque decoration from a pair of mysterious Italians who were active in Andalucía much earlier in the sixteenth century and

Fig. 13   Unknown artist. COMPOTE OF PLUMS. 27.5 × 27.5 cm. 1590s. Fundación Santamarca, Madrid.

Fig. 14   Unknown artist. COMPOTE OF PEARS. 27.5 × 27.5 cm. 1590s. Fundación Santamarca, Madrid.

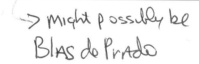

→ might possibly be Blas de Prado

are known in the sources simply by their first names, Julio and Alejandro.[20] But he was too young to have known them personally.

Pacheco mentions the influence of Julio and Alejandro in a chapter entitled "On Illumination, Stucco and Fresco Painting—Their Antiquity and Duration," in the context of discussing the renaissance of interest, during the reign of the Emperor Charles V, in the ruins of Roman Spain and in the practice of the fine arts (*"buenas artes"*) of antiquity:

> In this I think that things were enriched by Julio and Alejandro (presumed to be disciples of Giovanni da Udine or Raphael of Urbino), valiant men who came from Italy to paint the houses of [Francisco de los] Cobos, Secretary of the Emperor, in the city of Úbeda and from there went to the Royal Palace of the Alhambra in Granada [painting] (in tempera in one place and in fresco in the other), whose paintings have been the source of the good light that we have today that has been taken advantage of by all the great Spanish *ingenios:* Pedro Raxis, Antonio Mohedano, Blas de Ledesma and many others....[21]

Pacheco does not say, of course, that these Spanish painters studied with Julio and Alejandro, only that they profited by their works. Palomino saw their decorative frescoes at the Alhambra in 1712 and was very impressed by them. Their activity in Spain is referred to in Cristóbal de Villalón's *Ingeniosa comparación entre lo antiguo y lo presente,* published in Valladolid in 1539.[22] Writing a century before Pacheco, Villalón cites Julio and Alejandro in the context of his attempt to demonstrate that

Fig. 15   Unknown artist. PLATE OF PEARS. 23 × 32.5 cm. Private collection.

possibly Blas de Prado

in the arts, as in every other aspect of life, modern times far exceed antiquity. The works of these artists are obviously important to the history of decoration in Spain, but there is no indication that they painted anything approximating an independent still life. Nevertheless a series of grotesque decorations that has been attributed to Antonio Mohedano does manifest an attitude toward the imitation of natural objects that parallels that of the earliest still-life painters in Spain.

In the 1983–84 exhibition of still lifes in Madrid, Pérez Sánchez brought to public attention for the first time a series of long, narrow paintings in tempera and oil on linen which form part of the decorated ceiling executed shortly after 1600 in the Prelate's Gallery in the Archbishop's Palace of Seville (figs. 17, 18).[23] These narrow bands of grotesque decoration are mounted into wooden frameworks that separate the painted scenes on the coffered ceiling. The other ceiling paintings in the Prelate's Gallery are by several different artists and represent allegories of the Four Seasons and the Four Elements and scenes from the life of Noah, mostly secular subjects that were currently in vogue at the Spanish court (see Schroth here following). Pérez Sánchez reviews the circumstantial evidence that suggests that Mohedano was possibly the author of the grotesque panels in this ceiling but remains cautious about the attribution.

The authorship of the paintings is of less interest than the insight they provide into the painting of fruit around 1600. On each of the long, narrow strips of canvas, the artist has painted in muted, matte colors of green, rose and ivory an intricate

Fruit still life ➔ *Birds* ➔ *still life* ➔

Fig. 17 Unknown artist. Grotesque decoration from the Prelate's Gallery, PEARS AND GRAPES. 39×221 cm. Archbishop's Palace, Seville.

pattern of vegetal festoons and volutes; fanciful abstractions of foliage, flowers and swags of drapery are intertwined with tiny dragonlike beasts characteristic of grotesque decoration. The decorative scheme conforms to the Roman tradition of the grotesque that was brought to southern Spain by Julio and Alejandro, except in one unusual element: each panel includes two cartouches that hold trompe l'oeil panels of fruit—pears and grapes (fig. 17), cucumbers and quinces (fig. 18)—painted with a naturalism that is dramatically at odds with the surrounding decorative motifs. The trompe l'oeil images of fruit in the midst of self-consciously antique grotesques are allusions to the naturalism of the ancient painters. The artist's intention in these grotesques to illustrate Pliny's famous tale about the grapes painted so realistically by Zeuxis that birds came to peck at them is clear from the motif of a bird repeated in the central shell niche of each panel.

The grotesque decorations in the Archbishop's Palace in Seville are emblems that bespeak the preoccupation of painters at the turn of the seventeenth century with creating images that move men by their lifelikeness. Such a naturalistic attitude—mixed with a sense of competition with the artists of antiquity—was at the core of the emergence of the still life as an independent art form.

After citing Antonio Mohedano's skill at painting frescoed festoons, Pacheco mentions another painter who sometimes worked with him:

> Alonso Vázquez was not far behind, as can be seen in the famous canvas of Lazarus and the Rich Man, now in the possession of the Duke of Alcalá. There, in a cupboard with containers of silver, glass and clay, he placed a wide variety of food and fruit, and a copper flask immersed in water for chilling, all painted with much dexterity and decorum. But he did something that other painters of fruit do not do; namely he did the figures as skillfully as the other things. I have also tried this exercise, as well as flower painting, and I do not judge it to be very difficult.[24]

Alonso Vázquez's career in Seville was cut short by his departure for Mexico in 1603 in the service of the Viceroy, the Marquis of Montesclaros, and his untimely death there on May 24, 1608. He was not a painter of still lifes, but to the conservative Pacheco he was an ideal painter of objects because his illusionistic virtuosity was married to the human figure and, therefore, to narrative content. In 1959 Martin Soria rediscovered in a Madrid private collection the famous LAZARUS AND THE

[handwritten annotations: "✓ still life", "↳ Birds", "↳ still life"]

Fig. 18   Unknown artist. Grotesque decoration from the Prelate's Gallery, CUCUMBERS AND QUINCES. 39×221 cm. Archbishop's Palace, Seville.

RICH MAN that Pacheco described (fig. 19). Indeed, the large, mannerist composition—which Bergström (1970) has associated with the style of the Flemish painter Lodewijk Toeput, who worked in Italy under the name of Ludovico Pozzoserrato—shows remarkable skill in the execution of the elaborate display of fruit, sweets and tableware. The painting must date from around 1600.

Pacheco's familiarity with the new subject matter of art and his interest in it were not confined to pure still lifes and flowerpieces, or banquet scenes like Vázquez's. In a chapter entitled "On the Painting of Animals and Birds, Fish-Stalls and *Bodegones* and the Ingenious Invention of Portraits from Life," he discusses at length the painting of low-life subjects that depict both people and food. These important passages, which are fully quoted in Chapter III below, describe the type of composition at which Pacheco's disciple and protégé, Diego Velázquez, excelled during his early career. In his discussion of such paintings, Pacheco predictably bases himself upon ancient precedent. He asks:

> Do we find perhaps some antique painter who was inclined to paint these ordinary and comic things? It appears so; Pliny mentions one called Dionisio, with the nickname Anthropographos, who painted only figures with amusing names... And in the same way Peiraikos also painted humble things like barbershops, stalls, meals and similar things, for which they called him Riparographos; these paintings caused great delight and by them the artist achieved greatest glory.[25]

It is no mere coincidence that we find a learned painter like Pacheco discussing the lost works of Peiraikos at the very time when such subjects were being painted for the first time since antiquity. In the changing world at the turn of the seventeenth century, we find that artists were re-examining historical forms—as they do today—to find a meaningful vehicle for the expression of their most urgent concerns. The inspiration of the works of ancient Greece for the brilliant paintings of Velázquez's youth (Plates 7 and 8, figs. III.6,9) in no way diminishes the vibrant sense of the here-and-now that was the primary focus of his brush.

Typical of Pacheco's openness to experimentation, which led him to try painting still lifes of flowers and fruit, he relates that when he was in Madrid in 1625 he painted a *bodegón* "with two figures painted from life, some flowers, fruit and other trinkets, which today belongs to my learned friend Francisco de Rioja; and I suc-

ceeded to the extent that the other things by my hand appear in comparison to be merely painted."[26]

Forging a Terminology

BY THE EARLY SEVENTEENTH CENTURY, a number of different formats existed in which a painter could express his interest in natural objects, yet no fixed terminology existed for referring to such pictures. The words commonly applied today either did not exist then or did not have the meanings they have today. The French term *nature morte*, which came into common usage only in the middle of the eighteenth century, was not manifested in its Spanish counterpart, *naturaleza muerta*, until after the War of Independence in the early nineteenth century. The word commonly used in Spain today to denote a still life is *bodegón*, yet this word had a different and very specific meaning in the seventeenth century. The word was defined by Sebastián de Covarrubias in his *Tesoro de la lengua castellana* (1611) as: "The basement or low portal, within which is a cellar where he who does not have anyone to cook for him can find a meal, and with it a drink." Pacheco uses the word *bodegón*, in a derivation of its original meaning, to describe the sort of paintings done by the young Velázquez which depicted a meal with figures eating or preparing food. The first usage of the word in this way was Pantoja's reference in 1599 to the *bodegones de Italia* he had painted seven years earlier. In his case, it is clear that he must have been imitating the kind of paintings made famous by Vincenzo Campi, which depicted figures eating or selling food. Throughout this book, when the term *bodegón* is used, it will be meant in this seventeenth-century sense. By the time Palomino wrote in the early eighteenth century, the term *bodegoncillos* was already being used to refer to still lifes without figures.

In seventeenth-century inventories and texts, still lifes were referred to by their contents, as Pacheco did when he recalled Blas de Prado's *lienzos de frutas* (paintings of fruit), or as did the makers of Sánchez Cotán's inventory of 1603 when they referred to a *lienzo de caza* (painting of game). Other terms that came into common usage were derived from the containers in which flowers and fruit were placed: *florero* or *ramilletero* for flowerpiece, and *frutero* for still life of fruit.[27]

The Development of the Still Life Before 1650

THE FIRST STILL LIFES IN SPAIN were painted in the intellectual capital of Toledo. By the time that Juan Sánchez Cotán made his decision to retire from secular life in 1603, independent still lifes had been painted there for at least ten years. It is possible that the first ones were even done before that, but the idea, once rooted, may have developed quickly. If the hypothesis that Blas de Prado's early *lienzos de frutas* were similar in their format to contemporary Lombard still lifes is correct, that still does not explain the extraordinary originality of those by his pupil Sánchez Cotán. The explanation of that must lie partly in the reception of Prado's early explorations of naturalism by Toledan intellectuals and by Sánchez Cotán himself. At the same time that El Greco was successfully espousing a personal philosophy of art dedicated to the enhancement of nature through the application of extremes of artifice,[28] the earliest still lifes must have represented an alternative focal point for discussions of the illusionistic powers of art—discussions that surely ranged, like the treatises of the time, in an erudite way over the entire history of art, drawing parallels and making comparisons to the examples of the ancients. In the context of such a dialogue, which might have included, as Schroth demonstrates in the following essay, some of the most learned humanists in the inner circle of the Toledo Cathedral Chapter, Sánchez Cotán's haunting images of fruits and vegetables suspended and silhouetted against the sheer blackness of space and illuminated by a searing light must have been seen as *ingeniosidades*—paradigms of cleverness and skill, testaments of the power and permanence of art in a mortal world.

It has always seemed curious and difficult to explain that Sánchez Cotán's figural style (fig. 20)—with its idealized forms, bland modeling and pale colors reminiscent of the Italianate painters of El Escorial—was so completely unaffected by the intense naturalism of his still lifes. This strongly suggests the experimental character of his pictures of fruit, vegetables and game, works which were obviously not subject to the same rules that governed his religious paintings. They were subject to no rules at all, in fact, and provided a free rein to his imagination in seeking ways to enact the drama of art imitating nature. The far-reaching implications of this naturalism were never fully assimilated into his style, as happened with his Italian contemporary Caravaggio, or his Spanish followers like Van der Hamen. Once he had withdrawn from the intellectual atmosphere of the Imperial City, Sánchez Cotán's activity as a still-life painter appears to have diminished, while he continued to paint

Fig. 20 Juan Sánchez Cotán. BAPTISM OF CHRIST. 278 × 186 cm. The Charterhouse, Granada.

Fig. 21 Juan Esteban. MARKET SCENE.
128 × 167 cm. Signed, 1606. Museo de Bellas
Artes, Granada.

religious works in the same style he had pursued before. But the legacy of the still lifes he left behind totally altered the course of art in Spain.

In the early years of the seventeenth century, a few painters elsewhere began accepting the challenge posed by an artist's confrontation with objects in isolation or with scenes of low life. One was a modest Granadan painter named Blas de Ledesma (see Chapter II), who may have known Sánchez Cotán in his retirement. Another indication of such activity is the MARKET SCENE (fig. 21) signed in 1606 in the Andalusian city of Úbeda (Jaén) by a painter named Juan Esteban, who had also been active in Madrid in 1597.[29] Somewhat awkward in his command of the figures, Esteban seems to delight in the description of fruits and vegetables, meat, fur and feathers. Despite the obvious limitations of his painting, which is the earliest surviving *bodegón* by a Spaniard, Esteban managed to endow his work with freshness and immediacy. The picture demonstrates how this Italian genre was transformed in Spain fully twenty years before Alejandro de Loarte painted his POULTRY VENDOR (Plate 11) in Toledo in 1626.

In Seville, where the pure still life does not seem to have been widely practiced early in the century, Pacheco encouraged the natural inclination of his disciple Diego Velázquez to develop his skill at imitating the earthy appearances of people and things in *bodegones* that were inspired in part by the ancient low-life pictures of Peiraikos. Unlike the case of Sánchez Cotán, however, Velázquez's exploration of the power of art to mimic natural appearances was not an experiment in isolation from the rest of his oeuvre. Instead, the painterly pursuit of reality became his deepest artistic motivation, affecting his religious works and his portraits as well. In the greatest of his youthful *bodegones* (fig. III.9), however, we see that the mere mastery of appearances did not satisfy the subtlety of his mind. An interest in human nature elevates these works far above the level of their technical facility. Long after he had ceased to indulge in the tours de force which the *bodegón* represented in his formative years, this searching vision in the service of his intellect remained the guiding force of Velázquez's art.

Madrid, with its early Habsburg taste for collecting Flemish and Italian *bodegones,* lagged somewhat behind the intellectual circles of Toledo in encouraging the painting of pure still lifes. Certain artists active in the second and third decades of the seventeenth century, including Juan Bautista de Espinosa and Alejandro de Loarte (see Chapters IV and V), seem to have had ties in both cities. As the court and seat of government, Madrid was a thriving and eclectic place, populated by talented and ambitious professionals, merchants and emissaries from all over Europe. Revolving around the person of the king, life at the court was propelled by the aristocracy, many of whom erected palaces of their own during the reign of Philip III, following the king's brief and abortive attempt to relocate the court to Valladolid (1601–1606), and began collecting on a grand scale and with international scope.

It was in this atmosphere that a genteel young Spaniard of part-Flemish descent, Juan van der Hamen y León (1596–1631), was captivated by the innovation of Sánchez Cotán and brought the still life to its full prominence in Madrid in the 1620s (see Chapter VI). His works from the early twenties (fig. 22), with their hanging branches of fruit, are the closest to Sánchez Cotán's, but even they reveal an elegance in their subject matter (often depicting costly Venetian-style crystals and imported porcelains) that relates to court life. Of noble birth and belonging to a family of writers, Van der Hamen was himself a member of the intellectual elite of Madrid and wrote verses on the philosophy of art. His works, as Sánchez Cotán's had surely been in Toledo, became a focus of discussion on the mimetic powers of art and the superiority of the painted image over the things it depicts (see Chapter VI).

Within a broad European context, Van der Hamen's rather large and varied oeuvre establishes him as one of the major still-life painters of his time. During the brief span of his career, and no doubt largely due to his influence, the collecting of still lifes became extremely fashionable in court circles and among the well-to-do bourgeoisie. Nevertheless, because of the lowly status of the still life in the theoretical hierarchy of genres, Van der Hamen did not like to be thought of as a specialist in such pictures and he himself attached great importance to his portraits and figural works. The latter are barely known today, however, and the judgment of history has come down strongly on the side of his still lifes.

As far was we know, Juan Fernández, El Labrador, came the closest of any of his contemporaries in Spain to specializing in still lifes (see Chapter VII). In his lifetime, El Labrador was one of the best-known still-life painters of Spain, even though he lived a reclusive life away from the court, only occasionally bringing his pictures to Madrid to sell. The fame of his delicate works reached beyond the borders of Spain as far as England, where his still lifes (Plate 23) were eagerly sought by King Charles I and the nobles of his court. Long thought to have been a contemporary of Blas de Prado, Labrador is now known to have lived later. His activity is documented in the 1630s, and his paintings, with their dramatic light and satiny chiaroscuro, reveal the certain knowledge of Caravaggio's naturalism. Yet so personal and so extraordinarily skilled is his depiction of fruit and flowers that one can readily understand and agree with the assessment of his contemporaries, who considered him to be among the foremost still-life painters of Europe.

In the wake of Van der Hamen's phenomenal success with his still lifes, and simultaneous with that of El Labrador, a number of minor artists took advantage of the vastly increased demand for pictures of fruit and flowers. Some of them may have been protégés of Van der Hamen. Such painters as Antonio Ponce (see Chapter IX) and Francisco Barrera (see Chapter X) were not just still-life painters, but they nevertheless addressed a large part of their practices to creating series of the Seasons and the Months, as well as straight still lifes of fruit, flowers and comestibles. Rarely reaching an inspired level of quality, such works were no doubt aimed at a segment of the market that required such paintings for largely decorative purposes. While made with competence, they do not reveal their painters to be great masters and perhaps served to encourage the view of Pacheco and others that the still life was an easy thing to paint, attracting those with little talent for subtle narrative subjects. The still lifes of Juan de Espinosa (see Chapter VIII), on the other hand, occasionally rose far above the ordinary (Plate 27).

The most important legacy of Sánchez Cotán was not that certain artists chose

Fig. 22   Juan van der Hamen. STILL LIFE WITH FRUIT AND FLOWERS. 78 × 41 cm. Signed, 1622. Real Academia de San Fernando, Madrid.

Fig. 23 Unknown artist. STILL LIFE
WITH BOOKS AND AN HOURGLASS.
34 × 55 cm. Gemäldegalerie, Berlin.

to become specialized still-life painters (which they rarely did in Spain), but, as José López-Rey (1964) has observed, that most Spanish painters of real stature in the seventeenth century found it difficult to resist, at least once, accepting the challenge to their abilities which the still life represented. Not only did it pose a test of skill, but, as it had done to Sánchez Cotán, it also posed a challenge to their inventiveness, or *ingenio,* to their deepest instincts as artists alone, without rules or conventions upon which to rely. Regardless of the appeal the genre may have had to collectors— either as decoration or as technical tours de force—this challenge to the painter's *ingenio* was the source of its appeal to artists. Curiously, it is among the works of such non-specialists that we find some of the great Spanish still lifes.

In the generation of artists born around 1610–15, a number of artists who built successful careers as figural painters have left one or more remarkable still lifes signed with their names. Two of them were disciples of Velázquez, Francisco de Burgos Mantilla and Francisco de Palacios (see Chapters XII and XIII). Both are said to have been portrait painters, and there is no indication that either painted many still lifes. The only signed work by Burgos Mantilla that is known today is an

Fig. 24   Francisco de Zurbarán. STILL LIFE WITH LEMONS, ORANGES AND A CUP OF WATER. 60 × 107 cm. Signed, 1633. The Norton Simon Foundation, Pasadena.

exquisite small still life (Plate 36) which he signed in 1631, at the age of twenty-two. Two of the three surviving signed works by Palacios are still lifes (Plates 37 and 38) which reveal the unmistakable influence of his master.

The greatest still-life painter of this generation was an artist whose career was built mainly upon his work as a religious painter, Antonio de Pereda (see Chapter XIV). Patronized as a young man by some of the most sophisticated collectors at the court, Pereda had access to the great collections of Madrid. During his formative years, these collections were being enriched by still lifes imported from Italy and Flanders. He assimilated the best of what he saw into a baroque style that left behind the formal sobriety of Sánchez Cotán and Van der Hamen and inaugurated a style of painterly richness that characterized much of the art from the second half of the century. Through his exposure to still lifes from abroad, Pereda also adopted something that had been absent from Spanish still lifes before him—the tendency to make an explicit moral comment. In the 1630s, he introduced into Spanish still lifes the Vanitas theme (Plates 40 and 41), which he and later artists, such as Juan de Valdés Leal and Andrés Deleito, continued to elaborate.

Fig. 25 Francisco de Zurbarán. EDUCATION OF THE VIRGIN. 128.2 × 106.6 cm. Stanley Moss Collection, New York.

As a result of non-specialists painting still lifes and not signing them, we occasionally encounter an anonymous masterpiece. The history of attempts to attribute two such works, the well-known BODEGÓN KEEPER in Amsterdam and the beautiful PEARS IN A CHINA BOWL in Chicago, is reviewed in the discussions accompanying Plates 45 and 46. Another such painting is the masterly STILL LIFE WITH BOOKS AND AN HOURGLASS in Berlin (fig. 23). Once attributed to Pereda and even associated with the name of Velázquez, it has been tentatively ascribed by Gaya Nuño to Francisco Collantes,[30] whose signed landscapes recall the works of Paul Brill and whose figural compositions reflect a knowledge of Ribera. According to Palomino, Collantes painted *bodegoncillos,* and Gaya Nuño based his attribution on the resemblance of the books in this still life to those in a painting of Saint Jerome signed by Collantes. The attribution is not implausible, but the fact remains that this splendid work does not resemble any signed still life that is known.[31] It treats the theme of the vanity of learning, with its hourglass marking the passage of time, while the strong light entering from the left underscores the age, wear and perishability of the books. Such still lifes had been painted by Jan Davidsz. de Heem and others in the Netherlands in the 1620s and 1630s, but some northern examples seem prosaic in comparison to the poetic grandeur of this small canvas.

The best-known still life painted by a non-specialist is Francisco de Zurbarán's STILL LIFE WITH LEMONS, ORANGES AND A CUP OF WATER (fig. 24), the only such painting which bears the great painter's signature. This work, first mentioned in print in 1924 and not exhibited publicly until 1930,[32] has since that time lent Zurbarán enormous fame as a still-life painter. As Gállego has written, "Surely it seems excessive to speak of a painter as excelling in a genre in which we have only one work unquestionably from his hand."[33] When August L. Mayer first referred to this painting in 1924, he wrote that the objects are presented like flowers on an altar, linked to one another in a kind of litany. This often-quoted assertion has led to the widespread tendency to see the painting as a symbolic expression of religious devotion[34] a view that certainly cannot be disproved but the significance of which may have been exaggerated.

Throughout his career, Zurbarán exhibited a kind of genius for the use of objects in his religious compositions to express subtle shades of symbolic meaning. For example, in an early version of the EDUCATION OF THE VIRGIN (fig. 25), painted about 1627, he used the motif of a pewter plate with a cup of water and a rose to express the idea of the Virgin's purity. Around the same time, he used this motif again in THE MIRACULOUS CURE OF THE BLESSED REGINALD OF ORLEANS—again to denote purity. It would, therefore, be impossible to deny that he may have intended this same meaning when he included the plate, the cup and the rose at the right of his great still life of 1633. The motif, an extremely elegant one regardless of its symbolic potential, was obviously well known, because some years later Pedro de Camprobín (1605–1674) incorporated it into a flower still life of rather decorative character (fig. 26) in which there is no reason to believe that it means anything.

It has often been noted that Zurbarán's monumental, symmetrical composition follows the formula that had been employed in Madrid by Juan van der Hamen since about 1620. Certainly Zurbarán's still life surpasses the works of Van der

Fig. 26   Pedro de Camprobín. STILL LIFE WITH FLOWERS AND A CUP OF WATER. Signed. Count of Ibarra, Seville.

Hamen in its grandeur and eloquence, but it can hardly be doubted that he knew the Madrilenian artist's works. As Pérez Sánchez (1983) has pointed out, the close ties between the Sevillian aristocracy and the court suggest that there were ample opportunities to know Van der Hamen's still lifes in Seville. On the other hand, as Young (London 1979) hypothesizes, it is entirely possible that Zurbarán knew the artist's works in Madrid and that he even painted this picture there during an undocumented trip to the court in 1633 in anticipation of his commission received the following year to work with Velázquez at the Palace of the Buen Retiro. Whether or not that is the case, Zurbarán may have painted this work in the same spirit in which Pacheco executed a *bodegón* at the court in 1625—to prove that this new genre, so fashionable in Madrid, was not so difficult, or at least that he could do it better than those whose practice of it in Madrid earned them such acclaim for their skill. Another still life that is attributed to Zurbarán (fig. XV.1) may also have been painted in Madrid, but years later, when the artist had moved there in his old age.

   With the exception of Zurbarán's signed still life of 1633 and Pacheco's assertion that he also tried his hand at pictures of flowers and fruit, there is no evidence that the genre was widely practiced in Seville until the end of the 1630s, when Zurbarán's son Juan began to make a specialty of it (see Chapter XV). Pedro de Camprobín, who was trained in the Toledan studio of Luis Tristán, moved to Seville around 1630. Many signed still lifes by him are known from the 1650s on, and certain undated ones may have been painted earlier. A beautiful signed still life of game fowl by Camprobín (fig. 27) has, until now, been thought to date from 1623. Recent technical examination, however, revealed that, while the signature on the

Fig. 27 Pedro de Camprobín. STILL LIFE WITH
GAME FOWL. 68.5×76.8 cm. Signed, 1653.
The Meadows Museum, Southern Methodist
University, Dallas.

Fig. 27, detail Date photographed
with infrared light.

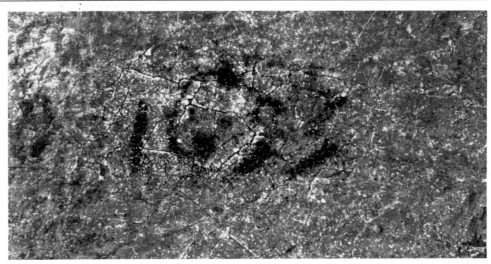

painting is in almost pristine condition, the slightly damaged date had been strengthened and altered by a restorer. Removal of the repaint uncovered the original date of the picture, unquestionably 1653 (fig. 27, detail). This date conforms much more logically to the painting's very fluid technique, which had always seemed out of place in the context of the naturalism of Toledo in the 1620s, when Alejandro de Loarte's pictures of game still adhered to the example set by Sánchez Cotán at the turn of the century. The stepped composition which Camprobín used in this painting was first employed by Van der Hamen only in 1626 (Plate 16). That Camprobín was using it in the 1650s is confirmed again by another signed and dated still life of 1652, which recently appeared in a private collection.

In the second half of the seventeenth century, the cities of Seville and Valencia also became important centers of still-life painting in Spain, but, after it was developed in Toledo, the new genre was primarily practiced close to the court until 1650. This reflected its origins in sophisticated circles. From its beginnings, as the focus of a new kind of engagement between the artist and the world around him, artists quickly developed its potential as a vehicle for the expression of a quasi-poetic response to nature, one unimpeded by the necessity for specific iconographic references. If any single thing about the still life can be said to have contributed the most to the great flourishing which the form experienced in the seventeenth century and which has sustained its development throughout successive generations, it is this capacity of the genre to allow the artist to set his own expectations for the work of art. In this sense it represented an important step in the development of a modern attitude toward art—one that could not have existed in the Renaissance and one that opened a new era in the history of art. In the pages that follow, we shall examine in detail how a pioneering generation of painters in Spain explored and developed their own potential as artists in a changing world.

Notes

1. Longhi 1950, pp. 34–39 on origins of the still life, see Sterling 1959, López-Rey 1964.

2. M. de Iriarte, *El Doctor Huarte de San Juan y su Examen de ingenios,* Madrid, 1948, p. 224.

3. See Margaret Mann Phillips, *Erasmus on His Times: A Shortened Version of 'The Adages of Erasmus,'* Cambridge, 1967, p. 142: Ollas ostentare (to make a show of kitchen pots). See also Keith P. F. Moxey, "Erasmus and the Iconography of Pieter Aertsen's Christ in the House of Martha and Mary in the Boymans-van Beuningen Museum," Journal of the Warburg and Courtauld Institutes, XXXIV, 1971, pp. 335–36.

4. Sterling 1959, pp. 39, 42, 139, note 83. The humanist Hadrianus Junius likened Aertsen to Peiraikos in his *Batavia* (Antwerp, 1588).

5. Spike 1983, p. 22.

6. Sánchez Cantón 1947, p. 102; María Kusche, *Juan Pantoja de la Cruz,* Madrid, 1964, p. 231; Jordan 1967, p. 36; Perez Sánchez 1983, pp. 18, 24.

7. Sterling (1952b, 1959 and 1981) has reviewed the history of still-life painting in antiquity and the important role that discussion of it played after the Renaissance.

8. Sterling 1959, pp. 40, 42; New York 1985, p. 264.

9. Bergström 1956, p. 99, fig. 189.

10. Madrid, 1956 ed., vol. 2, pp. 124–25: *"Es muy entretenida la pintura de las flores imitadas del natural en tiempo de primavera; y algunos han tenido eminencia en esta parte, particularmente en Flandes el famoso Florencio cuyo retrato se ve entre los ilustres pintores flamencos; y la antigüedad no careció desta*

gracia, que el primero en esta especie de pintura fue Pausanias [sic] *Sicionio el cual en su juventud, aficionado a Glisera, su ciudadana, inventora de las guirnaldas, a su imitación redució a la arte una innumerable variedad de flores; y pintó a su dama sentada componiendo una guirnalda; la cual pintura fue llamada 'stephanopoli,' porque Glisera, sustentaba su vida a vender guirnaldas. Y Lucio Lúculo compró por dos talentos en Atenas una copia desta tabla . . . ."* The remainder of the quotation is cited in the original Spanish in Chapter VI, note 17.

11. Hibbard 1983, p. 346.

12. Hibbard (1983, p. 84) has observed that, although Caravaggio expressed his view that flower painting was as difficult as figure painting, he all but abandoned still life after 1599 (just as Velázquez abandoned the *bodegón* after 1623), so we cannot assume that he thought that a still life was as worthy a subject as a figure painting.

13. Madrid, 1956 ed., vol. 2, pp. 125–26: *"Por el mesmo camino va la pintura de las frutas, si bien pide más caudal y tiene más dificultad su imitación, por servir, en algunas ocasiones, a graves historias. Pintólas muy bien Blas de Prado, y cuando pasó a Marruecos por orden del Rey, llevaba unos lienzos de frutas, que yo ví, muy bien pintados; y su dicípulo el P. Juan Sánchez, antes de ser religioso en la Cartuja de Granada, tenía mucha fama en esta parte."*

14. J. C. Gómez Menor, in several articles in *Boletín de Arte Toledano*, vol. 1 (1966) and vol. 2 (1967), has published significant documentation on the activity of Blas de Prado.

15. I am grateful to Mr. Serrera for sharing his manuscript with me.

16. Fernando Marías, "El cigarral toledano del Cardenal Quiroga," *Goya*, no. 154 (1980), p. 219.

17. Longhi 1967, pp. 18 ff.

18. Pacheco does mention Blas de Ledesma (vol. 2, p. 43) but only in the context of the painting of grotesque decoration. He does not mention his still lifes.

19. Pacheco, *op. cit.*, vol. 2, p. 126: *"Pintólas muy bien Antonio Mohedano, como muestran los festones que hizo a fresco en el Claustro de San Francisco . . ."*

20. They have been identified in modern times as Giulio de Aquiles and Alessandro Mayner whose activity at the Alhambra is documented between 1539 and 1546. See Gómez Moreno, 1919, p. 20.

21. Pacheco, *op cit.*, vol. 2, p. 43: *"De aquí pienso yo que se enriquecieron Julio y Alexandro (si ya no es que fuesen dicípulos de Juan de Udine o de Rafael de Urbino), los cuales valientes hombres vinieron de Italia a pintar las casas de Cobos, Secretario del Emperador, en la ciudad de Ubeda y de allí a la Casa Real del Alhambra en Granada (en una y otra parte a temple y fresco), la cual pintura ha sido la que ha dado la buena luz que hoy se tiene y de donde se han aprovechado todos los grandes ingenios españoles; de aquí, Pedro Raxis, Antonio Mohedano, Blas de Ledesma y otros muchos que has sido aventajados en esta parte . . . ."*

22. Cristóbal de Villalón, *Ingeniosa comparación entre lo antiguo y lo presente*, Valladolid, 1539; La Sociedad de Bibliófilos Españoles, Madrid, 1898 ed., p. 170: *"El Comendador mayor de León, Francisco de los Cobos, traxo aquí asalariados de Italia dos ingeniosos mancebos, Julio y Alexandro, para labrar sus casas, los quales hizieron obras al gentil y antigüedad, que nunca el arte subió á tanta perfeción."*

23. The grotesques were temporarily removed from the ceiling and exhibited in the exhibition. See Madrid 1983, pp. 79–82, nos. 48–52. Pérez Sánchez gives the entire plan of the ceiling's iconographic program and discusses the problems of attributing these paintings. The ceiling of this long passageway is conceived similarly to that of the Great Hall of the same palace, which was commissioned in 1604 by Cardinal Archbishop Fernando Niño de Guevara. The latter ceiling is discussed and reproduced by Valdivieso and Serrera 1979, pp. 14–40.

24. Pacheco, *op. cit.*, vol. 2, p. 126: *". . . Alonso Vásquez no quiso quedarse atrás, haciendo demonstración en el famoso lienzo de 'Lázaro y el rico avariento', que tiene hoy el Duque de Alcalá; donde, en un aparador de vasos de plata vidrio y barro, puso mucha diversidad de colaciones y otras frutas, y un frasco de cobre puesto en agua a enfriar, todo pintado con mucha destreza y propriedad. Pero, hizo lo que no hacen otros pintores de frutas, que dió a las figuras igual valentia que a las demás cosas. También he probado este exercicio, y el de las flores, que jusgo no ser muy difícil."* Quoted in translation from Enggass and Brown 1970, p. 216.

25. Pacheco, *op cit.*, p. 136. For original Spanish text, see Chapter III, note 4.

26. Pacheco, *op. cit.*, p. 137: "... *con el cual me aventuré una vez, a agradar a un amigo estando en Madrid, año 1625 y le pinté un lencecillo con dos figuras del natural, flores, y frutas y otros juguetes, que hoy tiene mi docto amigo Francisco de Rioja; y conseguí lo que bastó para que las demás cosas de mi mano pareciesen delante dél pintadas.*"

In sharp contrast to Pacheco's attitude of openness was the extremely negative posture on the subject of *bodegones* of his conservative counterpart in Madrid, Vincencio Carducho, whose archrivalry with Velázquez no doubt contributed to the vehemence with which he expressed himself on the subject. See Carducho 1633, 1979 ed., p. 338.

27. Pérez Sánchez (1983, pp. 18–19) gives an excellent review of the various terms used to refer to still lifes in the seventeenth century.

28. For El Greco's ideas on art, see Marías and Bustamante, *Las ideas estéticas del Greco*, Madrid 1981; Brown 1982a.

29. Pérez Pastor 1914, p. 73.

30. Gaya Nuño 1956, p. 227.

31. This painting has sometimes been associated with a still life representing books, an inkwell and a skull, which is inscribed "Æ°GV" (Madrid 1983, no. 47). Erroneously assumed to be by Alonso Vázquez (Torres Martín 1971, p. 65, pl. 45), who was long dead when the picture was painted, the painting's author remains unknown. Its style is quite different from the Berlin picture and its tonal range is earthy—ochre, grey, brown, black. Beyond a superficial level, the two paintings have nothing in common.

32. Rome, Galleria d'Arte Moderna. *Gli antichi pittori spagnoli della collezione Contini Bonacossi*, no. 65. Catalogue by Roberto Longhi and August L. Mayer, 1930.

33. See Gállego and Gudiol 1977, p. 49.

34. *Ibid.*

EARLY COLLECTORS OF STILL-LIFE PAINTING IN CASTILE

Sarah Schroth

A systematic study of the early history of still-life collecting in Spain has never been undertaken. The pioneering effort of Julio Cavestany (1936–40) to document the still lifes in the Spanish royal collections has recently been expanded by the excellent archival research of seventeenth-century private collections by Alfonso Pérez Sánchez (1967, 1977, 1983) and Mercedes Agulló Cobo (1978, 1981). These studies, however, concentrated on collections that were formed after the still life had become a fashionable and accepted part of palace and domestic decor. The question remained: who first collected still lifes when the genre was brand new? Some interesting patterns emerge in the present study, which encompasses inventories of some thirty-five important estates drawn up in Toledo and Madrid between 1590 and 1630.[1] The most significant pattern is that the first collectors of the independent still life were not at the court circles in Madrid and Valladolid, but rather in Toledo. These early collectors were a small group of Toledan nobles, many of them intellectual members of the clergy at the Toledo cathedral, who continued a long tradition of advanced taste associated with that prestigious institution. By purchasing or commissioning still lifes for their private collections, two archbishops and other lay members of the Cathedral Chapter encouraged the bold experiments in still-life painting that artists from their own city initiated before 1590. Court inventories of the same period, from 1590 to 1630, reveal that nobles in Madrid and Valladolid were more conservative in their tastes and did not admit the new genre as quickly. When they finally did, the evidence strongly suggests that the shift was due to the influence of the more progressive taste of the Toledan intellectuals.

An inventory of the collection of the Toledan nobleman Alonso Tellez Girón de Silva, taken on July 9, 1590,[2] lists some of the earliest recorded still lifes in the history of art. Tellez Girón's collection consisted mainly of devotional paintings, but also included "*nueve lienzos de verduras*" (nine canvases of vegetables). These paintings were unattributed in the inventory,[3] but it is likely that Blas de Prado and perhaps his pupil Juan Sánchez Cotán were painting such works in Toledo before 1590. Three years later, in 1593, when Blas de Prado was on his way to Morocco at the behest of Philip II and the Duke of Medina Sidonia, he stopped off in Seville, where Pacheco saw and admired several of his "*lienzos de frutas.*"[4] Despite the inevitable drawback of being unable to identify the authors of Tellez Girón's paintings, the inventory nevertheless indicates that still lifes occupied a place in the collections of Toledan nobles at the very moment the genre was being invented. Another reason for the significance of this 1590 inventory is that there is not yet any documentary evidence of patronage of still-life painting as early as 1590 elsewhere in Europe, although, of course, the genre was being developed simultaneously in the north and in Italy.

In August 1603, the testament of the still-life painter Juan Sánchez Cotán and an inventory of his belongings were recorded before he left Toledo to enter the Carthusian Order. Although knowledge of these documents has existed since 1940,[5] a composite portrait of the prestigious Toledan nobles who patronized Sánchez Cotán has never been compiled. Among the twenty-two individuals listed as owing the artist money are a dean of the cathedral, two canons, a chaplain of Los Reyes Nuevos Chapel in the cathedral, a lawyer and two high-ranking Dominicans. As an active member of Toledo's artistic community, Sánchez Cotán enjoyed the patronage of the Imperial City's intellectual and clerical elite.

Cardinal García de Loaysa Girón (1534–1599), an ardent collector of books and paintings, was an important member of that elite (fig. 28). A noted scholar who studied Latin, Greek, philosophy and theology at the universities of Salamanca and Alcalá de Henares, Loaysa was appointed canon of the Toledo Cathedral Chapter in 1564, and in 1577 became *obrero*, canon in charge of the cathedral's artistic patronage.[6] An *obrero* is a presbyter fundraiser who also superintends the repair and improvement of church buildings. He left Toledo in 1584 to assume duties as private almoner and chaplain to Philip II. Loaysa had considerable success at court. He was tutor to the future Philip III, and in 1594 was appointed by the king as acting governor of the Archdiocese of Toledo. Four years later he became archbishop of Toledo and primate of Spain.

The extensive inventory of over 3000 books and several hundred pictures[7] taken at Loaysa's death in 1599 reveals that he collected largely religious subjects and portraits, but that his private collection also included still lifes, hunting pictures, maps[8] and landscapes. The description of these works and their location in his residence in relation to other pictures are of special interest to those studying the early development of the still life.

Assuming that the sequence of the inventory followed the distribution of pictures on the walls of Loaysa's residence, the installation of Loaysa's paintings began with two small pictures of saints, followed by three panels of Flemish landscapes.

Fig. 28 Luis de Velasco. García de Loaysa Girón. 80 × 59 cm. 1599. Toledo, Cathedral Chapter Hall.

[Handwritten margin note: Cardinal GARCIA De LOAYSA GIRON (1534-1599) became "obero" CANON in charge of the cathedral's artistic patron-age]

Fig. 29   Luis Tristán. CARDINAL BERNARDO SANDOVAL Y ROJAS. 80 × 59 cm. 1619. Toledo, Cathedral Chapter Hall.

The Flemish landscapes that hung in the first room, directly after religious subjects and followed by four large maps and two *tablas de caza* (panels of dead game),[9] suggest that Loaysa regarded the newer genres—landscapes, maps and still lifes of dead game—to be no less important than traditional religious subjects. Indeed, the inventory describes one of the game pieces as: "*Una tabla de caça que dizen que hizo y pintado de su mano el rey dn F^e...que esta en gloria*" (a panel of game which they say was made and painted by the hand of the king, Philip...who is in heaven). While the Spanish monarchs and their families are known to have been amateur painters, Philip II's attempts at still-life painting are unrecorded except for this reference.

The pattern of mixing still lifes with other subjects on the walls is repeated throughout Loaysa's collection and is also indicated by the inventories of other early collections in Toledo and Madrid. The third still life listed in Loaysa's 1599 inventory hung between two portraits of unidentified cardinals in a room with other portraits and some religious paintings. Described as "*otro quadro en q[ue] [h]ay fruta pintada de melon membrillo granada naranja çanaorias y cardo*" (another picture in which there is fruit painted—a melon, quince, pomegranate, orange, carrots and cardoon), the picture may have been by Sánchez Cotán because it includes most of the elements that appear regularly in his still lifes. The cardoon was a particularly frequent subject of Sánchez Cotán's paintings, although identifying the artist on this evidence is admittedly guesswork. A fourth still life, described as "*otro quadro de pinturas de frutas melon datiles*" (another picture of fruits, melon, dates), also hung among portraits. Following a series of religious works was another still life: "*otra pintura en quadro de cossas de cocina y frutas*" (another painting of things of the kitchen and fruits).

The installation of these still lifes as independent works of art in Loaysa's collection suggests that they served more than a decorative function and were collected by Loaysa as art that could properly be displayed with the traditional genres of history painting (including religious works) and portraiture. While the "hierarchy of genres" that relegated still lifes to minor status may have been operative in theoretical discussions in Toledo, it had little effect on the installation of collections. In Toledo, the subject matter of the still life did not restrict its placement to dining rooms or other places for purely decorative purposes. Intellectuals in this academic center were schooled in Renaissance art criticism that referred to the ancient Greek precedent for such pictures as demonstrations of painterly skill and wit.[10] This classical reference doubtless appealed to a humanist like Loaysa, but the primary appeal of collecting still lifes was the sense of modernity they embodied. As Jordan points out in the preceding essay, these paintings were products of the new naturalism in Spanish art. Paintings without figures and without a narrative content were strikingly novel and were obviously viewed by artists and collectors in Toledo as an important and sophisticated new genre. When, in 1593, Blas de Prado transported his still lifes from his native Toledo to Morocco, it was presumably to display his new work—to Pacheco, perhaps to the *Xarife* of Morocco and others—and thus to seek broader recognition of a genre that had gained new status in Toledo.

Toledo's clerics and intellectuals seem to have remained in the vanguard as collectors of still lifes. Loaysa's successor as archbishop, Bernardo Sandoval y Rojas

(1546–1618) (fig. 29), was, according to Marcus Burke, a "connoisseur with modern tastes,"[11] that is, a patron of contemporary Italian and Spanish Caravaggesque painting. Although a death inventory has not been found, Sandoval's progressive role in the artistic life of Toledo is well documented. For example, during his tenure as archbishop, the cardinal commissioned three paintings from Carlo Saraceni for the cathedral of Toledo, commissions that have been viewed by some scholars as influencing the careers of such Spanish artists as Luis Tristán in the direction of tenebrist naturalism. Sandoval's progressive taste also extended to still lifes. In 1619 Juan van der Hamen received a commission from King Philip III to paint a still life of fruit and dead game for the South Gallery in the Pardo Palace "...to correspond to the other canvases that were bought at the estate sale of the cardinal of Toledo as overdoors of the said gallery."[12] The cardinal of Toledo, Bernardo Sandoval y Rojas, had died in the previous year.

Several still lifes from the cardinal's estate were purchased by the king in 1618, but many of Sandoval's pictures passed into the Oviedo family collection, part of which was inventoried in 1663.[13] Don Luis de Oviedo was Sandoval's *contador mayor*, or principal comptroller, and his sons were also employed by the cardinal. The 1663 inventory of the pictures belonging to Francisco de Oviedo, one of the sons, contained seven still lifes and one flower painting. Four of the still lifes were listed as "copies of Juan Sánchez [Cotán]." While it cannot be considered certain that these came from Sandoval's estate, most of the other pictures in the collection did. In any case, they conform to what we know of his taste. In collecting still lifes, Sandoval shared the inclinations of other members of the Toledan intellectual and clerical elite.

The progressive tastes of Loaysa and Sandoval fit the portrait of a late sixteenth-century Toledan patron given in various recent studies.[14] A circle of enlightened clergyman, intellectuals and aristocrats connected with the Toledo Cathedral Chapter sustained El Greco's successful career. Evidence suggests that later members of the same circle patronized the earliest painters of independent still lifes in Toledo. Thus, in the waning years of its temporal power, Toledo was a vital creative center where still-life painting flourished and received some of its earliest support.

THE SITUATION WAS DIFFERENT IN MADRID. Collectors there were slower to encourage the development of independent still-life painting. Indeed, in a preliminary study of fifteen estate inventories of important nobles who died in Madrid between 1590 and 1610, not a single still life was found.[15] One can document, instead, that Madrilenians before around 1615 collected the *bodegón* with figures,[16] an art form that had originated in Flanders in the 1550s and 1560s and spread to Italy around 1570. Therefore, collectors at the court seemed to be following the more conservative taste prevalent at other Habsburg courts, such as Vienna and Brussels. A taste for the independent still life finally took hold in Madrid in the second decade of the new century, whereas in Toledo collectors and artists had already developed a thirty-year history of the genre. In fact, the first known Madrilenian artists to practice this genre adopted the pictorial formula of their Toledan predecessors. The early still lifes of Van der Hamen (Plate 12 and fig. VI.4), who seems to have been

Fig. 30   Lucas van Valckenborch. SEPTEMBER
AND OCTOBER. 1590. Kunsthistorisches
Museum, Vienna.

the first successful painter of the new subject matter at the court, were clearly
inspired by the Toledan Sánchez Cotán.

The court portraitist Juan Pantoja de la Cruz (1553–1608) painted three
"*bodegones de Italia*" in 1592 for the courtier Agustín Álvarez de Toledo, a member
of the Council of the Indies.[17] Despite Philip II's preference for religious subjects in
art, which is also reflected in private collections during his reign, Pantoja's venture
into the secular *bodegón* was probably inspired by a taste for such pictures at court.
Indeed, by the end of Philip II's reign in 1598, a new type of patron had begun to
appear. His collection typically had a high secular content, contained many Flemish
works and almost always had a few *bodegones*.

An inventory drawn up in 1600 of the paintings of Juan de Borja, Count of
Ficallo, listed 281 paintings,[18] thirty-nine of which were Flemish. Only sixty-two
pictures (about one-fifth of the collection) were religious in content; the rest were
portraits, landscapes and genre paintings. The genre paintings included renditions
of the Four Seasons and Five Senses, and four *bodegones* described as "*tres tablas de
bendedores de fru[ta]s*" (three panels of fruit sellers) and "*otro lienzo de la cocina de
flandes*" (another kitchen canvas from Flanders). The paintings described cannot be
specifically identified, but they fall into the category of subject matter employed by
Pieter Aertsen (1508–1575), Joachim Beuckelaer (c. 1530–c. 1573) and Lucas van
Valckenborch (c. 1535–1597), a German artist who painted for the Habsburg court

(fig. 30). At his death in 1605, Francisco de Rojas, Marquis of Pozo, owned 299 paintings,[19] of which only one-quarter were religious subjects. His collection included thirty-two paintings of seasons or months of the year and four *bodegones*. These inventories are typical and connect collecting taste at the Spanish court to that prevalent in the courts of northern Europe and Italy.

Nine *bodegones* were listed in the 1601 death inventory of 349 paintings owned by Iñigo López de Mendoza de la Vega y Luna y Fonseca, V Duke of El Infantado (fig. 31).[20] Of the four *bodegones de cocina* (kitchen scenes), one was described as from Flanders, a second as "*cocina nueva*" (new kitchen [scene]) and a third as "*cocina vieja de Marta y Maria*" (old kitchen [scene] with Martha and Mary). This last was probably an inverted still life similar to those of Pieter Aertsen (fig. III.2) or Vincenzo Campi (fig. 4), in which the enlarged still-life element dominates the foreground and tiny human figures are relegated to a background scene. This citation in the inventory proves that the theme of Martha and Mary in the format of a *cocina* was in a Spanish collection prior to Velázquez's later treatment of the same theme (Plate 7). One of the *bodegones* was described as "*otra tabla de un villano y villana vendiendo huevos y gansos*" (another panel of a peasant man and woman selling eggs and geese). This market scene calls to mind the subjects painted by Vincenzo Campi (c. 1530–1591) (fig. 32). Later, such pictures were still being painted in Spain by Alejandro de Loarte (Plate 11). Others were described as: "*un bodegón con tres figuras de hombres y frutas y hortalizas*" (a *bodegón* with three men and fruits and vegetables); "*un bodegón que el Señor Cardenal de Mendoza envió al Duque mi Sr. que esta en el cielo, desde Roma*" (a *bodegón* that the Lord Cardinal Mendoza sent from Rome to my lord the Duke who is deceased). The latter could refer to a painting by Campi whose works were said by his brother to have been sent to Spain.[21] Until now, no specific document has been found that cites the existence of a Campi *bodegón* in collections of this early period.[22]

The high secular content of the Infantado collection—only one-eighth of the paintings had religious subjects—and the great number of Flemish pictures—142 out of 349—follows the clear pattern of the collections in Madrid that included *bodegones* surveyed for this study. The nine *bodegones*, as well as the duke's many landscapes, maps, cityscapes, pictures of animals and the seasons, were interspersed on the walls among portraits and mythological paintings.

In all probability the fashion for collecting *bodegones* originated at the court during the reign of Philip II. Loaysa, the influential Toledan cleric who held several important posts at court in the 1580s and 1590s, owned three *bodegones* in addition to the still lifes mentioned above. They were described as: "*un quadro grande y largo de pinturas de cosas de comidas y cocinero y otras figuras*" (a large picture painted of edible things and a cook and other figures) and two more "*de lo mismo y de mismo tamaño*" (of the same subject and size). These kitchen scenes correspond to the *cocinas* described in the Madrilenian collections of Ficallo, Pozo and Infantado, and it seems likely that Loaysa had purchased them between 1584 and 1594, when he was at the court before he returned to Toledo. Loaysa may have shared this taste with the king himself if the reference in his inventory to a *tabla de caza* by the monarch's own hand is valid.

Fig. 31   Unknown artist. Iñigo López de la Vega y Luna y Fonseca, V Duke of El Infantado. After 1594 (date of receiving the *Toisón de Oro*). Duke of El Infantado, Madrid.

Fig. 32   Vincenzo Campi. POULTRY VENDORS. Accademia di Brera, Milan.

Brown and Elliott[23] have established that Spanish nobles connected to the court of Philip IV often followed the taste of the king in the formation of their private art collections. Although art collecting as an aristocratic endeavor was still in its early stages during the reign of Philip III[24] (fig. 33), this king also exerted considerable influence on the type and extent of art collections formed under his monarchy. His taste is best evaluated by the major artistic project undertaken during his reign—the redecoration of El Pardo.[25] After fire swept through the Pardo Palace in 1604, Philip III ordered his court architect, Francisco de Mora, to rebuild the palace. An inventory of the new palace taken in 1623[26] is an important historical record of Philip III's acquisitions that suggests his influence on the collecting habits of his courtiers. The scheme of redecoration included the addition of many new paintings, all of which were secular in content. The subjects chosen by the king for addition to the palace collection followed the same pattern seen in Madrilenian inventories of the period: genre pictures, the Four Elements and Seasons, more hunting pictures and seven *bodegones*. Of the seven, six were Flemish market scenes:

> "*otro lienço de un bodegon con dos mugeres que estan sobre la puerta*" (another canvas of a *bodegón* with two women that is over the door)

> "*otro lienço al olio flamenco en que se benden pescados y en el esta pintado un hombre con un cuchillo en la mano derecha y quatro mugeres*" (another Flemish canvas in oil in which fish are sold and a man with a knife in his right hand is painted with four women)

> "*otro lienço de flandes pintado al olio en que estan pintadas dos mugeres y un hombre bendiendo quesos y guebos y otras cosas*" (another canvas from Flanders painted in oil in which are painted two women and a man selling cheeses and eggs and other things)

> "*otro lienço flamenco en que se bende pescado pintado al olio esta un hombre bendiendo pescado*" (another Flemish canvas in which fish are sold, painted in oil is a man selling fish)

> "*dos lienços de flandes pintados al olio flamencos en el uno estan bendiendo dos mugeres pescados y en el otro berduras y frutas que estan encima de la puerta...*" (two canvases from Flanders painted in oil. In one of them, two women are selling fish and in the other vegetables and fruit. They are over the door...)

> "*otro lienço al olio de flandes de unas mugeres que estan bendiendo algunos generos de pescados*" (another canvas in oil from Flanders of some women who are selling various types of fish).

Unquestionably the most important member of the court of Philip III was Francisco Gómez de Sandoval y Rojas, Duke of Lerma (fig. 34).[27] Lerma's influence on Philip and his court is legendary; his status as the king's favorite enabled him to amass a private fortune for himself and his relatives. When Rubens visited the Spanish court at Valladolid in 1603, he wrote to his patron, the Duke of Mantua, that Lerma's picture collection outranked any he had seen in Spain, including El Escorial's.[28] Rubens's impression of Lerma is expressed in the magnificent equestrian portrait now in the Prado (fig. 35), which Lerma hung in his ducal palace in the village of Lerma.

Fig. 33 Pedro Antonio Vidal. PHILIP III. 200 × 135 cm. 1617. Museo del Prado, Madrid.

Fig. 34 Pedro Antonio Vidal (here attributed).[27] FRANCISCO GÓMEZ DE SANDOVAL Y ROJAS, DUKE OF LERMA. 151 × 129 cm. Duke of El Infantado, Madrid.

Fig. 35 Peter Paul Rubens. EQUESTRIAN PORTRAIT OF THE DUKE OF LERMA. 289 × 205 cm. Signed, 1603. Museo del Prado, Madrid.

Although knowledge of Lerma's entire art collection is still fragmentary, inventories of two of his estates provide a barometer of taste at the court of Philip III. Like the prototype of the courtly collector already drawn, Lerma decorated his palaces mainly with secular works—landscapes, cityscapes and maps, genre paintings, the Four Seasons, months of the year and *bodegones*. In his palace La Ribera in Valladolid, a 1607 inventory of 401 paintings listed only seven religious pictures.[29] The number was slightly higher in the 1617 inventory of the ducal estate in the village of Lerma,[30] where thirty-two of 225 pictures were of religious subjects. Although the general pattern of Lerma's holdings resembles that of other noble collections at court, his was different in a significant regard: he owned still lifes. Nine "*lienzos de frutas*" (canvases of fruit) were listed in the 1607 inventory of La Ribera. This is the earliest reference to independent still lifes thus far identified in inventories of courtiers during the reign of Philip III.

Lerma's taste for this kind of picture must have derived from his connections to the clerical elite in Toledo, where still lifes were first painted in Spain. In 1599 his uncle, Bernardo Sandoval y Rojas, was appointed archbishop of Toledo, principally on the strength of Lerma's influence with the king. Sandoval, and Loaysa before him, were patrons of still-life painting in Toledo and possibly among the first patrons of Sánchez Cotán. Perhaps Lerma exercised his influence upon Philip III regarding the purchase of still lifes from the collection of his recently deceased uncle. The six still lifes in the 1623 inventory of the South Gallery of the Pardo Palace, "*mas seis tablas pequenas de frutas diferentes y abes que estan sobre las puertas,*" (plus six

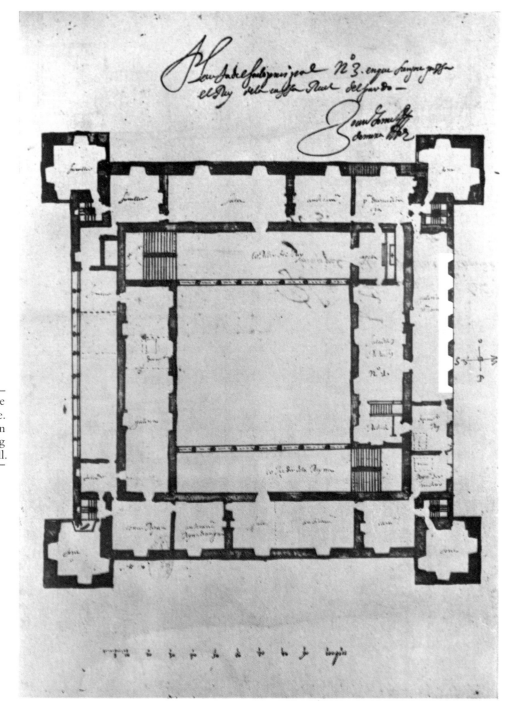

Fig. 36 Juan Gómez de Mora. Plan of the Pardo Palace. Biblioteca Vaticana, Rome. Placement of the six still lifes as overdoors in the South Gallery visible where indicated along the right exterior wall.

small panels of different fruits and birds which are over the doors), included those acquired from the estate sale of Sandoval's collection for which in 1619 Van der Hamen was paid to produce a pendant.

The floor plan of the Pardo (fig. 36) reveals that the group of six still lifes were displayed prominently within the palace, in the South Gallery directly accessible from the king's bedroom and from the portrait gallery. The still lifes were hung as overdoors but this does not imply a merely decorative role since portraits of Spanish royalty and history paintings also served as overdoors in the palace.

The royal commission in 1619 of a Van der Hamen painting for the Pardo Palace to match the still lifes acquired by the king from Sandoval's estate may have been an event of some importance in the development of the taste for the independent still life in Madrid because it signified the king's official approval of such pictures. Lerma's role as an early collector of still lifes at court, and his possible influence on the king to buy still lifes for a royal site from his uncle's estate, may indicate that he helped to promote the genre in court circles.

During the second decade of the seventeenth century, the inventories of other Madrilenian nobles also reflect a shift in taste toward the independent still life. In 1611, the VIII Count of Benavente's collection consisted entirely of religious paintings; by 1614, he had added a still life.[31] Juan de Acuna, the Marquis of El Valle, whose collection was inventoried in 1617,[32] owned fourteen still lifes, in addition to seven *bodegones*. The arrival at court in 1617 of the Italian nobleman and painter Giovanni Battista Crescenzi (c. 1577–1635) may have served to speed this trend. Crescenzi came to Madrid on behalf of his brother Pietro Paolo Cardinal Crescenzi—who needed the support of Philip III for his candidacy to the papal throne—and decided to stay. As an artist from a noble Roman family connected to the Church, Crescenzi rose quickly at court and played an influential role in the art world surrounding it. In Rome, Crescenzi, an enthusiast of the Caravaggesque style of painting, had formed a kind of academy in his home to encourage artists to paint still lifes from nature.[33] Crescenzi's presence at court may also have encouraged Philip III and others to expand their collecting taste beyond that prevailing at other Habsburg courts and to develop an interest in the independent still life. This development and the emergence of a great still-life painter at the court in the person of Van der Hamen ultimately led to the flowering of still-life painting in Madrid after 1620.

NOTES

1. This essay is preliminary to a study in more depth, which is my proposed doctoral dissertation on collecting during the reign of Philip III, New York University, The Institute of Fine Arts. I wish to acknowledge Professor Jonathan Brown's contribution in suggesting the approach for this investigation.

2. AHP T P#2120, fol. 1335v. I am indebted to Richard Kagan for pointing out the still life paintings in Tellez Girón's and Loaysa's inventories.

3. Attributions to specific artists, especially Spanish ones, are extremely rare in late sixteenth- and early seventeenth-century inventories. The general practice of the time was to mention by

name only such foreign artists of great renown as Titian or Bosch. Often the origin of a painting was noted if it was Flemish or Italian.

4. Pacheco 1649, vol. 2, p. 126; J. M. Serrera (in press) has discovered documentation of Prado's trip to Morocco that reveals that he undertook the journey while on the payroll of Medina Sidonia.

5. Cavestany 1936–40, pp. 134–38.

6. For an outline of Loaysa's career see Kagan 1982, pp. 48–49.

7. AHP M P#1811, fols. 1494–1666.

8. Kagan (1984, p. 89) has noted that map collecting first became popular in the sixteenth century. In the 1629 inventory of the collection of Pedro de Salazar de Mendoza of Toledo, one-third of the items listed were maps or cityviews. Map collecting therefore reflected a spirit of modernity in Spanish collections of this period. See also R. A. Skelton, *Maps: A Historical Survey of Their Study and Collecting*, Chicago, 1972.

9. The exact terminology used in the 1599 inventory is *"una tabla de caça"* and *"mas otra tabilla de caças,"* which could be interpreted as panel paintings of either dead game or trophies of the hunt. On the other hand, *una caza* would mean a painting of the hunt, a hunting scene with live game, figures and a landscape.

10. Pliny the Elder praises Peiraikos among the Greek painters who treated foodstuffs and other lowly subjects. He also tells the famous tale of Zeuxis, whose painted grapes were so realistic that they deceived live birds into pecking at them. Other ancient painters of still lifes were Antiphilos, Nealkes, Philiskos and Simos. See Sterling 1959, p. 135, note 6.

11. Burke 1984, vol. 1, p. 21. Both the novelty of the still life and the tenebrist naturalism of its earliest examples no doubt appealed to Cardinal Sandoval.

12. AGS, Contaduría Mayor, tercera época, leg. 784. First published by Saltillo 1953, p. 168 and later by Azcárate 1970, p. 60. The document reads that on September 10, 1619, 100 *reales* were dispatched to *"Juan Banderrame pintor vezino de esta dicha villa...por pintar al olio un lienço de frutas y caça que se hiço por mandado de su magestad para la galeria del medio dia de la Casa Real del Pardo en correspondencia de otros lienços que se compraron de la almoneda del cardinal de Toledo para sobre las puertas de la dicha galeria."*

13. Burke 1984, vol. 1, pp. 16–22. The Oviedo inventory was discovered and published by Barrio Moya 1979, pp. 163–71.

14. See Toledo, Ohio, 1982; and Brown 1982, pp. 19–30.

15. In addition to those inventories discussed in the essay, others consulted included: Rodrigo de Silva, Duke of Pastrana (AHP M P#1617, fols. 1832–36, March 23, 1596); Gómez Dávila, Marquis of Velada (AHP M P#1810, fols. 1291–1322, February 15, 1596); Luis Hurtado de Mendoza, Marquis of Mondéjar (AHP M P#2109, fols. 1592–1612, October 3, 1604); Antonio Fernández de Córdova, Duke of Sesa (AHP M P#1900–02, fols. 1173, 1604); Juan de la Cerda, Duke of Medinaceli (AHP M P#2001, fols. 1386–1449, July 7, 1605).

16. See Jordan's introductory essay above for a clear distinction between the still life and the *bodegón*.

17. Sánchez Cantón 1947, p. 102.

18. AHP M P#933, fol. 379ff. June 27, 1600. Cited by Pérez Pastor 1914, p. 83, no. 410, and Burke 1984, vol. 2, doc. 2.34.

19. AHP M P#2176, fol. 206ff. January 20, 1605. Cited by Pérez Pastor 1914, p. 111, no. 559.

20. AHN, Sección Osuna, leg. 1948. Cited by Burke 1984, vol. 2, doc. 2.14a.

21. In *Cremona fidelissima* (1585), Antonio Campi wrote that his brother Vincenzo had brought fame to their native city of Cremona and that his paintings were prized "also in Spain, where many of his pictures had been sent." For recent literature on Campi, see New York 1983, and Munich 1984.

22. Pérez Sánchez 1967, p. 312, demonstrates that the Campi *bodegón*, MESA ALEGRE (Happy

Table) in the Prado, can be traced to the 1666 inventory of the Alcazar in Madrid. A second Campi, called the COCINA (Kitchen [scene]), now in the Dirección General de Bellas Artes in Madrid, has long been in Spanish private collections, which suggests to Pérez Sánchez an ultimate Spanish provenance.

23. *Palace for a King*, Yale University Press, 1980.

24. If we search the geneology of those families who were noted for their art collections by Cassiano dal Pozo in 1626 or Carducho in 1633—such as the Dukes of Pastrana and Sesa, the Count of Benavente or the Marquis of Mondéjar—we observe that their fathers' generation either owned only devotional images or no pictures at all. The references for these inventories are cited in note 15.

25. The history of the Pardo Palace has been treated by Iñiguez Almech (1952, pp. 108–13) and Calandre (1953). A detailed discussion of the damages caused by the 1604 fire can be found in Pita Andrade (1962). An inventory taken in 1564 during the reign of Philip II (first published by Sánchez Cantón, *AEA y A* (1934), pp. 69ff, and reproduced in Calandre 1953, pp. 151–55, note 8) shows that the interior decoration of the palace then included nearly 100 paintings located in the chapel, portrait gallery and in another unspecified hall. The majority of the pictures were portraits of the royal family and other Spanish, Flemish and Italian dignitaries, including a self-portrait by Titian. Religious paintings were part of the decor. A later, detailed description of the palace by Gonzalo Argote de Molina in his *Discurso sobre la montería* (1582) reveals that Philip II had added more religious paintings to the walls, as well as a series of hunting and animal pictures reflecting the purpose of the estate. Philip III added *bodegones* and still lifes, but no religious paintings, between 1604 and 1623.

26. AGS TMC leg. 1560. My thanks to Jonathan Brown for informing me of this inventory and to Steven Orso for his photocopy of it.

27. Jordan has [orally] identified this portrait of Lerma as the work of Pedro Antonio Vidal on the basis of its formal similarities to the portrait of Philip III in the Prado (fig. 33) signed by Vidal. An entry in Lerma's inventory of 1617 supports this attribution: *"un retrato del duque, mi senor, con marco dorado de los que hizo Pedro Antonio"* (a portrait of the duke, my lord, with its gold frame, of the ones made by Pedro Antonio [Vidal]). Cervera Vera 1967b, p. 81, note 249.

28. Cruzada Villaamil, *Rubens diplomático español*, Madrid, 1874, p. 72.

29. AGS leg. 8. Published by Florit 1906, pp. 153–56.

30. Published by Cervera Vera 1967b.

31. AHN Sección Osuna 429–51, Caja 2, for the 1611 inventory; AHN Sección Osuna 430–39, Caja 2, for the 1614 inventory.

32. AHP M P#2661, fols. 687–954. January 6, 1617. Cited by Pérez Pastor (1914, p. 155, no. 796).

33. Baglione 1642, p. 365.

I. JUAN SÁNCHEZ COTÁN

(1560–1627)

Ju.sanchez cotan.f.
1602

The central event in nearly every account of the sixty-seven-year life of Juan Sánchez Cotán was his decision in 1603, at nearly the age of forty-three, to leave the city of Toledo, where he had been a successful painter patronized by the church and by members of the aristocracy and the educated elite, in order to become a lay brother of the Carthusian Order and reside in the Charterhouse of Granada. We do not know the circumstances that led to that decision, but it was not a particularly uncommon one in seventeenth-century Spain. As a lay brother, he was free to come and go outside the monastery walls and he never became a cloistered monk of the order nor wore its distinctive white robes.[1] The fact of his profession as a Carthusian, however, has become for subsequent generations seeking to understand the artist's works in the absence of many other clues, a lens through which even his earlier life could be viewed.

The biographical sketch of Sánchez Cotán written by Antonio Palomino in 1724 and somewhat amplified by Ceán Bermúdez in 1800 was more or less accurate in its broad outlines. Minor errors of place and date have since been corrected as a result of archival research, but the prevailing sentimentality of Palomino's account of the *"Santo Fray Juan"* was so appealing that it persists to the present day in Orozco Díaz's conception of the *"fraile pintor."*[2] By far the most thorough and objective modern study of the artist is that by Angulo and Pérez Sánchez (1972), which presents a balanced view of his life based on available documentation.

Sánchez Cotán was born in the town of Orgaz in the environs of Toledo on

June 25, 1560.[3] Nothing for sure is known of his early training, but Pacheco (1649) calls him a disciple of Blas de Prado, and documents that are known today confirm the friendship and collaboration of the two artists. To judge by his figurative works alone, his training was clearly within the stylistic orbit of El Escorial, with a certain Venetian orientation not far from Navarrete "El Mudo." Pacheco says that prior to becoming a friar, Sánchez Cotán had become very famous for his *"lienzos de frutas"* and that he followed Blas de Prado in this respect. According to the practice of the time, his apprenticeship must have begun by at least 1575, and by about 1580 he could have been an independent painter. We have no documentary knowledge of these years, however. On July 9, 1599, Blas de Prado named him, together with Pedro Sánchez Delgado, guarantor of a contract he had signed with the church in Madridejos (province of Toledo).[4] On December 13, 1599, Dr. Martín Ramírez de Zayas, a professor of theology at the University of Toledo who had commissioned from El Greco a magnificent family chapel dedicated to Saint Joseph, signed a document settling on a payment of 2,850 ducats for the work. Of this amount, 636 ducats were ordered to be withheld and paid directly to El Greco's creditors: 136 ducats were to go to a linen merchant and 500 ducats to Sánchez Cotán.[5] The nature of the debt was unspecified, but it is interesting to note that the two artists had dealings with one another. Sánchez Cotán's career as a painter, then, had lasted for about twenty years, when, on August 10, 1603, he signed his testament on the eve of departing Toledo. This document and the inventory of his belongings made three days later, when he had already left for Granada, are the most important sources of information about his career before that date.[6]

In his testament he names as executors Juan de Salazar, a manuscript illuminator active at El Escorial and Toledo, and Diego de Valdivieso, a well-known silversmith who had executed important commissions for the Cathedral of Toledo.[7] Most of the document is a list of debtors—ecclesiastics, professional men and a few nobles—who owed the artist money for works of art. These included a large number of religious paintings, but also others of a secular nature. For instance, Fernando de Monsalve, a canon of the cathedral, owed him for a large canvas described as *"una caza"* (a hunt). Six portraits were also listed, in addition to nine imaginary portraits of the kings of Castile. In the inventory of his studio, fifteen other portraits were itemized, among them the curious likeness of Brígida del Río, the Bearded Lady of Peñaranda (fig. I.1), whom he had portrayed in 1590. An unfinished portrait of the Cardinal Archbishop Quiroga, the guiding force of the Counter-Reformation in Toledo, must have been started before his death in 1594, if it was done from life. Also included were portrait sketches of the Archduke Albert of Austria, the nephew of Philip II, and the Infanta Isabel Clara Eugenia, the king's daughter, which must in some way have been connected with the celebration of the couple's marriage in 1599 just prior to their departure for Brussels. Among the other portraits listed were one of Queen Mary Tudor, surely a copy executed for some iconographic series, and a sketch of Queen Ana of Austria, perhaps also a copy of some official likeness. More likely to have been painted from life were a portrait of the Countess of Barajas, that of an unnamed Jewish woman, three small portraits on paper of a daughter of Juan de Salazar and a self-portrait. Although the only portrait that we know, that of Brígida del Río, falls far short of being a great work of art, the inventory and testament suggest that Sánchez Cotán continued to cultivate this genre, as did his master, Blas de Prado, until leaving Toledo.

It is evident from these documents that Sánchez Cotán also supported himself to some extent as a copyist of works by famous masters. A good number of paintings identified as Bassanos were described as unfinished, or only sketched. There were two copies after Titian—St. Francis and Europa—in addition to a reputedly original Madonna by the master. The Crucifixion by El Mudo (Juan Fernández de Navarrete) was surely a copy, as was the Agony in the Garden by Luqueto (Luca Cambiaso) described as unfinished. He also owned two evidently original paintings by El Greco—Veronica and Crucifixion—a book of drawings by Blas de Prado and two other books—one on painting and one on music—that belonged to the latter.

The documents also suggest that Sánchez Cotán had an active and fairly traditional career as a painter in Toledo, apart from his still lifes. This is, indeed, borne out by examining his only retable that can be reconstructed today, that of the Assumption of the Virgin (figs. I.2–9), which was in the Chapter Room of the monks at the Charterhouse of Granada and was executed shortly after his removal there in 1604.[8] As described by Palomino, the altarpiece contained six canvases and two panels. The latter, representing the Nativity and the Epiphany, occupied the predella from which rose the columnar framework, now destroyed. The central canvas, the Assumption of Our Lady, related to the dedication of this particular monastery, Santa Maria de la Asunción. Flanking the Assumption of Our Lady on the same level were Saint John the Baptist and Saint Bruno, the hermit saint who founded the Carthusian Order. Capping the retable, as was traditional for Toledan altarpieces, was The Crucifixion. In Toledan practice, however, this image was usually sculpted rather than painted. As Palomino made a special point of noting, Sánchez Cotán has painted it as though it were a sculpture casting a shadow upon a trompe l'oeil landscape. The Crucifixion was flanked by oval effigies of the Virgin and Saint John the Evangelist. In its overall organization and iconography, this is a completely conventional work. Stylistically, the paintings betray the range of influences operative within the environment of Toledo/Madrid/El Escorial. Their softened naturalism and harmonious colors reveal none of the intensity and sense of drama that characterize the artist's remarkable still lifes.

Within the context of Castilian art around 1600, the still lifes of Sánchez Cotán must have seemed amazing. Their intense naturalism could have had few parallels in the experience of those who saw them. Indeed, the roots of that naturalism were not to be found in art itself, but in a new outlook on nature that surely struck a receptive chord among sympathetic intellectuals. From all indications, it was among educated people at the highest levels of society in Toledo that such pictures found their first audience in Spain. The earliest reference thus far known to what was perhaps one of Sánchez Cotán's still lifes is to be found in the death inventory of Pedro Girón García de Loaysa (1542–1599), confidant of Philip II, longtime preceptor of Prince Philip (III), and briefly archbishop of Toledo before his death: *"Otro quadro en q[ue][h]ay fruta pintada de melon, membrillo, granada, naranja, çanaorias y*

Fig. I.1   Juan Sánchez Cotán. Portrait of Brígida del Río, the Bearded Lady of Peñaranda. 102×61 cm. 1590. Museo del Prado, Madrid

Figs. I.2–9   Juan Sánchez Cotán. ALTAR OF THE ASSUMPTION OF THE VIRGIN (reconstruction). Formerly Charterhouse, Granada. (2) NATIVITY. Panel, 61 × 102 cm. Adanero Collection, Madrid; (3) EPIPHANY. Panel, 61 × 102 cm. Adanero Collection, Madrid; (4) ASSUMPTION OF THE VIRGIN. 255 × 180 cm. Museo de Bellas Artes, Granada; (5) SAINT JOHN THE BAPTIST. 156 × 66 cm. Museo de Bellas Artes, Granada; (6) ST. BRUNO. 156 × 66 cm. Museo de Bellas Artes, Granada; (7) CRUCIFIXION. 220 × 120 cm. Museo de Bellas Artes, Granada; (8) VIRGIN. Oval, 88 × 67 cm. Museo de Bellas Artes, Granada; (9) SAINT JOHN THE EVANGELIST. Oval, 88 × 68 cm. Museo de Bellas Artes, Granada.

cardo."[9] (Another picture in which there is fruit painted–a melon, quince, pomegranate, orange, carrots and cardoon.)

In the artist's inventory of 1603, twelve paintings related to his activity as a still-life painter were described as follows:

    I. *Una* [sic] *ánade en tabla* (A duck on panel)

    II. *Un lienzo adonde estan un menbillo* [sic] *melón pepino y un repollo* (A canvas on which are a quince, melon, cucumber and a cabbage) See Plate 3.

    III. *Otro con un cardo y un francolin* (Another with a cardoon and a francolin [African partridge])

Although this picture is lost, both of the items mentioned are depicted in the still life signed by Felipe Ramírez in 1628, which has always been compared to the compositions of Sánchez Cotán (fig. I.10). Indeed, the cardoon in the Ramírez is exactly like the one represented in Plate 1, a work that has been identified with number VI in this list. Since number VI refers to "*the* cardoon" and is the second reference to one in the inventory, it could be inferred that the two cardoons were the same. It would not be unreasonable, therefore, to theorize that the Ramírez might be an exact copy of Sánchez Cotán. Were that the case, the failure of the inventory to mention the grapes and the silver gilt goblet with irises would not be inconsistent with the lack of thoroughness seen in others of these entries. Nevertheless, there is insufficient evidence to make such an assumption of fact. It would, after all, have been unusual for Ramírez to sign and date a copy of a revered artist's work. It may be, as has been assumed, that he merely borrowed a single form from one of his works.

    IV. *Un lienzo de frutas adonde está una taza de castañas y unos ajos y zebollas* (A canvas of fruit in which is a cup of chestnuts and some garlics and onions)

Gudiol (1977) published a still life corresponding to this description, formerly in the collection of the Marquis of Viana, Toledo (fig. I.11). In addition to the items mentioned, it includes a cardoon, some cherries, hanging apples and lemons. The point of view seems to be somewhat higher than that in the other window still lifes, with the compote tilting toward the viewer, but the composition is perfectly consistent with the autograph works. The lemons are the same as those in the still life discussed here as Plate 2. Nevertheless, the apparent quality of the execution is not on the same level as the autograph works. This could be due to the abrasion to which the picture has been subjected, or, perhaps, to its being a copy of the work inventoried here. In either case, there can be little doubt that this is Sánchez Cotán's composition.

    V. *Un lienzo de frutas adonde está el ánade y otros tres pájaros ques* [de] *Diego de Valdivieso* (A canvas of fruit in which are the duck and three other birds which belongs to Diego de Valdivieso) See Plate 4.

    VI. *Otro lienzo del cardo adonde están las perdizes ques el original de los demás ques de Juan de Salazar* (Another canvas of the cardoon in which are the par-

tridges which is the original of the rest which belongs to Juan de Salazar)
See Plate 1.

VII. *Un lienzo de frutas donde está un canastico con uvas y es de Diego de Valdivieso*
(A canvas of fruit in which there is a small basket of grapes and it belongs
to Diego de Valdivieso)

In 1850, a painting resembling this and belonging to the temporarily confiscated
collection of the Infante Sebastián Gabriel de Borbón was catalogued as number 834
in the Museo Nacional de la Trinidad, Madrid: *"Un frutero en que se ve un canastillo
con uvas y sobre una mesa aves muertas y fruta."* The painting (69 x 107 cm. in size) had
not appeared in the 1835 inventory of the Infante's collection.[10] It was supposedly
returned to the Infante but did not appear in the 1876 Pau catalogue.[11]

VIII. *Otro lienzo de frutas ques como el de Juan de Salazar* (Another canvas of fruit
which is like that of Juan de Salazar) This is a copy of number VI above.

IX. *Un lienzo emprimado para una ventana* (A primed canvas for a window)

This unfinished work conforms to the visual evidence in the finished still lifes that
the windows were painted first and then the objects were added on top.

X. & XI. *Dos cartones uno con una ganga y otro con dos ánades* (Two cartoons, one with
a pin-tailed grouse and another with two ducks)

This suggests that in some cases painted models may have existed from which the
same forms could be copied repeatedly in different still lifes.

XII. *Un lienzo de un zenacho de Zerezas y cestilla de albarcoques* [sic] (A canvas
with a hamper of cherries and basket of apricots)

This entry calls to mind a composition, most likely a pastiche, which is known in at
least two old copies (fig. I.12).[12] In addition to the two items mentioned in the
inventory, it also depicts two bunches of asparagus, some pea pods and crab apples,
a brace of game birds and what appears to be a rather misunderstood ear of corn.
The composition is more or less consistent with the works of Sánchez Cotán, but
the spatial relationships are rather clumsy, and the execution of neither copy is on a
very high level. Both the hamper of cherries and the bunches of asparagus, however, appear in a superb still life which is surely a genuine work of the artist (fig.
I.13). It is therefore possible that this painting in some way reflects elements of the
work referred to in the inventory entry.

In addition to the five still lifes that are catalogued in the following pages, it is
necessary to consider one other which I agree with Lafuente (1953) must be an
autograph work of Sánchez Cotán. This is the painting formerly in the Martínez de
la Vega collection which was included in the 1935 exhibition in Madrid (fig. I.13).
At that time, Cavestany very tentatively attributed it to Zurbarán, though he
acknowledged in the brief entry in the catalogue-guide that the painting displayed
strong stylistic similarities to the works of Sánchez Cotán.[13] By the time that the

Fig. I.10 Felipe Ramírez. STILL LIFE WITH CARDOON AND FRANCOLIN. 72 × 92 cm. Signed, 1628. Museo del Prado, Madrid.

Fig. I.11 Juan Sánchez Cotán (copy?). STILL LIFE WITH ONIONS, GARLIC AND CHESTNUTS. 67.5 × 78 cm. Private collection, Paris (formerly Marquis of Viana, Toledo).

Fig. I.12   Copy or pastiche of Juan Sánchez Cotán. STILL LIFE WITH A HAMPER OF CHERRIES AND A BASKET OF APRICOTS. Private collection, Madrid.

definitive catalogue of the exhibition was published in 1940, he had formed the opinion that the painting could be a work by Van der Hamen.[14] At the time, neither the San Diego nor the Chicago pictures by Sánchez Cotán (Plates 3 and 4) had yet been discovered. Today, when the styles of all three artists are much better understood, it seems impossible that this painting could be by Van der Hamen or Zurbarán. Yet it remains a work of spectacular brilliance. Its naturalism is more empirical and less conceptualized than Van der Hamen's. The graceful arcs and rhythms of the lilies, roses and irises extending beyond the edge of the window recall the spatial subtleties observed in the other authentic still lifes of Sánchez Cotán that we now know. The point of view is very low, indicating that the picture was intended as an overdoor. While it differs from the other known still lifes in this respect, that is no reason to exclude the probability of his authorship, for no other painter of still lifes active at that date could have painted it.[15]

All of the known still lifes by Sánchez Cotán display the objects within a window setting. This shallow, precisely defined, perspectival space allowed the artist to achieve, through the strong modeling of forms in light, a truly compelling sense of space. He connected this space to the viewer's by purposefully arranging certain objects so that they overlap the front edge of the window sill and protrude sharply into the space in front of it. A sense of great depth is also given by the dark space on the other side of the window, the shadowed background against which the objects are silhouetted. Xavier de Salas made the suggestion to Eric Young (1976) that this space is not a simple niche or window, but rather a *cantarero*, a typical cooling space in a Spanish house located in a corridor connecting the front and back doors, through which air passes and keeps foodstuffs fresh. Held (1979) called it a *despensa*, or niche in a cellar used for the same purpose. None of the compositions suggests the random order of a pantry shelf. Regardless of the original utilitarian function of the space, the artist's inventory calls it a window, and we continue that tradition. The window became for the artist a sort of stage on which the high drama of art imitating nature could be played out. As such, it was one of the most effective compositional devices in the whole development of naturalism in Spain.

Within the confines of the window setting, Sánchez Cotán employed two basic compositional types in the known still lifes: one characterized by a *horror vacui*, in which almost the entire space is filled with objects (Plates 1, 2 and 4); and one in which most of the background space is open (Plates 3 and 5). One might guess that, in the overall development of his career, the open mode was invented later, but it is likely that for some time he was painting both types of compositions simultaneously. It would, therefore, be ill-advised to try to deduce from so little information, as Gudiol (1977) does, a firm chronological sequence for the known works.

It is apparent from the inventory and from the examinations of the paintings that follow that Sánchez Cotán made a practice of studying a given object—a cabbage, a cardoon or a lemon—and, once he had cast it in a satisfying form, would repeat it in various combinations in more than one painting. Obviously, he did not return to the original model, but was able to endow the repeated image with the same conviction as the first one. Juan van der Hamen adopted this working method as well, and the results were similarly remarkable.

Fig. I.13 Juan Sánchez Cotán. STILL LIFE WITH ROSES, LILIES AND IRIS. 90 × 109 cm. Present location unknown (formerly Martínez de la Vega Collection, Madrid).

In a misguided effort to see Sánchez Cotán's still lifes as expressions of simple Carthusian values, much has been made of the "humble" subject matter they depict. It ought to be stressed, however, that raw vegetables, fruit, game and flowers were the subject matter of every early still life painter in Spain. To be sure, there is no evidence that Sánchez Cotán painted the courtly pastries and sweetmeats that Van der Hamen sometimes did, but there is nothing innately austere about the objects he did paint. Van der Hamen and Loarte painted the same kinds of fruit, vegetables and game—even the *cardo*, which has been cited so often as an almost penitential meal. The fact is that people of all classes ate *cardos*, not raw but braised long and seasoned. What Sánchez Cotán did not show in any of his still lifes is what was done by cooks to any of these things. He never depicted prepared food—only the products of nature held up for scrutiny by the artist. His pictures are about seeing and painting, not about eating, and in this they differ from northern still lifes. Neither is the sense of drama and seriousness they convey simply a reflection of the presence of God in the things depicted—though who can say that was not also on his mind?—but rather a reflection of the artist's confidence and pride in the lofty act of painting itself.

Although Pacheco's statement that Sánchez Cotán was famous for his still lifes before his profession as a Carthusian suggests that his activity as a still-life painter was curtailed afterward, we cannot infer from this, as has been done, that he painted none after 1604.[16] There is, in fact, evidence to the contrary. The STILL LIFE WITH CARDOON AND PARSNIPS in the Museo de Bellas Artes, Granada (Plate 5) was transferred there directly from the Charterhouse at the time of the deamortization of the monasteries in the 1830s. Furthermore, according to Ceán Bermúdez's corrective notes at the end of volume six of his dictionary, which have often been overlooked by art historians, two *"hermosos fruteros"* by Sánchez Cotán were said to be at the Monastery of El Paular in 1800.[17] These were no doubt painted while the artist was resident there at an undetermined time, painting about a dozen religious paintings as well. Nevertheless, it is probable that he painted few still lifes after leaving Toledo.

BIBLIOGRAPHY

Pacheco 1649, vol. 1, p. 175 and vol. 2, p. 126; Palomino 1724, pp. 845–47; Ponz 1776, vol. 10, pp. 80, 85–88, 90; Ceán Bermúdez 1800, vol. 4, pp. 337–41 and vol. 6, p. 379; Cruz y Bahamonde 1812, vol. 12, p. 29; Quilliet 1816, p. 324; Stirling-Maxwell 1848, vol. 2, pp. 506–11; Mayer 1915, p. 125; Mayer 1922, pp. 361–62; Lafuente Ferrari 1953, pp. 226–27, fig. 138; Cavestany 1936–40, p. 70; Vroom 1943; Soria 1944a, pp. 135–36; Soria 1945, pp. 225–30; Gallego Burín 1946, p. 556; Orozco Díaz 1946, pp. 159–64; Angulo 1947, pp. 146–47; Orozco Díaz 1952a, pp. 18–28; Orozco Díaz 1952b, pp. 69–74; Caturla 1953, pp. 15–18; Orozco Díaz 1954a, pp. 19–29; Orozco Díaz 1954c; Kubler and Soria 1959, pp. 221–22; Sterling 1959, pp. 56, 69–74, 76, 88, 90; Grate 1960, pp. 111–30; Santos Torroella 1962, pp. 62–63; Orozco Díaz 1965, pp. 224–31; Orozco Díaz 1966a, pp. 133–38; Salas 1966, pp. 198–201; Jordan 1967, vol. 1, pp. 32–34; Orozco Díaz 1967, pp. 111–20; Pérez Sánchez 1968, pp. 172–73; Bergström 1970, pp. 18–23; Torres Martín 1971, pp. 47–48; Bayón 1971, pp. 25–31; Angulo 1971, pp. 23–24; Angulo and Pérez Sánchez 1972, pp. 39–102; Young 1976, pp. 204–05; Gudiol 1977, pp. 311–18; Camón Aznar 1978, pp. 202–07; Marías 1978, pp. 418–19; Bergström 1979, pp. 137–42; Bergström et al. 1979, p. 212; Matsui 1980, pp. 123–33; Münster/Baden-Baden 1979, pp. 382–90; Toledo 1982, pp. 189–91; Brown 1982, p. 105; Haraszti 1983, pp. 73–75; Madrid 1983, pp. 28–29, 217; Orozco Díaz 1984, pp. 125–30.

NOTES

1. See Fray Juan de Madariaga, *Vida del seráfico Padre San Bruno*, Valencia, 1596, on the hierarchy and structure of the Carthusian monastic community. Sánchez Cotán professed as a lay brother *(lego)* on September 8, 1604 and remained in that station until his death. Although lay brothers took the same vows and followed the same general rules as the monks *(monjes)*, they had their own chapels and refectory, wore brown habits instead of the white monks' robes, and kept separate from the monks in most activities. They performed most of the menial tasks that were thought to inhibit the higher spiritual life of the monks.

2. Orozco Díaz 1965.

3. Orozco Díaz 1966.

4. Gómez Menor 1966, Document 5.

5. Brown 1982, p. 105.

6. Cavestany 1936–40, pp. 134–38. Palomino recorded the presence of paintings by Sánchez Cotán at El Paular in 1724. By 1800, Ceán Bermúdez was under the impression that the artist had taken his vows and passed the years of probation there, transferring later to Granada. In his notes to volume six (p. 379), however, Ceán corrects this error on the basis of a document of July 29, 1604, whereby Sánchez Cotán was proving the purity of his Christian lineage *(limpieza de sangre)* requisite to professing in Granada. This mistake is widely repeated throughout the later art

historical literature. Although it is certain that the artist was at El Paular for a period of time, it is not certain when, or whether he went there for a purpose other than painting the works he left there.

7. See Angulo and Pérez Sánchez 1972, pp. 40–41, for identification of Salazar and Valdivieso.

8. Palomino ed. 1947, p. 846; Angulo and Pérez Sánchez 1972, p. 68.

9. See Schroth essay above.

10. See Agueda 1982.

11. Angulo and Pérez Sánchez 1972, p. 99, no. 212.

12. A third version which appears from photographs to be possibly a modern fake was auctioned in London several years ago.

13. Madrid 1935, pp. 29–30, no. 7.

14. Cavestany 1936–40, p. 150, no. 7.

15. A seventeenth-century copy of this painting was sold by the Galería Ispahan, Madrid in 1978.

16. Newark 1964 (catalogue introduction by José López-Rey), p. 2; Jordan 1965, p. 59; Young 1976, p. 204–05.

17. In an inventory of the paintings at El Paular made on January 10, 1821—that is, several years after the French invasion and before the deamortization of the monasteries—no such pictures were listed, although two *floreros* with rounded tops did appear without attribution. See Juan J. Luna, "Las pinturas del Monasterio del Paular: Un inventario inédito de 1821," *Anales del Instituto de Estudios Madrileños*, vol. 13, 1966, pp. 1–20.

1. GAME FOWL, FRUIT AND CARDOON

Signed and dated lower center: *Ju°sánchez cotán. f. 1602*

Oil on canvas

26¾ × 35¹/₁₆ in. (68 × 89 cm.)

Private Collection, Madrid

THIS WELL-PRESERVED PAINTING WAS FIRST referred to in the art historical literature in 1848 by Sir William Stirling-Maxwell, who had seen it on display in the Museo de la Trinidad in Madrid. It had come to the museum along with other paintings forcibly taken in 1835 from the collection of the Infante Sebastián Gabriel de Borbón, a member of the Carlist branch of the royal family, to whose heirs it was later returned. The history of the painting before that time is unclear.[1]

As Pérez Sánchez notes (1974), this is almost certainly the still life described in the artist's 1603 inventory: *"Otro lienzo del cardo adonde están las perdizes ques el original de los demás ques de Juan de Salazar."* The brief entry informs us that the artist had either given or sold the painting to Juan de Salazar, manuscript illuminator and executor of his testament. By saying that the painting was "the original of the others," the entry also indicates that copies of the painting (and probably of others) were made in the studio. Indeed, a copy of it was listed in the same inventory. A rather imprecise copy of this work is known,[2] which is a more horizontal canvas in which the relative proportions of objects and intervals between them are altered.

The subtle play with visual elements in this work is remarkable. In the simple window setting customarily used by the artist, the forms are silhouetted against a profound blackness. A large, pinkish-white cardoon rests against the right wall of the opening, casting a strong shadow and curving outward beyond the window's edge into the viewer's space. Beside it lie two white radishes, the ends of which also seem to pierce the picture plane, and three parsnips (often misidentified as carrots). The play of light and half-shadow on these root vegetables and the heavy shadows on the window ledge underneath them create a clear and precise sense of space that heightens the illusion of reality caused by the sedulously observed forms. Leaning against the left edge of the window is a split cane containing six small sparrows with plucked bodies and tail feathers that seem to serrate the blackness of the void. At the upper left, three suspended lemons and their leaves are strongly modeled by the light. Their precise outlines vibrate against the black space. A cluster of red apples is suspended by strings. In the center of the space, hangs a brace of partridges and two other small birds. The interrelationship of forms and the brilliant balancing of colors are so carefully planned—so seemingly inevitable—that it is impossible to imagine the composition any other way. Therefore, a copy such as the one mentioned above, which so completely misses the point, makes one wonder if it could even be a studio copy.

In 1915, August L. Mayer, betraying how little was known then about Spanish still lifes, made the suggestion that this work was intended as the signboard of a grocery or poultry shop. By 1922, he had dropped that idea and wrote of the painting's "great plastic sense and extraordinarily zealous objectivity." In 1971, Angulo considered it equal to, if not superior to, any still life produced in Italy by the date of its execution.

PROVENANCE
Juan de Salazar, Toledo, 1603 (?); Infante D. Sebastián Gabriel de Borbón y Braganza (1811–1875); Museo Nacional de la Trinidad, no. 393 (the Infante's collection was appropriated by the government in 1835 because of his Carlist political affiliations and placed on public view; it was eventually restored to his heirs); Infante D. Pedro de Borbón y Borbón, Duke of Durcal; Infante D. Alfonso de Borbón, Madrid; D. Manfredo de Borbón, Duke of Hernani and of Ansola, Madrid.

EXHIBITIONS
Pau 1876, no. 648; Madrid 1935, no. 9; Madrid 1981–82a, no. 60; Madrid 1983–84, no. 3.

BIBLIOGRAPHY
Stirling-Maxwell 1848, vol. 2, p. 507; Mayer 1922, p. 361, fig. 267; Lafuente Ferrari 1935, pp. 173–74, fig. 6; Cavestany 1936–40, pp. 150–51, no. 9, pl. XIV; Oña Iribarren 1944, pp. 23, 91, no. 2; Mayer 1947, p. 384, fig. 297; Caturla 1953, pp. 15–18; Lafuente Ferrari 1953, p. 226, fig. 137; Orozco Díaz 1954a, p. 27, ill.; Grate 1960, p. 117, ill.; Bergström 1970, p. 20, pl. 4; Angulo 1971, pp. 22–24, fig. 4; Torres Martín 1971, p. 48; Angulo and Pérez Sánchez 1972, pp. 58, 60, 97, no. 206, pl. 74; Pérez Sánchez 1974, p. 80; Gudiol 1977, pp. 311–17, fig. 3; Camón Aznar 1978, p. 203; Münster/Baden-Baden 1979, pp. 382–90, ill.; Madrid 1981, p. 93, cat. no. 60; Agueda 1982, p. 108, no. 77; Madrid 1983, p. 31, cat. no. 3.

NOTES
1. For a history of the Infante's collection, see Agueda 1982.
2. *Colecciones españolas*, E.M.S.A. Barcelona, 1946, p. 117, pl. XXIX.

PLATE 1

GAME FOWL, FRUIT AND CARDOON

2. STILL LIFE WITH FRUIT AND VEGETABLES

Oil on canvas
27⅜ × 38 in. (69.5 × 96.5 cm.)
José Luis Várez Fisa Collection, Madrid

THE EXISTENCE OF THIS STILL LIFE WAS FIRST pointed out by Lafuente Ferrari in a footnote in 1935, when it was in the collection of the Viscount of Roda in Madrid. It was not reproduced, however, until Angulo and Pérez Sánchez included it in their 1972 study of the artist. Those authors then knew the painting only from a photograph made in 1937 and expressed reservations about its authenticity. Shortly thereafter the painting changed hands, was cleaned, and came to the attention of the same authors. In 1973, it was included in the exhibition *Caravaggio y el naturalismo español* in Seville. In the catalogue, Pérez Sánchez withdrew any doubts about the attribution and declared it an outstanding example of Sánchez Cotán's work roughly contemporary with the Hernani still life of 1602. In a series of reviews of the exhibition which followed, authorities generally agreed with this assessment. Also inspiring a general echo among the critics was Pérez Sánchez's observation that the naturalism of this and other still lifes by the artist had no direct relation to that of Caravaggio, but was instead probably inspired by Lombard innovations which preceded him. Gudiol (1977) regarded this as one of the earliest of the extant still lifes by Sánchez Cotán, dating prior to 1602.

The rather stark composition, with the isolation and even spacing of each form and a somewhat less complex play of shadows, betrays a certain earnestness, or ingenuousness, that does suggest an earlier date than the more sophisticated Hernani still life (Plate 1). The hanging objects form a clear diagonal descending from the upper left to the lower right of the composition. The two lemons hanging at the left, one halved and the other whole, are carefully studied, with special definition given to the translucency of the pulp, the white zest and seeds. As was the

artist's pattern of working, this motif was repeated in the still life with garlic, onions and chestnuts, which may be a contemporary copy (fig. I.11). Next to the lemons is suspended an enormous, golden citron, dense and monumental. The bright green cabbage is baroque in its movement, its crinkled leaves forming traps for shadow and reflectors of light. At the right, a bunch of parsnips and carrots hangs slightly in front of the window, their pointed tips teasing the space around them. On the shelf below, a pink-and-white cardoon lies on its side. Its ribbed surface richly contrasts the plain gray stone around it. As is the case in all Cotán's still lifes, the transparency of the paint in the cardoon reveals that the window was completely painted before the vegetable itself was superimposed. The form of the cardoon swells upward to fill the void and curves outward to pierce the picture plane. The orange slice and escarole to the right fulfill the same functions. Putting an end to the composition, like the final note of a musical composition, is the solitary orange.

Jutta Held, in her 1979 essay on the still lifes of Sánchez Cotán and Van der Hamen, constructs an elaborate sociological and moral interpretation of these works that is not completely convincing as an application of seventeenth-century thought. She attempts to place the simple, indigenous subject matter in historical context, citing a 1687 treatise on the five senses by Lorenzo Ortiz and interpreting from it that such Spanish monarchs as Isabel la Católica and Emperor Charles V had simple eating habits and were indifferent to fineries of the culinary arts. In the case of the emperor, at least, that is simply not historically correct. Moreover, the argument would seem to be irrelevant.

PROVENANCE
Adanero Collection, Madrid; Viscount of Roda, Madrid.

EXHIBITIONS
Seville 1973, no. 87; London/Paris 1976, no. 14; Bordeaux 1978, no. 73; Münster/Baden-Baden 1979–80, no. 206; Madrid 1983–84, no. 4.

BIBLIOGRAPHY
Lafuente Ferrari 1935, p. 174, no. 1; Angulo and Pérez Sánchez 1972, p. 98, no. 210, pl. 73; Seville 1973, no. 87, ill.; Harris 1974a, pp. 242–43; Lehmann 1974, p. 350; Steingräber 1974, p. 104, ill.; London 1976, pp. 37–38, no. 14, ill.; Young 1976, pp. 204–05, fig. 13; Gudiol 1977, pp. 312–18, fig. 2; Camón Aznar 1978, p. 204; Bordeaux 1978, pp. 117–18, no. 73; Bergström et al. 1979, p. 212, ill.; Münster/Baden-Baden 1979, pp. 382–90, no. 206, ill.; Madrid 1983, p. 32, no. 4, ill.

PLATE 2

STILL LIFE WITH FRUIT AND VEGETABLES

Signed lower center: *Ju° Sãchez Cotan F.*
Oil on canvas
27¼ × 33½ in. (69.21 × 85.09 cm.)
San Diego Museum of Art
Gift of Misses Anne R. and Amy Putnam, 1945

SINCE ITS ACQUISITION BY THE SAN DIEGO Museum of Art in 1945 and its publication that year by Martin Soria, this painting has become one of the most famous works of Spanish art and has inspired more than a few soaring interpretations. Its irresistible impact upon the viewer results from a riveting naturalism and disarming simplicity of design. In a way that can only be called ingenious, the artist has made the strongly modeled, spherical or conical shapes conform to a mathematically pure, hyperbolic curve within the space of the window. That curve, as a single shape, arrests our attention. Once engaged, we begin to examine the minutia of each of the forms illuminated by the scorching light and contrasted in richness of detail to the black void behind. It would be hard to imagine a more self-consciously artful composition. As Pérez Sánchez (1983) has noted, its mathematical rigor calls to mind the Neo-Pythagorean preoccupations of El Escorial. Indeed, if a single painting could be chosen to help define the seventeenth-century usage of the word *ingenio* and its adjective, *ingenioso,* it ought to be this one. It reveals that quality of mind and imagination intended to dazzle by its brilliance, its cleverness and originality. Without the startlingly original design, we would not be so impressed with the artist's skilled and deliberate imitation of nature, which Pacheco had called the principal aim of still-life painting.[1] Bergström's theory (1979) that this composition was inspired by sixteenth-century Italian marquetry panels is not convincing.

Soria pointed out in 1945 that this still life corresponds to the one described in the artist's inventory of 1603: *"Un lienzo adonde estan un menbillo* [sic] *melón pepino y un repollo."* Therefore, we can be certain that it dates prior to 1603. Soria later published (1959), without acknowledging the source of his information, that the painting came to Philadelphia about 1820. He must have been relying on the published research of Anna Wells Rutledge (1955) into the lists of artists whose works had been shown at the Pennsylvania Academy of Fine Arts. According to the Academy's catalogue of July 1818, item 215 was: "Juan Sánchez Cotán, *Still Life—Quince, Cabbage, Melon, &c."* Another by Cotán was listed in the same exhibition as item 191: "Sánchez Cotán, *Still Life—Celery, Birds, Lemons &c."* Although the Academy's ledger for 1818 is lost and the catalogue did not identify the lender of the paintings, the mystery of how these works got to Philadelphia is now perhaps a little closer to being solved. Like so many masterworks that have left Spain, these were surely dislodged by the upheavals of the Peninsular War and either came to America around 1815 with Joseph Bonaparte or with the collection of Mr. and Mrs. Richard Worsam Meade shortly thereafter.[2]

Bonaparte, the elder brother of Napoleon, had been made king of Spain by the emperor in 1808. With the empire disintegrating, he and his troops fled Madrid on May 26, 1813, with 1500 wagonloads of booty destined for France. Defeated a few days later at the Battle of Vitoria by the forces of the Duke of Wellington, Bonaparte escaped to France with only part of his enormous treasure, which may have included still lifes by Sánchez Cotán that he had already appropriated. On December 3, 1809, Frédéric Quilliet, a dealer who became the new king's art expert, placed his signature on a long list of paintings that had been confiscated from El Escorial and brought to Madrid for inclusion in the proposed Real Museo de Pintura, the Museo Josefino. Among them were *"Dos naturalezas muertas, de Cotán,"* another described as *"Cotán: Frutas y Cardos,"* and yet another listed as *"Copia de Cotán."*[3] Among Bonaparte's paintings inventoried after his arrival in France were two—numbers 133 and 134—which were described simply as *"Fruits divers"*[4] and could conceivably have been the Sánchez Cotáns. In 1815 he came to the United States and the following year, going by the name of Comte de Survilliers, bought an estate called Point Breeze near Bordentown, New Jersey, where he had sent to him from France the collection of around 200 paintings he had brought out of Spain. The Comte de Survilliers, realizing that he had some of the few important Old Master paintings then in the United States, loaned pictures to the Pennsylvania Academy.[5] In 1832, 1835 and 1839, he sold many of the important pictures in London. In 1841, he returned to Europe where he died in Florence in 1844.

Bonaparte's grandson, the Comte de Musignano, inherited the house, which he sold in 1847, and the remaining paintings, which he began to sell in 1845. It may not be a coincidence that in the year that Point Breeze was sold, a still life by Sánchez Cotán was exhibited at the Pennsylvania Academy and said to be for sale.[6] According to the practice of the time, this could either have been something placed there on consignment by someone or something that had been given to the Academy itself which it had decided to sell. In either case, what was probably the same picture was shown again in 1849, listed as belonging to the Academy. But the situation becomes more complicated at this point by an American collector who also owned still lifes by Sánchez Cotán.

In a second exhibition at the Pennsylvania Academy in 1847, two other paintings by our artist were exhibited as numbers 398 and 414, both described as "Fruit and Vegetables, Cotán," and loaned by Mrs. Richard Worsam Meade of Washington. While these two paintings might be the same ones that were exhib-

PLATE 3

Quince, Cabbage, Melon and Cucumber

ited in 1818, they are clearly distinct from the one exhibited for sale just months before in 1847 and again in 1849. Richard Worsam Meade was a wealthy American merchant who established a commercial house in Cádiz and took up residence there with his family in 1804. He remained in Spain throughout the Peninsular War and functioned as a major supplier to the Spanish forces. During this time he built an important collection of paintings, while the Spanish government ran up an enormous debt to him. Following the war, in his efforts to collect the debt owed him, which approximated a half-million dollars, Meade was arrested in 1816 and imprisoned for two years. In the meantime, he sent his family back to the United States with their belongings. He was released in 1818 and went to Madrid, continuing his effort to recoup his loss. In the following year under the Treaty of Florida, the United States agreed to pay all just claims of American citizens then existing against Spain. Meade returned to Philadelphia and later moved to Washington in order to prosecute his claim more vigorously. He never received his money and he died in 1828. His widow maintained their home in Washington and continued to lend generously from her collection to the Pennsylvania Academy. She was already back in Philadelphia by 1818 and, therefore, could have been the lender of the two Sánchez Cotáns to the Academy in that year.

To summarize this complex, and at this point insoluble, set of possibilities: Joseph Bonaparte, who had the opportunity to own paintings by Sánchez Cotán, may have brought them to America and loaned them to the Academy in 1818; Mrs. Meade, who did own two paintings by Sánchez Cotán and did loan them to the Academy on several occasions after 1847, either acquired them when in Spain with her husband or from Bonaparte or his grandson after returning to the United States. In either case, there appears to have

been a third Sánchez Cotán at the Academy in those years, which may be an indication that both collectors had owned works by the master.

The San Diego painting has been slightly cut down at the sides. The right side, especially, has been trimmed very close to the edge of the window opening. The resulting strip of the original canvas was added to the top of the painting at some time in the distant past in an example of misplaced priorities, to make it fit a particular antique frame. In 1976, when the painting was last cleaned, the strip of canvas was temporarily replaced in its original position along the right edge and a radiograph made (see x-ray detail, fig. I.14). It was then replaced at the top so that the frame would not have to be altered. Thus, the composition remains today somewhat distorted by the excessive height (with the extension of the cords at the top) and uneven width of the two sides of the window opening.

A pastiche involving all of the elements of this composition along with others, including a cut watermelon and a cat, was published by Angulo and Pérez Sánchez (1972, no. 211) as by an imitator of Sánchez Cotán. It appears to be much later in date.

PROVENANCE
Artist's inventory, 1603; Private collection, United States, by 1818 (see discussion above); Private collection, Boston; Newhouse Galleries, New York (jointly owned with Mondschein Gallery, New York); sold to Misses Putnam in 1945 through Jacob Heimann, New York.

EXHIBITIONS
Philadelphia 1818, no. 215; Philadelphia 1847, no. 398 or 414 (?); Santa Barbara 1940, no. 13, ill.; Paris 1952, no. 71; Seattle 1954; Milwaukee 1956 and Cincinnati 1956; Atlanta 1958.

BIBLIOGRAPHY
Philadelphia 1818, no. 215; Philadelphia 1847, p. 21; Saltillo 1933, pp. 59, 69, 72; Soria 1945a, pp. 225–30, fig. 2; Seckel 1946, vol. 30, p. 296; San Diego, Andrews, 1947, p. 82, ill.; Paris 1952, pp. 94–95, no. 71, pl. 27; Orozco Díaz 1952, p. 23, ill.; Orozco Díaz 1954a, p. 25, ill.; Rutledge, 1955, p.

193; Gaya Nuño 1958, p. 300, no. 2609; Kubler and Soria 1959 p. 221, pl. 116B; Sterling 1959, p. 71, pl. 61; Grate 1960, p. 114, ill.; Jordan 1965, p. 59, fig. 19; Jordan 1967, vol. 1, p. 45, fig. 4; *Master Works from the Collection of the Fine Arts Gallery of San Diego,* 1968, s.p.; Bergström 1970, p. 19, pl. 3; Angulo and Pérez Sánchez 1972, p. 99, no. 213, pl. 71; Gudiol 1977, p. 316, fig. 4; Bergström 1979, pp. 137–42, pl. 1; Madrid 1983, p. 34, no. 6, ill.

NOTES
1. Pacheco 1649, ed. 1956, vol. 2, pp. 125–26.
2. For information on Joseph Bonaparte in America, see Georges Bertin, *Joseph Bonaparte en Amérique,* Paris, 1893; Michael Benisovich, "Sales of French Collections of Paintings in the United States During the First Half of the Nineteenth Century," *Art Quarterly,* vol. 19 (1956), p. 296. For information on Meade, see *Dictionary of American Biography* (ed. by Dumas Malone) New York, 1943, vol. 12, pp. 477–78. I am indebted to William Hutton of the Toledo Museum of Art and to Dodge Thompson of the National Gallery of Art for having suggested and facilitated this avenue of research concerning the provenance of this painting. I am also grateful to Cathy Stover, former Archivist of the Pennsylvania Academy of Fine Arts, for her kind assistance.
3. Saltillo 1933, pp. 59, 69, 72.
4. Bertin 1893, p. 418.
5. *Catalogue of…Paintings…Belonging to the Estate of the Late Joseph Napoleon Bonaparte, Ex-King of Spain,* Bordentown, New Jersey, June 25, 1847, p. 5, no. 44.
6. Rutledge 1955, p. 193.

Fig. I.14   X-ray detail of Plate 3 showing original strip of canvas along right edge.

4. STILL LIFE WITH GAME FOWL

Oil on canvas
26¹¹/₁₆ × 34¹⁵/₁₆ in. (67.8 × 88.7 cm.)
The Art Institute of Chicago,
Gift of Mr. and Mrs. Leigh B. Block

THE EXISTENCE OF THIS STILL LIFE WAS NOT generally known until its acquisition by the Art Institute of Chicago in 1955 and its subsequent publication for the first time. Because it repeats the hyperbola motif of the San Diego picture and also probably because it has always been exhibited under glass, making careful examination difficult, several scholars have been skeptical of its authenticity. All of them eventually changed their minds, however. Bergström (1970), noting the *horror vacui* that prompted the artist to fill the void present in the San Diego version, felt that the picture lacked the intensity of the latter and must, therefore, be a good replica of the workshop or possibly the work of a disciple. By 1979, he accepted the work as autograph. In 1972, Angulo and Pérez Sánchez expressed the view that the Chicago picture was the work of a *"discípulo muy inmediato"* attesting to the prestige of the painting now in San Diego. By 1983, Pérez Sánchez accepted the painting and noted that, while it lacks some of the austerity of the San Diego painting, its "matrix of subtle equilibrium" is in keeping with the other autograph works. Gudiol (1977) considered the painting to be of excellent quality and associated it with the composition referred to in the artist's 1603 inventory as *"Un lienzo de frutas adonde está el ánade y otros tres pájaros ques* [de] *Diego de Valdivieso."* Gudiol further put forth the novel theory that the Chicago painting is the earliest extant still life by Sánchez Cotán and that the San Diego version, in what he felt must have been the artist's usual creative method, was distilled from it. This is not a convincing argument.

As was more probably Sánchez Cotán's accustomed practice (which would later become Van der Hamen's as well), he frequently repeated the same objects in varying combinations. In this design, Cotán used the open hyperbola of the San Diego picture to accommodate the added objects in the composition. The melon and its slice have both been moved forward so that they clearly overlap the front edge of the ledge and cast strong shadows to the right. By bringing the melon forward, the artist has also lowered it in relation to the top of the canvas, thereby creating slightly more space in the background for the critical placement of the grouse, whose feet barely touch the melon. To counterbalance the strong vertical of the magnificent duck at the right, he has added at the left a plump squash that overhangs the edge of the ledge, as does the cucumber. These two vertical accents recall the STILL LIFE WITH ROSES, LILIES AND IRIS (fig. I.13), which I believe to be a work by Sánchez Cotán.

The quality of the Chicago painting is indeed superb, and its state of preservation is superior to that of the San Diego still life. Although its surface is at present still covered with a heavy layer of old varnish, it has never been subjected to as harsh a cleaning as the other painting has received on more than one occasion.

PROVENANCE
Munich, Hohenthal Sale, November 24, 1933; Frederick Mont and Newhouse Galleries, New York, 1955.

EXHIBITIONS
Los Angeles, 1960; Caracas, 1967.

BIBLIOGRAPHY
Art Institute of Chicago Bulletin, vol. 50, no. 2 (1956), p. 37; *Art Quarterly*, vol. 19 (1956), p. 73, ill.; Gaya Nuño 1958, p. 300, no. 2611; Grate 1960, pp. 111–30, ill.; Chicago, The Art Institute, 1961 cat., p. 409; Jordan 1965, p. 59, fig. 18; Jordan 1967, vol. 1, p. 45, fig. 6; Bergström 1970, pp. 20–21; Torres Martín 1971, p. 48, pl. 7; Angulo and Pérez Sánchez 1972, p. 97, no. 204; Gudiol 1977, pp. 311–18, ill.; Bergström et al. 1979, p. 212, ill.; Münster/Baden-Baden 1979, p. 384; Madrid 1983, pp. 28–29, ill.

PLATE 4

STILL LIFE WITH GAME FOWL

5. CARDOON AND PARSNIPS

Oil on canvas
24¹³/₁₆ × 33⁷/₁₆ in. (63 × 85 cm.)
Museo de Bellas Artes, Granada

THIS IS GENERALLY THOUGHT TO BE THE latest of Sánchez Cotán's surviving still lifes and was found in the Carthusian monastery of Granada following the act of government which legally suppressed the monasteries in 1835 (Gallego Burín 1946). It and twenty-three other paintings by the artist were taken to the newly founded Museo Provincial de Bellas Artes in the Alhambra in 1836. Included in the still life exhibition in Madrid in 1935, it has since become one of Sánchez Cotán's best-known works. Most scholars have accepted that it was painted in the early years after the artist's arrival in Granada. Young (1976), however, insists that it must have been taken with him from Toledo in 1603. This is probably not so. Sánchez Cotán did instruct that certain items included in his inventory of 1603, such as his eyeglasses and painting equipment, be sent to him in Granada. This painting did not appear in the inventory. It is not likely that he would have left his equipment to be sent after him and taken a painting with him.

The composition of this work is similar to that of the San Diego still life (Plate 3). In this case, the curving forms of the pink cardoon leaning against the right wall of the window initiate the gentle arc of the design, which is continued by the cluster of purplish parsnips (often misidentified as carrots). As in the instance of the Hernani still life (Plate 1), the light and shadow are extraordinarily subtle. The cardoon casts a strong shadow against the right corner of the window, but the reflected light among its stalks takes on a rosy hue that causes the darkest of them to glow warmly. The parsnips range in color from the same whites and pinks as the cardoon to a purplish black. The resulting chromatic scale is extremely limited but, within that self-imposed limitation, extremely rich. The contrast between that richness, on the one hand, and the utter void of space, on the other, creates the impression of great monumentality. The nobility of the artist's vision of reality, a plausible enough end in itself, has, in the case of this still life more than any of the others, inspired some truly acrobatic attempts at religious interpretation.

Orozco Díaz (1952, 1954a) has been the most persistent in attempting to develop a religious basis for Sánchez Cotán's realism. He sees this painting as an invitation to abstinence painted expressly for the refectory of the Carthusians, an idea that fails to account for the still lifes painted before 1603, at least one of which (Plate 3) approaches this one in austerity. Don Denny (1972) would have us see the instruments of the Passion of Christ in the vegetables depicted in Sánchez Cotán's still lifes. Specifically in this one, he proposed that the cardoon represents the scourge of the Flagellation and the parsnips the nails of the Crucifixion. In support of his theory, he cites Pacheco's dictate that four nails be used in representations of the Crucifixion instead of three, a practice that was common among Sevillian painters under Pacheco's influence. He overlooked, however, that Sánchez Cotán, formed as a painter in Toledo, invariably used three nails in all of the Crucifixions that he painted in Granada. Angulo and Pérez Sánchez (1972) reject Denny's interpretation, since such symbolic allusions have never appeared in Spanish ascetic or mystical writings, adding that if such iconographical readings of paintings were current at the time, the pious Pacheco would not have failed to comment on it in his remarks on the artist, whose still lifes he clearly considered to be secular works executed, for the most part, prior to his taking religious vows.

PROVENANCE
Charterhouse of Santa María de la Asunción, Granada, until 1836.

EXHIBITIONS
Barcelona 1929, no. 3397; Madrid 1935, no. 14; Granada 1953; Bordeaux 1955, no. 21; Stockholm 1959–60, no. 97; Münster/Baden-Baden 1979–80, no. 205; Madrid 1983–84, no. 5.

BIBLIOGRAPHY
Lafuente Ferrari 1935, pp. 173–74, fig. 3; Cavestany 1936–40, pp. 28, 151, no. 14, pl. XI; Soria 1945, p. 226; Gallego Burín 1946, p. 715; Mayer 1947, p. 384; Orozco Díaz 1952a, p. 26, fig. 27; Caturla 1953, p. 20, ill.; Orozco Díaz 1954a, pp. 24, 28; Bordeaux 1955, p. 15, no. 21; Stockholm 1959, p. 76, no. 97, ill.; Grate 1960, p. 112, ill.; Bermejo 1960, pp. 329–30, ill.; Gaya Nuño 1964, ill.; Orozco Díaz 1966b, pp. 44–45, pl. 12; Jordan 1967, vol. 1, p. 44, fig. 6; Bergström 1970, p. 21, fig. 5; Torres Martín 1971, p. 48; Denny 1972, pp. 48–53, fig. 2; Angulo and Pérez Sánchez 1972, pp. 60–61, 97, no. 205, pl. 70; Young 1976, pp. 204–05; Gudiol 1977, p. 316, fig. 5; Camón Aznar 1978, pp. 203–04; Bergström et al. 1979, p. 142, pl. 133; Münster/Baden-Baden 1979, pp. 382–90, no. 205, ill.; Haraszti 1983, p. 73, fig. 45; Madrid 1983, p. 33, no. 5, ill.

PLATE 5

CARDOON AND PARSNIPS

II. *BLAS DE LEDESMA*

(Documented in Granada, 1602 and 1614)

BLAS DE LEDESMA. Ẽ granada.

Blas de Ledesma is one of the few painters now known to have painted still lifes who is mentioned by Pacheco in *Arte de la pintura* (1649), although he does not refer to such works by him. In a chapter entitled "On Illumination, Stucco and Fresco Painting—Their Antiquity and Duration," he cites Ledesma, along with Pedro Raxis (d. 1626) and Antonio Mohedano (c. 1563–1626), as a painter who practiced fresco decoration in the manner of the Italian grotesque painters Julio de Aquilis and Alejandro Mayner, who came to Spain in the 1530s and worked in the palace of Charles V in the Alhambra.[1] The only other mention of Ledesma in seventeenth-century literature is by the Granadan poet Pedro Soto de Rojas in a lyric description of his own house and gardens in El Albaicín. In his 1652 *Paraíso cerrado para muchos, jardines abiertos para pocos*, Soto de Rojas praised Ledesma's ability as a still-life painter by rallying the cliché of Pliny's famous story about Zeuxis and the birds deceived by his skill:

> *Vitrubio en tanto asseo su elegancia.*
> *Acusa de ignorancia,*
> *Viendo de Zeusis el pincel facundo,*
> *Que aplaudido en los términos del mundo,*
> *Por mano de Ledesma en sus fruteros,*
> *Buelve a engañar los pájaros ligeros.*[2]

From this reference, we know that Ledesma had something of a reputation for his fruit still lifes. Not a single picture by him was known, however, before 1943, when

Fig. II.1   Blas de Ledesma. STILL LIFE WITH
GRAPES, FRUIT AND BIRDS. 85 × 136 cm.
Signed. Private collection.

Fig. II.2   Blas de Ledesma. STILL LIFE WITH
POMEGRANATES AND BIRDS. 85 × 136 cm.
Signed. Private collection.

Julio Cavestany published the painting that now belongs to the High Museum of
Art in Atlanta (Plate 6). This work, which is fully signed, but not dated, is still our
touchstone for knowledge of the artist. To this day, few facts have been added to his
biography beyond what Cavestany was able to pull together then. He still believed
that Ledesma's works were painted in the sixteenth century. In addition to the
signed still life, which Cavestany related to the tradition of Italian grotesque painting because of its "decorative" quality, he also reproduced another unsigned painting of exactly the same dimensions and belonging to the same Sevillian collection,
which he considered to be its pendant despite the fact that its composition was quite
different. Acknowledging that it appeared at first glance to be by another hand, the
author was convinced, after examining both side by side, that it too was by
Ledesma. In 1947, three more still lifes of this second type were exhibited in Barcelona (figs. II.1–3).[3] All three are signed, but the manner of signing resembles in
no way the large, Roman letters with which the Atlanta picture is signed. It has
more in common with, but does not imitate, a signature reproduced in facsimile by
Bénézit, which had been noted by Cavestany.[4] Although signatures on some paintings attributed to Ledesma have been justly called into question recently,[5] there was
no reason in 1947 to have faked these, and they appear to be genuine. Unless proof
to the contrary is forthcoming, it would be wise to keep an open mind about these
particular paintings.[6]

  The three still lifes exhibited in Barcelona in 1947 all have analogous compositions and are distinctly provincial in their lack of a secure naturalism. All have
repoussoir curtains in one corner of the foreground, balanced on the other side by
branches with exotic birds. All are asymmetrical in design: one depicts sweets and
nuts together with metal plates, wooden boxes, ceramic vessels and glassware; the
other two depict fruit. In all of the foregrounds, certain elements are arrayed in a
row with a degree of naïveté. Except for their subject matter, these works have
nothing to do with the sophisticated achievements of Sánchez Cotán and painters
nearer the court, but they have a certain decorative charm.

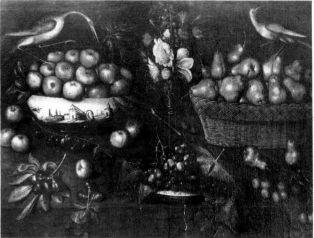

Fig. II.3   Blas de Ledesma. Still Life with
Sweets. 84 × 136 cm. Signed. Private
collection.

Fig. II.4   Unknown artist. Still Life with
Fruit and Birds. 88 × 131 cm. Private
collection.

In 1952, Charles Sterling mistakenly assumed that Blas de Ledesma, whose surname Cavestany had observed was of Castilian origin, was actually the Blas de Prado mentioned by Pacheco as the teacher of Sánchez Cotán and skilled painter of fruit still lifes. Reiterated by Sterling in 1959, this assumption was widely diffused throughout the secondary literature. Yet it was not accepted by everyone[7] and, in 1965 and 1966, Eric Young[8] and Chandler Post[9] refuted the claim without giving substantiating reasons. In 1967, I pointed to a document that proved the two artists could not be the same.[10] While Blas de Prado had already died in Toledo by 1600, Blas de Ledesma was active as a painter in Granada and Málaga in 1602.[11] In 1614, he designed a stucco vault decoration for the Sala de Mozárabes in the Alhambra, an example of just the kind of work for which Pacheco recognized him.[12] We do not know the date of Ledesma's death, but it is reasonable to assume that he was of the same generation as Mohedano and Raxis. While his still lifes probably date from the first two or three decades of the seventeenth century, they are surely later than once thought, and we can no longer assume with certainty that they were painted before 1600.

That is all that we know about Blas de Ledesma, but, unfortunately, the story does not end there. Due to the misguided labors of the late Ramón Torres Martín, aptly criticized by Pérez Sánchez,[13] the public perception of this artist has been so confused that his name has become a meaningless label to hang on anonymous Spanish still lifes of indifferent quality. In a series of articles, exhibition catalogues and books published between 1967 and 1978, Torres Martín expanded the attributed oeuvre to a staggering total of 115 works clearly by many different hands. In a pamphlet of 1967, he first augmented the oeuvre to a total of twenty-four pictures, some of them obviously by the same hand as the three exhibited in Barcelona in 1947, but others related neither to them nor to each other, and some with signatures that eventually proved to be false. In a 1976 exhibition catalogue, the attributed oeuvre grew to a total of sixty-nine works. The major "innovation" here was the addition of a sizeable number of paintings representing fruit and birds that had all been recently, or were at the time, on the art market in Barcelona or Madrid (fig. II.4). By a single, recognizable hand, quite superior to that of Ledesma as seen in the works exhibited in Barcelona in 1947, these charming, somewhat provincial paintings have, as Pérez Sánchez has noted, nothing to do with the Granadan artist.[14] The biggest "innovation" of Torres Martín's 1978 catalogue of Ledesma's oeuvre was the decision that he had painted a group of derivative pictures based on the still lifes of Juan van der Hamen y León, which are in the Cerralbo Museum in Madrid, and others like them. Works of extremely base quality, they have nothing to do with Ledesma or with the other paintings attributed to him by Torres Martín.

One of the few credible works in Torres Martín's catalogue is the half-length VIRGIN AND CHILD in the collection of Angel de la Riva in Málaga.[15] Signed with Roman capitals like the Atlanta still life, it is a very modest painting indeed, suggesting, together with the few still lifes which can be considered his, that Blas de Ledesma was, after all, a minor provincial talent whom Pacheco, perhaps rightly, recognized for his architectural decorations rather than his easel paintings.

BIBLIOGRAPHY
Pacheco 1649, vol. 2, p. 43; Soto de Rojas 1652; Ceán Bermúdez 1800, vol. 3, p. 6; Gómez Moreno 1892, p. 60; Bénézit, 1911–23 [1966, vol. 5, p. 471]; Allende-Salazar in Thieme Becker 1928, vol. 22, p. 536; Cavestany 1936–40, p. 23; Cavestany 1943, pp. 16–18; Barcelona 1947, pp. 7–17; Paris 1952, pp. 36–38; Sterling 1959, pp. 38, 49, 69–70; Llordén 1959, pp. 118–19; Jordan 1967, vol. 1, pp. 37–39; Torres Martín 1967, pp. 5–9; Barnard Castle, The Bowes Museum, 1970 cat., pp. 42–43; Bergström 1970, pp. 23, 89; Torres Martín 1971, pp. 39–42; Bergamo 1971, pl. 46; Pérez Sánchez 1972, p. 75; Torres Martín 1974, pp. 217–23; Torres Martín 1976; Torres Martín 1978; Camón Aznar 1978, p. 213; Hernández Díaz 1978, pp. 449–51; Bergström et al. 1979, p. 197; Sterling 1981, pp. 17, 19–20; Madrid 1983, pp. 70–71, 83, 210.

NOTES
1. See Introduction for more on these artists.

2. Quoted in Cavestany 1943, p. 17.

3. Barcelona 1947, pp. 7–17, signatures reproduced in facsimile.

4. Cavestany lamented that Bénézit did not indicate the source of the signature.

5. Pérez Sánchez 1983, p. 70.

6. Sterling (1952) and Bergström (1970) accepted the authenticity of the paintings and their signatures. Pérez Sánchez in his 1972 review of Bergström indicated that he found it hard to accept them because of the dissimilarity to the Atlanta still life.

7. For example, the oral opinion of Orozco Díaz.

8. Eric Young, "Renaissance and Mannerist Painters in Spain," *Apollo*, March 1965, p. 214.

9. Chandler R. Post, *A History of Spanish Painting*, vol. 14, Cambridge, 1966, p. 205.

10. Jordan 1967, pp. 38–39.

11. Llordén 1959, pp. 118–19.

12. Gómez-Moreno 1892, p. 60, cited by Bergström 1970, pp. 23 and 89, note 23.

13. Pérez Sánchez 1983, p. 70.

14. Pérez Sánchez 1983, p. 84, no. 55. It should be noted here that old photographs of a number of these paintings in the archive of the Instituto Amatller in Barcelona indicate that they have a Mallorcan provenance, information that might be helpful in tracking the painter.

15. Torres Martín 1978, no. 115.

6. STILL LIFE WITH CHERRIES AND FLOWERS[1]

Signed lower left: *Blas de Ledesma. Ē granada.*
Oil on canvas
22⅛ × 30⅞ in. (56.2 × 78.4 cm.)
High Museum of Art, Atlanta
Great Painting Fund Purchase

SINCE ITS PUBLICATION FOR THE FIRST TIME in 1943, and especially since its exhibition at the Orangerie des Tuilleries in 1952, this haunting painting has been associated with the earliest origins of still life in Spain. Its conspicuous signature confirms not only the identity of the painter, but also boldly proclaims that it was made in Granada, where Pacheco said that Ledesma benefitted from the tradition of good light in painting established years earlier by Julio and Alejandro, who painted wall decorations in fresco and tempera. Charles Sterling (1952), like Julio Cavestany, believing that the painting was executed prior to 1600, saw it as an outgrowth of the kind of grotesque panel painting practiced in Italy by Giovanni da Udine. This is a modern assumption, and there is no evidence that Julio and Alejandro painted this kind of picture.

The composition features a finely woven basket of cherries placed in the center of a narrow stone plinth. The cherries are delicately modeled and several of them have fallen from the basket on either side, establishing a certain symmetry and a pyramidal focus of the overall design. The light enters gently from the left; the basket and each of the fallen cherries cast soft shadows to the right. The most unusual aspect of the composition, which puzzled and disappointed Cavestany but has delighted others, is the presence of flowers in the background. Rising on either side of the basket, as if growing behind a garden wall, the flowers reinforce the symmetrical orientation of the composition. Yet this suggestion of flowers naturally growing is disturbing, because the setting is dark, and no landscape is visible. Has the artist led us with a torch into a garden at midnight? Hardly anything so like García Lorca as that. Instead, as in the still lifes of Sánchez Cotán, the objects depicted have been removed from their natural context and rearranged within the context of art, where the conventions of naturalism required a dark background and a strong light to give relief to the natural forms. Indeed, Pérez Sánchez, thinking afresh about this painting, has made the original and valuable suggestion that Ledesma was probably influenced by Sánchez Cotán, present in the Charterhouse of Granada from 1603, in the "almost magical silence" of the picture and in its quality of light.[2] Although the painting's symmetry resembles nothing in Sánchez Cotán's known still lifes, the disposition of the objects along a stone ledge and the acute observation of detail in the cherries do call to mind the Toledan tradition.[3]

The painting differs greatly in these respects from the three signed paintings that were exhibited in Barcelona in 1947 (figs. II.1–3). If all of these paintings are indeed by him, then some strong differentiating force must have intervened.

Two still lifes (figs. II.5, 6) belonging to the Marquis of Deleitosa, Madrid, which follow very much the same format as STILL LIFE WITH CHERRIES AND FLOWERS, were exhibited in the 1983 Madrid exhibition (Plates 53 and 54). These paintings were first published by Torres Martín (1971) with an attribution to Pedro de Medina, but that author subsequently (1978) gave them to Blas de Ledesma. Pérez Sánchez accepted that attribution with reservations owing to their relatively poor state of preservation, which has led to a hardening of the shadows and a general flattening of the surface.

PROVENANCE
Juan Gómez Castillo Collection, Seville, 1943; Private Collection, Barcelona, 1952; Durlacher Bros., New York; acquired by Atlanta Art Association (now High Museum of Art), 1957.

EXHIBITIONS
Paris, 1952, no. 18, ill.; Syracuse, 1957, no. 15; Atlanta, 1958; Los Angeles / San Diego, 1960; New Orleans, 1962–63, no. 41, ill.; Indianapolis / Providence, 1963, no. 4, ill.; Newark, 1964–65, no. 14, ill.; Atlanta, 1966, no. 14, ill.

BIBLIOGRAPHY
Cavestany 1943, pp. 16–18; Oña Iribarren 1944, pp. 23, 91, no. 1; Paris 1952, pp. 36–38, no. 18; Poland 1958; Sterling 1959, pp. 38, 49, 69–70, pl. 24; López-Rey 1963a, p. 512, fig. 2; López-Rey 1963b, pp. 420–23; Newark 1964, p. 4, no. 14, ill.; Jordan 1965, pp. 61–62, fig. 5; Jordan 1967, vol. 1, pp. 37–39, fig. 10; Torres Martín 1967, p. 8, fig. 16; Bergström 1970, pp. 23, 89, pl. 7; Torres Martín 1971, p. 41, pl. 6; Torres Martín 1974, pp. 217–23, ill.; Young 1976, pp. 207–08; Torres Martín 1976, no. 46; Bergström et al. 1979, p. 197, ill.; Torres Martín 1978, pp. 119–20, no. 100, ill.; Sterling 1981, pp. 69, 93, pl. 24; Madrid 1983, p. 70, ill.

NOTES
1. The title usually given this painting is STILL LIFE WITH CHERRIES, IRIS AND LUPIN. The tiny flowers were identified by Poland (1958) as lupin [sic]. Pérez Sánchez (1983) identified them as larkspur. They seem instead to be Spanish Broom *(Spartium Junceum)*, characterized by its long spine and tiny petals.
2. Pérez Sánchez 1983, p. 70.
3. Pérez Sánchez probably made too much of the resemblance between the irises in this painting and those in Sánchez Cotán's IMMACULATES painted in Granada. Certainly the draughtsmanship and modeling of the flowers in his IMMACULATE in the Museo de Bellas Artes in Granada (Orozco Díaz 1954c, p. 55) is vastly more skilled.

Fig. II.5 Attributed to Blas de Ledesma. BASKET OF FRUITS AND FLOWERS. 60 × 80 cm. Marquis of Deleitosa, Madrid.

Fig. II.6 Attributed to Blas de Ledesma. BASKET OF EGGPLANTS. 60 × 80 cm. Marquis of Deleitosa, Madrid.

PLATE 6

STILL LIFE WITH CHERRIES AND FLOWERS

III. DIEGO VELÁZQUEZ
(1599–1660)

B etween the ages of about sixteen and twenty-four, the young Velázquez painted in Seville a number of true *bodegones*—that is, still lifes with figures—which have never been surpassed. These remarkable works of the artist's youth depict the people and things in his immediate surroundings; it was obvious to those who knew him best, by the time he completed his education in 1617, that his talent was off the scale of ordinary experience. "After five years of education and training, impressed by his virtue, integrity and excellent qualities, and also by the promise of his great natural genius, I gave him my daughter in marriage," wrote Francisco Pacheco of his pupil *(Arte de la pintura,* 1649).[1]

Elsewhere in his book, in a chapter entitled "On the Painting of Animals and Birds, Fish-Stalls and *Bodegones* and the Ingenious Invention of Portraits from Life," Pacheco discussed the importance of a painter's ability to imitate the natural qualities and movements of animals and birds, citing as examples of those who have done it well Bassano in Venice, and Orrente and Navarrete "El Mudo" in Spain.[2] He went on to say:

> Others have been inclined to paint fish-stalls with much variety; others, dead fowl and game; others, *bodegones* with varieties of food and drink; others, ridiculous figures with diverse and ugly subjects that provoke laughter, and all these things, made with boldness and quality *(buena manera),* entertain and demonstrate inventiveness *(ingenio)* in composition and in lifelikeness.[3]

In a subsequent paragraph Pacheco set up the opportunity to underscore the legitimacy and ingenuity of his son-in-law's early paintings of this sort by citing the ancient precedents for them:

> Do we find perhaps some antique painter who was inclined to paint these ordinary and comic things? It appears so; Pliny mentions one called Dionisio, with the nickname Anthropographos, who painted only figures with amusing names… And in the same way Peiraikos also painted humble things like barbershops, stalls, meals and similar things, for which they called him Riparographos; these paintings caused great delight and by them the artist achieved the greatest glory.[4]

Pacheco commented specifically on the *bodegones* of the young Velázquez in the spirit of the then relatively common belief that "modern times" offered equal, if not superior, talents and achievements to those of antiquity:[5]

> Well, then, are *bodegones* not worthy of esteem? Of course they are, when they are painted as my son-in-law paints them, rising in this field so as to yield to no one; then they are deserving of the highest esteem. From these beginnings and in his portraits…he hit upon the true imitation of nature, thereby stimulating the spirits of many artists with his powerful example.[6]

Barry Wind has recently stressed with good reasons the importance of these passages to an understanding of certain of Velázquez's early paintings which, Pacheco left no doubt, were intended as "modern" examples of these amusing genres of antiquity.[7] To be sure, the spirit of competition with antiquity was involved with the beginnings of naturalism in Europe, and Pliny's reference to Peiraikos was cited by other sixteenth- and seventeenth-century authors.[8] But these ancient precedents only justified the strong inclination among creative people at the turn of the seventeenth century to focus on the events and values of common people in everyday life. Nowhere was this tendency more noticeable than in Spain, with the development of the picaresque tradition in literature and the visual arts.

Pacheco continued his recollection of Velázquez's early training in his discussion of drawing and the importance of outlines in the realization of a truly lifelike image:

> In this doctrine my son-in-law Diego Velázquez de Silva was brought up when he was a boy. He used to bribe a young country lad who served him as a model to adopt various attitudes and poses, sometimes weeping, sometimes laughing, regardless of all difficulties. And he made numerous drawings of the boy's head and of many other local people in charcoal heightened with white on blue paper, and thereby he gained assurance in portraiture.[9]

If Pacheco's own paintings are somewhat academic and dull, his most appealing works of art are his own portrait drawings, made for his *Libro de retratos,* or book of portraits of the famous men of his time (fig. III.1).[10] In these incisive likenesses, we can see the analytical bent of the master who guided his pupil to learn by using his eyes. But nature and antiquity were surely not Velázquez's only examples. His second published biographer, Antonio Palomino (1724), writing almost a century later, tried with the aid of hindsight to establish a plausible artistic milieu in his account of the young artist's life. Besides mentioning the names of several well-

Fig. III.1   Francisco Pacheco. PORTRAIT OF FRIAR JUAN BERNAL from *Libro de retratos.*

Fig. III.2 Pieter Aertsen. CHRIST IN THE
HOUSE OF MARTHA AND MARY. 60 × 101.5 cm.
Signed. Kunsthistorisches Museum, Vienna.

known artists of Italy and Spain whose works he assumed Velázquez might have
known and admired, Palomino wrote:

> Velázquez rivaled Caravaggio in the boldness of his painting and was the equal of
> Pacheco on the side of the theoretical. He admired Caravaggio for his extraor-
> dinary and subtle talent and he chose Pacheco as his teacher because of his knowl-
> edge of the field, which made him worthy of the choice… He was called a second
> Caravaggio because he imitated nature so successfully and with such great propri-
> ety, keeping it before his eyes in all things and at all times.[11]

For nearly the past hundred years, art historians have debated how, whether,
and which works by foreign artists might have inspired the young Velázquez. A
very few religious paintings by Caravaggio, and perhaps copies of others, had
reached Spain by then, but, despite Palomino's account, there is no true resemblance between Velázquez's early works and the paintings of Caravaggio.[12] He
probably did know other types of paintings, however, whose subject matter at least
had a bearing on his *bodegones. Bodegones de Italia,* as they were called, paintings of
daily life of the type done by Vincenzo Campi (c. 1530–1591) and Bartolomeo
Passarotti (1529–1592), were surely known: elsewhere in Andalucía, in the city of
Úbeda (Jaén), the painter Juan Esteban had signed such a work in 1606 (fig. 21).
Also familiar was the even older Flemish tradition, dating from the middle of the
sixteenth century, of paintings in which a superabundance of foodstuffs in the foreground often dominates a tiny religious scene in the background. Paintings by
Pieter Aertsen (1508–1575) and Joachim Beuckelaer (c.1530–c.1573), or at least

engravings after them, were in Sevillian collections (fig. III.2). In Pacheco's house, which Palomino called "a gilded cage of Art," all of these things were surely known of and were probably talked about for whatever examples they might offer a young artist. But Velázquez's *bodegones* actually resemble none of them, except in the most general ways. Nor do his works resemble those of Pacheco's other disciples or of the other young artists of Seville at the time. The singular, self-propelled talent of Velázquez seems to have launched itself from the *idea* of imitating nature, an idea that in Spain was still largely identified with the Venetian tradition of the Bassanos and with the fabled artists of antiquity.

Fig. III.3   Velázquez. MUSICAL TRIO. 87 × 110 cm. c. 1615–17. Gemäldegalerie, West Berlin.

Fig. III.4   Velázquez. THREE MEN AT TABLE. 107 × 101 cm. c. 1618. The Hermitage, Leningrad.

By far the earliest *bodegón* generally accepted as by Velázquez's hand is the MUSICAL TRIO in Berlin (fig. III.3). Usually dated about 1616–17, it is surely a work from his apprentice years and may very well date a year or two earlier than usually thought. In it we can see several of the preoccupations of which Pacheco wrote in describing the young artist's development: the striving after lively facial expressions, each one studied to the point of being frozen and psychologically isolated from the rest; and the strong contour of each form, which contributes to an emphatic sense of volume and which Pacheco had insisted was essential to a lifelike image. There are awkwardnesses in drawing and perspective, as in the body of the guitar and the round of cheese. Each form is acutely observed as the light falls upon it, yet the picture does not hold together. Such subject matter as this was common among the Dutch followers of Caravaggio in Rome, but Velázquez's treatment of it appears as though he had only heard about such works, grounded as it is entirely in the costumes, accoutrements and experience of his immediate surroundings.[13]

Fig. III.5   Velázquez. A Girl and Two Men at a Table. 96 × 112 cm. c. 1618–19. National Museum of Fine Arts, Budapest.

Considerably more advanced is the painting known as Three Men at Table in the Hermitage at Leningrad (fig. III.4), in which three male figures of different ages are seated around a simple table spread with a white cloth. The principal advance is in the handling of light, which much more subtly defines the forms—especially the still-life objects on the table and the cloth itself—and seems to unify the composition. Although the facial expression of the boy lifting the flask is still somewhat forced, and both of the younger figures look out of the picture conveying the sense of a private joke, the theatrics of the scene are better managed.[14]

A further development of this composition is found in the *bodegón* in the Museum of Fine Arts, Budapest (fig. III.5). In the slightly horizontal composition, the place of the young boy has been taken by a maidservant who fills a glass of water from an earthenware pitcher and presents it to the old man. The younger man, rather than looking out of the painting as in the Leningrad picture, gestures with his thumb toward the maid and says something to his companion, who in turn looks across at him while reaching for the glass. The air of a joke addressed to the viewer has been shed in favor of a dramatic interaction among the figures themselves. This represents a tremendous advance on the young artist's part and suggests a somewhat later date. Unfortunately, the painting is too damaged and restored to be able to judge from its subtler pictorial qualities how much later it might be.

One of Velázquez's few dated paintings is The Old Woman Frying Eggs in the National Gallery of Scotland, Edinburgh (fig. III.6). It was painted in 1618, the year after his acceptance into the Guild of Saint Luke and the year of his marriage to Juana Pacheco. Among the masterpieces of his youth, it is a *bodegón* in the truest sense of the word, depicting an old woman assisted by a young boy in the preparation of a meal. The figures and articles of the kitchen are united in a tightly knit, rhythmical design characterized by a hyperbolic curve similar to the famous design of Sánchez Cotán's Quince, Cabbage, Melon and Cucumber (Plate 3). The curve begins with the boy's head at the left and descends through the melon he is holding to the vessel of congealing eggs and ends with the group of objects on a plinth in the foreground—a white saucer with a knife casting a shadow on its concave surface, a brass mortar and pestle, two pottery pitchers, a red onion and some garlic. This ingenious composition is unusual enough to make one wonder if Velázquez did not know and admire some work of his Toledan predecessor. Certainly the interchanges between Seville and Toledo were sufficient for this to be possible. The firmly anchored composition gives the painting a sense of arrested motion. In this shadowed stillness, our eyes are lured to explore the tactile qualities of every form, which, in their variety, have been captured with spectacular virtuosity. Indeed, we cannot escape the impression that the artist was blatantly showing off his ability. Only in this sense does the immaturity of his nineteen years reveal itself.

In two oblong canvases of the Sevillian period, Velázquez couched familiar religious subjects in compositional terms of *bodegones*. Christ in the House of Martha and Mary (Plate 7), painted in the same year as The Old Woman Frying Eggs, shares the same model for the figure of the old woman and is painted in much the same manner. Christ at Emmaus in the Beit Collection (fig. III.7) is often dated somewhat later but is conceived in a similar way.[15] Both of them have been com-

Fig. III.6 Velázquez. THE OLD WOMAN FRYING EGGS. 99 × 116.9 cm. 1618. National Gallery of Scotland, Edinburgh.

pared to the elaborate "inverted" still lifes of Aertsen and Beuckelaer, because the religious scenes are relegated to tiny background vistas into other rooms, while the scenes of daily life with prominent still-life elements occupy the foregrounds. In CHRIST AT EMMAUS, the Negro maidservant pauses in her work, leaning on the table as though weary, staring blankly as though her mind is wandering, unaware that behind her the risen Christ has revealed himself to his two disciples. The supernatural event in the background heightens the viewer's awareness of the earthbound reality of the foreground scene, and, conversely, the mortality of the maidservant underscores the miracle of Christ's resurrection.[16]

Velázquez already had an apprentice by 1618, and he was, as Pacheco proudly noted, beginning to influence other artists in Seville at the time. The large number of derivative works which presuppose a knowledge of his paintings attest to his prominence on the Sevillian art scene. One in particular is the *bodegón* (fig. III.8) signed by Francisco López Caro (1598–1661) which makes use of both Velázquez's compositional format and several objects that appear in the works we have just examined.[17] López Caro was one year Velázquez's senior and knew him, as proved by a document of 1622 in which he served as a witness to a power of attorney

Fig. III.7 Velázquez. CHRIST AT EMMAUS. 55.8 ×118 cm. c. 1620. Sir Alfred Beit Collection, Blessington, Ireland.

between Velázquez and Pacheco executed on the eve of the former's departure for Madrid. A work of modest quality, it may nevertheless help to bring order into the chaos of anonymous pastiches after Velázquez's *bodegones* by giving us a name we can associate with one of the hands.

The culminating work of Velázquez's youth is the great THE WATER SELLER OF SEVILLE (fig. III.9), painted sometime between 1620 and 1622, when he made his first trip to Madrid. The most esteemed of his paintings from the Sevillian period, the picture was probably brought with him to the court, where it belonged in 1627 to his friend and protector Juan de Fonseca y Figueroa. Upon Fonseca's death in that year, when Velázquez appraised his collection, the work was valued by the artist more highly than any other. Within a few years, it had been acquired by the king's brother, the Cardinal Infante Don Fernando. It was catalogued in the royal collection in 1701 and remained there until it was carted off with many other treasures by Napoleon's brother, the intrusive King Joseph, from whom it was rescued by the Duke of Wellington and the allied forces in 1813.

The painting depicts an introspective old man wearing a tattered jerkin, one hand resting on an enormous clay water jug, while with the other he offers a young boy a goblet of water containing a fig for the purpose of clarifying and freshening the water.[18] Barely sketched in the shadows, a young man staring directly at us drinks from an earthen mug. The boy, whose eyes avoid the water seller's, appears to be the same model as the boy in THE OLD WOMAN FRYING EGGS; in fact, all of the models rather resemble those who have appeared in earlier paintings. Yet this work speaks to us with utter authority, fulfilling every conceivable goal of this kind of painting. With unparalleled skill and imagination, the artist has simulated the palpable reality of matter—that of fired clay, glazed and unglazed, dry or wet with drops and runnels of condensed water; of human flesh; of fabric and wood; of glass behaving like a prism. But the sum of these effects, and the artist's pride in his achievement, have been subordinated to the larger aim of revealing the mute interaction of men in daily intercourse as well as their individual dignity in the course of ordinary human experience.[19]

As Pacheco proudly recounted, among the outstanding achievements of Velázquez's youth were his portraits from life, which he cultivated at the same time and in the same spirit as the *bodegones*. Probably shortly after he completed THE WATER SELLER OF SEVILLE, he journeyed to Madrid where, according to Pacheco, he made one of his most important early portraits:

> Desirous, then, of seeing El Escorial, he left Seville for Madrid about the month of April in the year 1622. He was very well received by the two brothers don Luis and don Melchior del Alcázar, and especially by don Juan de Fonseca, His Majesty's royal chaplain, who was an admirer of Velázquez's paintings. He made at my request a portrait of don Luis de Góngora, which was very much praised in Madrid....[20]

The portrait of Góngora (fig. III.10) was no doubt made with the intention of serving as a model to Pacheco for his *Libro de retratos*.[21] It has the same plastic strength as some of the figures in the *bodegones*. Its dramatic light, faceted planes and incisive contours reveal the lessons he learned from his master, but its sense of dignity and its authority in the portrayal of character have no peers among Spanish portraits up to that time. With this work and with THE WATER SELLER OF SEVILLE, Velázquez was ready to capture the stage of art at the court of Madrid, and he would not release it until he died. In October of 1623, as a result of a similar portrait he had made of the king, Velázquez was appointed painter to Philip IV, the first of many honors and titles that the monarch would bestow upon him throughout their long working friendship. From that point on, the emphasis on portraiture, already established in Velázquez's youth, would predominate. The *bodegón* played little or no role in his mature oeuvre.

Fig. III.8   Francisco López Caro. BODEGÓN. 58.5 × 98 cm. Signed. Private collection.

BIBLIOGRAPHY

Pacheco 1649, vol. 1, pp. 149, 155–66, vol. 2, pp. 134–37, 146, 154; Palomino 1724, pp. 891–936; Ceán Bermúdez 1800, vol. 5, pp. 155–80; Stirling-Maxwell 1848, vol. 2, pp. 671–736; Beruete 1906, pp. 6–12; Mayer 1927b, p. 562; Harris 1935, pp. 258–59; Mayer 1936, pp. 21–30; Cavestany 1936–40, p. 75; Trapier 1948, pp. 57–77; London, National Gallery, 1952 cat., pp. 74–75; Soehner 1955, pp. 1–39; López-Rey 1963c, pp. 29–33; Steinberg 1965, pp. 274–94; Bergström 1970, pp. 53–59; London, National Gallery, 1970 cat., pp. 121–25; Steinberg 1971, p. 54; Haraszti 1973, pp. 21–48; Gudiol 1974, pp. 17–24; Gállego 1974, pp. 97–104; Kahr 1976, pp. 12–28, 40–43; Kemenov 1977, pp. 15–59; Moffitt 1978, pp. 5–23; López-Rey 1979, pp. 12–17; Moffitt 1979, p. 214; Kinkead 1980, pp. 185–86; Moffitt 1980, pp. 82–95; London, Apsley House, 1982 cat., pp. 138–41; Harris 1982, pp. 37–56; Haraszti 1983, pp. 79–102; Moffitt 1984, pp. 13–24; Wind in press, pp. 64–102.

Fig. III.9 Velázquez. THE WATER SELLER OF SEVILLE. 106.5×82 cm. c. 1620–22. The Wellington Museum (Apsley House), London.

NOTES

1. Pacheco, 1956 ed., vol. 1, p. 155: *"…despues de cinco años de educación y enseñanza casé con mi hija, movido de su virtud, limpieza y buenas partes, y de las esperanzas de su natural y grande ingenio."* Quoted in translation from Harris 1982, p. 191.

2. *op. cit.*, vol. 2, pp. 134–35.

3. *op. cit.*, vol. 2, p. 135: *"Otros se han inclinado a pintar pescaderías con mucha variedad; otros, aves muertas y cosas de caza; otros, bodegones con diferencias de comida y bebida; otros, figuras ridículas con sugetos varios y feos para provocar a risa y todas estas cosas, hechas con valentía y buena manera, entretienen y muestran ingenio en la disposición y en la viveza."*

4. *op. cit.*, vol. 2, p. 136: *"Hallaremos acaso algún pintor antiguo que se inclinase a estas cosas ordinarias y de risa? Parece que si; pues Plinio hace mención de uno llamado Dionisio, por sobre nombre Antropógrafo, que pintó, solamente, figuras con nombre jocoso… Y, en el mesmo lugar, también Pireico pintó cosas humildes, como barberías, tiendas, comidas y cosas semejantes, por lo cual le pusieron por nombre riparógrafo; estas pinturas causaban gran deleite y en esta parte alcanzó el artífice suma gloria."*

5. This notion was first promoted in Spain by Cristóbal de Villalón in his *Ingeniosa comparación entre lo antiguo y lo presente* (Valladolid, 1539).

6. *op. cit.*, vol. 2, p. 137: *"¿Pues qué? ¿Los bodegones no se deben estimar? Claro está que si, si son pintados como mi yerno los pinta alzándose con esta parte sin dexar lugar a otro, y merecen estimación grandísima; pues con estos principios y los retratos…halló la verdadera imitación del natural alentando los ánimos de muchos con su poderoso exemplo…."* Quoted in translation from Harris 1982, p. 194.

7. Barry Wind, *Velázquez's Bodegones: A Study in Seventeenth-Century Genre Painting*, Association of University Presses (in press; expected date of publication 1985). I am very grateful to the author for sharing his manuscript with me.

8. Peiraikos is cited by Felipe de Guevara, *Comentarios de la pintura*, written in the mid-sixteenth century and published only in 1788, with annotations by Antonio Ponz; he is also cited by the humanist Hadrianus Junius, *Batavia* (Antwerp, 1588), in relation to Pieter Aertsen. See Sterling 1959, pp. 39–40, note 83.

9. Pacheco, *op. cit.*, vol. 2, p. 146: *"Con esta doctrina se crió mi yerno, Diego Velásques de Silva, siendo muchado, el cual tenía cohechado un aldeanillo aprendiz, que le servía de modelo en diversas acciones y posturas, ya llorando, ya riendo, sin perdonar dificultad alguna. Y hizo por él muchas cabezas de carbón y realce, en papel azul, y de otros muchos naturales, con que granjeó la certeza en el retratar."* Quoted in translation from Harris 1982, pp. 194–95.

10. *Libro de descripción de verdaderos retratos de ilustres y memorables varones* (facsimile edition), Seville, n.d. (1886).

11. Palomino 1724, 1947 ed., p. 894: *"Compitió Velázquez con Caravaggio en la valentía del pintar; y fué igual con Pacheco en lo especulativo. A aquél estimó por lo exquisito, y por la agudeza de su ingenio; y a éste eligió por maestro, por el conocimiento de sus estudios, que le constituían digno de su elección… Diéronle el nombre de segundo Caravaggio, por contrahacer en sus obras a el natural felizmente, y con tanta propiedad, teniéndole delante para todo, y en todo tiempo."* Quoted in translation from Harris 1982, p. 198.

12. The question of Caravaggio's purported influence on Velázquez has been laid to rest by, among others, Richard Spear (*Caravaggio and His Followers,* New York, 1975, pp. 19–20), who firmly rejects any meaningful connection between the two artists.

13. Soehner (1955, p. 6) proposed a more concrete link between Velázquez and these painters than can be accepted.

14. Wind (in press) relates this painting to the *"figuras ridículas"* mentioned by Pacheco, which, he believes, had erotic connotations, and he disagrees with Kahr (1976, p. 19) and Moffitt (review of Kahr 1976 in *Art Journal,* vol. 38, 1979, p. 214) that the scene has Eucharistic symbolism.

15. A version of this composition without the background religious scene, in the collection of the Art Institute of Chicago, is generally accepted as an autograph work, but it is so generally abraded and strengthened by restoration that it is difficult to tell.

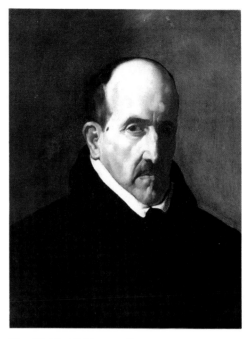

Fig. III.10   Velázquez. PORTRAIT OF LUIS DE GÓNGORA Y ARGOTE. 50 × 40 cm. 1622. Museum of Fine Arts, Boston.

16. López-Rey (1963, pp. 30–33) treats the idea of baroque dualisms in Velázquez's early works.

17. This painting, once in a private collection in England, was first published by Enriqueta Harris, "Obras españolas de pintores desconocidos," *Revista Española de Arte,* 1935, pp. 258–59.

18. López-Rey 1963, p. 163.

19. Such values, of course, were fundamental to the picaresque literature of seventeenth-century Spain. Parallels between art and literature are explored in detail by Haraszti (1973, 1983). As Harris (1982, p. 47) notes, a water seller appears as a character in the picaresque novel *Vida y hechos de Estebanillo González,* published in Seville in 1646.

Moffitt (1978), following the lead of Gállego (1974), argued in detail that the painting represents the three ages of man and can be interpreted as an allegory of Prudence. The evidence for such an emblematic reading of the picture is not convincing, however. In a brief but sensitive article, Steinberg (1971) already pointed out that the painting embraces, among other things, the universal theme of the three ages of man.

20. Pacheco, *op. cit.,* vol. 1, p. 156: *"Deseoso, pues, de ver el Escorial, partió de Sevilla a Madrid por el mes de abril del año de 1622. Fué muy agasajado de los dos hermanos don Luis y don Melchior del Alcázar, y en particular de don Juan de Fonseca, sumiller de cortina de Su Majestad (aficionado a su pintura). Hizo, a instancia mía, un retrato de don Luis de Góngora, que fué muy celebrado en Madrid...."* Quoted in translation from Harris 1982, p. 191.

21. Velázquez originally painted a laurel wreath on Góngora's head, which would have been in keeping with the style of many of Pacheco's portrait drawings of poets. The drawing, if it was ever made, is not known today, however. Velázquez later repented of the laurel wreath and painted the background over it, giving the portrait a much greater sense of modernity. As an indication of the importance of the portrait to Velázquez, it was still in his own apartment in the royal palace when he died in 1660.

Inscribed at right with fragmentary date: *1618*
Oil on canvas
23⅝ x 40¾ in. (60 x 103.5 cm.)
The Trustees of The National Gallery,
London

ALTHOUGH A FEW AUTHORS (JUSTI 1933, Ortega y Gasset 1943, Trapier 1948, Pantorba 1955) have held that this is little more than a realistic genre scene, most acknowledge that it deals in some way with the biblical story of Christ in the house of Martha and Mary. From the relative emphasis on the foreground scene, in which a maidservant works at preparing a meal, over the tiny background scene, in which Christ is seen seated in a room with two women, it is easy to understand how a literal reading of the painting could lead to the conclusion that it is fundamentally a profane work. But, as Martin Soria insisted (1949), Velázquez was not so literal a painter as that. The work, in fact, has profound religious meaning, expressed in terms of a compelling rendition of earthly reality.

The story of Christ in the house of Martha and Mary occupies an important place in Christian exegetical literature, being one of the biblical texts most frequently commented upon in the controversy over whether "faith" or "good works" is more efficacious in the salvation of man's soul.[2] This controversy had gone on since the time of Saint Augustine, but it took on renewed intensity during the Reformation and Counter-Reformation of the sixteenth century. The story, oddly enough, was used by both sides in the bitter debate to defend their respective positions. Told in the Gospel of Luke, it goes as follows:

> Now it came to pass as they were on their journey that he entered a certain village; and a woman named Martha welcomed him to her house. And she had a sister called Mary, who also seated herself at the Lord's feet, and listened to his word. But Martha was busy about much serving. And she came up and said, "Lord, is it no concern of thine that my sister has left me to serve alone? Tell her therefore to help me." But the Lord answered and said to her, "Martha, Martha, thou art anxious and troubled about many things and yet only one thing is needful. Mary has chosen the best part, and it will not be taken away from her."[3]

According to Saint Augustine, Martha's concern about her work in preparing a meal for the Lord establishes her as the "type" for the *vita activa* (temporal life), while Mary's wish to sit at the feet of the Lord and listen to his words establishes her as the "type" for the *vita contemplativa* (spiritual life)—two poles that were seen not as good and bad, but rather as good and best. Augustine wrote:

> …doubtless Martha had chosen that part, which shall be taken away from her. Manifestly, there shall be taken away from every man, who ministers to the saints such things as are necessary for the body, shall be taken away from him that which he doeth. For he will not minister to the saints for ever. For to what doth he minister, but to infirmity? to what doth he minister, but to mortality? to whom doth he minister, but to the hungry and the thirsty? All these things shall not be when this corruptible shall have put on incorruption, and this mortal shall have put on immortality. For when the necessity itself shall have passed away, there shall be no ministering to necessity…And when one fed the Lord what did he give?…He gave food to the Bread…A great ministry this, a great work this, a great gift. And yet Mary chose the better part which shall not be taken away from her. Martha's part therefore passeth away.[4]

As Kenneth M. Craig observed, Augustine has thus utilized food as a symbol of earthly transience in the context of the story of Martha and Mary.[5] In the context of the Counter-Reformation, Catholics did not deny the primacy of faith but, unlike Luther and his reformers, they insisted on the efficacy of a life of service. Thus, while Martha's work was seen as transitory, it was not unimportant.

Christ's message was not that she should want not to work, but that she should gladly work and not begrudge her sister her thoughtful inclination.

As Martin Soria finally concluded in 1959, after several previous attempts to interpret Velázquez's painting, it represents a "moral admonition," or, as Braham called it in 1965, a *bodegón moralisé,* or "general application" of the biblical story to contemporary life. Neither of the two figures in the foreground can be seen as Martha or Mary, but rather, the color and style of their clothing, as opposed to those of the women in the background, suggests that they are contemporary women whose daily lives we are encouraged to think about in terms of the biblical example. The young maid, whose sullen face is brilliantly characterized, seems to resent her chores, while the old woman—certainly not her sister but just another, wiser woman in the kitchen— looks out at the viewer and points with her finger toward the biblical example. Velázquez has lavished his virtuoso skill on the still life in the foreground, endowing those symbols of earthly transience with a heightened physicality that sharply contrasts the sketchy rendition of the biblical scene immediately above.[6] With acuity and skill, Velázquez has charged this image of quotidian reality with a bristling religious significance and, as a consequence, has made it vibrant.

In 1918–19, August L. Mayer suggested that Velázquez's source for this composition was a print of CHRIST AT EMMAUS by Jacob Matham after Pieter Aertsen (fig. III.11), a work in which the religious scene is also depicted as a tiny vignette in the background while the principal activity in the foreground is that of cleaning fish.[7] It has frequently been stated since then that Velázquez was inspired by the "inverted" still lifes of the Antwerp School.[8] There can be no doubt Velázquez knew such engravings, and probably paintings of that school, and that he was

PLATE 7

CHRIST IN THE HOUSE OF MARTHA AND MARY

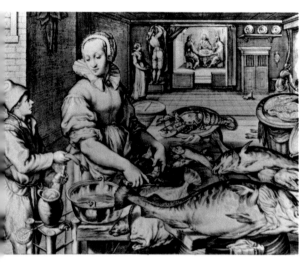

g. III.11   Jacob Matham after Pieter Aertsen.
HRIST AT EMMAUS.

taking advantage of the device of inverted emphasis. Beyond the general use of this device, however, the differences underscored by such comparisons far outweigh the similarities, and no single source that has been suggested is truly relevant.

One of the main points of disagreement among scholars about this painting is whether the scene in the background is a view through a wall into another room,[9] or whether it is a small, framed painting hanging on the wall.[10] A third possibility, apparently first suggested by the English critic Kaines Smith, is that the image is a reflection in a mirror of a scene in the same room as the two servant women.[11] A further development of the last idea by Mestre Fiol (1973) presupposes, not at all convincingly, the presence of two mirrors in the same room and is predicated on the assumption that Velázquez was visually just as literal as some would have him be intellectually. After the cleaning of the painting in 1964, when repaints in this area were removed, it is now clear from visible perspective lines running through the window opening, that this is an aperture in a wall similar to the one depicted by the artist in his CHRIST AT EMMAUS (fig. III.9) though without the shutter door used to clarify the form in the latter painting.

All of the literature prior to 1965 reproduces the painting with the excessive repaints that were removed the previous year, and many early authors mention its damaged condition. The repaints were especially noticeable in the faces of the two women in the foreground. A fragmentary date was also discovered during the cleaning. Located on the rear wall at the right, just below the window, it can be deciphered as *1618,* making it roughly contemporary with THE OLD WOMAN FRYING EGGS (fig. III.8), dated in the same year. Beruete (1906) was the first to point out that the model for the older maid in this work appears to be the same as that for the old woman in the Edinburgh picture. Radiographs made at the time of cleaning determined that this painting was executed on the same type of open-weave canvas as other works from the same general period, including THE OLD WOMAN FRYING EGGS, THE IMMACULATE CONCEPTION, SAINT JOHN WRITING THE APOCALYPSE and THE WATER SELLER OF SEVILLE. In contrast, TWO YOUNG MEN AT TABLE (Plate 8) was painted on a fine, tightly woven canvas.[12]

PROVENANCE
Collection Lt. Col. Packe, Twyford Hall, Norfolk;[1] sale, London, June 18, 1881, lot 18; Sir William H. Gregory, until 1892 (when bequeathed to the National Gallery).

EXHIBITIONS
London, 1946, no. 21; London, 1947, no. 28; Madrid, 1960–61, no. 35; London, 1981, no. 12.

BIBLIOGRAPHY
Buchanan 1824, p. 235; Armstrong 1896; Picón 1899, p. 36; Beruete 1906, pp. 12, 157, pl. 7; Gensel 1908, p. 175, pl. 5; von Loga 1914, no. 10; Mayer 1918–19, pp. 236–37; Allende-Salazar 1925, p. 273, pl. 16; Justi 1933, p. 153; Mayer 1936, p. 5, no. 9, pl. 38; Lafuente Ferrari 1943, no. 5, pl. 4; Ortega y Gasset 1943, p. 20; Soria 1945, p. 215; London 1946, no. 21; London 1947, p. 17, no. 28; Trapier 1948, pp. 72–73; Angulo 1948, p. 16; Soria 1949, pp. 124–27, fig. 5; London, National Gallery, 1952 cat., pp. 74–75, no. 1375; Gaya Nuño 1953, no. 14; Soehner 1955, p. 14, fig. 15; Pantorba 1955, p. 72, no. 14; Gerstenberg 1957, p. 28; Gaya Nuño 1958, p. 319, no. 2823; Birkmeyer 1958, p. 67; Kubler and Soria 1959, p. 254, pl. 133A; Madrid 1960, p. 49, no. 35, pl. 25; de Tolnay 1961, pp. 31–45; López-Rey 1963c, pp. 32–33, 125, no. 8, pl. 5; Camón Aznar 1964, pp. 230–33, 1003, ill.; Steinberg 1965, p. 279; Braham 1965, pp. 362–65; Asturias and Bardi 1969, no. 13; Bergström 1970, pp. 55–56; London, National Gallery, 1970 cat., pp. 121–25, no. 1375; Braham 1972, pp. 7, 11–13, pl. 4, 5; Haraszti 1973, pp. 30, 32, figs. 25, 26; Mestre Fiol 1973, pp. 15–36; Gudiol 1974, pp. 22, 323, no. 9, figs. 18, 20, 21; Gállego 1974, pp. 100–01, 135–36, pl. 4; Kahr 1976, pp. 19–23, fig. 2; López-Rey 1979, p. 190, no. 7, pl. 62; London 1981, p. 57, no. 12, fig. 64; Harris 1982, pp. 45–46, ill.; Haraszti 1983, pp. 222–23, no. 212, pl. 80; Madrid 1983, p. 72–74, ill.; Moffitt 1984, pp. 13–24.

NOTES
1. See London, National Gallery, 1970 cat., pp. 123, 125, note 11, for identification of owner.

2. Leo Steinberg (1965, p. 289), in his review of López-Rey 1963, was the first even to suggest this aspect of the painting's meaning by his observation that the seated figure of Mary in the background scene is clearly based on Dürer's MELANCOLIA I, whose posture signifies meditation, and therefore alludes to the contemplative life. Kahr (1976, p. 23) mentions this aspect of the picture's iconography, as does Harris (1982, p. 46). Moffitt (1984) pursues this line of thought to extreme lengths. An important and excellent new study of the iconography of Christ in the house of Martha and Mary and its relation to Christian literature can be found in Craig (1983, pp. 25–39), which has been the source of the biblical and Augustinian quotes made here.

3. Luke 10:38–42, from the Douay-Confraternity Bible; quoted from Craig 1983, p. 26.

4. Augustine, Sermon 179; quoted from Craig 1983, pp. 28–29.

5. Craig 1983, p. 29.

6. Moffitt (1984, p. 16) ascribes a symbolic meaning to every object in the still life.

7. Bergström (1979, pp. 55–56) observes that Matham's print is a pastiche rather than a copy of any one work by Aertsen and points out, as others had done, that Velázquez's work has none of the mannerist qualities of Aertsen's.

8. Haraszti (1973, p. 39) suggests that another engraving by Matham, LAZARUS AND THE RICH MAN, was possibly Velázquez's source. Kahr (1976, p. 22), without citing Haraszti, makes the same point.

9. Among those who have adopted this view are: Beruete (1906); Mayer (1918–19); Soria (1945, 1949, 1959); Angulo (1948); MacLaren (1952); de Tolnay (1961); Braham (1965, 1970, 1972); Steinberg (1965); Bardi (1969); Bergström (1970, 1979); Haraszti (1973, 1983); Kahr (1976); Harris (1982).

10. Among those taking this view are: Trapier (1948) and Camón Aznar (1964).

11. This idea was subscribed to by: Pantorba (1955); Orozco Díaz (1960); López-Rey (1963, 1979); Gállego (1974).

12. London, National Gallery, 1970 cat., p. 124, note 1.

Oil on canvas
25¾ × 41 in. (65.3 × 104 cm.)
The Wellington Museum (Apsley House), London

MOST WRITERS ON VELÁZQUEZ HAVE concluded that this painting is one of the latest and most advanced of his *bodegones*. Along with THE WATER SELLER OF SEVILLE, it is one of two surviving paintings of this type mentioned in Palomino's text of 1724: "He painted another picture of two poor men eating at a humble little table, where there are different earthenware vessels, oranges, bread and other things, everything observed with rare thoroughness."[1]

In 1768 the painting was purchased from the Marquis of La Ensenada by King Charles III, and in 1772 it was inventoried in the new royal palace in Madrid, where it is said to have been in the *retrete del rey,* the king's private drawing room. Recorded in the palace by Ponz (1776), Cumberland (1787) and Ceán Bermúdez (1800), it was found, along with THE WATER SELLER OF SEVILLE, among what is euphemistically called the "baggage" of Joseph Bonaparte when he was attempting to flee the country with more plunder than he could carry in 1813. Rescued by the Duke of Wellington at the Battle of Vitoria, it was among 165 paintings which the duke took back to London with the intention of returning them to the Spanish Crown once order was restored. Upon receipt in London, this painting and THE WATER SELLER OF SEVILLE were catalogued as by Caravaggio.[2] In 1816 Wellington made good his intention to offer the return of all the captured paintings to King Ferdinand VII. The Count of Fernán-Núñez, Spanish Minister in England, replied, however, that, "His Majesty, touched by your delicacy, does not wish to deprive you of that which has come into your possession by means as just as they are honourable."[3] The duke did not argue.

For some reason, Stirling-Maxwell, who recognized the presence of THE WATER SELLER OF SEVILLE at Wellington's Apsley House in 1848, did not know the whereabouts of TWO YOUNG MEN AT TABLE either then or in 1855, when he published his *Velázquez and His Works.* When the French translation of this book was published in Paris ten years later with a catalogue of the artist's paintings by W. Bürger, the oversight was corrected, and the painting entered the modern literature with its correct provenance. In 1885, however, Cruzada Villaamil still listed the painting as lost. Justi (1889) recognized the Apsley House picture as the one Palomino had described and considered it a study of foreshortened faces. He thought the young man drinking from a bowl was perhaps partaking of chocolate, while his companion, "his head resting on his arm, seems dosing over the table, taking a *siesta* after the meal and the wash-up of plates and dishes." Typical of his nineteenth-century point of view, this literal, or realist, interpretation shows little sympathy for the baroque subtleties of the picture. The first attempt to see the painting in the context of seventeenth-century ideas was that of López-Rey (1963c, p. 30), who considered the *bodegones* to be portrayals of "the drowsing of the senses."

The composition of TWO YOUNG MEN AT TABLE is much more complex than that of any of the other *bodegones* except THE WATER SELLER OF SEVILLE. In CHRIST IN THE HOUSE OF MARTHA AND MARY (Plate 7) and CHRIST AT EMMAUS (fig. III.7), the tabletops supporting the still-life elements tilt right out of the bottom of the picture. In this later work, as in THE WATER SELLER OF SEVILLE, we can see the leg supports and empty space underneath the table, which open the pictorial space and make it more vivid.

The composition, which is built on interlocking diagonals, is divided into two halves. The left half is comprised of a still life that is the most artfully arranged in all of Velázquez's oeuvre. An overturned brass mortar and its pestle shine warmly in the strong light that enters from the left and catches the shiny surfaces of a neat stack of upturned pottery bowls. The ceramic jug stoppered with a radiant orange is one of the grandest inventions of the artist's youth, and the greenish glaze on the wine pitcher at the right completes the muted but elegant chromatic scale.

Seated on a stool to the right of the table, a young man turned away in vanishing profile lifts what is no doubt a cup of wine to his lips. In front of him, somewhat slumped down, is another young man, his lips slightly parted, seemingly suspended in a drunken stupor.[4] Rather different from the portrayal of chocolate-drinking dishwashers described by Justi, and more akin to the portrayal of the "drowsing of the senses" advanced by López-Rey, the picture presents us with a dualism between the alcohol-numbed senses of the men and the heightened sensuousness of the still-life objects. This is not unlike the dualistic interplay seen in CHRIST AT EMMAUS. As the artist manipulates the viewer to perceive both sides of the coin, he brings him to a fuller awareness of its shape.

Somewhat abraded in places, TWO YOUNG MEN AT TABLE was cleaned in 1958. Trapier (1948) was the first modern author to speculate that the background was repainted. Crombie (1973) called attention to Cumberland's description of the painting when it hung in the royal palace in 1787: "Peasant Boys, eating and drinking, of the size of life; half-length: In the back-ground a clear and beautiful landscape." As there is no landscape visible in the painting today, Crombie suggested that an x-ray might help to resolve the issue of whether any landscape had been painted out. To be sure, the right side of a window or door opening is visible in the background just to the right of the orange. There is no indication, however, that a landscape was ever visible through

the opening: it would be hard to justify the drama of the lighting effects if one were. Cumberland, who was not particularly reliable, may have been writing from a faulty recollection.

According to Braham (1970, p. 124), the canvas on which this picture is painted is of a finer weave than that of other paintings of the Sevillian period. It may be, as the painting's style would tend to support, that this work was actually painted early in Velázquez's residence in Madrid, where he habitually used a finer weave of canvas. This dating (1623–24) approximates that proposed by Camón Aznar (1964, p. 310).

Di Stefano (1954) proposed that a small version of this composition in an Italian private collection is a sketch made by Velázquez for this painting. Although I have not seen the small version, it would appear to be a later copy. It was certainly not Velázquez's practice to make such preparatory studies in oil.

PROVENANCE
Marquis of La Ensenada until August 25, 1768; Charles III, 1768; Royal Palace, Madrid (1772 inventory); Joseph Bonaparte, 1813; Duke of Wellington, taken from Joseph Bonaparte at the Battle of Vitoria, 1813; presented to the Duke of Wellington by King Ferdinand VII, 1816; Duke of Wellington Bequest, 1947.

EXHIBITIONS
London, 1888, no. 125; London, 1895–96, no. 73; London, 1901, no. 103; London, 1913–14, no. 45; London, 1947, no. 39; London, Arts Council, 1946, no. 14; London, 1981, no. 14.

BIBLIOGRAPHY
Palomino 1724, p. 893; Ponz 1776, vol. 6, p. 34; Cumberland 1787, p. 54; Ceán Bermúdez 1800, vol. 5, p. 178; Stirling-Maxwell 1848, vol. 2, p. 678; Stirling-Maxwell 1865, p. 270; Curtis 1883, p. 37, no. 85; Cruzada Villaamil 1885, p. 326, no. 166; Justi 1889, p. 72; Mesonero Romanos 1899, p. 195; Beruete 1906, pp. 7, 151, 157, pl. 1; Gensel 1908, p. 9, pl. 3; Sánchez Cantón 1916, p. 83; Allende-Salazar 1925, p. XIII, 273, pl. 5; Mayer 1936, p. 25, no. 109, pl. 38; Cavestany 1936–40, p. 75; Toledo, Ohio 1941, p. 95; Lafuente Ferrari 1943, no. VII, pl. 9; Trapier 1948, p. 69; di Stefano 1954, pp. 257–59; Pantorba 1955, pp. 71–72, no. 13; Soehner 1955, p. 7, pl. 9; Gaya Nuño 1958, p. 317, no. 2813; López-Rey 1963c, pp. 26–30, 158, no. 105, pl. 25; Camón Aznar 1964, pp. 309–11, 1004; Steinberg 1965, p. 279; Asturias and Bardi 1969, p. 87, no. 4, ill.; London, The National Gallery, 1970 cat., p. 122; Haraszti 1973, pp. 25, 29, 46, fig. 24; Crombie 1973, pp. 212–13, ill.; Gudiol 1974, pp. 18, 323, no. 3, fig. 10; Gállego 1974, pp. 98, 113, no. 3; Kahr 1976, pp. 41–42, fig. 12; López-Rey 1979, p. 232, no. 24, pl. 84; London 1981, p. 59, no. 14, fig. 66; Harris 1982, p. 44, ill.; London, Apsley House, 1982 cat., pp. 139–40, no. 182, ill.; Haraszti 1983.

NOTES
1. *"Otra pintura hizo de dos pobres comiendo en una humilde mesilla, en que hay diferentes vasos de barro, naranjas, pan, y otras cosas, todo observado con diligencia extraña."* Translation quoted from López-Rey 1963c, p. 158, no. 105. The inclusion of bread among the things depicted is generally assumed to be just one of Palomino's occasional inaccuracies.

2. "Catalogue of the principal pictures found in the baggage of Joseph Bonaparte, Made by Mr. Seguier on their arrival in London," 1813 (Reprinted from the 1901 Catalogue of The Wellington Museum), London, Apsley House, 1982 cat., pp. 157, 159.

3. London, Apsley House, 1982 cat., p. 6.

4. Barry Wind, *Velázquez's Bodegones: A Study in Seventeenth-Century Genre Painting* (in press), is the first to my knowledge to observe that the figures in this painting are inebriated.

PLATE 8

Two Young Men at Table

IV. JUAN BAUTISTA DE ESPINOSA

(Documented in Madrid and Toledo between 1612 and 1626)

The first notice of Juan Bautista de Espinosa in art historical literature was provided by the Count of La Viñaza (1889), who, basing himself on notes made by Valentín Carderera in his copy of Ceán Bermúdez's dictionary, referred to two signed works by the artist then existing in Toledo. One was a "good picture" representing Saint James the Greater, signed in 1626 with an indication that its maker was painter to the king.[1] The picture was in the chapel of the Castrejón Commons, a property in the patrimony of the Cathedral of Toledo. Viñaza also recorded Carderera's knowledge of "an excellent portrait of a jurist, painted by this Espinosa in 1616." A life-size, half-length image of a man beside a table on which were books by Covarrubias, the portrait was tentatively identified as representing "one of the Narbonas, who flourished and wrote at that time." Neither picture is known today.

In 1935, Enriqueta Harris published a still life by him (Plate 9), then in a private collection in England, which is fully signed, *Joannes Bap^ta Despinossa faciebat anno D, 1624.* This alerted Julio Cavestany in the same year that a pair of still lifes then belonging to the Duchess of Valencia, one of them signed simply *Espinosa ft.,* must be by the same artist.[2] No other works have been firmly attributed to him.

Although part of Espinosa's activity took place in Toledo, what have been assumed to be the earliest documentary references to him are found in Madrid. In 1612, a painter of that name was received as a brother into the Confraternity of the Sacrament in the parish of Saint Sebastian in Madrid.[3] On October 12, 1614, "Juan

Fig. IV.1   Juan Bautista de Espinosa. Vases of
Flowers and Basket of Fruit. 63 × 85 cm.
Signed. Present location unknown (formerly
Duchess of Valencia, Madrid).

Bautista Espinossa, *pintor*," was named among the debtors of Juan Andrés de la Roble, another artist, who signed his testament on that day.[4]

In October 1616, Espinosa was described as a resident of Toledo in a contract which he and another painter signed with the Old Tribunal *(Santa Hermandad Vieja)* of Toledo to undertake a restoration of the architectural decor of the interior of its premises.[5] The Toledan archives also record in January 1618 Espinosa's contract to execute an altar for the town of Navalagamella in the Province of Madrid;[6] and in September 1620, he vouched for the "honorability" of the painter Francisco Granelo, with whom he had worked on the previous job, in a contract the latter was seeking for an altar at the parish church of Villaluenga de la Sagra.[7]

On December 1, 1624, a newborn daughter of "Juan Baptista, *pintor*," died in the parish of Saint Sebastian in Madrid. Although the surname of the father is not given in the Book of Enterments, he has been assumed to be the same "Juan Bauptista Despinosa" who was living there in 1612.[8]

On July 5, 1641, one Magdalena Muñoz, "widow of Juan de Espinosa, painter, resident of Madrid," signed her last will and testament in the parish of Saint Justus.[9] If this Espinosa is indeed the same painter, then the date of his death can be placed somewhere between his dated painting of 1626 and 1641. The date of his birth is unknown but has been assumed to be about 1590 or before.[10] Documents relating to another artist known as Juan de Espinosa, dating from 1645 to 1677, no doubt concern the life of a different painter treated here in Chapter VIII.

Like most Spanish still-life painters of his time, Juan Bautista de Espinosa seems to have been an artist of traditional formation who, to a large extent, made his living painting religious pictures and portraits and performing sometimes menial tasks for which his training equipped him. And, like some other painters of the reign of Philip III and early in the reign of Philip IV, he seems to have divided his time between the court of Madrid and the old Imperial City of Toledo, some thirty miles away.

The two still lifes exhibited by Cavestany in Madrid in 1935 (figs. IV.1, 2) cannot be assumed with certainty to have been a pair originally, since their equal size is the result of severe cropping. Their compositions are similarly symmetrical but do present significant differences. The signed one of the two, known to me only through Cavestany's publication, features a central basket of open-weave straw containing quinces and plums. It has been placed near the edge of a table spread with a green cloth bearing fold creases and trimmed with lace. Flanking the basket are a pair of jasper and gilt bronze urns, each filled with a bouquet of morning glories, sunflowers, jasmine and primroses. The painting's rigorous symmetry and the rather ingenuous rendition of the basket and the lace are relieved by the gentle fall of light that produces soft shadows on the tabletop. It is a rather impressive painting, making the more lamentable the sacrifice of space around its edges, which was doubtless once important to its overall grandeur.

The unsigned painting, which was recently exhibited in Madrid, is not as fine a work as the other appears to be, though some of its original qualities may have been lost as a result of damage. The basket, of the same general design, is a bit more heavy-handed, but the grapes that fill it are skillfully modeled. The almost shadowless support on which the basket rests simply runs off the bottom of the picture, with no front edge visible. The result is a more "primitive" sense of space. The fanciful crystal vases of hexagonal shape have lost some of their form over the years, but the flowers seem to be painted in a way similar to those in the signed painting. Pérez Sánchez expressed indecision on whether this painting is by the Espinosa under consideration here or by the homonymous painter active some years later in Madrid.[11] The juxtaposition of this work with examples by the later artist in the recent exhibition in Madrid made it clear that it could not be by the latter.

Based on the signed painting discussed above and the one catalogued in the following pages, Juan Bautista de Espinosa appears as one of the more interesting minor figures to emerge during the reign of Philip III. Although his activity encompassed both Toledo and Madrid, he seems to have grown out of a different tradition than that of Sánchez Cotán. His subject matter relates, as Van der Hamen's does, to affluence and courtly life, and, as Van der Hamen often does, he inclines to a symmetrical ordering of things. Although not uniquely Spanish, symmetrical design is often found in Spanish still lifes. One could search for the sources of this symmetry in art historical precedent, but the more meaningful source is likely to be found in age-old, perhaps subconscious, patterns and hierarchies. A composition like Espinosa's, in fact, best conforms to the sense of the Spanish noun *gala* (ostentation, show), a concept that was central to the conduct of public life in seventeenth-century Spain.[12]

Fig. IV.2 Juan Bautista de Espinosa. BASKET OF GRAPES AND FLOWERS. 63 × 85 cm. Private collection, Madrid.

BIBLIOGRAPHY
Viñaza 1889, vol. 2, p. 162; Sánchez Cantón 1915, p. 61; Harris 1935, p. 259; Lafuente Ferrari 1935, p. 176; Cavestany 1935, p. 42; Cavestany 1936–40, p. 76; Oña Iribarren 1944, pp. 29, 92; Kubler and Soria 1959, p. 235; Sterling 1959, p. 74; Harris 1967a, pp. 154–55; Torres Martín 1971, p. 35; Angulo 1971, p. 319; Agulló 1978, pp. 65–66, 118, 136, 156, 183; Marías 1978, pp. 425–26; Bergström et al. 1979, p. 187; Agulló 1981, pp. 72, 77; Madrid 1983, pp. 45, 58.

NOTES
1. Sánchez Cantón (1915, p. 61) picks up Viñaza's information, but, it should be stressed, there is no other reference to Espinosa as among the king's painters. To be sure, he was not among the salaried painters. Perhaps he did paint on royal commission occasionally and so noted on the picture seen by Carderera.
2. Cavestany 1935, p. 42.
3. Agulló 1981, p. 77.
4. Agulló 1978, p. 136.
5. Harris 1967, pp. 154–55.
6. Marías 1978, pp. 425–26.
7. *Ibid.*
8. Agulló 1981, p. 77.
9. Agulló 1978, pp. 65–66.
10. Pérez Sánchez 1983, p. 45.
11. Pérez Sánchez 1983, p. 58, cat. no. 31.
12. Jordan 1965, p. 64; Joaquín Casalduero, *Sentido y forma del teatro de Cervantes*, Madrid, 1951, p. 191.

9. Still Life with Silver Gilt Salvers

Signed on shelves above table: *Joannes Bap^{ta} Despinossa faciebat anno D, 1624*

Oil on canvas

38⅝ × 46½ in. (98 × 118 cm.)

The Hilmar Reksten Foundation,
Bergen, Norway

Exhibited only once in England since its discovery by Enriqueta Harris in 1935, this spectacular still life is known to most art historians only through black-and-white reproduction. The brief discussions of it in the literature are mostly summed up in Young's description of it as "the one most rigidly symmetrical composition that we know."

Rather dry in its execution, as are the figural works of such contemporaries as Bartolomé González, the picture, nevertheless, achieves a certain grandeur through its emphatic symmetry and rather showy color contrasts. The focus of attention is the pyramid of three silver gilt salvers resting on the crisp white tablecloth. The artist has achieved a spectacular evocation of light reflecting from the surfaces of these and the other gilded metal objects. The design of the salvers, probably of Toledan craftsmanship, gives us a rare glimpse of domestic opulence of the period. Contrasting vividly in color is the pair of red clay bowls containing one of those special alcoholic concoctions popular at the time.[1]

The artist has tried to vary the symmetry in subtle ways: for example, one of the two crystal flasks of liquid flanking the central salver is filled with water, the other with white wine; of the two oranges at the front edge of the table, the one on the left is placed with its navel pointing up, the one on the right with its navel pointing straight out of the picture. Through such self-conscious maneuvers as these we can see the artist manipulate the elements of his picture in a search for just the right visual presentation of his subject matter. This intensely artificial, even precious, sensibility is akin to the verbal play of Spanish poets of the epoch. It differs diametrically from the utilitarian naturalism of Dutch still life and, most importantly, prefigures the purely formal concerns of the modern artist.

Provenance
Art Market, London, 1920; Sir Anthony Doughty-Tischborne, Hampshire, 1955; Sale, Christie's, London, June 21, 1968; A. R. Lunde, New York.

Exhibitions
Winchester/Southhampton 1955, no. 10.

Bibliography
Harris 1935, p. 259, figs. 3, 4; Lafuente Ferrari 1935, p. 176; Cavestany 1936–40, p. 76; Gaya Nuño 1958, p. 142, no. 694; Kubler and Soria 1959, p. 235; Bergström 1970, p. 47; Torres Martín 1971, p. 35, no. 5; Young 1976, pp. 213–14, fig. 30; Bergström et al. 1979, p. 187; Madrid 1983, p. 45, ill.

Note
1. The most common such "cocktail" was the *hipocrás*, which was composed of good wine, sugar, cinnamon, ambergris and musk. A cone of cinnamon sticks rests on the tabletop. See José Deleito y Piñuela, *Sólo Madrid es corte*, Madrid, 1953, pp. 155–57.

PLATE 9

STILL LIFE WITH SILVER GILT SALVERS

V. ALEJANDRO DE LOARTE

(Late 1590s–1626)

AlexanDro De loarte. f.^{at} 1523

Few Spanish artists have been so poorly understood in modern times as a result of misattributions as Alejandro de Loarte has. This was due in part to the imprecise idea of his style promulgated by Méndez Casal (1934, 1936) and to permissive attributions in the United States art market. An illustration of the resulting confusion is the American museum exhibition in the 1960s that contained four still lifes attributed to Loarte that were by four different painters—none of them Loarte, and not all of them Spanish.[1] Nevertheless, what little documentary knowledge we have of the life and work of Loarte we owe to the archival research of Méndez Casal, who in 1934 published the only significant documents yet known. The earliest of these is the dowry contract signed by the artist on October 16, 1619, in which he described himself as a painter resident in Madrid, the son of Jerónimo de Loarte, also a painter. His wife was María del Corral, widow of one Gaspar Carrillo, a court notary. The artist then lived in rented quarters in the Calle de los Gitanos. According to the social practices of the time, his age at the time of his marriage might have been little more than eighteen or nineteen. It would be reasonable to assume, therefore, that the date of his birth was perhaps between 1595 and 1600, making him the contemporary of Juan van der Hamen.[2]

Following up on the scant information provided by Ceán Bermúdez (1800) to the effect that Loarte had worked in Toledo (Ceán erroneously thought he had been a pupil of El Greco), Méndez Casal found the artist's testament, signed in that city on December 9, 1626, and the inventory of his studio made eight days later. In his testament, indicating that he was ill, he named his father as his universal heir and appointed as executors his wife, María del Corral, and the painter Pedro Orrente, who at the time was also living in Toledo. He died on December 12th and was buried in the parish of Saint Justus. On January 15, 1627, Jerónimo de Loarte, declaring himself to be "sick in bed, worn-out and poor," renounced his inheritance from Madrid, perhaps fearing that his son's debts would exceed his assets.

Knowing that Loarte's father was also a painter, Méndez Casal made the logical assumption that the artist's early training was probably received from him.[3] Perhaps the most significant fact that we can glean from his testament, however, is that, at the time of his early death, he was on the friendliest of terms with Pedro Orrente, fifteen to twenty years his senior and an influential painter who, according to a reliable seventeenth-century source, had studied in Venice with Leandro Bassano.[4] Knowledge of the friendship of the two artists is not enough to warrant an assumption of a master-disciple relationship, which Allende-Salazar (1929) had done even without knowing the artist's testament, but it does indicate at least that he was a respected member of the artistic community of Toledo.

From the inventory of Loarte's studio (assuming that most of the paintings were his), we can see that he had a busy practice as a painter. A total of 149 paintings were itemized: nearly half of them were religious works; eight were portraits; fifteen were landscapes; only thirty-eight, or about twenty-five percent of the total number, were still lifes in any sense of the word. Most of these were described as *"lienzos de frutas,"* although four of them were flower paintings. In his testament, Loarte claimed payment for another fifteen such works, twelve of them already in the possession of one client, Antonio Martínez Heredia. Among those was a *"Gallinera* signed with my name," perhaps the famous THE POULTRY VENDOR dated 1626 (Plate 11). The number of still lifes found in Loarte's studio far exceeded the twelve such paintings underway or completed in Sánchez Cotán's studio twenty-three years earlier. This was due in part to a diffusion of the taste for such pictures from the aristocracy and the intellectual elite to the middle class, which created a bigger, less exacting demand on the part of the public. Still, by far the largest part of Loarte's activity was comprised of those subjects that had always been the mainstay of a painter's practice.

As a painter of religious subjects, Loarte brought an earthy, anti-mannerist naturalism to his pictures which relates him to other artists of his generation active in the area of Toledo and Madrid and which has parallels in Italian painting.[5] From the few such pictures that are known, however, his talent does not appear to have been a great one. Ceán Bermúdez referred enthusiastically, nevertheless, to a large painting, now lost, THE MIRACLE OF THE LOAVES AND FISHES in the refectory of the Monastery of Los Minimos in Toledo, which was dated in 1622 and which he described as being well drawn and in the Venetian taste as regards its color.

The few known still lifes and one *bodegón* with figures that Loarte signed all date within the brief span of only four years—from 1623 to 1626. The earliest of these is the STILL LIFE WITH GAME AND FRUIT (fig. V.1) belonging to the Fundación Santamarca in Madrid, first published by Mayer (1927). Signed *Alexandro de Loarte, fat. 1623,* it is perhaps the *"lienzo de caza"* painted in that year that was mentioned by Ceán in 1800 as belonging then to Nicolás de Vargas. It is a symmetrical com-

Fig. V.2 Alejandro de Loarte. STILL LIFE WITH FRUIT. 81.5 × 108 cm. Signed, 1624. Plácido Arango Collection, Madrid.

Fig. V.1 Alejandro de Loarte. STILL LIFE WITH GAME AND FRUIT. 84 × 105 cm. Signed, 1623. Fundación Santamarca, Madrid.

Fig. V.3 Alejandro de Loarte. STILL LIFE WITH FRUIT BOWL. 81.5 × 108 cm. Plácido Arango Collection, Madrid.

position with a basket of quinces and pomegranates as its center. The fruit is modeled in a fluid and sensuous manner. At the edges of the composition, hanging from metal hooks in a horizontal rail, is a brace of dressed hares, one with its back to the viewer and one turned so that the slit in its belly shows. Just to the inside of these are a pair of doves on the left and two partridges on the right. The plumage of the fowl, especially the gray-and-white doves, is palpably evoked by a skillful manipulation of light and shadow. Accentuating the central axis of the composition is a slab of cured pork hanging over the basket and a hen and a fish flanking it on the brown countertop. The principles of symmetry have been unflinchingly adhered to, but at the same time the artist has done everything possible to underscore the uniqueness and individuality of each component of the rigid design. This seeming contradiction, which has the effect of implying a dualism of nature and art, was a common feature of Castilian still life in the 1620s and can also be seen in the works of Juan Bautista de Espinosa and Juan van der Hamen.[6]

Dating from 1624 is the signed STILL LIFE WITH FRUIT (fig. V.2) that was one of the works published in 1934 by Méndez Casal. Since most of the still lifes described in Loarte's inventory were *lienzos de frutas,* we should take special notice of this work which was exhibited for the first time in Madrid in 1983. Very similar to the compositions of Van der Hamen of comparable date, the elements are arranged within a window setting, following the practice of Sánchez Cotán. As Méndez Casal noted, the two birds attracted to the fruit were inspired by Pliny's story of the ancient painter Zeuxis, a reference intended to call attention to the artist's skill which was also employed by Van der Hamen (figs. VI.7, 8). But Loarte's performance is less impressive here than in the STILL LIFE WITH GAME AND FRUIT. His fluid brushwork in this case fails to achieve the illusion of reality which the symbolic birds lead one to expect.

The unpublished pendant of this work (fig. V.3), which has always been in the same collections with it, further enlarges our knowledge of the artist and his fruit still lifes. A painted ceramic bowl containing quinces and pomegranates occupies the center of the composition, flanked by a branch of quinces on the left and a cut melon on the right. Branches of small apples suspended from above accentuate the symmetry of the design, but in a lively way. The modeling of the fruit is similar to that in the STILL LIFE WITH GAME AND FRUIT, and the treatments of the melon and the foliage of the apples resemble those in the STILL LIFE WITH FRUIT of 1624.

These three paintings and the two catalogued on the following pages are the only still lifes or *bodegones* that can be accepted as by Loarte at this time. They reveal a distinct personality, less sophisticated than Van der Hamen's, but one clearly aware of its own identity.[7]

BIBLIOGRAPHY
Ponz 1776; Ceán Bermúdez 1800, vol. 3, pp. 42–43; Quilliet 1816, p. 184; Parro 1857, vol. 2, p. 94; Cruz y Bahamonde 1813, vol. 10, p. 571; Poleró 1898; Mayer 1927a, pp. 116ff; Allende-Salazar in Thieme Becker 1929, vol. 23, p. 300; Méndez Casal 1934, pp. 187–202; Lafuente Ferrari 1935, pp. 174–75; Méndez Casal 1936, p. 9; Cavestany 1936–40, p. 70–71; Valentiner 1950, pp. 34–37; Orozco Díaz 1954a, p. 26; Sterling 1959, pp. 41, 63, 75; Kubler and Soria 1959, p. 235; Madrid 1960, pp. 31–32, no. 4; Jordan 1967, vol. 1, pp. 73–77; Bergström 1970, pp. 33,

58–59; Torres Martín 1971, p. 50; Angulo 1971, p. 24; Angulo and Pérez Sánchez 1972, pp. 207–26; Young 1976, p. 207; Camón Aznar 1978, pp. 208–10; Marías 1978, p. 422; Bergström et al. 1979, pp. 150,199; Toledo 1982, p. 170; Haraszti 1983, pp. 91–92; Madrid 1983, pp. 29, 210; Cherry 1984, p. 60.

NOTES

1. Newark 1964–65, nos. 15–18. The attributions in this exhibition were made by the lenders.

2. The surname Loarte is thought to be of Basque origin (Méndez Casal 1934, p. 194), and there are records of other individuals in the late sixteenth and early seventeenth centuries with that name. One such reference, curiously, is found in a document relating to the career of Juan van der Hamen y León, who, when he petitioned the Crown to be made salaried painter to the King in 1627, declared that he had an uncle named Matheo LoArte [sic], who was an *Archero del Rey,* or a member of the Burgundian Guard of the King. (Archivo Histórico de Simancas. Casa y Sitios Reales, Legajo 333 [antiguo 28], folio 150; Jordan 1967, vol. 2, pp. 185–86.) This largely ceremonial position, which Van der Hamen himself and his father before him held, was limited to those of Flemish heritage. While the handwriting of the document is quite clear and precise, it could be that the orthography was not and that we are dealing with two distinct names. Although similarities between the works of the two artists can be seen, there is no verifiable evidence at this time to suggest that Van der Hamen and Loarte were distantly related.

3. He went on to suggest, however, that the most significant part of Loarte's training must have been in Seville, where, he hypothesized, he must have been a pupil of Pacheco alongside Velázquez. This completely groundless theory of a relationship with the young Velázquez threw off many other writers, including Bergström (1970, p. 59). Orozco Díaz (1954), however, had already pointed out the error of this assumption and had stressed the Castilian origin of Loarte's style.

4. Jusepe Martínez, *Discursos practicables del nobilísimo arte de la pintura.* Madrid, 1866 ed., p. 154.

5. See Angulo and Pérez Sánchez 1972, pp. 207–26, for the most complete account of Loarte's life and works in which all of the religious paintings are reproduced.

6. It has frequently been noted (e.g., Sterling 1959, p. 75) that a similarity exists between certain of Loarte's pictures and still lifes being painted at the same time in Florence by Jacopo da Empoli (1551–1640). These similarities, which are not nearly as significant as the peculiar characteristics of Loarte's style mentioned above, have not been satisfactorily explained.

7. A pair of unsigned still lifes with human figures in tiny background scenes, very much in the manner of the Italian followers of Pieter Aertsen, were reproduced by Méndez Casal (1934, pls. I and II) and attributed to Loarte's early years. Still in the collection of the Marquis of Casa Torres in Madrid, one of the pair represents game fowl and the other fish. Both excellent paintings and surely Spanish, the one with fowl especially resembles Loarte's way of painting. When these works are cleaned, perhaps the matter of their attribution can be resolved.

Three other paintings attributed to Loarte in Méndez Casal's 1934 article cannot be accepted as by him. These include the famous COOK in Amsterdam, catalogued here as Plate 45, and a pair of rather crude *bodegones* with figures. In his 1936 article, he ascribed to Loarte two other still lifes in Scandinavian collections. To judge from the reproductions, neither attribution is convincing.

Signed on cartellino lower left: *Alexandro de Loarte fat. 1625*

Oil on canvas

31⅞ × 42 in. (81 × 108 cm.)

José Luis Várez Fisa Collection, Madrid

IN THIS STILL LIFE LOARTE HAS GIVEN A rather realistic view of the way in which food was stored in a pantry, or *despensa,* but his irresistible impulse to order things has led him to arrange the objects he is painting in a symmetrical way, which endows them with a certain monumentality. At the center is a robust cardoon that lies there rather grandly between two heads of salad greens casting a strong shadow on the support. Echoing this symmetry, but at the same time diffusing its rigidity, are a chicken, some sausages and cuts of meat suspended from hooks in a horizontal rail across the top. This rail with metal hooks was never depicted by Sánchez Cotán, who, as Held pointed out (1979), preferred to let the source of his suspended game and vegetables remain a mystery. But such a device was no doubt a common feature of every household larder. It was also shown in the contemporary still lifes of the Florentine painter Jacopo da Empoli, to whose works Loarte's have been compared, but the Spaniard's compositions are much simpler and more direct. Like Sánchez Cotán, Loarte has also depicted the side walls of the window opening, barely visible in the shadows at either side of the composition, but he fails to achieve the sense of spatial clarity which the use of that device made possible in the older artist's works.

Loarte's painting technique is also quite different from Sánchez Cotán's. His contours are not as sharp, his medium is more fluid and his use of the brush is broader by comparison. Overall, it is a direct and vigorous technique. The red ground and earthy colors lend a sensuous warmth that generally characterizes the artist's works.

PROVENANCE
Private Collection, Cáceres, 1935.

EXHIBITION
Madrid, 1983–84, no. 10.

BIBLIOGRAPHY
Cavestany 1936–40, p. 71; Cavestany 1942, pp. 97–100, ill.; Angulo and Pérez Sánchez 1972, pp. 209, 221, no. 93; Madrid 1983, p. 37, no. 10, ill.

Signed on cartellino bottom center:
Alexandro de Loarte Ft. 1626

Oil on canvas

63¾ × 51³⁄₁₆ in. (162 × 130 cm.)

Private Collection, Madrid

SIGNED IN THE YEAR OF HIS DEATH AND probably not yet paid for when he wrote his testament, this painting is Loarte's most important work and makes us regret that the young artist did not live to fulfill the promise it contains. Set in the Zocodover Plaza, the hub of mercantile life in Toledo, the painting depicts a young woman presiding over a poultry stall where a boy wearing a hunting cap is buying a live hen. This type of painting was popularized in the second half of the sixteenth century by Vincenzo Campi of Cremona, whose works were certainly known in Spain by this time.[1] But Loarte has adapted the genre freely and arrived at a convincing scene of daily life in Castile of a sort that few others cultivated.

Méndez Casal (1934), in his misguided belief that Loarte had studied together with Velázquez in Pacheco's studio in Seville, claimed a relationship between this painting and the *bodegones* of Pacheco's pupil. As early as 1935, Lafuente Ferrari refuted that claim and defended the Castilian roots of the picture.

It is not difficult to see which parts of this picture the artist enjoyed painting the most. Indeed, he seems to have had a bit of trouble bringing much of a sense of life to the figures. They are a bit stiff and dryly modeled, and the drapery in places is dull. But this serves, perhaps not intentionally, as a foil for the skill with which the plumage of the fowl is rendered. Loarte has brought the viewer very close within the compass of this scene: we seem to be standing right in front of the table in the foreground and looking down upon it. A loose net containing four live hens is spread out in the foreground. Beside it are several dead birds and a plate of giblets,

PLATE 10

KITCHEN STILL LIFE

PLATE 11

The Poultry Vendor (La Gallinera)

placed on the central axis of the composition. In the interval between the two human figures, we catch a glimpse of a basket of straw that cradles some eggs. The most impressive part of the picture, however, is the array of fowl hanging from the beam overhead, silhouetted against the sky and the architecture. Roosters, turkeys, ducks, grouse and other game birds challenge the artist's skill and create a rich feast for the eye. But surely the painting must not be looked at in a formal sense only, as the twentieth-century eye is apt to do. At its core, after all, is a transaction—a sale, or purchase. It is possible that this is presented in a very straightforward spirit. It may also be, however, that this activity in the context of the poultry stall has some hidden significance of which we are not aware.

According to the artist's testament of 1626, a painting described an *"un lienzo de dos varas y media de una gallinera firmado de mi nombre el cual no está concertado"* (a canvas two and half *varas* [in size] of a hen seller signed with my name, the price of which has not been set) was in the possession of a client named Antonio Martínez Heredia. He ordered that the painting be appraised and that its value be collected. In spite of the fact that two and one half *varas* is somewhat larger than the dimensions of THE POULTRY VENDOR,[2] the painting has usually been considered to be the one mentioned in the inventory. Recently, however, another signed version of this composition, also dated in 1626, was discovered in a private collection in Spain. As Pérez Sánchez (1983) notes, this appears to make it less certain that the painting catalogued here was the one documented on the artist's deathbed. The newly discovered version (fig. V.4) is an exact replica of the well-known one, but the execution is dryer and somewhat in-ferior. Whether this replica was painted by Loarte himself or by a member of his studio is difficult to know on the basis of our limited knowledge of him and his working situation. A peculiarity of the signature of the second version is that underneath the artist's name is painted a skull crowned with a laurel wreath (fig. V.4, detail). Pérez Sánchez suggests that this detail was added by a member of the artist's studio after his death as a sign that his fame would live on after him. If this is the case, which it must be, then the replica could not be the painting that at the time of the artist's death was already in the possession of Martínez Heredia.

PROVENANCE
Antonio Martínez Heredia, 1626 (? according to the artist's testament); Marquis of Santa Marca, 1857; Duchess of Valencia, Madrid; her heirs, until 1984.

EXHIBITIONS
Madrid, 1935, no. 6; Stockholm, 1959–60, no. 67; Madrid, 1960-61, no. 4; Madrid, 1983–84, no. 11.

BIBLIOGRAPHY
Cruz y Bahamonde 1812, vol. 10, p. 571; Poleró 1857, p. 82, no. 150; Allende-Salazar 1925, p. 300; Méndez Casal 1934, pp. 196, 200, pl. VII; Cavestany 1936–40, p. 150, no. 6, pl. 13; Oña Iribarren 1944, pp. 21, 91, no. 6; Mayer 1947, p. 424; Lafuente Ferrari 1953, p. 228, pl. 139; Sterling 1959, p. 63; Kubler and Soria 1959, p. 235; Stockholm 1959, pp. 60–61, no. 67; Grate 1960, p. 61, ill.; Bermejo 1960, pp. 328–30; Madrid 1960, pp. 31–32, no. 4, pl. 13; Jordan 1967, vol. 1, pp. 72–76, fig. 43; Bergström 1970, p. 59, fig. 42; Torres Martín 1971, p. 50; Angulo and Pérez Sánchez 1972, pp. 209, 222, no. 97, pl. 163; Camón Aznar 1978, p. 208, fig. 175; Münster/Baden-Baden 1979, p. 323, ill.; Haraszti 1983, pp. 91–92, 174–75, no. 48; Madrid 1983, p. 38, no. 11.

NOTES
1. Sterling 1959, p. 75; see also Schroth essay above.
2. Two and half *varas* are equivalent to 2.07 meters, one *vara* equaling .836 meters, or 33 inches. Such measurements, probably only approximated, were never very precise and sometimes included the frame.

Fig. V.4   Alejandro de Loarte. THE POULTRY VENDOR (replica). 167.5 × 128 cm. Signed, 1626. Private collection, Spain.

Fig. V.4, detail   Cartellino with signature.

VI. JUAN VAN DER HAMEN Y LEÓN
(1596–1631)

T he passage of three and a half centuries has done much to dim the fame of Juan van der Hamen y León, who in his lifetime was one of Madrid's best-known painters. Indeed, Van der Hamen inspired more encomiums in prose and verse from his Golden Age literary peers than did any of his artist contemporaries. While his oeuvre embraced the entire range of subject matter ushered in with the seventeenth century, it is clear that his still lifes were what his admirers valued most. The academic taste of later years relegated the still life to the sidelines of art, whereas, in fact, its emergence in the early years of the seventeenth century was one of the things that signaled for some discerning witnesses the dawning of a new Golden Age of painting whose brilliance vied with that of antiquity about which they had read.

The "Phoenix" of Madrid's intellectuals, the prodigious Lope de Vega (fig. VI.1), devoted two sonnets to his friend Van der Hamen. In one of them, he evoked the image of Olympian Jupiter being forced to adjudicate a complaint brought against the "New Apelles" by Nature herself, who complained that the artist's "peregrine genius" had stolen her brushes to make fruits: that he did not paint, but rather created carnations, as she in the earth, he on white linen. Jupiter, having a canvas brought to him and seeing that the painted fruits were equal to the natural ones, ruled in favor of the artist and ordered that Van der Hamen paint the natural ones, leaving them in the sky as originals for Nature to copy:

Fig. VI.1 Pedro Perret. PORTRAIT OF LOPE DE VEGA. Engraving, 1625. Biblioteca Nacional, Madrid.

Fig. VI.2 Anonymous engraver. PORTRAIT OF JUAN PÉREZ DE MONTALVÁN. Engraving, 1631. Biblioteca Nacional Madrid.

SONETO
A Juan de Vander Hamen Valderrama,[1]
Pintor Insigne

Al Olimpo de Júpiter divino,
donde rayos de sol forman doseles,
a quejarse de vos, oh nuevo Apeles,
con triste vos Naturaleza vino.

Dijo que vuestro ingenio peregrino
le hurtó para hacer frutas sus pinceles;
que no pintáis, sino criáis claveles,
como ella en tierra, vos en blanco lino.

Júpiter las querellas escuchadas
hizo traer un lienzo y viendo iguales
con las que ella crió las retratadas;

Mandó, que vos pintéis las naturales,
y ella pueda sacar de las pintadas,
quedándose en el cielo, originales.

Two years after Van der Hamen's death, Lope's principal protégé, Juan Pérez de Montalván (fig. VI.2), published his *Índice de los ingenios de Madrid,* a kind of *Who's Who* of the court intellectuals. Van der Hamen was the only artist included in this comprehensive list of over 500 persons which was otherwise clearly limited to men of letters. He wrote of the artist:

> Juan de Vanderhamen y León, among the most celebrated painters of our century, because in drawing, in painting, and in narrative works *(lo historiado)* he exceeded Nature herself: aside from being unique in his art, he wrote extraordinary verses, with which he proved the relationship that exists between Painting and Poetry; he died very young, and from what he left us in fruits, as well as in portraits, and large canvases, it obtains that if he were living, he would be the greatest Spaniard of his art.[2]

This praise, echoed again and again by other writers, is important not only to the biography of Van der Hamen, but also to an understanding of his times. The brief span of Van der Hamen's activity fell mostly within the decade of the 1620s and coincided with a period of crisis in the visual arts in Madrid. The established artists were, for the most part, pursuing styles that were outdated and leading nowhere. The appearance on the scene of Velázquez in 1623 represented a threat to the status quo that, together with the enlightened patronage of Philip IV, was largely responsible for the rebirth of the School of Madrid in the 1630s. But in that critical period of transition, Van der Hamen represented one of the more vital forces. By examining the full range of his development mentioned by Montalván, we can gain valuable insights into the artistic climate of those years, as well as a better understanding of the part of his oeuvre that is best known today, his still lifes. Although a taste for Van der Hamen's still lifes lived on throughout the eighteenth and nineteenth centuries, a true insight into that elite society of men whose favorite artist he was seems to have died with them. It is only with much effort now that we can begin to reconstruct his biography and his wide-ranging and sometimes eclectic oeuvre.[3]

The biography of Van der Hamen published by Palomino in 1724 and amended by Ceán Bermúdez in 1800 led—as did Palomino's characterization of Velázquez as a "second Caravaggio"—to oversimplifications by later art historians. Palomino, who believed that Van der Hamen's father had been a painter from Flanders, wrote that it was "held to be certain" that the youth studied with his father. The later eighteenth-century writer Álvarez y Baena hardened that assumption into a statement of fact, which was repeated by all subsequent writers on the subject until I questioned its reliability in the 1960s. In all of the copious documentation relating to the artist and his family that is now available, and in the entire corpus of documentation relating to Spanish art, there is not a single known reference to the elder Van der Hamen as a painter. While that does not rule out the possibility that Palomino was right, we should not use his statement to build an easy interpretation of Van der Hamen's style as a hybrid of "inherited" Flemish characteristics and "acquired" Spanish ones. The truth of the matter is much more complex, and much more interesting, than that.

Juan was baptized in the parish of Saint Andrew in Madrid on April 8, 1596,[4] the son of Juan van der Hamen, who had immigrated to Spain from Brussels before 1586, and Dorotea Bitman [sic] Gómez de León, a half-Flemish/half-Spanish native of Toledo whose noble ancestry in Spain is traced back to the reign of Ferdinand and Isabella.[5] The elder Van der Hamen, a man of means and of noble birth, whose father before him had served both Philip II and the Emperor Charles V, held the position of *Archero del Rey* under both Philip II and Philip III. This meant that he was a member of the Burgundian Guard of the King, a group of nobles of Flemish ancestry who accompanied the monarch in full regalia on all public and ceremonial occasions at the court. His son Juan would also hold this title and function. In 1607, the elder Van der Hamen signed a power of attorney in Madrid in connection with his wish to sell a property he owned in the Duchy of Brabante in the Low Countries; a few days later, he revoked the agreement without explanation.[6] In 1609, he received from Utrecht a document he had requested which certified and described the family's ancestral coat-of-arms.[7] Nothing else is known of his activity or his fortunes.

Juan was reared with his two brothers in comfortable circumstances with the advantages of education and a stimulating intellectual environment. His elder brother Lorenzo (fig. VI.3), an ecclesiastic who was a scholar and historian, was one of the most respected men of letters of Madrid in his day and the intimate friend of Quevedo and Lope de Vega.[8] We know nothing about Juan's education as a painter, but he had surely completed it before March 6, 1615, when, declaring that he had never left Madrid, he petitioned the Vicar General of the city to allow him to marry Eugenia de Herrera immediately, without giving the customary three weeks' public notice to those who might object. He gave as the reason for his hurry that he had pressing business that would take him away from Madrid for a period of time

Fig. VI.3 Pieter de Jode. Portrait of Lorenzo van der Hamen y León. Engraving. Biblioteca Nacional, Madrid.

Fig. VI.4   Juan van der Hamen. Still Life
with Cardoon and Basket of Apples.
75 × 109 cm. Signed, 1622. Private collection,
Mexico.

Fig. VI.4, detail   Cardoon.

Fig. VI.4, detail   Oranges.

and that, if he waited until his return to marry, his relatives would "maliciously impede" the marriage because they wanted him to wed someone else who was richer and had a larger dowry.[9] Several witnesses swore that this was the case and the Church approved the wedding. We do not know where he went on business, or how long he was gone, but the couple's son Francisco was born sometime prior to June 5, 1617.[10] On April 5, 1622, their daughter María was born.[11]

The first record of Van der Hamen's activity as a painter is found in the accounts of the royal household of El Pardo. There it is recorded that on September 10, 1619, he was paid 100 *reales* for painting a "picture of fruit and game for the South Gallery in the Royal Palace of El Pardo, to go with others which were bought at the auction of the Cardinal of Toledo as overdoors."[12] As Schroth points out above, this Cardinal of Toledo was no doubt Archbishop Bernardo Sandoval y Rojas, Primate of Spain, who had died the year before. The pictures referred to were surely the kind of still lifes painted in Toledo by Sánchez Cotán, if indeed they were not by Sánchez Cotán himself.

Although the particular game and fruit still life painted by Van der Hamen for El Pardo cannot be identified today, other still lifes which are among his earliest dated works confirm that the example of Sánchez Cotán was a very important influence on the formation of his style. Still Life with Cardoon and Basket of Apples (fig. VI.4), signed with initials and dated 1622, shows the artist adopting the window setting of Sánchez Cotán. As in Cotán's Still Life with Fruit and Vegetables (Plate 2), Van der Hamen has placed two predominant elements on the horizontal plane of the window opening. The cardoon at the left casts a strong shadow and overhangs the edge of the shelf in the manner of the older artist. Van der Hamen has stylized the pattern of light and shadow on its ribbed surface, however, which renders the image somewhat harder and more abstract than a cardoon by Sánchez Cotán (fig. VI.4, detail). The apples in the basket at the right are drawn with precision and are modeled in clear planes that give them a strong plasticity. The two parsnips in the corner, one of them pointedly overhanging the edge of the window ledge, are a clear quotation from Sánchez Cotán. The large citron and three oranges hanging by strings from above, although compositionally derived from Sánchez Cotán, are modeled much more generically. The oranges are treated as simple spheres in strong shadow and their leaves are reduced to a series of planes caught by the light (fig. VI.4, detail). Van der Hamen's way of painting natural forms is less empirical than the meticulous approach of Sánchez Cotán. His sense of form is more conceptualized.[13]

The roots of Van der Hamen's style, however, are complex and also have a great deal to do with the cosmopolitan taste of the capital, where individuals and objects of art from practically everywhere abounded. Indeed, the magnates of Van der Hamen's time vied with each other and the king in building fabulous collections of Flemish and Italian art as well as that by local masters. An artist with entrée to such collections could easily become familiar with most recent developments from those countries.[14] At the same time that Van der Hamen was painting still lifes inspired by Sánchez Cotán, he was also painting others with a Flemish compositional derivation. The SERVING TABLE (Plate 13), an undated painting from the early 1620s, follows a compositional type employed earlier by several Dutch and Flemish artists—among them, Clara Peters, Floris van Schooten and Floris van Dijck—but Van der Hamen's carefully ordered and restrained manner of arranging and painting the objects on his table could hardly differ more from the opulent abundance of the northern examples.

A pair of still lifes from the royal collection at El Escorial shows well how Van der Hamen would appropriate and hispanize a contemporary Flemish format. In 1621 and 1623, he painted two *fruteros* with window vistas (figs. VI.5, 6). Both of them depict blue-and-white porcelain fruit bowls on tables spread with sumptuous cloths—one a red silk damask, the other a blue and gold striped brocade. Each painting has, at opposite corners, a window with a distant landscape view, as in paintings executed at Antwerp by Frans Snyders (1579–1657) (fig. VI.7). Yet both of Van der Hamen's works achieve a severity and monumentality that set them apart from the flourishing sensuality of such a Flemish prototype. In the painting with the striped cloth, the recession of those stripes in strict perspective has the effect of thrusting the bowl of fruit forward and making it loom large, while adding a note of theatricality to the two linnets attracted to the open pomegranate at the left. The rigorous geometry that the painter has used to achieve his dramatic effect proved to be a characteristic trait.

As Sánchez Cotán had done, Van der Hamen maintained a repertory of still-life motifs which he used over and over again in varying combinations throughout his career. In a signed still life of 1622 (fig. VI.8), which is now located in a private collection in Paris, he took the same arrangement of fruits and birds that he had

Fig. VI.5   Juan van der Hamen. STILL LIFE WITH FRUITS AND BIRDS. Panel. 56 × 74 cm. Signed, 1621. Patrimonio Nacional, El Escorial.

Fig. VI.6   Juan van der Hamen. STILL LIFE WITH FRUITS AND BIRDS. 56 × 74 cm. Signed, 1623. Patrimonio Nacional, El Escorial.

Fig. VI.7   Frans Snyders. Still Life. 58×82 cm. Koninklijk Museum Schone Kunsten, Antwerp.

Fig. VI.8   Juan van der Hamen. Still Life with Basket of Fruit. 67×100 cm. Signed, 1622. Private collection.

used in the 1621 Escorial panel (fig. VI.5), transferred it to a wicker basket of distinctly Spanish design, arranged everything symmetrically within a shadowy window setting in the manner of Sánchez Cotán, added hanging apples and grapes, and transformed the motif from one of Flemish reference to one of Castilian reference. Similarly, the 1623 Escorial still life (fig. VI.6) contains a motif that the artist used in quite another context. The open pomegranate being attacked by birds seems at home in this painting in a Flemish mode. The year before, however, Van der Hamen had used the same pomegranate as part of a very "Castilian" symmetrical still life featuring a large Venetian glass and ormolu fruit bowl filled with pears and grapes (fig. VI.9). This fruit bowl, with various arrangements of fruit in it, was an object that Van der Hamen used in numerous still lifes over a period of years (Plates 15 and 16).

A gradual "hispanization" of an initial "Flemish" tendency in Van der Hamen's oeuvre, that some modern writers have asserted, is not supported by the chronology of the artist's work.[15] Instead, he intermittently painted works of a Flemish compositional type throughout his career, no doubt responding to an important element of taste for such pictures in Madrid.

A similar case, involving a different type of subject matter, is the oval landscape surrounded by a garland of flowers (fig. VI.10), signed and dated 1628. To argue whether these flowers are closer in style to those of Jan Breughel or Osias Beert the Elder, as Bergström (1970) has done, is wholly beside the point. Drawn with precision and given an emphatic plasticity by the blazing light and deep shadow, they are unique creations that could only have been painted by Van der Hamen. In his derivation of the garland motif from Flanders, he relied on no particular artist's work and could have painted this picture as a result of having seen a garland by either, or neither, of the artists mentioned above.

Fig. VI.9 Juan van der Hamen. STILL LIFE
WITH FRUIT BOWL. 57.2 × 94 cm. Signed, 1622.
Stanley Moss Collection, New York.

Lope de Vega's long poem *Laurel de Apolo* (1630) praises Van der Hamen as a
painter of flowers.[16] Pacheco (1649), in an extended discussion of flower painting
that reveals the prevailing ranking of still-life subjects at the bottom of the hierarchy
of genres, mentions only Van der Hamen as a Spanish practitioner of the art:

> …In our time there is no want of painters who are fond of the entertainment
> afforded by this genre, which can be easily learned and gives delight by its variety.
> Among those who have done it with power and skill can be counted Juan van der
> Hamen, archer to Philip IV.

> Oil painting is most suitable for this genre, because you can retouch over and over
> again and refine the colors so that they truly imitate natural flowers. You must also
> master the painting of vases of glass, clay, silver, and gold, and the little baskets in
> which flowers are usually placed, and the use of lighting and the arrangement of all
> these things. And occasionally good painters can amuse themselves this way,
> although it does not lead to artistic glory….[17]

Until recently, very few paintings with flowers by Van der Hamen, apart from
the OFFERING TO FLORA (Plate 22), were known but of late several have come to light
that bear witness to the contemporary praise they inspired. Of special interest is a
pair of very large paintings from the royal collection that were clearly part of some
specific palace decor (figs. VI.11, 12). Perhaps, as Orihuela Maeso (1982) suggests,
they are the two of the same size and subject matter inventoried in 1666 in a room,
referred to as "the room where His Majesty dined," of the royal palace in Madrid.
Each canvas depicts a serving table, spread with green damask, supporting an
elaborate green glass flower vase with gilt mountings that is filled with a large,
mixed bouquet. The flowers are executed with precision and have a certain hard-

Fig. VI.11 Juan van der Hamen. STILL LIFE WITH VASE OF FLOWERS AND A PUPPY. 228 × 95 cm. Museo del Prado, Madrid.

Fig. VI.12 Juan van der Hamen. STILL LIFE WITH VASE OF FLOWERS AND A DOG. 228 × 95 cm. Museo del Prado, Madrid,

Fig. VI.10   Juan van der Hamen. LANDSCAPE
WITH GARLAND OF FLOWERS. 85 × 107 cm.
Signed, 1628. Dartmouth College Museum of
Art, Hanover, New Hampshire.

ness, an almost artificial quality, that is characteristic of the artist (Plate 21). In the foreground of each painting, where the receding perspective of the floor tiles dramatically enlarges the pictorial space, a royal pet is portrayed. In one, there is a hearty, full-grown dog; in the other, what may be that dog's puppy is shown playing with a ball. Odd but interesting paintings that conform to no common type in the artist's oeuvre, they give the impression of having been made to fulfill some special purpose, perhaps both decorative and personal.

Following his discussion of painting flowers, Pacheco discusses the painting of fruit. He says:

> I have also tried this exercise, as well as flower painting, and I do not judge it to be very difficult. Juan van der Hamen did it extremely well, and was even better with sweetmeats, surpassing in this part the figures and portraits that he did. Thus he became more renowned for this, much to his displeasure.[18]

Other indications that Van der Hamen did not have the success he sought with his figure paintings, or that he did with still lifes, are a matter that deserves further discussion, but we cannot let pass Pacheco's remark that what he did best was the painting of sweetmeats. Indeed, his paintings of the luxurious sweets and delicate desserts of courtly society and the Venetian-style crystals that accompanied them brought him his greatest distinction.

The STILL LIFE WITH SWEETS AND GLASSWARE in the Prado Museum (fig. VI.13) is one of his best-known works. Recorded in the royal collection since 1702, we do not know if it was acquired by Philip IV in the seventeenth century. The painting exemplifies a compositional type not only associated with Van der Hamen but also one that had a profound effect on Spanish still-life painting in general. Its mark on Zurbarán (fig. XV.1), especially, has been noted frequently. On a narrow stone ledge of brownish color, the artist has arranged his objects in a zig-zag that fills the shallow depth. A footed plate of dark green glass is piled with the pastries we call Lady Fingers, intermixed with candied figs. Beside this dish a roll of wafers, or *barquillos,* overhangs the edge of the shelf, establishing with clarity the pictorial space, just as a cucumber or a parsnip would in a Sánchez Cotán. Behind this is a glazed terra-cotta honey pot. At each end of the composition are Venetian-style crystals rendered by the artist with consummate skill, especially the pair at left which he has placed on a fluted ceramic dish. The flask at the right does not contain wine, as often stated, but rather *aloja,* an aromatic infusion composed of honied water with such spices as cinnamon, clove and ginger, often scented with the essence of jasmine or roses. The flies depicted on the flask call attention to the sweetness of its contents. The fashion for drinking these infusions and eating elaborate sweets had swept the upper levels of Madrid society in the early years of the seventeenth century, and such delicacies were usually served at the *merienda,* or tea time.

Contemporary accounts of social functions and prescriptions for etiquette point out that it was customary for servants to pass round trays and baskets of confections, and it was considered proper form for the guest not only to consume them zealously but to fill his pockets as well.[19] Lope de Vega gives this advice on entertaining in Act I of his comedy *El cuerdo en su casa:*

Una caja de perada
algún vidrio de jalea,
cidra en azúcar, jalea,
o con ambos nuez moscada,
es lo que habéis de tener
para honradas ocasiones.[20]

Fig. VI.13   Juan van der Hamen. STILL LIFE
WITH SWEETS AND GLASSWARE. 52 × 88 cm.
Signed, 1622. Museo del Prado, Madrid.

The boxes of pear conserves, glass jars of jelly, candied citron and nutmeg which he prescribes for honored occasions seem like a list of the things depicted in certain still lifes by Van der Hamen (Plate 17).

Van der Hamen's still lifes of confections run the gammut of his compositional repertory. Of 1622 is the unusual composition of desserts in the Cleveland Museum of Art (Plate 14). From 1627 are two surpassing works in this vein: one is the symmetrical still life that formerly belonged to Julio Cavestany, Marquis of Moret (Plate 18), in which the empty space at the top of the composition contributes a new sense of monumentality; the other is the stepped composition in the National Gallery of Art, Washington (Plate 17), in which Van der Hamen has challenged his brush to depict a wide variety of textures—stone, clay, wood, metal, glass, cloth, wicker and pastries—and at the same time worked in a daring new compositional format. This bold experiment with new spatial effects, in which symmetry plays no role, is a radical departure from his accustomed approach to composition, first noticeable in 1626 but yet to be adequately explained. It is clear that something in his own life or experience widened his horizon in the mid-1620s and led to a dramatic new direction. (See discussion accompanying Plate 16.)

Paintings of the quality of the ones just described were collected by the king and by aristocratic collectors such as the Marquis of Leganés and the Marquis of El Carpio. But the large demand for Van der Hamen's still lifes extended from wealthy bourgeois collectors—some of whom collected works of great quality too—to those of smaller means. This demand was met by a workshop that produced both autograph repetitions of successful works and signed paintings of a lower quality that were no doubt executed by assistants and sold for a lower price. The difference in quality is easily discernible and, while Van der Hamen may have supervised the production of everything that left his studio with his name on it, it is impossible to believe that some of the works bearing his signature were actually painted by him. In addition, Madrid abounded in hack painters who blatantly imitated his style in unsigned works.

DESPITE THE PRAISE and financial success that still lifes brought Van der Hamen, he, like most painters of his time in Spain, was unsatisfied by that success alone. The still life, notwithstanding the *ingenio* it was seen to reflect, was ranked near the bottom of the accepted hierarchy of subject matter. Van der Hamen desired to succeed as a painter of "higher" themes, and to this end he applied for the position of salaried painter to the king vacated by the death of Bartolomé González in 1627.[21] The eleven other candidates for the position were Francisco de las Cuevas, Juan de la Corte, Antonio de Monreal, Felipe Diriksen, Julio César Semini, Antonio de Salazar, Pedro Núñez del Valle, Angelo Nardi, Félix Castello, Antonio Lanchares and

Fig. VI.14   Juan van der Hamen. VISION OF THE APOCALYPSE. 300 × 237 cm. Signed, 1625. Museum of the Convent of the Incarnation, Madrid.

Fig. VI.14, detail   Lorenzo van der Hamen as St. Lawrence.

Francisco Gómez, none of them a painter of still lifes. The king commanded his three principal salaried painters, Vincencio Carducho (1576–1638), Eugenio Caxés (1577–1634) and Velázquez to inform him of the respective merits of the candidates and to choose from among them the one most worthy of the post. Although we are not privy to the reasons behind their decision, Van der Hamen was not among the finalists. He had, nevertheless, quite an active career as a painter of religious subjects and portraits. Palomino (1724) knew and admired religious paintings by him in the Monastery of Saint Giles in Madrid, the Charterhouse of El Paular near Segovia, the Monastery of the Shod Trinitarians in Madrid, and "many others in different locations that are little known." To that list, Ponz (1772–94) added others in the Monastery of the Barefoot Trinitarians and the Convent of the Incarnation in Madrid. Ceán Bermúdez (1800) recorded those plus others at Alcalá de Henares.

The only religious paintings by Van der Hamen that are known today are the ones he executed for the Convent of the Incarnation in 1625.[22] Founded by Queen Margaret of Austria, consort of Philip III, the convent was situated on a plot of land adjacent to the royal palace, with which it was eventually connected by a tunnel. Its privileged relationship to the Crown may have helped its contents to survive intact the suppression of the monasteries in the 1830s, that led elsewhere to the dispersal of Van der Hamen's religious paintings. The most important of his paintings in the Convent of the Incarnation is the large canvas known as THE VISION OF THE APOCALYPSE (fig. VI.14), which reveals certain strengths as well as weaknesses. The iconography of the painting is unusual and appears to be based upon ideas espoused by the artist's brother Lorenzo, who is portrayed as the figure of Saint Lawrence at the far left of the painting (fig. VI.14, detail). In his theological treatise on Saint John entitled *Al hijo segundo de María Santíssima, al solo en sus regalos y favores, a San*

Juan Evangelista (Granada, 1652), Lorenzo developed a detailed comparison between the Incarnation of the Word of God in the body of Christ and the cloud that shrouded the sun-face of the Seventh Angel of the Apocalypse when the Word was revealed to Saint John[23]—and "then is finished the mystery of God."[24] This iconographic connection makes the subject of the painting especially suitable for the devotional focus of the institution. In the upper part of Van der Hamen's composition, which is rather stiff and unimaginative, the relationship of the Lamb of God to the four symbols of the Evangelists is loosely derived from Dürer's woodcut, the ADORATION OF THE LAMB. The lower part of the composition, however, is a rather remarkable example of tenebrist naturalism. The foreground figures—Saint Lawrence, Saint Paul, Saint Peter, Saint John and Saint Augustine—are nobly conceived and executed in a rich and sensuous palette with a dramatic use of light and shadow. The painting has been ineptly restored in parts but gives a valuable glimpse, nonetheless, of an essential aspect of Van der Hamen's personality as an artist.

ANOTHER PART OF THAT PERSONALITY, which can be revealed here for the first time, concerns his activity as a painter of *bodegones* with figures. Cavestany (1936–40) mentioned that he had seen a photograph of a painting then on the New York art market which he described as representing a man seated at a table on which were plates and victuals, with fish hanging from above; behind him was another man carrying a large vessel of meats; and in the distance a landscape. The whereabouts of this painting is unknown today, but a photograph of it (fig. VI.15) is known to me. When the picture was sold on the London market in 1923, it was described as signed and dated 1647.[25] Both from the standpoint of the painting's style and the biography of Van der Hamen, this is impossible. The date must have been restored or

Fig. VI.15   Juan van der Hamen. MAN EATING. Signed. Location unknown.

Fig. VI.16   Juan van der Hamen. PORTRAIT OF FRANCISCO DE LA CUEVA Y SILVA. 117 × 105 cm. 1625. Real Academia de Bellas Artes de San Fernando, Madrid.

Fig. VI.17   Juan van der Hamen. PORTRAIT OF LORENZO VAN DER HAMEN. 55 × 43 cm. Instituto de Valencia de Don Juan, Madrid.

FRANCISC⁹ S.R.E. CARD. BARBERINVS.

Sᴜᴘᴇʀᴏᴄ ɪᴩᴍ. 1624. Eques Octaui⁹ Leo Rom! pictor fecit.

Fig. VI.18 Ottavio Leone. Portrait of Cardinal Francesco Barberini. Engraving, 1624.

misread and probably should have been read as 1617 or 1627—the latter being the more likely in terms of what we know of the artist's development.

The painting represents a low-class eating place, or *bodegón*. The man seated at the table is coarse-featured, plainly dressed, and eats ravenously from a bowl lifted to his mouth. The other man, no doubt an employee of the establishment, appears to be coming out of the kitchen with a steaming dish and glancing in the direction of the client. The corner of a brick wall over his right shoulder creates an emphatic receding perspective leading to a landscape in the background. The landscape is of the same general type as that in the background of Pomona and Vertumnus of 1626 (fig. VI.24). The face and hands of the seated man, as well as the joint of meat, bowls and utensils are modeled with a sensuous naturalism not unlike that in The Vision of the Apocalypse (fig. VI.14). The scene probably reflects very accurately what one could see on any day in certain quarters of Madrid, but the ravenous appetite of the eating man is so emphatic that it suggests the artist may have intended another level of meaning as well. Perhaps he was alluding to the Sense of Taste or to the Sin of Gluttony. With the knowledge of the photograph of this signed work, one must reconsider Martin Soria's idea that the so-called Cook in the Rijksmuseum (Plate 45) is by Van der Hamen.[26] Despite the indication that the artist did paint figurative *bodegones*, the Amsterdam painting reveals none of the stylistic features that we now associate with his works. (See discussion accompanying Plate 45.)

One of the most significant aspects of Van der Hamen's career, and one that is barely known today, was his considerable activity as a portraitist. It has always seemed curious that, despite the relative mediocrity of Spanish portraiture—apart from the works of Velázquez—during the reign of Philip III and the early reign of Philip IV, no period of Spanish literature has left more thoughtful and imaginative reflections on the art of portraiture than the period of the 1620s and early 1630s. Historians of the period have also been impressed by the unusually large number of references to Van der Hamen as a portraitist by the major literary figures of his time. Yet with one exception, Van der Hamen's portraits have remained unknown until recently. That one exception, a posthumous portrait of the jurist Francisco de la Cueva y Silva (d. 1624) painted in 1625 (fig. VI.16), although it contains a dramatic still life of books, has such a stiff and labored quality that it would lead one to wonder why Van der Hamen was so praised as a portraitist. Now that question can be answered, at least in part.

When Van der Hamen died in 1631, a series of twenty bust-length portraits of "illustrious persons" was catalogued among his belongings.[27] That series, which constituted only one entry in the inventory, was clearly regarded as an entity and was distinguished from other portraits listed separately. In the appraisal of the paintings made afterward by Pedro Núñez del Valle (early 1590s–1657) and Angelo Nardi (1584–1665) the sitters of the portraits were identified. Included were portraits of such men as Lope de Vega, Francisco de Quevedo, Luis de Góngora, José de Valdivielso, Juan Pérez de Montalván, Juan Ruiz de Alarcón, Lorenzo van der Hamen, Francisco de Rioja, etc. Among these men are the authors of most of the surviving literary references to Van der Hamen. Valdivielso refers to Van der Hamen's portrait of him in this way: "A portrait with which he honored me, by placing me in the company of the *ingenios*…even if among them I seem out of place."[28] Valdivielso's reference makes it clear that the portraits on which the artist had been working for several years were a series like Pacheco's *Libro de retratos,* that they were a visual counterpart to Montalván's *Índice de los ingenios de Madrid,* or Lope de Vega's *Laurel de Apolo.* The painting of these portraits of the artist's friends and the sitters' responses to them, usually with verses, represented a focusing of some of the most fertile minds of his time on the subject of portraiture. If he had done nothing other than this, Van der Hamen's contribution to the creative climate of his time would have been significant. Since Montalván said that the artist wrote "extraordinary verses" on the doctrine *ut pictura poesis,* he no doubt took an active part in the dialogue himself.

After Van der Hamen's death, his portrait series was split up, but eight of the portraits were later reunited in the collection of the Marquis of Leganés.[29] The only one of the series that can be identified with reasonable certainty today is the portrait of the artist's brother Lorenzo (fig. VI.17).[30] A sensitive likeness that is more fluid in its execution than one would expect on the basis of the portrait of de la Cueva, it indicates that the other bust portraits were perhaps in the same, more spontaneous style. This portrait, or a more developed version of it, seems to have served as the model for the elegant engraving of Lorenzo by Pieter de Jode (fig. VI.3). The engraving is identical to the painting in costume detail although in it the sitter seems somewhat older, but perhaps his features have been hardened by the engraver's stylus, not age.

A telling indication of Van der Hamen's stature as a portraitist that was discovered fairly recently by Enriqueta Harris is the diary kept during a journey to Spain by the Cavaliere Cassiano dal Pozzo, the famous Roman antiquarian and connoisseur, described by Francis Haskell as "the most cultivated and learned of all Italian art patrons."[31] From late May until October of 1626—in the promising, early years of Philip IV's reign—dal Pozzo accompanied Cardinal Francesco Barberini (fig. VI.18), nephew of Pope Urban VIII, on his Legation to the Spanish court. Following by only a few months a similar Legation to the Court of Louis XIII, the ostensible occasion was the baptism of the short-lived Infanta María Eugenia. While these Roman visitors were in Madrid, Velázquez painted portraits of the Cardinal and of the Count-Duke of Olivares, perhaps at the suggestion of the latter, which the two gentlemen were going to exchange as mementos of the visit. As it turned out, Velázquez's portrait of Barberini, which he finished on July 13th, did not please the sitter. In his diary entry for July 28th, Cassiano dal Pozzo records:

> After I had asked my lord and patron the Cardinal whether he would be pleased to have himself portrayed by Giovanni Vander Gumen de Gualdarama [sic], a native Spaniard of Madrid, who obtained excellent results in the painting of portraits, of flowers, and of fruit; and after he had seen that the portrait done by Giovanni [sic] Velasquez for my lord the Count of Olivares had achieved a melancholy and severe air, he was pleased that he [Van der Hamen] should come, and in half an hour, or a little more, he did it very well, not, however, having completely finished it….[32]

Fig. VI.20 Juan van der Hamen. PORTRAIT
OF A DWARF. 122 × 87 cm. c. 1625.
Private collection, Madrid.

A few days later, on August 1st, after the artist had completed his portrait, Cassiano dal Pozzo records further:

> And then he finished the portrait, for which he [the Cardinal] gave him an Audience. While he worked on the portrait, the brother of the painter, Don Lorenzo Vander Hammer [sic], who presented some of his books to my lord the Cardinal, read some chapters of the Life of Don Giovanni of Austria, which he had composed, and which he was about to have printed.[33]

None of these portraits, neither Velázquez's nor Van der Hamen's, is known today. It is difficult, of course, to believe that Velázquez's portrait of Barberini was not as fine as his other early portraits, but it is not difficult to understand how the Cardinal might have preferred another painter's likeness of him when we take account of the heated atmosphere of professional rivalry that existed among the king's painters at the time of his visit. The two Roman patrons could hardly have avoided being made privy to the resentment of Velázquez's rapid rise in the king's favor on the part of the established painters at the court. This partisan air no doubt extended to others in the community, including many of Van der Hamen's literary friends and sitters for his portrait series, who were also the close friends of Velázquez's archrival, Vincencio Carducho. That rivalry must have been reaching an acrimonious pitch around this time, for, within a year, the king ordered a competition between Velázquez, Carducho, Caxés and Nardi to determine once and for all who was the superior artist.[34] The victor, adjudged by Juan Bautista Maino (1578–1641) and Giovanni Battista Crescenzi (c.1577–1660; in Madrid from 1617) was Velázquez, whose EXPULSION OF THE MORISCOS (the assigned subject) won for him the appointment as Usher of the King's Chamber and thus effectively stopped the public sniping. Both Cardinal Barberini and Cassiano dal Pozzo eventually became admirers of Velázquez's art when he visited them in Italy, but on this occasion, perhaps as a result of palace intrigues, their opinion of his performance was less favorable. The important thing for our purposes is that, in this highly charged situation, Van der Hamen was perceived by Cassiano dal Pozzo as the logical alternative to Velázquez as a portraitist.

The appraisal of Van der Hamen's studio made after his death in 1631 included a canvas described as "A portrait sketch of the Legate"[35] that may have been the likeness executed on July 28, 1626, in half an hour's time, of which Cassiano dal Pozzo wrote. In the four days that lapsed before his return to the Cardinal on August 1st, the artist probably worked from that sketch to create a fully developed portrait, on which he put the final touches in the presence of the sitter. But this was evidently not all that Van der Hamen did for Barberini. Among the unpublished accounts of the Cardinal's expenses on the Legation to Spain, which are preserved in the Vatican Library, is an undated entry among the payments for 1627 that reads: "To a painter, with the brief of the lord Cavaliere del Pozzo [sic] for three portraits made by Giovanni de Guardarama [sic], painter."[36] Presumably his own portrait was one of these. It is also known that Barberini owned portraits of the kings of Spain and a portrait of Lope de Vega, which he may have acquired while he was in Madrid.[37]

Fig. VI.19   Juan van der Hamen. KNIGHT OF THE GOLDEN FLEECE. Signed, 1626. 206 × 120 cm. Private collection, Madrid.

Fig. VI.19, detail KNIGHT OF THE GOLDEN
FLEECE.

In 1971, Diego Angulo published a full-length portrait KNIGHT OF THE GOLDEN
FLEECE, fully signed by Van der Hamen and dated in the year of Barberini's visit to
Madrid (fig. VI.19). Owing to its strong plasticity, the painting has a rather star-
tling presence. The sitter, who must have been one of the powerful grandees of the
reign of Philip IV, is clad in gilded armor trimmed in red, with gold-embroidered
trousers and tan leather boots.[38] He stands firmly with one hand on his baton, the
other on the hilt of his sword. A dalmatian is sleeping at his feet. The effect of light
reflecting off the surface of the metal and the bold way in which light and shadow
are used to model the hands, the trousers and the boots parallel the ways in which
Van der Hamen uses light to create solid volumes in his still lifes. This very strong
sculptural quality, however, is not a particularly subtle vehicle for the portrayal of
character. The painting, therefore, has more developed plastic qualities than psy-
chological ones.

Recently, a remarkable unpublished portrait has come to light which, although
unsigned, is without doubt by the same hand as KNIGHT OF THE GOLDEN FLEECE.[39] It
represents a mature male dwarf wearing a *golilla*[40] and a green and red suit embroidered with gold bands on the sleeves and trimmed with gold buttons and a long
gold chain (fig. VI.20). At his left side is a sword, and in his right hand he holds a
baton of authority which lends him the comic air of a mock-general. The way of
modeling the faces and costumes is as similar as two portraits of different individuals by the same artist could be (figs. VI.19, 20, details). The generally high-keyed
color of each portrait and the definition of the spatial setting by a warm, brownish
floor and a gray background wall are also common to both works. Perhaps because
of its more intimate scale, the portrait of the dwarf lacks some of the stiffness of the
larger painting. Executed in the mid–1620s, it antedates any of Velázquez's known
portraits of dwarfs but follows in a long tradition of such paintings at the Spanish
court.

It is impossible to confirm the identity of the dwarf at this time, but, information published by Moreno Villa,[41] does suggest one plausible candidate, the dwarf
Bartolo, or Bartolillo, who was documented in the royal palace between 1621 and
1626. Described as a member of the king's retinue when the Prince of Wales visited
El Escorial in 1623, palace accounts indicate that he was provided with twenty-four
pairs of shoes in that year. Other entries record the making of his clothes in 1625.
Of course, the sitter of this portrait might not have been a palace dwarf at all and
could have been instead a member of some noble household. Regardless of the identity of the sitter, however, the portrait reveals the hand of an accomplished artist.
Van der Hamen's performance as a portraitist may have been somewhat uneven
overall but, if he often performed on this level, the praise of his contemporaries is
perfectly understandable.

KNIGHT OF THE GOLDEN FLEECE and PORTRAIT OF A DWARF were conceived with
a naturalism completely independent of that which Velázquez brought from Seville
in 1623 (fig. III.10). Their style is considerably more advanced than anything being
practiced in the 1620s by the other court portraitists, who for the most part were
carrying on the exhausted traditions of the sixteenth century. Van der Hamen's
naturalism seems to have more to do with post-Caravaggio Italian taste than it does

with the prevailing tendencies at the Spanish court or with any Flemish strain of naturalism. It is not surprising, therefore, that it would have found a sympathetic admirer in Francesco Barberini, whose uncle Maffeo, then Pope Urban VIII, had been one of Caravaggio's important early patrons in Rome. Young Barberini's devotion to the more decorative style of Pietro da Cortona eventually put an end to the influence of Caravaggio on Roman art, but at this stage in his life he much admired the early, Caravaggesque works of Simon Vouet and Valentin de Boulogne. Although his own more florid taste would eventually lead Vouet and Valentin to transform their styles, in 1626 Barberini would understandably have found Van der Hamen's portrait style a pleasing one.

Fig. VI.20, detail   PORTRAIT OF A DWARF.

IN TWO LARGE ALLEGORIES, Van der Hamen combined his flair for painting fruits and flowers with representations of the human figure. In one of them, the OFFERING TO FLORA (Plate 22), painted in 1627, the principal figure appears to be a portrait. But, while the figure's refined face, with its almond-shaped eyes, gives the impression that it was painted from a live model, we cannot be sure that it was a commissioned portrait of a lady in the guise of Flora. Certainly the related composition representing POMONA AND VERTUMNUS (fig. VI.24) of 1626 does not have the same portrait-like quality.

These paintings, exquisite in their execution and unlike anything by his Spanish contemporaries, present another example of Van der Hamen's purposeful eclecticism. He has applied his characteristic naturalism with its emphatic plasticity to the representation of goddesses with spilling cornucopias, a motif that is Flemish in its derivation. But he has also employed the effects of chiaroscuro and of light shimmering on the surface of irridescent fabrics, which are devices associated with the followers of Caravaggio, including Juan Bautista Maino in Spain. While these works reveal a painter conversant with artistic developments in Rome and Antwerp, no doubt through the great collections of Madrid, they also reveal the mind of a Spaniard who was, as Montalván suggested, a painterly poet of refined sensibility. None of Van der Hamen's fellow artists in Madrid so successfully delved into the classical imagery to which his poet peers were so devoted. Thus these paintings reveal yet another level on which he earned the respect of the intellectual community.

HAVING EXAMINED THE WHOLE SPECTRUM of Van der Hamen's oeuvre, we are reminded in the end of Pacheco's remark that his still lifes surpassed his figure paintings and portraits and that, to his displeasure, they brought him greater renown. Lope de Vega, too, seems to have captured the essence of Van der Hamen's dilemma, in which his talent and innovativeness as a still-life painter were at odds with his aspirations as an artist. In the last six lines of one of his sonnets to the artist, Lope de Vega said that, if his figure paintings failed to conquer his detractors and his portraits hushed his favors, then: "Let there return to you, Vander, so many dawns,/ That they crown you with your own flowers."

Soneto
A Juan de Vander Hamen Pintor Excelente[42]

Si quando coronado de Laureles,
Copias, Vander, la Primavera amena,
El lirio azul, la candida azucena,
Murmura la ignorancia tus pinceles:
Sepa la embidia, Castellano Apeles,
Que en una tabla, de tus flores llena,
Cantó una vez, burlada, Filomena,

Y libaron Abejas tus claveles.
Pero si las historias vencedoras
De quanto admira en unicos pintores,
No vencen las embidias detractoras,
Y callan tus retratos sus favores;
Vuelvan por ti, Vander, tantas Auroras,
Que te coronan de tus mismas flores.

Notes

1. Sánchez Cantón 1923–41, vol. 5, p. 399. The use of the name Valderrama in the dedication of this sonnet is an example of the Castilianization of Van der Hamen's name, which one often encounters in inventories and other informal records. Another form which this sometimes took was Guadarrama, the name of the mountain range north of Madrid.

2. Pérez de Montalván 1633, fol. llr, no. 215: *"Juan de Vanderhamen y Leon, Pintor de los mas celebres de nuestro siglo, porque en el dibuxo, en la pintura, y en lo historiado excedió a la misma Naturaleza: fuera de ser unico en su Arte, hizo extremados versos, conque provó el parentesco que tienen entre si la Pintura, y la Poesia, murio muy moço, y de lo que nos dexo assi en frutas, como en retratos, y lienços grandes, se colige, que si viviera, fuera el mayor Español que huviera avido de su Arte."*

3. Much of the information and documentation incorporated into this study first appeared in my doctoral dissertation at the Institute of Fine Arts, New York University, in 1967, which is available to scholars through University Microfilms, Inc., of Ann Arbor, Michigan. Since that time, several scholars have made valuable contributions to knowledge of the artist, and these are recognized here at the appropriate places. Since 1967, only one general study of Van der Hamen's still lifes has been undertaken, that of Joan-Ramón Triadó published in 1975. It is primarily a stylistic analysis of the still lifes which adheres to a pseudo-scientific methodology employing charts and graphs and resulting in completely unreliable conclusions concerning authenticity and attribution. See, for example, discussion of Plate 22, note 8 below.

4. Cavestany 1936–40, p. 133.

5. The genealogy of both sides of the artist's family is given in the *limpieza de sangre* of Lorenzo van der Hamen. See Jordan 1967, pp. 163–75. It is evident from this document, as it is in Van der Hamen's signatures, that the brothers were proud of their Gómez de León lineage and never used their maternal grandfather's name. Even Juan's son Francisco retained use of the name León two generations later.

6. Agulló 1978, p. 171.

7. Jordan 1967, p. 171.

8. For biographical information on Lorenzo van der Hamen, see Jordan 1967, pp. 21–25. For additional information, see Luis Astrana Marín, *Epistolario completo de D. Francisco de Quevedo-Villegas,* Madrid, 1946, p. 108; P. Gregorio de Andrés, "La descripción de 'S. Lorenzo el Real de la Victoria' del Escorial por Lorenzo Van der Hamen (1620)," *Anales del Instituto de Estudios Madrileños,* 1966, vol. 9, pp. 1–26.

9. The marriage document is preserved in the archive of the Archbishop's Palace, Madrid. See Jordan 1967, pp. 176–83. As noted by Pérez Sánchez (1983–84, p. 43), Eugenia de Herrera was of the prominent Herrera Barnuevo family of sculptors and painters. His source for this, not cited, is Saltillo 1947b, p. 376.

10. This date can be deduced from statements Francisco made in the accounts of his guardianship by Alonso Pérez de Montalván in 1634–35. See Jordan 1967, pp. 250–79.

11. Cavestany 1936–40, p. 134.

12. Saltillo 1953, p. 168: *"Consta que en ese año, a 10 de septiembre, se le libraron 100 reales por pintar un lienzo de frutas y caza para la galería del mediodía de la Casa Real de El Pardo, en correspondencia de otros que se compraron de la almoneda del Cardenal de Toledo para sobrepuertas...."*

13. Another autograph version of this composition, fully signed and also dated 1622, is known to me. The same cardoon is also depicted in several workshop pictures. Among these must be included the signed still life in the collection of the Marquis of Casa Torres, Madrid. See Pérez Sánchez 1976, pp. 53–54, no. 29; Held 1979, p. 390.

14. Vincencio Carducho discusses at length the great collections of Madrid in the VIIIth Dialogue of his *Diálogos de la pintura* (1633), 1979 ed., pp. 417–27. See also Burke 1984.

15. Cavestany 1936–40, p. 37; Sterling 1952, p. 66; Soria 1959, pp. 273–80. Bergström (1963, 1970, pp. 30–31, figs. 12–14), basing his argument on a pastiche of Van der Hamen which could not possibly be of his own hand, sought to prove that he was influenced in his youth by the still lifes of Osias Beert the Elder.

16. Sánchez Cantón 1923–41, vol. 5, p. 419: *"Vanderhamen, a quien Flora sustituyó el oficio de la Aurora...."*

17. Madrid, 1956 ed., vol. 2, p. 125: *"Tampoco falta en este tiempo quien se aficione al entretenimiento desta pintura, por la facilidad con que se alcanza y el deleite que causa su variedad, y entre los que lo han hecho con fuerza y arte se puede contar Juan de Vanderramen, archero del Rey Filipo cuarto.*

"La pintura a olio es más acomodada a este género, porque se puede retocar muchas veces y subir con la fineza de los colores a la verdadera imitación de las flores naturales. Puede haber maestría en los vasos de vidrio, de barro, de plata y oro y cestillos en que se suelen poner las flores y en la eleción de las luces y diminución y apartamiento destas cosas entre si. Y alguna vez se pueden divertir en ellas buenos pintores, aunque no con mucha gloria...." Quoted in translation from Engass and Brown 1970, pp. 215–16.

18. Madrid, 1956 ed., vol. 2, p. 126: *"También he probado este exercicio, y el de las flores, que juzgo no ser muy difícil. Juan de Vanderramen las hizo extremadamente, y mejor los dulces, aventajándose en esta parte a las figuras y retratos que hacía y, así, esto le dió, a su despecho, mayor nombre."* Quoted in translation from Engass and Brown 1970, p. 216.

19. Deleito y Piñuela 1954, p. 126.

20. Deleito y Piñuela 1954, p. 127.

21. For the most extensive published information on the competition, which is far from complete, see J. J. Martín González 1958, pp. 59–66. Van der Hamen's petition is preserved in the Archivo Histórico de Simancas, Casa y Sitios Reales, Legajo 333 (antiguo 28), fol. 150. See Jordan 1967, pp. 185–86.

22. Tormo 1917, pp. 131–34; López Serrano 1965, pp. 12–30; Lozoya 1965, pp. 376–83; Junquera 1966, p. 389; Jordan 1967, pp. 119–43; Ruiz Alcón 1977, pp. 29–36.

23. *Op. cit.,* fol. 36v.

24. *Revelation* 10:7.

25. Sale by Messrs. Robinson, Fisher and Harding (Willis's Rooms), London, May 31, 1923, lot 59.

26. Kubler and Soria 1959, p. 235.

27. Jordan 1967, pp. 81–85, 189–94.

28. José de Valdivielso, "En favor del arte de la pintura" (1632), appended to Carducho's *Diálogos de la pintura,* Madrid, 1633, fol. 183: *"...Un retrato con que me honró graduandome en el numero de los ingenios..., si bien entre ellos me estraño...."*

29. López Navio 1962, nos. 344, 583–90.

30. Jordan 1967, pp. 342–44, no. 32. A poor copy of this portrait is in the Archbishop's Palace, Granada, inscribed on the back: *"Dⁿ Juan de Valderamen y Leon."* Cavestany (1936–40, pp. 38, 73, fig. 16) reproduced the copy, suggesting that it was a self-portrait of the artist.

31. Harris 1970, pp. 364–73; Haskell, *Patrons and Painters,* New York, 1963, p. 44.

32. Harris 1970, p. 364: *"Hauendo io pregato il Signore Cardinale Patrone si compiacesse di lasciarsi*

ritrarsi a Gio: Vander Gumen di Gualdarama [sic] *spagnolo naturale di Madrid che per fare ritratti fiori frutti e simili riusciua eccellentemente; hauendo visto che l'ritratto fatto da Gio:* [sic] *Velasquez per il Signore Conte d'Olivares riusciua d'aria malinconica e seuera si contentò che uenisse, e in una mez'hora ò po più lo fece assai bene, non essendo però finito di tutto punto…"*

33. *Ibid.: "El poi si finì l'ritratto, ne si dè Vdienza. Mentre si fece il ritratto il fratello del Pittore D. Lorenzo Vander Hammer* [sic] *che presentò al Signore Cardinale alcuni suoi libri, lesse alcuni capitoli della uita di D. Giouanni d'Austria, che esso haueua composto, e staua in punto di uoler stampre."* I was kindly assisted in the translation of the Italian by the late Megan Comini of the Department of Italian, Southern Methodist University.

34. López-Rey 1979, p. 39.

35. Jordan 1967, p. 365, no. 130.

36. Biblioteca Vaticana, Archivio Barberini: Giustificazioni of Card. Francesco Barberini Sr., no. 501–820: *"779. Partito del conto con Illmo. S. Card$^{e\cdot}$ Prone nella Legaz$^{ne\cdot}$ di Spagna: Ad un pittore, con uiglietto del Sr Caualier del Pozzo per tre ritratti fatti da Gio de Guardar^{ma}. pittore."* I am indebted to Enriqueta Harris and Jennifer Montagu for kindly giving me this information.

37. Harris 1970, p. 367, note 7.

38. At some time long after the painting's execution a crudely painted crest was added to the background in an attempt to identify the sitter. It is emblazoned with the name "Don Gastón de Peralta 3er Marqués de Falces." Gastón de Peralta, who did not possess the Golden Fleece, was the third Viceroy of New Spain, serving in that post from October 1566 until March 1568. He could not possibly be the sitter of this portrait. The picture belonged to a group of five portraits of very disparate style and date, all from the same collection. All were inscribed in a similar manner with the name of some member of the Peralta family.

39. The owners of both of these portraits facilitated this research by allowing them to be placed side by side for comparison.

40. This kind of platelike collar was adopted as a result of the sumptuary edicts issued by Philip IV in 1623, which forbade the wearing of elaborate ruffs.

41. José Moreno Villa, *Locos, enanos, negros y niños palaciegos,* México, 1939, p. 75.

42. Palomino, 1947 ed., p. 887.

BIBLIOGRAPHY
Pérez de Montalván 1633, fol. 11r.; Pacheco 1649, 1956 ed., vol. 2, pp. 125–26; Palomino 1724, 1947 ed., pp. 886–87; Álvarez y Baena 1789–91, vol. 3, p. 212; Ponz 1776–79, 1947 ed., pp. 119, 430, 456, 878, 972; Viñaza 1899, vol. 4, p. 12; Sánchez Cantón 1916, p. 58; Tormo 1917, pp. 131–34; Sánchez Cantón 1923–41, vol. 2, p. 369, vol. 5, pp. 169–70, 399–400, 419; Mayer 1927a, pp. 230ff; Madrid 1935, nos. 1, 5, 10, 16, 21, 29, 31, 32, 34, 40; Lafuente Ferrari 1935, pp. 169–83; Cavestany 1936–40, pp. 37–38, 72–73; Entrambasaguas 1941, pp. 1–4; Cavestany 1942, pp. 97–102; Oña Iribarren 1944, pp. 27, 92; García Chico 1946, vol. 3, pt. 2, p. 66; Orozco Díaz 1947, pp. 39–50; Mayer 1947, p. 464; Longhi 1950, p. 39; Sterling 1952a, p. 96, pl. 28; Sterling 1952b, p. 66; Saltillo 1953, p. 168; Martín González 1958, p. 59; Soria 1959, pp. 273–80; Kubler and Soria 1959, pp. 225, 228, 235, 282; Sterling 1959, pp. 49, 69–70, 72–74; López Navio 1962, nos. 96, 97, 108–110, 124, 144, 344, 351, 353, 583–90; Bergström 1963, pp. 24–32; López-Rey 1963c, pp. 2–5; Jordan 1965, pp. 52–69; López Serrano 1965, pp. 12–30; Lozoya 1965, pp. 376–83; Salas 1965, p. 212; Junquera 1966, p. 389; Jordan 1967; Gállego 1968, p. 193, pl. 23; Harris 1970, pp. 364–73; Bergström 1971, pp. 29–38, figs. 11–21; Angulo 1971, pp. 24–26, figs. 8–10; Torres Martín 1971, pp. 55–60, figs. 9, 10, pls. 13–15, 17; Ruiz Alcón 1973, pp. 71–72; Pérez Sánchez 1973, nos. 69, 70; Pérez Sánchez 1974, p. 83, figs. 12–13; Triadó 1975, pp. 31–76; Valdivieso 1975, pp. 402–03, fig. 7; Bergström 1978, pp. 238–41; Agulló 1978, pp. 171–72; Bergström et al. 1979, pp. 139–45, pls. 136, 37; Held 1979, pp. 380–400; Agulló 1981, pp. 96, 214, 216; Orihuela Maeso 1982, p. 11–14; Lurie 1983, pp. 115–22; Pérez Sánchez 1983, pp. 41–43, nos. 15–29; Burke 1984, vol. 2, pp. 206, 434.

Signed and dated lower right: *Juan Banderamen/fa*[t], *1621.*
Oil on canvas
14¾ × 19⁵/₁₆ in. (37.5 × 49 cm.)
Museo de Bellas Artes, Granada

THIS IS ONE OF THE EARLIEST SIGNED STILL lifes by Van der Hamen, and in it we see his style already fully formed. Adapting to his own purposes the pictorial formula of Sánchez Cotán, he has arranged four containers of sweets and a silver spoon on a narrow stone ledge. Although his picture deals with the courtly subject matter of the dessert, he actually depicts in this case only the containers of the delicacies—two wooden boxes of marzipan, a glass jar of preserved cherries, and a glazed terra-cotta honey pot. Each one is a simple geometrical shape—a cylinder or a sphere. The stack of boxes and jar at the left creates overall a conical form that is mirrored by the globular honey pot on its narrow leg. Both the boxes and the spoon hang over the edge of the shelf and cast strong shadows, just as comparable forms would do in a work by Sánchez Cotán. The honey pot, pushed to the back of the shelf, creates a sense of shallow depth. The strong light boldly models the simple forms, and emphasizes the surface texture of each—the grain of the wood and the tiny black nails, the rough glaze of the pot, and the dull sheen of the silver spoon. The surface of the painting has never been deformed by relining or overcleaning, so that it reveals better than most extant paintings by Van der Hamen the richness of his brushwork.

As was Van der Hamen's usual practice, the principal forms in this painting were employed in other paintings of a later date. The stack of boxes with the jar of cherries appears in several works, among them the large BASKET AND BOXES OF SWEETS formerly belonging to the Marquis of Moret (Plate 18) and the large, stepped composition of sweets and pottery in the National Gallery of Art, Wash-

ington (Plate 17), both painted in 1627. The honey pot also appears in other signed still lifes, notably in the elegant STILL LIFE WITH SWEETS AND GLASSWARE of 1622 (fig. VI.11), which is in the Prado Museum.

The Granadan provenance of this painting, and particularly its connection with the Archbishop's palace, suggests that it may have belonged to the artist's brother Lorenzo, who served as Chaplain of the Royal Chapel in Granada from April 7, 1650 until his death around 1665.

PROVENANCE
Archbishop's Palace, La Zubia (Granada); acquired in 1946 by the *Ayuntamiento* (city government) of Granada and deposited in the provincial museum, where it was finally put on display in 1958.

EXHIBITIONS
Münster/Baden-Baden 1979–80, no. 207; Madrid 1983–84, no. 18.

BIBLIOGRAPHY
Cavestany 1936–40, p. 73; Orozco Díaz 1966a, p. 49, pl. 15; Jordan 1967, pp. 326–27, no. 2, fig. 20; Triadó 1975, p. 40, no. 3, ill.; Held 1979, p. 392, no. 207; Pérez Sánchez 1983, pp. 51–52, no. 18.

Signed upper right: *Ju VanderHamen/de Leon, factore*
Oil on canvas
24⁷/₁₆ × 48¹/₁₆ in. (62 × 122 cm.)
Private Collection

THE SERVING TABLE, OR *APARADOR,* IS A subject treated by Van der Hamen or his studio on several occasions in the early part of his career. In turning to it, he adopted a compositional type that was common among certain Dutch and Flemish painters in the second and third decades of the seventeenth century. The differences between his works and theirs, however, are more significant than the similarities. The present still life, which must date from the early 1620s, is the finest and best preserved of this type that is known, and the only one that is signed.

The dominant feature of the composition is the table spread with a white damask cloth. The receding in precise perspective of the two ends of the table establishes the pictorial space with a clarity that is absent in the Dutch and Flemish paintings of the type. The strong contrast of light and shadow dramatically emphasizes the reticular creases in the cloth, as well as the luscious sheen and pattern of its weave, and gives the picture an architectonic base. The stable composition is further reinforced by the solid modeling and carefully ordered placement of the objects on the table.

An instructive comparison can be made between Van der Hamen's still life and almost any of the northern paintings of a table, such as Clara Peeters's STILL LIFE WITH MEAT PIE AND OLIVES from the second decade of the seventeenth century, which is in the Prado Museum (fig. VI.21).[1] In the studied disarray of Peeters's work, every unoccupied space on the damask cloth has been filled with petals and leaves of flowers, which lends a certain temporality to the picture and its meticulous rendition of detail. In Van der Hamen's composition, the Talavera plates

PLATE 12

STILL LIFE WITH SWEETS

PLATE 13

SERVING TABLE

Plate 13, detail   SERVING TABLE.

Fig. VI.21   Clara Peeters. STILL LIFE WITH MEAT PIE AND OLIVES. Panel, 55 × 73 cm. Museo del Prado, Madrid.

of fruit are placed at almost even intervals. The square, brown bottle is turned at a forty-five degree angle to the grid of the fold pattern in the cloth; the bottle's stopper, carefully placed at the left, is the starting point of a zig-zag pattern in the arrangement of the rest of the objects, which results in the full articulation of the shallow depth of the tabletop. The modeling of the objects, such as the silver gilt compote (Plate 13, detail) is rather generalized and is aimed at defining the forms in broad, plastic terms. This connects the painting more with the Venetian heritage of Spanish art than with the polish and sharp focus of northern painting.

An unsigned version of this composition, that does not show the ends of the table and has certain other very slight changes, is in the collection of the Marquis of Casa Torres in Madrid. A work of lesser quality, it was probably executed by the workshop of the artist.[2]

PROVENANCE
Art market, Madrid, early 1960s.

EXHIBITION
Bergamo 1971, no. 45.

BIBLIOGRAPHY
Jordan 1965, p. 61, fig. 4; Jordan 1967, p. 327, no. 4, fig. 22; Bergström 1971, no. 45; Triadó 1975, p. 39.

NOTES
1. First recorded in the 1746 inventory of La Granja Palace, this is one of numerous Flemish paintings acquired in the eighteenth century by Isabella Farnese, consort of King Philip V.
2. Jordan 1967, pp. 327–28, no. 5.

Signed and dated lower left: *Juº VanderHamen/de Leon faᵗ, 1622.*
Oil on canvas
22¾ × 38¼ in. (58 × 97 cm.)
The Cleveland Museum of Art, John L. Severance Fund

THIS STILL LIFE, WHICH CAME TO LIGHT only recently, is one of Van der Hamen's most daring compositions. It depicts a stone niche containing a rectangular wooden confectionary box placed toward the right, parallel to the picture plane. On top of the box is a footed plate of dark green glass piled with sweets and an exotic Venetian-style goblet of new wine or some wine-laced infusion. Just to the left of center on the gray stone shelf, is a dark glass bottle half-filled with liquid and turned on a nearly forty-five degree angle to the picture plane. At the left, is another plate of sweets in front of which, near the very edge of the niche, are several walnuts, one whole and others halved. These are carefully modeled with an effort to differentiate between the texture of the shells and that of the meat of the nuts. The rectangular sweets on the plates are a mixture of pine nuts, honey, almonds and hazelnuts called *turrones*. Each plate also contains a large, cubical sweet containing more pine nuts in a sugary, white concretion.

The daring interplay of bold, primal shapes in this painting was undertaken at great risk of failure, so fine is the line between the representational and the abstract in these particular forms. But few paintings reveal so clearly the architectonic aims of the artist as he subtly manipulates those shapes. The vivid sense of space that he achieves within the niche is further enhanced by the irregular pattern of shadows and half-lights around and under the plates.

The painting was cleaned and relined prior to its acquisition by the museum. Aside from a hole in the background about 2.5 centimeters in diameter, which was easily and successfully repaired, the only significant damage that the painting has sustained is a slight weakening of the form of the brown bottle due to abrasion. At the time of cleaning, the old inventory number "13" was removed from the lower left corner.

Although the elements of this still life were not used in any other signed work that is now known, the right-hand two-thirds of the composition (from the bottle to the right) were employed in a derivative pastiche that I know only from a photograph.

PROVENANCE
Private collection, Mexico, D. F. (Sale, Christie's, New York, January 11, 1979, no. 65); Newhouse Galleries, New York (with Eugene V. Thaw) 1979–80.

EXHIBITION
Cleveland 1981

BIBLIOGRAPHY
The Bulletin of the Cleveland Museum of Art, 1981; Lurie 1983.

Signed and dated lower left: *Ju° Vander Hamen/de Leon fa^t. 1623.*
Oil on canvas
21½ × 41⅜ in. (54.5 × 105 cm.)
Plácido Arango Collection, Madrid

THIS OPULENT FRUIT BOWL OF DEEP GREEN Venetian glass with ormolu mounts must have been one of Van der Hamen's favorite objects, for he painted it on several occasions, and his assistants and imitators repeated it even more often. The quality of this work sets it apart as one of the finest examples of its type.

Van der Hamen has used as his setting for this still life the architectural niche initiated by Sánchez Cotán. But he has organized his composition with a strict symmetry that this particular fruit bowl would almost seem to dictate. Flanking the *frutero* are two fine plaited baskets, one filled with cherries and persimmons and the other filled with figs. The basket at the right is brought forward so that its perimeter overhangs the edge of the shelf, articulating the space between the image and the viewer. One fig, bursting with ripeness, rests near the edge of the shelf. Hanging at the upper corners of the canvas, further accentuating the symmetry of the design, are two tiny sprigs of fruit—one of plums at the left and one of cherries at the right. A small interval separates these from the branches of plums that extend like graceful wings from the bowl of fruit in the center.

The emphatic artifice with which this composition is conceived completely sets it apart from the studied informality of contemporary Dutch and Flemish still lifes. Van der Hamen's fruits are arranged purely for show, to be looked at and to be painted, with no hint of their consumption through the depiction of citrus peel or other waste. While the artificiality of the composition may seem to link the painting with the sixteenth-century Italian tradition of the grotesque, the naturalistic intent of the artist aligns it firmly behind

the example of Sánchez Cotán.

Four years later in 1627, Van der Hamen took up the same motif of the fruit bowl with an almost identical arrangement of fruit, yet achieved an even grander effect of opulence and spaciousness (Plate 19) due to a fundamental change in his artistic outlook.

PROVENANCE
Ceballos Collection, Madrid; Newhouse Galleries, New York, twice in the 1960s; Clowes Collection, Indianapolis; Newhouse Galleries, New York, 1982.

EXHIBITION
Madrid 1983–84, no. 22.

BIBLIOGRAPHY
Cavestany 1942, p. 100; Bergström 1962, p. 26, fig. 8; Jordan 1965, pp. 63, 69, fig. 9; Jordan 1967, p. 331, no. 11; Bergström 1970, p. 32, fig. 18; Torres Martín 1971, p. 56, pl. 14; Triadó 1975, p. 50, no. 16; Bergström 1978, pp. 240–41, fig. 2; Pérez Sánchez 1983, p. 54, no. 22.

PLATE 14

STILL LIFE WITH SWEETS

PLATE 15

STILL LIFE WITH FRUIT BOWL AND BASKETS

Signed and dated lower left: *Ju vander Hammen faᵗ./1626.*
Oil on canvas
33 × 44⅛ in. (83.8 × 112.1 cm.)
The Museum of Fine Arts, Houston, Samuel H. Kress Collection

THE YEAR 1626 MARKED A DECISIVE TURNing point in Van der Hamen's career. This extraordinary painting is his earliest dated composition that employs an expansive new format. In it, he departs from the simple window or niche of his early works and arranges the objects on a stepped ledge, adding another plinth in the foreground which further opens the space to the viewer. This and all the compositions like it are asymmetrical in their internal design. It is certain, however, that they were sometimes used as pairs in which the asymmetry of one mirrored that of the other.[1]

Roberto Longhi, who first published this painting, noted the parallel that exists between the stepped composition and still lifes of classical antiquity. Sterling (1952b) specifically compared it to certain frescoed still lifes from Pompeii that have been known only since the eighteenth century.[2] These could not have affected Van der Hamen, but, since stepped still lifes occur in both Spain and Italy, it is likely that knowledge of other such ancient prototypes existed in the early seventeenth century. More importantly, as Bergström (1970) notes, such architectural forms actually existed in the pantries of seventeenth-century houses. But, as in the case of Sánchez Cotán's windows, they ceased to have for Van der Hamen the literal function they might have had for a servant and became stages for the pursuit of his art. It may not be just a coincidence that this dramatic change in style, which incorporated a compositional format with antique precedent, occurred in the very year that Cassiano dal Pozzo and Cardinal Francesco Barberini visited Madrid. During their four-month stay, the learned antiquarian and the Roman patron, whose

taste effected changes in the styles of several artists he admired, got to know and admire Van der Hamen. The Cardinal commissioned several portraits from him (see Chapter VI above).

Pérez Sánchez (1974, 1983) has sought to relate the stepped compositions of Van der Hamen to the large KITCHEN by Pietro Paolo Bonzi (c.1576–1636) formerly belonging to the Duchess of Valencia, which has been in Spain for an unknown period of time, or to the lost still lifes of Giovanni Battista Crescenzi (c.1577–1660), who lived in Madrid from 1617.[3] An interesting Italian still life (fig. VI.22), which has been erroneously attributed to a Spanish master of the seventeenth century,[4] suggests a more specific parallel to the stepped composition. It features a stepped plinth very similar to those used by Van der Hamen, on which the artist has arranged pieces of fruit and a vase of flowers. Instead of a lower plinth in the foreground, that Van der Hamen would have employed, the artist has placed a kitchen worktable spread with fruit and vegetables. The rather informal way of arranging the objects and the deep, saturated colors are very unlike Van der Hamen's style and appear to have more in common with the first-generation followers of Caravaggio in Rome, who were painting still lifes in the first two decades of the seventeenth century.[5] While we cannot speak of a direct influence on Van der Hamen of any one painting or artist, it is obvious that he did not work in a vacuum. There was, no doubt, an interaction going on with Italian painting that contributed to the decisive change in Van der Hamen's ideas about composition. Nevertheless, his way of painting—his color, his use of light, his sense of space—were completely different from those of any Italian contemporary.

Van der Hamen's still life at Houston is composed along subtly interlocking diagonals that recede into the picture's depth. This represents for the artist a completely new way of structuring a still life.

The dominant diagonal begins with the melon and pomegranates on the front ledge at the left and recedes, parallel to the branch of irridescent plums, through the large crystal jar and the small beaker with bubble shapes behind it. The secondary diagonal is formed by the same large jar and the silver plate of white grapes at the edge of the ledge. The large, plaited basket of pomegranates and quinces that overhangs the edge of the upper ledge establishes a diagonal with the plate of grapes that is parallel to the picture plane; it also creates a recession into space just above and behind the melon. A subtle shaft of light enters the composition from above and shines down toward the right, creating an atmospheric effect that had not been present in the artist's work previously, nor, for that matter, in the work of any Spanish still-life painter.

In addition to its spatial innovations, the technical mastery of this painting reaches a new level of sophistication for the artist. Pérez Sánchez (1974) suggests that this also may represent a diffused Caravaggesque influence transmitted through Crescenzi, whose still lifes were praised for their delicate representations of crystals, fruits and flowers. This influence is, of course, impossible to certify until still lifes by Crescenzi are definitely identified, but it is more than likely that the two artists knew each other and their respective works. But Van der Hamen's increased skill in the representation of subtle textures is more probably the outgrowth of tendencies already begun in his earliest works.

This still life is one of the few known today which can be traced with certainty to the great collection formed in Madrid by the Marquis of Leganés, who, at his death in 1655, owned nine still lifes (among eighteen paintings in all) by Van der Hamen. Visible at the lower right of the canvas is a partially erased inventory number "353." Number 353 in the appraisal of Leganés's paintings reads: "Another by Vanderhamen, of the same

PLATE 16

STILL LIFE WITH FRUIT AND GLASSWARE

Fig. VI.22   Unknown Italian artist. STILL LIFE WITH CABBAGE. 70×92 cm. Private collection, Bergamo.

size (*vara* and a quarter wide, and three quarters high), with fruits and pomegranates, quinces, melons and grapes and some glass vessels."[6]

PROVENANCE
Marquis of Leganés, Madrid, 1655; Victor Spark, New York, 1950; David M. Koetser Gallery, New York; Kress Collection, 1957.

BIBLIOGRAPHY
Longhi 1950, p. 39, pl. 15; Sterling 1952b, pp. 66, 132, no. 137; Sterling 1959, pp. 40, 139, note 88; Soria 1959, p. 277; López Navio 1962, p. 285, no. 353; Bergström 1962, pp. 25–26; Jordan 1965, pp. 52–69; Jordan 1967, p. 333, no. 15; Bergström 1970, pp. 35–36; Torres Martín 1971, p. 56; Angulo 1971, p. 29, fig. 8; Pérez Sánchez 1974, pp. 82–83, fig. 13; Triadó 1975, p. 57, no. 30; Eisler 1977, pp. 205–06, no. K2176.

NOTES
1. A pair of such paintings, in which the points of view are consistent and the various planes mirror each other exactly, is still preserved in a private collection in Barcelona. See Jordan 1967, p. 334, nos. 19 and 20, figs. 37 and 38.

2. See also Sterling 1959, fig. 10, pl. 3.

3. During his early career in Rome, Crescenzi conducted a kind of academy in his house, in which he encouraged younger artists to paint still lifes in the manner of Caravaggio (see Baglione 1642, pp. 364–67). Baglione admired a picture by Crescenzi that depicted a glass vase with fruit immersed in water. None of his still lifes, either from his Italian period or his Spanish one, has been convincingly identified. For hypothetical attempts to identify them, see Volpe 1973, pp. 25–36, and Gregori 1973, pp. 36–56. Crescenzi's taste is assumed to have exerted a strong influence in Madrid. He was particularly relied upon by Philip IV in such matters. In 1626, the king made him Marquis of La Torre.

4. Bergström 1971, n. p., pl. 50.

5. Spike 1983, pp. 15–16.

6. López Navio 1962, p. 285: "*353. otra de Vanderhamen, del mismo tamaño, con frutas y granadas, membrillos, melones y ubas y unos bidrios.*"

17. STILL LIFE WITH SWEETS AND POTTERY

Signed and dated at right: *Ju vanderHamen i Leon/faᵗ 1627*
Oil on canvas
33⅛ × 44⅜ in. (84.2 × 112.8 cm.)
National Gallery of Art, Washington, Samuel H. Kress Collection

ALMOST IDENTICAL IN SIZE TO THE STILL LIFE WITH FRUIT AND GLASSWARE in Houston (Plate 16) and discovered together with it in 1950, this painting has been considered its pendant by nearly all those who have written about it. Eisler (1977) rightly points out, however, that the compositions are not complementary, unless they were originally part of a series of four referring to the Seasons, with Houston's representing "Fall" and this one "Winter," a practice that was not at all uncommon in Spain at the time. A painting of this subject matter was recorded in the collection of the Marquis of Leganés in 1655, as the Houston picture was, but can only be considered as possibly the same work if we assume that the scribe made a serious error in the dimensions of the canvas: "97. Another banquet-piece by the same hand and the same size [2 *varas* more or less high and one and a half wide], with boxes of conserves, a little basket of different sweets and clay vessels."[1] Such errors in dimensions were not uncommon in inventories of the time, but this painting does not retain the inventory number that the Houston picture has, which could have resolved the matter.

The composition of this still life is structured in exactly the same way as that of the Houston picture, with crossing diagonals that converge on the fanciful shape of the brick-red stoneware bottle in the shape of a ring.[2] The hollow center of this bottle becomes the formal leitmotif of the entire composition—a play of circles, cylinders and spheres against the rectilinear severity of the stone ledges. But the ingenious geometry of the painting only serves as the underpinning of a virtuoso performance with the brush. The artist has skillfully noted such effects as the powdery surface of doughnuts and the crinkled, glistening surface of candied figs in contrast to the dull sheen of a silver plate. Perhaps the greatest tour de force in his entire oeuvre is the painting of the glass finger bowl filled with water, which casts not only a shadow but also a reflection of light onto the stone ledge. The interplay of the intellect and the senses in this painting is characteristic of Van der Hamen's works in general but perhaps reaches its most satisfying expression in this work.

PROVENANCE
Marquis of Leganés, Madrid, 1655[?]; Victor Spark, New York, 1950; David M. Koetser Gallery, New York; Kress Collection, 1955.

EXHIBITION
Paris 1952, no. 72.

BIBLIOGRAPHY
Longhi 1950, p. 39, pl. 16; Sterling 1952a, pl. 28; Sterling 1952b, p. 96; Sterling 1959, pp. 40, 74, 139, note 88; Suida and Shapley 1956, p. 104, no. 37; Soria 1959, p. 277; Evans 1959, p. 23; López Navio 1962, p. 274, no. 97 (?); Bergström 1963, pp. 25–26, pl. 29; Jordan 1965, pp. 52–69, fig. 16; Jordan 1967, p. 333, no. 16, fig. 34; Bergström 1970, p. 35; Torres Martín 1971, p. 56, pl. 13; Angulo 1971, p. 29; Pérez Sánchez 1974, pp. 82–83, fig. 12; Triadó 1975, p. 58, no. 31; Eisler 1977, pp. 206–07, no. K2109; Pérez Sánchez 1983, pp. 42–43.

NOTES
1. López Navio 1962, p. 274: "*97. otro banquete de la misma mano y tamaño [2 baras poco mas o menos de alto y una y media de ancho], con cajas de conserbas, un canastillo de diferentes dulces y bucaros.*" The *vara* was equivalent to .836 meters, or thirty-three British inches.

2. Eisler, p. 206, identified this vessel, with the aid of Dr. Konrad Strauss of Munich, as a *loch* originating from the lower Rhineland. It is definitely not of Spanish origin.

PLATE 17

Still Life with Sweets and Pottery

Signed and dated on jar at right: *Ju Bander hamen/de Leon fa. 1627.*

Oil on canvas

32¼ × 48¹³/₁₆ in. (82 × 124 cm.)[1]

Private Collection, Madrid

IN THIS WORK, WHICH FORMS A PAIR WITH STILL LIFE WITH FRUIT BOWL AND SWEETS (Plate 19), Van der Hamen returned to the symmetrical format of his still lifes before 1626 but on an even larger scale than that of the stepped compositions from the Kress Collection (Plates 16 and 17). He has also retained the overall proportion of those canvases, with a greater height relative to the width, resulting in more open space above the basket of sweetmeats. The effect of monumentality thus achieved has no parallel in his earlier work.

At the Madrid exhibition of 1935 and in the exhibition guide published on that occasion, Cavestany transcribed the date on this painting as "1627."[2] By the time that he wrote the definitive catalogue of the exhibition, which did not appear until 1940, he had changed his mind and decided that the date should be read "1622." While all subsequent scholars, including myself, have adhered to the earlier date, it now appears that Cavestany's first reading of it was correct. The signature (Plate 18, detail), which is written on the cloth cover of the jar at the right, is not as precise as those on other paintings and is somewhat erased in parts, but the date is intact. The last digit does lend itself to interpretation as either a two with the foot missing or a seven. Its angularity, however, supports the latter. The greater knowledge we have today of Van der Hamen's oeuvre also helps to resolve the matter in favor of the later date. While it repeats motifs introduced earlier, such as the stack of marzipan boxes topped with a jar of preserves pictured in the small painting in Granada (Plate 12), this painting resembles more in the general refinement of its execution the stepped STILL LIFE WITH SWEETS AND POTTERY of 1627 (Plate

17), which was not known to Cavestany. Furthermore, by 1940 Cavestany had not yet discovered the 1623 STILL LIFE WITH FRUIT BOWL AND BASKETS (Plate 15), which is clearly in an earlier style than this work or its pendant.

A painting that appeared on the London art market recently (fig. VI.23) reveals that the main features of this composition were worked out considerably earlier than 1627, or even 1622. Signed and dated 1620, the composition is much lower and more horizontal, a format more common in the early works. But the execution is dry and lifeless by comparison to that of the 1621 still life from Granada (Plate 12), which is a benchmark of Van der Hamen's early work. Therefore, this painting must certainly be by a lesser artist employed in Van der Hamen's workshop.[3] Nevertheless, it demonstrates that the basic arrangement of the sweets in the basket, as well as the flanking of the basket by a stack of marzipan boxes on one side and the wooden cask and jar of preserved quinces on the other, was established in the artist's earliest years and refined throughout his career.

PROVENANCE
Private collection, Játiva; Julio Cavestany, Marquis of Moret, Madrid.

EXHIBITION
Madrid 1935, no. 5.

BIBLIOGRAPHY
Lafuente Ferrari 1935, p. 175, fig. 7; Cavestany 1936–40, pp. 149–50; Bergström 1962, p. 25, fig. 5; Jordan 1965, pp. 52–69, fig. 7; Jordan 1967, p. 330, no. 9, fig. 27; Bergström 1970, p. 32; Triadó 1975, p. 44, no. 9.

NOTES
1. All scholars to write on this picture, including myself, have followed an error made by Cavestany in recording the dimensions of this canvas. Since 1935 they have been consistently given as 84 × 104 cm.

2. The 1935 exhibition guide is fairly rare today and is almost never referred to by scholars. There are, however, a number of significant differences between it and the large catalogue that make consulting it worthwhile.

3. Van der Hamen, who had been married for five years by 1620 and had been patronized by the king at least as early as 1619, surely had a workshop by 1620. A number of signed works of inferior quality which share certain stylistic traits with this painting must be considered as not by his own hand. Among them is another that repeats this composition, which is monogrammed but undated.

Fig. VI.23   Juan van der Hamen (workshop). STILL LIFE WITH BASKET OF SWEETS. 62.2 × 96.5 cm. Signed, 1620. Private collection.

Plate 18, detail   BASKET AND BOXES OF SWEETS.

PLATE 18

BASKET AND BOXES OF SWEETS

PLATE 19

STILL LIFE WITH FRUIT BOWL AND SWEETS

Unsigned.
Oil on canvas
32¼ × 48¹³/₁₆ in. (82 × 124 cm.)
Bank of Spain Collection, Madrid

THIS PAINTING AND ITS DATED PENDANT OF 1627, BASKET AND BOXES OF SWEETS (Plate 18), were obviously painted to decorate a large room, for their scale is without parallel among Van der Hamen's symmetrical still lifes. The artist has taken as his central motif the opulent fruit bowl made of dark green Venetian glass with ormolu mounts, an object which he painted on numerous occasions throughout the 1620s. On this occasion, he chose to fill the bowl with the same arrangement of fruit that had occupied it in the still life of 1623 (Plate 15). The differences between these two works reveal just how much the artist had changed in the intervening four years.

Due to the increased height of this composition, which allows more open space above the fruit bowl, Van der Hamen has completely rethought the two plum branches which extend from the fruit. In the earlier work, the rather bare branches extend almost horizontally from the bowl, due to the compression caused by the picture's lower height; while in this work, the more luxuriant branches stretch upward to fill the vast empty space above the bowl. Perhaps because of his need to command a larger spatial arena, Van der Hamen has also heightened the plasticity of the fruit in the bowl, particularly that of the citron in the center. He has accentuated the irridescence of the plums and done much more with the play of light and shadow on the leaves of the plum branches. Even the fruit bowl itself has been treated differently. In the earlier work of 1623, and in the still life of 1622 in which the same bowl appears (fig. VI.7), Van der Hamen meticulously rendered a delicate filagree pattern of relief on the gilt rim of the bowl, the ring around its foot and the handles. In this version of 1627, however, he has altered the design of the

orlomu trim, eliminating the filagree pattern and replacing it with a bold pattern of repeated circles. The greater contrast of light and shadow has increased the sense of relief in the sculptural detail of the gilt bronze, and the impact of this is altogether stronger.

Flanking the fruit bowl are footed glass plates of biscuits and candied fruit. As usual, the pattern of shadows and reflections around and under the plates, which the artist learned from Sánchez Cotán, helps to define the clarity of the space in this shallow window setting. Also in the manner of Sánchez Cotán, Van der Hamen has extended a candied carrot stick over the edge of the ledge to accentuate the space between the painting and the viewer. This was done in just the same way in the STILL LIFE WITH SWEETS AND POTTERY (Plate 17), also from 1627.

This painting and its pendant demonstrate that Van der Hamen continued to paint symmetrical still lifes in window niches even after adopting the stepped format usually associated with his later works. In so doing, however, he revealed that the changes that had affected him around 1626 were profound ones. In their greater sense of baroque grandeur these paintings are as different from the early ones as the stepped compositions are.

PROVENANCE
Private collection, Játiva; Julio Cavestany, Marquis of Moret, Madrid; Almudena Cavestany Bastida, Madrid.

EXHIBITION
Madrid 1983–84, no. 23.

BIBLIOGRAPHY
Jordan 1967, p. 331, no. 10, fig. 28; *Una visita a la planta noble*. Bank of Spain, Madrid, 1970, n. p.; Triadó 1975, p. 51, no. 18, ill. p. 47; Pérez Sánchez 1983, p. 54, no. 23.

Signed lower right: *Ju° vander Hamen fa ¹/[1]6[2]9*
Oil on canvas
34⅜ × 51½ in. (87.3 × 130.8 cm.)[1]
Williams College Museum of Art, Ruth S. Weston Fund, Williamstown, Massachusetts

THIS IS ONE OF VAN DER HAMEN'S LARGEST still lifes and one of his most skilled representations of fruit. The similarity of its size and construction to that of the Shickman still life (Plate 21), which is also dated 1629, suggests the two paintings may have been part of a series. In contrast to the somewhat smaller Kress paintings (Plates 16 and 17), the artist has lowered the foreground plinth, which has the effect of opening up the pictorial space even more. The perspectival recession of the edges of the upper and lower shelves, which converges on the great basket of fruit, is one of the most dramatic spatial devices Van der Hamen has used. It lends added monumentality to the already very sculptural plate of grapes and pears on the foreground ledge and creates a suitable setting in which the artist can display the emphatic plasticity of the pomegranates, quinces and grapes overflowing from the large basket. The peaches on the silver plate on the upper shelf and the three lying on the lower shelf are also firmly modeled so that their weight and volume are forcefully suggested. The solidity of the fruit is especially felt in contrast to the delicate Venetian glassware at the outer edges of the composition.

The large basket of fruit and the silver plate of grapes and pears are motifs that Van der Hamen obviously worked hard to perfect. He used them again in a pair of paintings dated 1629,[2] and his assitants and imitators used them as well.

For the possible association of this painting with the theme of the Seasons, see the discussion accompanying Plate 21, which follows.

PLATE 20

STILL LIFE WITH FRUIT AND GLASSWARE

PROVENANCE
Unknown.

EXHIBITIONS
London, Western Ontario 1955; Indianapolis/Providence 1963, no. 40; Newark 1964–65, no. 29.

BIBLIOGRAPHY
Bergström 1962, pp. 25–26, pl. 31; López-Rey 1964, p. 4; Jordan 1965, pp. 52–69, fig. 12; Jordan 1967, pp. 333–34, no. 18, fig. 36; Bergström 1970, pp. 35–36; Torres Martín 1971, p. 56; Triadó 1975, p. 57, no. 29; Bergström et al. 1979, p. 145.

NOTES
1. The measurements usually given for this painting are 83 × 129 cm. During a recent cleaning and relining, areas of the canvas which had been folded over the stretcher, including an old tacking edge, were re-exposed. This accounts for the current, larger measurements.

2. See Jordan 1967, p. 334, nos. 19 and 20, figs. 37 and 38; Bergström 1970, pp. 35–36, figs. 19 and 20.

Signed and dated lower right: *Ju° vander Hamen faᵗ, 1629*
Oil on canvas
33¼ × 51½ in. (84 × 131 cm.)
Lila and Herman Shickman Collection, New York

THIS PAINTING, WHICH CAME TO LIGHT only about fifteen years ago, is similar in size and format to the still life at Williams College (Plate 20). The lighter and brighter coloration may have been meant to evoke the spring or summer months of the year, as opposed to the autumnal character of the Williams picture. It is possible that both paintings were part of a larger series that evoked the seasons or months. While the perspectival point of view does not lend itself to the picture's being placed on the same wall with the Williams painting, it does accommodate placement on a perpendicular wall to the left. Series of this kind were common among such followers of Van der Hamen as Antonio Ponce and Francisco Barrera (see Chapters IX and X) and are part of a tradition originating in the sixteenth century.[1]

The principal ledge of the composition is the longest of any of the stepped still lifes and accommodates three main elements: a glass vase of flowers, a metal plate of figs and a basket of peaches, pears and plums. The flowers, which are precisely drawn and vividly colored, resemble those in Van der Hamen's OFFERING TO FLORA of 1627 (Plate 22). The lower ledge, like that of the Williams picture, is quite low indeed and contains two terra-cotta vessels, a metal plate of cherries, scattered fruit and a splendid black glass bottle. The shadows cast by the two bottles are the kind of subtle, abstract shapes that Van der Hamen delighted in painting. The upper step, which is the narrowest of any in the stepped compositions, supports a plaited basket of green pea pods and cherries.

As Bergström has pointed out, this type of picture has parallels elsewhere in Europe in the first third of the seventeenth century, but Van der Hamen's "severe construction of a 'scenario' in three planes" is a personal trait of the artist.[2] In his final works, as in his early ones, he proved himself to be one of the most original and sophisticated still-life painters of his age.

PROVENANCE
Dr. Fritz Rosenberg, Boulder, Colorado (auctioned at Parke-Bernet Galleries, New York, March 19, 1969, no. 28).

EXHIBITION
Amsterdam 1970, no. 30.

BIBLIOGRAPHY
Valdivieso 1975, vol. 48, pp. 402–03, fig. 7.

NOTES
1. For a review of this tradition, see Christian Klemm, "Weltdeutung—Allegorien und Symbole in Stilleben," in Münster/Baden-Baden 1979, pp. 140–218.

2. Bergström 1970, pp. 36–37.

PLATE 21

STILL LIFE WITH FLOWERS AND FRUIT

Signed and dated on stone at lower right:
Juᵒ vanderHamen faᵗ,/ 1627
Oil on canvas
85×55⅛ in. (216×140 cm.)
Museo del Prado, Madrid

FOR MANY YEARS VAN DER HAMEN'S OFFERING TO FLORA was his only published figural composition, although the Prado catalogues from 1945 made passing reference to the existence of another in a private collection. The painting referred to was no doubt POMONA AND VERTUMNUS (fig. VI.24) which the late Juan de Zavala Lafora bequeathed to the Bank of Spain in 1968.[1] Only slightly larger than OFFERING TO FLORA, which has probably been cropped, it is dated 1626.[2] The two paintings are complementary in their compositions and their subjects. It has been thought that they might have formed part of a series of the Four Seasons, but, while they indeed have seasonal overtones, it now seems more likely that they were intended as a pair. They should be considered together for the meaning of each to be fully apparent.

Flora, as is well known, was the Roman goddess of flowers, and Pomona the goddess of fruit trees. Together, they presided over much of nature's bounteous gift to man. But, beyond that, they have something else in common: both of them were beloved by many but were indifferent to the love of ordinary men. According to Antonio de Guevara's *Epístolas familiares*—a copy of which was in Van der Hamen's library—the Divine Flora, symbol of the noble courtesan, would give her favors only to "king, prince, dictator, consul, pontiff and questor."[3] The nude statue crowned with a laurel wreath, which stands in the background garden of Van der Hamen's painting, is an allusion to her discrimination as far as lovers are concerned.

So complete was Pomona's devotion to her orchards and gardens that she spurned all of the many suitors who wooed her. Vertumnus, the god of chang-

Fig. VI.24   Juan van der Hamen. POMONA AND VERTUMNUS. 229×149 cm. Signed, 1626. Bank of Spain, Madrid.

ing seasons, nevertheless, fell in love with her. To be nearer to her, he disguised himself as a laborer in her garden. Van der Hamen has depicted him in this disguise paying suit with a basket of fruits. Later, disguised as an old woman, Vertumnus told Pomona a parable of marriage about the interdependency of the grape vine and the elm tree, both depicted as a backdrop to the figure of the goddess in Van der Hamen's painting. Eventually, when the

young god revealed himself in his youthful beauty, Pomona fell in love with him and agreed to share her gardens with him in marriage.

Both of these paintings represent an idealized conception of love and an ennobling view of women that characterized much of Spanish literature in the sixteenth and seventeenth centuries—to the extent that Cervantes even used the goddess Flora to satirize it.[4] They function as

PLATE 22

OFFERING TO FLORA

visual poetry in which images of flowers and fruit, gardens and sylvan views, peopled by goddesses and youths, played an important role. In this sense, the paintings parallel the lyric poetry of the time. One such sonnet written by Pedro Espinosa and published in his *Flores de poetas ilustres* (1603), could easily have been entitled "Offering to Flora":

Estas purpúreas rosas, que á la aurora
Se le cayeron hoy del blanco seno,
Y un vaso de pintadas flores lleno,
Oh dulces auras! os ofrezco agora,

Se defendeis de mi divina Flora
Con vuestras alas el color moreno,
Del sol, que ardiente y de piedad ajeno,
Su rostro ofende porque el campo dora.

Oh hijas de la tierra peregrinas!
Mirad si tiene mayo en sus guirnaldas
Mas frescas rosas, mas bizarras flores.

Llorando les dió el alba perlas finas,
El sol colores, mi aficion la falda
De mi hermosa Flora, y ella olores.[5]

Van der Hamen's painting of the OFFERING TO FLORA depicts the same two figures that Espinosa's sonnet describes—the goddess herself and an unnamed mortal who returns to her in homage the "painted roses" and "bizarre flowers" that have "fallen with the dawn from her white breast." The young kneeling page is, no doubt, bringing the basket of roses from a suitor, probably the one whose statue we see in the background.

Compositionally, the two paintings function in tandem much as the paired, stepped still lifes of 1626 and 1627 must have done. Both are built along the opposing diagonals established by the laps of the principal figures. The fruit and flowers spilling from the cornucopias in the foregrounds function as the lower plinths did in those still lifes: indeed, the melon at the lower left of POMONA AND VERTUMNUS resembles closely the melon on the foreground plinth in the 1626 still life in the Kress Collection, Houston Museum

(Plate 16). The vivid, springlike colors of OFFERING TO FLORA are contrasted with the autumnal hues of POMONA AND VERTUMNUS, where the changing foliage in the background hints at the office of Vertumnus. The crisp folds and faceted planes of Flora's skirt, as well as the sharp angles of the garden architecture, parallel the precise linearity of the flowers in the foreground. In contrast, the heavy, rounded folds of Pomona's dress are compatible with the ripe, sculptural quality of the fruit issuing from her cornucopia.

Stylistically, these paintings reveal the complex eclecticism of Van der Hamen, who drew from the many sources available to him in the cosmopolitan artistic atmosphere of Madrid in the 1620s. There are Flemish parallels, as far as the subjects are concerned, in works by Rubens and his circle,[6] but Van der Hamen's crisp style, with its emphatic plasticity and architectonic structure, is completely his own and does not relate to that of any Flemish painter. He combines with this a concern for chiaroscuro and for the dramatic effect of light shimmering on the surface of irridescent fabrics, which represents a diffused Caravaggesque influence, no doubt received through Juan Bautista Maino in Madrid.[7]

Obviously painted for a great patron, these works may one day be identified in a seventeenth-century inventory, which will give us further insight into the forces that may have influenced their making. As a pictorial ensemble, they stand out as one of the more remarkable creations of the School of Madrid in the critical decade of the 1620s.[8]

PROVENANCE
Valentín Carderera y Solano, 1880; Count of La Cimera (bequeathed to the Prado in 1944).

EXHIBITIONS
Madrid 1935, no. 40; Seville 1973, no. 69.

BIBLIOGRAPHY
Cavestany 1936–40, p. 156, no. 40, pl. XIX; Orozco

Díaz 1947, p. 171; Soria 1959, p. 235; Bergström 1962, p. 26, fig. 9; Jordan 1965, pp. 67–69, fig. 23; Salas 1965, pp. 205–27, no. 69; Gállego 1968, p. 193, pl. 23; Bergström 1970, p. 33, pl. 11; Torres Martín 1971, p. 117, pl. 17; Angulo 1971, pp. 29–30; Gállego 1972, p. 237; Pérez Sánchez 1973, no. 69, pl. 69; Triadó 1975, p. 65, no. 40; Bergström 1978, p. 238, fig. 1.

NOTES
1. Jordan 1967, pp. 143–53, 337, no. 24, figs. 108–10.

2. As I pointed out in 1967, the last two digits of the date on this painting are damaged and had been restored to read "1620." The date has thus been given as 1620 in the subsequent literature, except Pérez Sánchez (1973), who, by error, gave it as 1622. The painting has since been cleaned. Recent reexamination of it revealed that enough of the original last two digits remains to be absolutely certain that the date is 1626.

3. See Julius S. Held, "Flora, Goddess and Courtesan," *Essays in Honor of Erwin Panofsky*, ed. Millard Meiss, New York, 1961, pp. 201–18.

4. Miguel de Cervantes Saavedra, *El ingenioso hidalgo, Don Quixote de la Mancha, Part One*, Madrid, 1605. Ed. Rodríguez Marín, 1947, vol. 1, p. 36.

5. *Biblioteca de autores españoles*, Madrid, 1856.

6. Bergström 1970, pp. 33–34, operating under the assumption that Van der Hamen was influenced by the works of Osias Beert the Elder, considers OFFERING TO FLORA in relation to Rubens's PAUSIAS AND GLYCERA, executed around 1613 with Beert (Ringling Museum, Sarasota). A painting of Flora by Rubens's workshop is in the Prado Museum (no. 1675). Neither painting resembles Van der Hamen's in any significant way.

7. Jordan 1967, p. 153; Pérez Sánchez 1973, no. 69.

8. Two third-rate paintings of similar subjects, one of which copies exactly Van der Hamen's figure of Vertumnus, first appeared on the art market in Madrid (Adolfo de Arenaza) in the spring of 1966. I pointed out at that time that the inventory numbers written on them (nos. 704 and 705) corresponded to unattributed paintings in the inventory of the Marquis of Leganés in 1655 (see Jordan 1967, pp. 153, 337, figs. 111 and 113). The paintings, very Rubenslike in character, were neither signed nor dated. These mediocre pictures have since been accepted as Van der Hamen originals by Bergström (1970, p. 30), who mistakenly described them as signed and dated 1620, and Triadó (1975, pp. 37, 64), who maintained, at least, that they were not dated. One of them was recently auctioned in Madrid for a very small amount of money. A third composition, corresponding to number 703 in the Leganés inventory, which represents Spring, is known to me from a photograph. Like the others, it was probably executed in the 1630s.

VII. JUAN FERNÁNDEZ, EL LABRADOR

(Active in the 1630s)

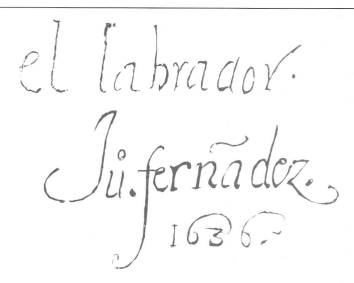

One of the most enigmatic figures in the development of Spanish still-life painting is the artist known in his lifetime and for more than three centuries thereafter by his nickname, El Labrador, which means "The Rustic," or someone who lives in the country.[1] He achieved international fame in his lifetime despite the simple life he chose to live away from the court, dedicating himself to his delicate pictures of fruit and flowers. In England, where his works were avidly collected by King Charles I and his court, he was known as "the Spanish Labrador." In France, where he was also represented in the royal collection, Félibien (1666) wrote of him:

> Although these sorts of works [pictures of fruit and flowers] are not the most considerable in the art of painting, nevertheless those who are the most outstanding at them have not failed to acquire a reputation, such as Labrador, de Somme, and Michel Ange des Batailles.[2]

By 1724, when Palomino attempted the first biography of Labrador, no one could remember his real name. Palomino called him Juan Labrador, though he obliquely suggested that Labrador was a sobriquet, reflecting his activity as a cultivator of the things he depicted. Ceán Bermúdez (1800) demurred at that and maintained that Labrador could also have been his true surname. Thereafter, almost no one questioned that Labrador was his name.[3]

Based on nothing more than the artist's works and on oral tradition, Palomino's life of Labrador also contained other inaccuracies that misled later generations. He mistakenly thought that Labrador was a painter active during the reign of Philip II and that he had been a disciple of Luis de Morales (c. 1520–1586). Follow-

Fig. VII.1   Unknown artist. PORTRAIT OF SIR ARTHUR HOPTON AT HIS DESK. 186.6 × 115.85 cm. 1641. Meadows Museum, Southern Methodist University, Dallas.

ing his statement to that effect, he said: "…whereby it is very possible that he was also Extremaduran, indeed if he did not come from the same city of Badajoz."[4] He wrote that he had died in Madrid around 1600 at an advanced age. As often happened, later historians attempted to harden Palomino's frank assumptions into fact. Nineteenth-century Extremaduran archivists searched the regional archives and found a baptismal certificate for someone named Juan Labrador in the small town of Jaraicejo (Cáceres), dated January 13, 1531. Published by Díaz Pérez (1884), this appeared to confirm the accuracy of Palomino's biography, including the likely death around 1600. Thereafter, in the early decades of the twentieth century, when the history of still-life painting as an independent genre was being systematically studied, Juan Labrador was considered to be, along with Blas de Prado, the earliest practitioner of the art.

The supposed early death date of Labrador, however, was at odds with the advanced, Caravaggesque style of the paintings that were attributed to him as early as 1639 in the inventory of the collection of Charles I (fig. VII.3, Plate 23). This led to either skepticism of those attributions or to bewilderment about how the artist could have been so powerfully influenced by Caravaggio at this early date. A resolution of the inconsistency did not seem imminent when, in the late 1960s and early 1970s, two important discoveries were made which opened an entirely new chapter in the study of Labrador.

In 1967, Elizabeth DuGué Trapier published the results of her research into the collected papers of Sir Arthur Hopton (d. 1650) which are preserved in the British Museum. Hopton (fig. VII.1) went to Spain in 1629 with Sir Francis Cottington, the English ambassador to the court of Philip IV from 1629 until 1631. During his extended stay, which lasted for years after Cottington had returned to England, Hopton acted as an agent of Charles I and was especially active in buying paintings for the English monarch's extraordinary collection. Later, from 1638 to 1644, he himself served as ambassador in Madrid. The exchange of letters (1631–36) between Hopton in Madrid and Cottington in London frequently concerned the purchase and shipping of works of art. Conspicuous in the correspondence is the eagerness on the part of the English king and his nobles to acquire still lifes by "the Labrador." Hopton was getting these directly from the artist himself; thus, the correspondence proves that he was active in the 1630s and did not die around 1600 as Palomino had written. Among the references to the painter there are a few that give further clues about him.

In a letter of November 10, 1631, Lord Cottington writes to Hopton: "You must remember to send the king the painted grapes which the poore fellow hath drawne for him." The use of the words "poore fellow" would seem to suggest someone in fairly abject circumstances, if not a little condescension on the part of the writer. In an undated letter probably written in 1632, Hopton writes to Cottington:

> I have not yet the Labradors pictures, I hope by his long stay hee will bring such store, as I shall steale some to send to my lady whoe Mr. Francis telles me desires them, & I beseech your Lordship by your next to send mee word, what you gave him for those your Lordship caryd.

As Trapier noted, this suggests that the traffic in Labrador's still lifes had been going on for some time. It also suggests that the artist had not been to Madrid for a long time. In another letter, Hopton writes: "The Labradors pictures are not yet come, though the time bee past wherein hee promised to bring them soe I suppose they cannot long tarry." And in an undated letter probably written in 1633, Hopton writes: "...the Labrador never comes hither but about Easter...." From these statements, we get the impression of a rustic who shunned the city, coming to Madrid as infrequently as once a year with a supply of pictures, some of them commissioned on previous trips, which he would sell to eager collectors. If the Spanish collectors experienced anything like the trouble the Englishmen had in securing what they wanted, then there must have been quite a spirit of competition among those seeking the artist's works.

It is curious that, with such a reputation, Labrador was not mentioned by Pacheco, whose *Arte de la pintura* was completed by 1638, though not published until 1649. It could be that Labrador was not yet active when Pacheco visited Madrid in 1625/26 and came to know Van der Hamen's works. In that case, he would have had no direct knowledge of his paintings in collections there. Labrador's paintings begin to appear in estate inventories in Spain in the 1640s and 1650s. In the inventory of the fabulous collection left by the Marquis of Leganés (1655), the artist is referred to as "*el labrador de las nabas* [sic]." This led Pérez Sánchez (1983) to suggest that he probably lived in Las Navas del Marqués, in the province of Ávila, or in one of the other towns of that name not far from Madrid. *Las navas*, which literally means "the plains," could, however, have been intended in a more generally descriptive way. Pérez Sánchez relates this preference for country life and its attendant sobriquet to the attitude expressed by the old phrase *"menosprecio de corte y alabanza de aldea,"* or "scorn of the court and praise of the village," which was expressed in contemporary life, as well as in literature.[5] Labrador may have been seen as an embodiment of this attitude.

Another of Labrador's patrons at the court was evidently the influential collector/painter/architect Giovanni Battista Crescenzi, Marquis of La Torre. In an unaddressed letter,[6] which Harris (1974) has convincingly shown was written to Sir Arthur Hopton in the early 1630s, Crescenzi offers to sell to Charles I nine paintings from his collection, apologizing that his financial need prevented him from giving them to the monarch. Included were paintings by Rosso, Paris Bordone, Caracciolo and Adam Elsheimer, as well as four landscapes by Labrador. In addition to enlarging our idea of his oeuvre, the letter connects Labrador with one of the most dedicated proponents of Caravaggesque painting in Madrid and one of the most enthusiastic supporters of still-life painting. The documentary reference places the taste for Labrador's works exactly where one would expect to find it; thus another piece of the puzzle falls into its logical place.

In 1971, the second major discovery in the reconstruction of Labrador's personality was made when the first signed and dated painting appeared on the art market. A flowerpiece painted on wood panel (Plate 24), the painting is inscribed on the back: *el labrador./Ju. Fernãdez./1636.* (fig. VII.2).[7] Its extraordinary quality justified the high praise historically accorded the artist's works, and its style resem-

Fig. VII.2 Juan Fernández, El Labrador. Signature from reverse of FLOWERPIECE (Plate 24).

bled that of the paintings which had been catalogued in the collection of Charles I. The inscription, unquestionably a signature and not a later addition, gives us Labrador's real name, and its date coincides with the time span covered by Hopton's correspondence with the artist's English patrons. The knowledge of the artist's name later led Harris and Troutman (1981) to suggest that he might be identified with one Juan Fernández, *labrador,* whose paintings were appraised following his death on December 14, 1657.[8] That identification is not correct, however. I have read the entire estate inventory of this Juan Fernández, and it is clear that he was a prosperous farmer living just outside Madrid. Only sixteen religious paintings of low valuation were among his possessions, and nowhere in the lengthy document is he referred to as a painter. Therefore, while the knowledge of Labrador's real name will surely one day lead to further discoveries concerning his biography, we still do not even know the dates of his birth or death. Nor do we know where he lived or how he arrived at his remarkable, naturalistic style.

If, in the eighteenth century, the details of Labrador's life had already been forgotten, his works had not been. Palomino and, especially, Ceán Bermúdez seem to have known exactly what they looked like. Palomino wrote:

> He dedicated himself especially to fruit and flowers…: painting them repeatedly from nature, he succeeded in delineating them with such superior excellence that none has equalled him, and thus his panels are so recognized for their delicacy and detail in the definition of fruits and other trifles, just as those of the Divine Morales are for the subtlety of the hair of his figures. He painted some still lifes *[bodegoncillos]* with different edible things, vessels, and other articles with singular skill.[9]

Enlarging upon what Palomino had said, Ceán Bermúdez appeared to express keen personal observation when he wrote:

> Few have equalled him in the merit and execution of flowers: the two pictures by his hand which are in the antechamber of the King in the new palace rival all those painted in this genre—in the contrast and good arrangement of the flowers, as well as in the thinness of the leaves and the brilliance of the color. Admirable is the transparency of a few drops of water that are represented on them [the leaves], which appear real. He also dedicated himself to painting fruits, still lifes *[bodegoncillos]* and trifles, which he discharged with the same effect.[10]

Well into the nineteenth century, collection inventories indicate that connoisseurs still recognized the style of Labrador. But by the 1935 still-life exhibition in Madrid, Cavestany could only describe his personality as "nebulous" and acknowledge that the few attributions made to him lacked firmness. With the great progress made recently in the study of the artist, it may be possible in the near future to identify a larger part of his oeuvre. As a background for that and for the discussions of specific paintings on the following pages, it may be helpful to review some of the documentary references to his paintings.

Chronological summary of Labrador's still lifes in collection inventories

1639 Catalogue of the collection of King Charles I, London

    I. The picture of several sorts of fruits in a white earthen vessel; grapes, apples, chesnuts [sic], and the like, painted upon the right light. Done by the Spanish Labrador; given to the King by my Lord Cottington. 2f. 9 in. x 2f. 3 in. (Van der Doort 1639, p. 4).

This is the painting still at Hampton Court (Plate 23).

II. Done by Labradore. Upon a cloth, upon a stone table, a wicker wine bottle, and a speckled white earthen wine pot, and a wine-glass, and a white earthen dish, wherein some seeteroome [sic], and a white napkin by, wherein some sausages de Bolonia, a napkin, a loaf of bread by, and some greens; which the King did change with the Lord Marquiss of Hamilton, giving him a piece of grapes for the same, done by the Labradore. 1f. 10 in. x 2f. 4 in. (Van der Doort 1639, p. 153).

Fig. VII.3   Juan Fernández, El Labrador(?).
STILL LIFE WITH A DISH OF LEMONS, SAUSAGES, BREAD AND A STRAW-COVERED BOTTLE.
54.6 × 72.4 cm. H. M. Queen Elizabeth II, Kew Gardens.

This is no doubt the heavily restored painting today at Kew Gardens Palace (fig. VII.3), which was sold for £10 by the Commonwealth following the execution of the king but later reacquired by the Crown. In the inventory of James II, the painting was attributed to "Michael Angelo." Law (1898, p. 174, no. 467) assumes this meant Michelangelo da Campidoglio. Harris (1967), among others, is skeptical that this painting and the one at Hampton Court are by the same hand. She suggests that the name Labrador was meant to apply to the painting of grapes which Charles I exchanged with the Marquis of Hamilton for this one. It appears clear from the marginal notation in Van der Doort's inventory, however, that the attribution applied to this painting and that the king had traded one picture by Labrador for another. Knowing as little as we do about the artist, it seems unwise to reject at this time an attribution made so near the time when the painting was acquired by the king.

III. A round turned wooden frame painted, a red Spanish wine pot, and some bunches of Spanish grapes, done upon a board, being brought from Spain by my Lord Cottington, and given to the King. Done by the Spanish Labradore. 9 in. (Van der Doort 1639, p. 160).

Law (1898, p. 195, no. 544) mistakenly assumed that this very small, possibly circular panel could be identified with a two-foot-high, rectangular canvas of some grapes bequeathed to the Crown at an unknown date by a Mrs. Mary Delayny. This painting is apparently lost.

1644   Appraisal of the paintings of Juana de Quevedo, wife of Juan Gómez Dávila, Madrid. November 17, 1944. AHP M P#9063, fols. 99v–103 (Agulló 1981, p. 98).

IV. *Más otro quadro pequeño de vnas vbas, del Labrador* (Another small picture of some grapes, by the Labrador)

1651   Declaration of the paintings of Bartolomé Barrilaro, on the occasion of his marriage to Ana Ramírez y Figueroa, Madrid. April 10, 1651. AHP M P#9074, fols. 41–44 (Agulló 1981, p. 211).

V. *Dos ramilleteros, el vno del Teatino y el otro del Labrador y dos tablas de dos batallas* (Two flowerpieces, the one by the Theatine and the other by the Labrador and two battle scenes)

1651   Inventory begun on June 1, 1651, of the collection of Don Gaspar Méndez de Haro y Guzmán, Marquis of Eliche. Archive of the Palacio de Liria, Madrid, Caja 221–22. (Cited in partial English transcription by Burke 1984, vol. 2, p. 221.)

> VI.   *139. Un lienço de Labrador con una jarra de Rossas claveles y azucenas con ottras flores y unos Racimos de uvas y unos granados aviertos de bara y quarta de ancho y una de cayda con su marco negro* (A canvas by Labrador with an earthen jar of roses, carnations and lilies with other flowers and some bunches of grapes and open pomegranates, one and a quarter *varas* wide and one in height with its black frame) See Plate 25.

1655   Inventory of the collection of the Marquis of Leganés and La Poza, Don Diego Felipez de Guzmán, Madrid. April 6, 1655. AHP M P#6267, fol. 616 (López Navio 1962, p. 294).

> VII.   *(605) una pintura de media bara en quadro, de una porçelana de hubas, dos bucaros, unas castañas y bellotas, de mano del labrador de las nabas* (A painting one-half *vara* square of a porcelain dish of grapes, two ceramic vessels, some chestnuts and acorns, by the hand of *el labrador de las navas*)

1662   Inventory of the collection of Don Francisco Merchant de la Zerda, Madrid. June 1, 1662. AHP M P#9149, fols. 669 ff. (Agulló 1981, pp. 214–15).

> VIII.   *Más vn lienzo pequeño redondo en que están pintadas vnas ubas, de mano de El Labrador* (Plus a small, round canvas on which are painted some grapes, by the hand of the Labrador)

> IX.   *…vn lienzo de dos terzias de alto y del mismo ancho, con sus marcos negros* [sic], *en que está pintado vn razimo de vbas, del Labrador* (…A canvas two-thirds *[vara]* in height and the same in width, with its black frames [sic], on which is painted a bunch of grapes, by the Labrador)

1682   Auction sale of the collection of Sir Peter Lely, London. April 8, 1682. Lely Catalogue, p. 187 (Talley 1984, p. 201).

> X.   A Piece of Fruit. Of Laberador. [sic]

1687–89   Inventory begun on December 23, 1687, of the collection of the VII Marquis of El Carpio, Don Gaspar Méndez de Haro y Guzmán, Marquis of Eliche, Madrid. AHP M P#9819, fol. 1019v. (Cited in partial English transcription by Burke 1984, vol. 2, p. 252k.) Numbers 196 and 198 were sold on October 10, 1691, to Francisco Travieirra [sic]. (Archive of the Palacio de Liria, Madrid, Caja 221–22.)

> XI.   *196. Un quadro de sobrepuerta con un Razimo de Ubas y abellanas y original de Labrador de Tercia en quadro.* (An overdoor picture with a Bunch of Grapes and hazelnuts an original by Labrador, One-Third *vara* square)

> XII.   *198. Otro del mismo tamaño y autor con un racimo de ubas y unas Villotas* (Another of the same size and author with a bunch of grapes and some Acorns)

XIII. 349. Chestnuts and a glass of wine, one-third *vara* by two-thirds. Labrador. (Fol. 1032, quoted in English transcription only by Burke 1984, vol. 2, p. 254.)

1767 Collection of the Earl of Pembroke, Wilton House, Salisbury, Wiltshire. From the description by Thomas Martyn, *The English Connoisseur,* 1767, vol. 2, p. 87 (Talley 1984, p. 201).

XIV. Still Life of Plate and Earthen Vessels. Wilton House. Dining Room, over the door.

1772 Inventory of the Buen Retiro Palace, Madrid. (Cavestany 1936–40, p. 142.)

XV. *No. 14513 (148). Un racimo de uvas en su vástago colgante tres cuartas de alto, dos tercios de ancho, de Juan Labrador* (A bunch of grapes on its stem hanging three-quarters *[vara]* in height and two-thirds in width, by Juan Labrador) See Plate 26.

1776 Description of the pictures in the New Royal Palace, Madrid. (Antonio Ponz, *Viaje de España,* vol. 6, p. 27.)

XVI. and XVII. *En la antecámara del quarto del Rey se hallan…dos floreros de Juan Labrador* (In the antechamber of the King's room are found…two flowerpieces by Juan Labrador)

These paintings are the same two described in more detail by Ceán Bermúdez in 1800 (quoted in full above).

1811 Among the paintings destined to be offered to the Emperor Napoleon as "national recompense" by the Minister of the Interior in the government of the intrusive King Joseph I; taken on June 6, 1811 from the apartment of the Queen of Etruria in the Royal Palace, Madrid. (Saltillo 1933, p. 31)

XVIII. *Las flores y frutas, de Labrador, de la segunda pieza de la Reina de Etruria* (The flowers and fruit, of Labrador, from the second room of the Queen of Etruria)

1835 Inventory of the collection of the Infante Don Sebastian Gabriel de Borbón. (Agueda 1982, p. 109.)

XIX. *(97). Otro en tabla de 1 pie de alto por 1 y 5 pies de ancho. Es un Frutero compuesto de una salvilla con brevas, y un melón. Juan Labrador* (Another on panel of 1 foot in height by 1 and 5 feet [sic] in width. It is a *Frutero* composed of a salver with figs, and a melon. Juan Labrador)

NOTES

1. *Labrador* can also mean a farmer who actually tills the soil himself, or one who simply owns a farm but does not work with his hands. The meaning of the painter's nickname most likely corresponds to the third definition given in the *Diccionario de autoridades* published by the Real Academia Española (1732): *"Se llama tambien a todo hombre o muger que vive en Lugar corto o Aldea, aunque no se ocupe en el ministerio del campo."*

2. Félibien 1666, ed. 1775, p. 179: *"Bien que ces sortes d'ouvrages ne soient pas les plus considerables dans l'art de peindre, toutefois ceux que s'y sont le plus signalez, n'ont pas laissé d'acquerir de la reputation, comme Labrador, de Somme, & Michel Ange des Batailles."* According to Baticle (Bordeaux 1978, p. 56), Labrador is mentioned in an inventory of Anne of Austria, consort of Louis XIII and elder sister of Philip IV.

3. In 1967, based on the reference to the artist as *"el labrador de las nabas"* in the inventory of the collection of the Marquis of Leganés (1655), I put forward the hypothesis that Labrador was the artist's nickname. Jordan 1967, pp. 34–35.

4. Palomino 1724, ed. 1947, p. 812: *"conque es muy posible, que fuese también extremeño, ya que no fuese de la misma ciudad de Badajoz."*

5. He cites as examples the comedies *El villano en su rincón* by Lope de Vega, and *Del rey abajo ninguno* and *Labrador más honrado García de Castañar* by Rojas Zorrilla.

6. This letter, which is inscribed with the heading "copie of a note given me by James Bap. Cresentio, touching pictures," was published by Sainsbury (1859, Appendix 103), who believed that it had been written c. 1614.

7. See Valdivieso 1972.

8. Agulló (1978, p. 182) cited the document in the Archivo de Protocolos in Madrid (AHP M P#6770), without transcribing it. Pérez Sánchez (1983) was skeptical of the identification.

9. Palomino 1724, ed. 1947, p. 812: *"Inclinóse más a las frutas, y flores, por ser de suyo labrador: que haciéndolas repetidamente por el natural, llegó a expresarlas con tan superior excelencia, que ninguno le ha igualado; y así son sus tablas tan conocidas, por la delicadeza, y puntualidad en lo definido de las frutas, y otras baratijas; como las del Divino Morales en las sutileza de los cabellos de las figuras. Pintó también algunos bodegoncillos con diferentes cosas comestibles, vasijas, y otros adherentes con singular primor."*

10. Ceán Bermúdez 1800, vol. 3, pp. 1–2. *"Pocos le han igualado en el merito y execucion de las flores: los dos quadros de su mano, que están en la antecámara del Rey en el palacio nuevo, desafian á todos los que pintáron en este género, así por el contraste y buena colocacion de las flores, como por la delgadez de las hojas y brillantez del colorido, y es admirable las transparencia de unas gotas de agua que figuró en ellas, pues parecen verdaderas. Se dedicó tambien á pintar frutas, bodegoncillos y baratijas, que desempeñaba con el mismo acierto."*

BIBLIOGRAPHY

Van der Doort 1639, pp. 4, 153, 160; Félibien 1666–85, vol. 4, p. 179; Palomino 1724, p. 812; Salas 1773, pp. 75–76; Ponz 1776, vol. 6, p. 27; Ceán Bermúdez 1800, vol. 3, pp. 1–2; Quilliet 1816, p. 173; Víu 1852; Sainsbury 1859, pp. 354–55; Díaz Pérez 1884, pp. 477–79; London, Hampton Court, 1898 cat., pp. 174, 194–95; Saltillo 1933, p. 31; Lafuente Ferrari 1935, p. 172; Cavestany 1936–40, pp. 66, 142, 150; Orozco Díaz 1954b, p. 30; Sterling 1959, p. 70; López Navio 1962, p. 294; Jordan 1967, vol. 1, pp. 34–35; Harris 1967b, pp. 483–84; Trapier 1967, vol. 164, pp. 239–43; Bergström 1970, p. 17; Barnard Castle, The Bowes Museum, 1970 cat., pp. 41–42; Torres Martín 1971, pp. 34–35; Valdivieso 1972, pp. 323–24; Harris 1974b, pp. 162–64; Young 1976, p. 211; Agulló 1978, p. 182; Bordeaux 1978, pp. 55–56; Bergström et al. 1979, p. 188; Agulló 1981, pp. 98, 211, 214–15; Harris and Troutman 1981, no. 35; Agueda 1982, p. 109; Haraszti 1983, pp. 72, 83; Talley 1984, p. 201; Madrid 1983, pp. 43–44; Burke 1984, vol. 1, pp. 222, vol. 2, p. 221.

23. STILL LIFE WITH QUINCES AND ACORNS
(usually titled STILL LIFE WITH APPLES IN A DISH)

Oil on canvas
33½ × 28 in. (85.1 × 71.1 cm.)
H. M. Queen Elizabeth II, Hampton Court
Palace

THIS IS CERTAINLY THE PAINTING CAT-
alogued by Van der Doort in 1639 in the
collection of Charles I: "The picture of
several sorts of fruits in a white earthen
vessel; grapes, apples, chesnuts [sic], and
the like, painted upon the right light.
Done by the Spanish Labrador; given to
the King by my Lord Cottington. 2f. 9 in.
x 2f. 3 in."[2] Although the subject matter
of the still lifes sent to Cottington from
Madrid by Sir Arthur Hopton is not speci-
fied in their correspondence, this is surely
one of those which arrived after much delay between 1633 and 1635.[3]

The dimensions of the painting today
are almost the same as those given in the
seventeenth century, which assures us that
it has not been cut down. As Sterling
(1959) noted, the composition reveals an
artist who abhors an empty space, for
every part of the rectangular canvas has
been filled with some form. Just slightly
to the left of center on a horizontal ledge is
a perforated ceramic dish filled with
grapes and quinces, which are often mistaken for apples. In the foreground, the
artist has painted some chestnuts and
acorns, a bunch of grapes and another
quince with a very conspicuous worm
hole. Near that quince is a branch of foliage from its tree. Behind the ledge on
which the fruit is placed rises a grapevine
whose pruned branches and leaves fill the
entire upper part of the composition.

The composition of the painting represents the very antithesis of the studied artificiality of Van der Hamen's still lifes in
which symmetry, perspective and pure
geometric shapes play such an important
role. Labrador seems concertedly to have
avoided the impression that artifice intervened at all. In the true spirit of Caravaggio, he seems to have caught nature
just as it is. Indeed, it is not without good

Fig. VII.4 Caravaggio. ST. JOHN THE BAPTIST.
173.5 × 132 cm. The Nelson-Atkins Museum
of Art, Kansas City

reason that Sterling and others have noted
the Italian's influence on Labrador. The
curled leaf at the left and the imperfections
of the fruit are definite Caravaggesque
traits. But the blazing light that illuminates the forms against utter darkness is
unlike the clear, even light in the famous,
early BASKET OF FRUIT in the Ambrosiana
(fig. 6) and is more like that found in
Caravaggio's mature religious paintings
(fig. VII.4). The porcelain-smooth finish
and satiny chiaroscuro of the quinces and
the ceramic dish reveal a greater refinement of facture than most Roman still lifes
in 1630, and this must have been the crux
of the artist's great success with Charles I,
who knew well the various followers of
Caravaggio. His style represents a personal and even eccentric adaptation of the
general features of Caravaggio's that could
understandably have developed far from
the master's coterie in Rome, but under
what stimulus we do not know.

PLATE 23

STILL LIFE WITH QUINCES AND ACORNS

Unfortunately, certain chemical and physical changes inherent in the artist's technique have altered the appearance of the painting from what it once was, resulting in the loss of some of its original coherence. The green leaves have oxydized, so that they now appear brownish. The delicate glazes that once defined the subtlety of the grapes in the dish have sunken into the ground, so that the quinces now seem to rest atop a rather ill-defined mass. But those forms which contain lead white —the quinces, the dish and the curled leaf at the left—retain their force. We can only imagine the original impact of the painting when the colors were in balance. It could be that this was among the pictures by Labrador which, after months of delay, departed San Sebastian for England in November 1632. On January 22, 1633, Sir Francis Cottington wrote to Hopton in Madrid of the king's reaction to them: "The paintings are extremely liked."[4]

Unquestionably by the same hand as the Hampton Court STILL LIFE WITH QUINCES AND ACORNS is STILL LIFE WITH GRAPES AND APPLES, formerly in the Hohenlohe Collection at El Quexigal, near Ávila (fig. VII.5).[5] The painting is fragmentary, cut off at the right through the middle of a stem of raisins. At the left, on a narrow ledge, is a bunch of grapes with one dramatic grape leaf caught in the light. To the right is a Venetian glass compote of apples which are modeled with strong chiaroscuro. Two of the apples have worm holes. Randomly strewn across the front of the ledge are several grapes, acorns and raisins. As in the case of the Hampton Court picture, the grapes have lost some of their form and the colors have generally darkened, but the quality of the work is still very high and gives us an important additional insight into the artist's style.

PROVENANCE
Lord Francis Cottington c. 1633–35 (sent by Sir Arthur Hopton from Madrid); King Charles I, by 1639; sold by the Commonwealth for £5 following the execution of Charles I but reacquired by the Crown; King James II; King William III.[1]

EXHIBITIONS
London, 1920; Barnard Castle, The Bowes Museum 1967, no. 26; Nottingham 1981, no. 35; London 1981, no. 56.

BIBLIOGRAPHY
Van der Doort 1639, p. 4; Law 1898, p. 194, no. 539; London 1920, pp. 65–66; Lafuente Ferrari 1935, p. 172; Cavestany 1936–40, p. 66, fig. 4; Sterling 1959, p. 70; Trapier 1967, p. 242, fig. 2; Barnard Castle, The Bowes Museum 1967, no. 26, fig. 63; Harris 1967b, p. 484, fig. 63; Barnard Castle, The Bowes Museum, 1970 cat., pp. 41–42; Young 1976, p. 211, fig. 22; Bergström et al. 1979, p. 188, ill.; Haraszti 1983, pp. 72, 82; Madrid 1983, p. 43, ill.; Talley 1984, p. 201.

NOTES
1. Law 1898, p. 194, no. 539.
2. Van der Doort 1639, p. 4.
3. Trapier 1967.
4. Trapier 1967, part I, p. 241.
5. Sale Sotheby Parke Bernet & Co., Spain, May 25–27, 1979, no. 39. The painting was probably given with the house "El Quexigal" to María de la Piedad, daughter of the Duchess of Parcent, on the occasion of her marriage to Prince Max von Hohenlohe-Langenburg. The Duchess of Parcent had personally built the collection prior to World War I. At the time of the sale in 1979, the lower right corner of the painting was overpainted with two figs in order to conceal the fragmentary state of the canvas. It was reproduced in that overpainted state in the sale catalogue.

Fig. VII.5   Juan Fernández, El Labrador. GRAPES AND COMPOTE OF APPLES. 38 × 49 cm. Private collection, Spain (formerly Hohenlohe Collection, El Quexigal).

Signed and dated on back of panel: *el. labrador./Ju. fernãdez./1636*

Oil on panel

16⅛ in. diameter (41 cm. diameter)

Private Collection, Europe

The discovery of this painting in 1971 was an event of the greatest importance for the study of Labrador, inasmuch as the signature on the reverse of the panel (fig. VII.2) gave us the artist's full name and a date for his activity. Valdivieso (1972) connected the painting with the Juan Labrador mentioned in the art historical literature. He pointed out that the discovery effectively nullified any previous sense of certainty about the dates of the artist's birth and death—which he erroneously attributed to Félibien (1666)—and proposed that his birth date might be approximately thirty years later than usually thought. Harris (1974b) concurred in that but repeated the error that Félibien had been the source of the traditional belief that Labrador had died around 1600. It was, in fact, Palomino (1724) who was responsible for that.

Harris (1974b) added an important fact for the artist's biography with the information that it was Sir Arthur Hopton, by his own account, who first persuaded Labrador to paint flowers. In a letter to Lord Cottington dated February 25, 1635, which had been overlooked by Trapier (1967), Hopton wrote: "I have had him [the Labrador] to try his hand at flowers, which I have not yet seen; if they turn out as good as his fruits, I shall send some of them to your Lordship."[1] None of the paintings by Labrador recorded in English collections represented flowers, so it is not certain that Hopton was ever able to send any back to England. This painting proves, however, that less than a year after Hopton's letter, Labrador did paint flowers with spectacular results. Several other flower paintings by him are recorded in Spanish collections (see the Summary of Collection Inventories above).

The composition of this painting reveals a tendency to fill the available space, as does the Hampton Court still life (Plate 23). Noting the way in which the forms press near the perimeter of the circle, Sterling (1981) suggested that the panel had been cut down from a larger size. Examination of the painting out of its frame, however, demonstrates that this is not true. Instead, the constriction of the space around the flowers serves to bring them closer to us and must be viewed as intentional on the part of the artist. Not a single blossom or leaf is cut off by the edge of the painting, and the arrangement of the flowers skillfully conforms to the shape of the tondo.[2] The round shape of the panel reminds us that one of the paintings of grapes belonging to Charles I was painted on a small, round panel.[3] In referring to Labrador's works, Palomino mentioned only panels. Cavestany (1936–40) noted this and pointed out that all of the paintings attributed to him at the time of his writing were canvases. Obviously, he worked on both kinds of surfaces. If this painting and the canvas at Hampton Court are evidence of any general tendency, it may be that his panel paintings are better preserved than his canvases.

In composing this flowerpiece, Labrador seems to have purposely avoided depicting the fancy sort of vase that was the standard in such pictures. Instead of Venetian glass, silver or silver gilt, he has arranged his bouquet in a simple pottery jar. The strong light entering from the left causes the handle, rotated at an oblique angle to the picture plane, to cast a shadow on the uneven surface of the jar. Its humble fabric provides the perfect contrast to the satin-smooth chiaroscuro of the flower petals above. Indeed, the range from bright light to deep shadow is great, and the transition is more subtle than the human eye usually perceives in nature. This lighting lends the flowers a haunting presence that immediately calls to mind Ceán Bermúdez's enthusiastic description of the delicate pair of *floreros* which in 1800 were in the antechamber of the king's room in the royal palace in Madrid.

Provenance
Lyversberg Collection, Cologne 1800–1971; Sale Kunsthaus Math. Lempertz, Cologne, May 26, 1971, no. 48; Private Collection, The Hague.

Exhibitions
Münster/Baden-Baden 1979–80, no. 178.

Bibliography
Lyversberg 1837, p. 225, no. 121 (attributed to Gottfried Schalken); Clemen 1930, p. 225; *AEA*, vol. 178 (1972), p. 232, no. 265, pl. II; Valdivieso 1972, pp. 323–24, ill.; Harris 1974b, pp. 162–64; Young 1976, p. 211; Bordeaux 1978, pp. 55–56; Bergström et al. 1979, p. 188; Münster/Baden-Baden 1979, pp. 336, 560, no. 178; Sterling 1981, p. 19; Madrid 1983, p. 43, ill.

Notes
1. Quoted by Harris in Spanish translation from *Clarendon State Papers*, vol. 1, 1967, pp. 240–41.

2. In some reproductions in books (e.g., Pérez Sánchez 1983, p. 44), the perimeter of the painting does unavoidably appear to crop some of the flowers, but this is not really the case.

3. Van der Doort 1639, p. 160.

PLATE 24

Vase of Flowers

Oil on canvas (fragment)
17⁵/₁₆ × 13⅜ in. (44 × 34 cm.)
Museo del Prado, Madrid

THIS PAINTING TRADITIONALLY HAS BEEN attributed to Francisco de Zurbarán and was exhibited as such in the 1935 still-life exhibition in Madrid. Included in several books and catalogues of Zurbarán's works, it was, nevertheless, doubted by Guinard (1960) and rejected by Gregori and Frati (1973). Following the discovery of Labrador's signed flowerpiece of 1636 (Plate 24), it occurred to me and to Pérez Sánchez independently that the painting is by Labrador. The porcelainlike smoothness of the surface, the intense chiaroscuro of the flowers, and the simple pottery vase are similar to those features in the signed flower painting (Plate 24). Pérez Sánchez (Madrid 1978) published the attribution, acknowledging that we had both reached the same conclusion.

Certain inherent problems in Labrador's technique are more evident in his works on canvas than in his panel paintings. In this painting on canvas, the dark tones have darkened considerably. This phenomenon is also observable in the Hampton Court STILL LIFE WITH QUINCES AND ACORNS (Plate 23) and the ex-Hohenlohe STILL LIFE WITH GRAPES AND APPLES (fig. VII.5). Both VASE OF FLOWERS and STILL LIFE WITH GRAPES AND APPLES are fragments. Pérez Sánchez (1983) noted that part of a bunch of grapes is barely visible at the left. Like those in the Hampton Court picture, these grapes have lost most of their formal definition. Obviously, the composition continued at the left, and it may have been larger in all directions. Although it cannot be confirmed, it is very likely that this is a fragment of the painting by Labrador that was described in the 1651 inventory of the collection of the Marquis of Eliche in Madrid: "A canvas by Labrador with an earthen jar of roses, carnations and lilies with other flowers and some bunches of grapes and open pomegranates, one and a quarter *varas* wide and one in height with its black frame." (See no. VI, Summary of Collection Inventories above.)

PROVENANCE
Marquis of Eliche, Madrid, 1651 [?]; Antonio Pons, Málaga (on loan to the Museo Provincial de Bellas Artes, Málaga, 1931–40); acquired from Pons by the Ministerio de Educación Nacional in 1946 for the Museo del Prado.

EXHIBITIONS
Madrid 1935, no. 13; Madrid 1978–79, no. 77; Madrid 1983–84, no. 30.

BIBLIOGRAPHY
Málaga, Museo Provincial de Bellas Artes, 1933 cat., pp. 22–34, pl. 15; Cavestany 1936–40, p. 151, no. 13, pl. 21; Seckel 1946, p. 287, fig. 6; Gaya Nuño 1948, p. 45, no. 95; Madrid, Prado, 1949–72 cats., no. 2888; Guinard 1960, p. 281, no. 607; Bergström 1970, pp. 41–42, pl. 25; Gregori and Frati 1973, p. 117, no. 566; Gállego and Gudiol 1977, p. 121, no. 543, fig. 486; Camón Aznar 1978, p. 264; Madrid 1978, no. 77; Angulo 1978, p. 174; Bergström et al. 1979, p. 146, pl. 138; Madrid 1983, p. 58, no. 30.

Oil on canvas
19¹³/₁₆ × 15⅜ in. (50 × 39 cm.)
Museo del Prado, Madrid

PEDRO DE MADRAZO ATTRIBUTED THIS painting to Juan de Espinosa in the Prado catalogue of 1872, and the attribution has remained unchallenged ever since. As recently as 1983, Pérez Sánchez defended the attribution in his catalogue of the still-life exhibition in Madrid; however, due to administrative difficulties, the painting was never sent from the Museum of Fine Arts in Seville, where it had been on loan from the Prado, and was not actually seen in the exhibition. I have had doubts that this painting is by Espinosa and believe that the matter of its attribution should be reconsidered in light of the somewhat clearer understanding of the art of Juan Fernández, El Labrador, that is emerging today. To be sure, the styles of the two artists have a number of congruencies that have been observed before.[1]

The painting in question depicts two bunches of grapes, one light and one dark, hanging from the top of the picture together with a sprig of oak and some acorns. Just underneath the grapes on a stone plinth are three large apples. The canvas appears to have been cropped all around, especially at the bottom, rendering the front part of the plinth no longer visible. This takes away the solid support the apples must have had once and creates a slight sense of instability in the composition. Nevertheless, a certain simplicity in the relationship of the grapes and apples is consistent with Labrador's approach in the Hampton Court painting (Plate 23), and is unlike the rather more artificial designs of Espinosa, as seen in the other still life attributed to him in the Prado (Plate 27).

While hanging grapes are represented in extant works by Espinosa, and in others by him known only from old inventory descriptions, the grapes in the painting under consideration lack the crystalline

PLATE 25

VASE OF FLOWERS

precision of Espinosa's grapes (see Plates 27 and 28 and fig. VIII.1). The dark ones have lost some of their formal definition, as in other works by Labrador, and the light ones have a sense of pliancy that is, in a subtle way, more lifelike than the polished grapes of Espinosa.

Grapes are also one of the most common subjects in still lifes attributed to Labrador, both recently and in old inventories. The extremely dirty STILL LIFE WITH SWEETS AND GRAPES in the Cerralbo Museum in Madrid (fig. VII.6), which has traditionally been attributed to Labrador, represents the grapes hanging in a similar way, together with oak leaves and acorns, beside a stone plinth like the one in the Prado painting.[2] The Cerralbo canvas was the only work attributed to Labrador that was included in the 1935 Madrid exhibition. It is so darkened by neglect today, however, that it is difficult to assess and cannot serve in its present condition as the basis for any attribution.

In support of the attribution of the Prado STILL LIFE WITH GRAPES AND APPLES to Espinosa, Pérez Sánchez cited an entry in the 1662 inventory of the collection of Francisco Merchant de la Zerda, who owned fifteen paintings by the artist: "A bunch of grapes by the hand of the same Juan de Espinosa."[3] However, one could also cite from the very same inventory a painting of that subject by Labrador: "A canvas…on which is painted a bunch of grapes, by the Labrador" (see no. IX, Summary of Collection Inventories above). Both of these entries may just illustrate how very common the subject was. A somewhat smaller painting of grapes and acorns by Labrador was also cited in 1688 among the paintings left by the VII Marquis of El Carpio (see no. XII, Summary of Collection Inventories above). The inventory entry that most likely refers to the Prado painting, however, is from the 1772 inventory of the Buen Retiro Palace: "A bunch of grapes on its stem hanging, three-quarters high,

two-thirds wide, by Juan Labrador" (see no. XV, Summary of Collection Inventories above). As the Prado painting is known to come from the royal collections, it could well be that one, whose dimensions at the time were approximately 63 by 55 centimeters. The larger size accounts for those parts around the edges which are obviously missing from the Prado picture today.

Recently, another version of this composition, which has not been cropped, appeared in a private collection. I know the painting only from a photograph, so I cannot judge if it is a copy, but it is inscribed on the back of the original canvas: "Orig./Juan Fdz Labrador." This would seem to add another bit of circumstantial evidence to the case linking this composition to Labrador. Although the Prado painting has not darkened as much as the Hampton Court still life (Plate 23), or the Prado VASE OF FLOWERS (Plate 25), there is reason to believe that it may be a rare example by this little-known artist.

PROVENANCE
Spanish royal collection; Museo del Prado since 1849 (Inv. #512).

EXHIBITIONS
Seville, 1970, p. 12, fig. 34; Madrid 1983–84, no. 34 (not actually exhibited).

BIBLIOGRAPHY
Madrid, Prado, 1843–58 cat., no. 512; 1872–1907 cat., no. 726; 1910–72 cat., no. 703; Cavestany 1936–40, p. 76; Kubler and Soria 1959, p. 235; Madrid, Prado, 1963 cat., pp. 198–99, no. 703; Torres Martín 1971, p. 35; Agulló and Pérez Sánchez 1981, p. 374, no. 60; Pérez Sánchez 1983, p. 60, no. 34, ill.; Cherry 1984, p. 60.

NOTES
1. Jeannine Baticle, "Bodegon ou 'la vérité dans le naturel,' " Bordeaux 1978, p. 56.

2. Without going so far as to attribute the Prado painting to Labrador, Sterling (1959, pp. 70, 143, note 150) noted its similarity to the Cerralbo still life and the one at Hampton Court.

3. Agulló 1981, p. 213: *"…vn razimo de vbas, de mano de el mismo Juan de Espinosa."*

Fig. VII.6   Attributed to Juan Fernández, El Labrador. STILL LIFE WITH SWEETS AND GRAPES. 43 × 61 cm. Museo Cerralbo, Madrid.

PLATE 26

STILL LIFE WITH GRAPES AND APPLES

VIII. JUAN DE ESPINOSA

(Active from the 1640s to the 1670s)

Since the mid-1930s, when Enriqueta Harris discovered the still life signed in 1624 by Juan Bautista de Espinosa (Plate 9), it has been apparent that there were two still-life painters with the surname Espinosa. Cavestany distinguished between Juan Bautista de Espinosa and the Juan de Espinosa to whom two rather more advanced still lifes in the Prado had been attributed since 1872. It is now believed that the earlier of these artists had died before 1641 (see Chapter IV). Nothing at all was known about the later of the two artists until the publication of the archival research of Mercedes Agulló y Cobo in 1978 and 1981 and the interpretation of that information by Pérez Sánchez in 1978 and 1983. It is likely that the later painter was the Juan de Espinosa who signed documents in Madrid between 1645 and 1677 on his own behalf and as a witness for his artist friends and whose still lifes begin to appear in collection inventories in 1646.[1]

On June 22, 1645, Juan de Espinosa appeared as a witness in the *carta de dote,* or marriage contract, between the painter Francisco de Burgos y Mantilla (see Chapter XII) and Manuela Márquez.[2] Francisco de Burgos was already in his mid-thirties by this date. On December 23, 1646, what must have been a painting by Espinosa was listed in the collection of another artist named Juan Bautista Santolus: "a small canvas of grapes made by the hand of Juan de Espinosa, on ordinary canvas."[3] On March 24, 1651, "Juan de Spinossa," master painter, resident of Madrid, declared that he had received 1,100 *reales* owed him by Doña Gregoria de Espinosa, widow of Onofre de Espinosa, a silversmith.[4] Onofre de Espinosa was probably a relative.

Two documents of the late 1650s were also signed by a Juan de Espinosa. Although the signator is not specifically said to be a painter, it was probably the

Fig. VIII.1   Juan de Espinosa. STILL LIFE WITH DEAD FINCH. Panel, 23 × 30 cm. Museo del Prado, Madrid.

same person, since in both cases he was serving as a witness for another painter or widow of a painter. On June 2, 1658, he signed as a witness to a promisary note for Luisa de las Cuebas, widow of Domingo Sobrino, painter.[5] On December 2, 1659, he witnessed the testament of Pedro Núñez, painter.[6] Very likely our painter was the same Juan de Espinosa who joined Antonio de Pereda and other *"profesores del arte de la pintura"* on May 13, 1677 in a continuation of the lengthy lawsuit against the Royal Brotherhood of Our Lady of the Seven Sorrows.[7] This places his death much later than has been previously thought.

On June 1, 1662, an inventory was taken of the collection of Francisco Merchant de la Zerda.[8] This bourgeois collector had a remarkable interest in still lifes. Apart from twenty-one still lifes by Van der Hamen and two by Labrador, he owned no less than fifteen *fruteros,* flowerpieces and *bodegones* by Juan de Espinosa. The concentration of his paintings in this rather select collection is probably an indication of the esteem in which his works were held.

Concerning the dates of Espinosa's activity, Pérez Sánchez (1978) once dated the remarkable still life in the Prado (Plate 27) to the decade of 1620–30. In 1983, he considered the painting to be somewhat later, suggesting a date around or just after 1630. There is nothing in the painting's style, however, to preclude a date in the 1640s (when the documentation of his activity begins) or even later. Baticle (Bordeaux 1978) suggested that Espinosa's refined style and polished facture may have been influenced by the works painted in the 1630s by Labrador.

One of Espinosa's most beautiful works is the small panel in the Prado which represents a red ceramic vase, a bunch of grapes, a seashell and a small dead bird (fig. VIII.1). Pérez Sánchez (1978) has astutely attributed the painting to Espinosa on the basis of its resemblance to those in the Prado (Plate 27) and the Louvre (Plate 28). The records of the Prado indicate that the panel came to the museum in 1847 from the Palace of Aranjuez. The painting has a seventeenth-century provenance, however, which has not been known until now. In 1651, it was described in the collection of Gaspar Méndez de Haro y Guzmán, Marquis of Eliche: "A *frutero* by Ju° despinosa painted on panel with a clay jar and a bunch of grapes and a dead finch."[9] The presence of the dead bird lends the painting a certain melancholy air typical of the baroque—an ironic twist on the cliché from classical antiquity of the bird deceived by the realism of Zeuxis's painted fruits.

NOTES
1. He should not be confused with the Juan de Espinosa from Navarra who, according to Ceán Bermúdez (1800, vol. 2, pp. 41–42), died in that province in 1653.
2. Agulló 1978, p. 183.
3. Agulló 1978, p. 156: *"vn lienzo pequeño de vbas echo de mano de Juan de Espinosa, en lienzo ordinario."*
4. Agulló 1978, p. 66.
5. Agulló 1981, p. 187.
6. Agulló 1978, pp. 117–18.
7. Saltillo 1947a, p. 664. For earlier references to this lawsuit, see Chapters IX and X.
8. Agulló 1981, pp. 213–14.
9. Archive of the Palacio de Liria, Madrid, Caja 221–22: "no. 18. *Un frutero de Ju° despinosa pintada en tabla con un barro y un racimo de uvas y un gilguerro muerto."*

BIBLIOGRAPHY
Carderera y Solano 1866, p. 32; Cavestany 1936–40, pp. 44, 76; Mayer 1947, p. 461; Kubler and Soria 1959, p. 235; Madrid, Prado, 1963 cat., p. 198; Bordeaux 1978, p. 56; Agulló 1978, pp. 66, 117–18, 156, 183; Pérez Sánchez 1978, no. 75; Agulló 1981, pp. 187, 213–14; Agulló and Pérez Sánchez 1981, p. 374; Madrid 1983, p. 45.

27. GRAPES, APPLES AND PLUMS

Oil on canvas
29⅞ × 23¼ in. (76 × 59 cm.)
Museo del Prado, Madrid

IN THE 1872 EDITION OF THE PRADO Museum catalogue, Pedro de Madrazo, the museum's director, noted that GRAPES, APPLES AND PLUMS was signed by Juan de Espinosa, an assertion which he did not repeat in any of the numerous editions of the catalogue that he prepared subsequently. As there is no signature visible now, it has been assumed by the Prado that Madrazo was mistaken. Based on the recent appearance of the signed painting which is now in the Louvre (Plate 28), however, the traditional attribution of the painting has been reinforced.

Espinosa was probably a generation younger than Van der Hamen, and his works reveal that he was basically unconcerned with the spatial clarity and architectonic structure of the older artist's still lifes. Responding perhaps to the inspiration of Labrador, he seems to prefer a shallow space to bring his forms under the viewer's close scrutiny. This particular still life features a narrow shelf on which is placed a silver plate of brilliant red apples and a stem of white grapes which Sterling (1959) noted are so translucent that they seem to be made of glass. Behind the grapes Espinosa has painted a fanciful red ceramic vase, a type of ware which Pérez Sánchez (1978) has observed was painted by such artists of the time as Pereda, Ponce and Palacios.

Hanging bunches of grapes and plums fill the upper space of the composition, like a frieze, against a neutral background. The effect of light on the iridescent surface of the fruit is a tour de force. Although such subtleties had been treated in Van der Hamen's late works, it is not impossible that Espinosa also benefitted from the example of northern still lifes, which by this time had begun to appear in some important Spanish collections.

To judge from the frequent references to grapes in the inventory descriptions of Espinosa's pictures, as well as from the presence of grapes in all of his recognized works, he seems to have made something of a specialty of this fruit, no doubt capitalizing on his ability to evoke the transparency and delicate color variations of their skin. Although today we can only identify a certain type of painting from Espinosa's repertoire, we know from the inventory of the collection of Francisco Merchant de la Zerda that he also painted flowerpieces and *bodegones,* which at this date may still have included human figures.

PROVENANCE
Spanish royal collection; Museo del Prado since 1849 (Inv. #55).

EXHIBITIONS
Madrid, 1978–79, no. 74; Madrid, 1983–84, no. 33.

BIBLIOGRAPHY
Madrid, Prado, 1854 and 1858 cat., no. 55; 1872–1907 cat., no. 725; Cavestany 1936–40, p. 76; Mayer 1947, p. 461; Kubler and Soria 1959, p. 235; Sterling 1959, p. 143, no. 150; Madrid, Prado, 1963 cat., p. 198, no. 702; Torres Martín 1971, p. 35, ill.; Bottineau 1975, p. 314; Pérez Sánchez 1978, no. 75, ill.; Agulló and Pérez Sánchez 1981, p. 374, no. 60; Pérez Sánchez 1983, p. 59, no. 33, ill.; Cherry 1984, p. 60.

PLATE 27

GRAPES, APPLES AND PLUMS

PLATE 28

STILL LIFE WITH GRAPES, FLOWERS AND SHELLS

28. STILL LIFE WITH GRAPES, FLOWERS AND SHELLS

Signed lower left: *J. Despinosa* (signature very effaced)

Oil on canvas

32⅝ × 24⅜ in. (83 × 62 cm.)

Musée du Louvre, Paris

THIS PAINTING, GIVEN TO THE LOUVRE IN 1973, is the first signed work by Espinosa to come to light in modern times. The extremely damaged signature has been cited by Pérez Sánchez (1983) as reading *Juan de Espinosa,* followed by a fragmented and illegible date. The Louvre catalogue, however, transcribes the signature as *J. Despinosa.* Pérez Sánchez suggests that this may be the work that was auctioned with the Pereire Collection in Paris in 1868, which was said at the time to be signed and dated: *J. Espinosa F. 1645.* The association of that date with the artist— whether it was on this work or not— coincides with the earliest known documentation of his adult life in Madrid.

The composition of this painting has much in common with GRAPES, APPLES AND PLUMS in the Prado (Plate 27), although there are significant differences. In both, the objects are arranged on a narrow tabletop, but in the Louvre painting, we see the right corner of the table; in the Prado picture, the artist has used direct frontal perspective. In addition to a bunch of white grapes, the Louvre composition features two seashells, in one of which the artist has arranged a spray of flowers. At the left he has placed a red stoneware bottle of a circular form similar to the type painted by Van der Hamen (Plate 17). The space above, as in the case of the Prado painting, is filled with two leafy branches from a grapevine laden with heavy bunches of grapes. Unlike the Prado painting, however, a pair of birds is attracted by the fruit and flowers.

Despite the similarities of composition between this painting and the one in the Prado, the notable differences in the execution of the two pictures cannot be explained simply by the superior state of

Fig. VIII.2   Juan de Espinosa. STILL LIFE WITH GRAPES AND APPLES. 60 × 43.5 cm. Private collection.

preservation of the Prado painting. The still life in the Prado is a subtler and finer painting. The modeling of forms in the Louvre still life is less richly developed, and the lapse of drawing skill in the foreshortening of the red stoneware bottle is noteworthy. This stylistic evidence suggests that the Louvre painting is an earlier work and that the Prado painting represents the artist in his full maturity.

A small painting which has recently come to light in a private collection (fig. VIII.2) reveals definite similarities to the Louvre picture and seems to be by Espinosa. On a stone ledge, the artist has grouped several apples, a walnut, a small bunch of grapes and a red ceramic dish of water; hanging from above is a bunch of grapes with a sprig of oak and two acorns. The modeling of the vase and the fruit is similar in style to the Louvre painting and,

likewise, inferior to the Prado work. Both paintings may therefore represent an earlier stage in Espinosa's development.

PROVENANCE
Pereire Collection, Paris (sale 1868, no. 19); Jean Riechers, who donated it to the Louvre in 1973.

EXHIBITION
Madrid 1983–84, no. 32.

BIBLIOGRAPHY
Revue du Louvre, vol. 23, no. 2 (1973), p. 135; *GBA,* vol. 83 (1974), p. 9, no. 25; Bottineau 1975, p. 314, fig. 2; Paris, Louvre, 1981 cat., p. 114, ill.; Madrid 1983, p. 59, no. 32, ill.; Cherry 1984, p. 60.

IX. ANTONIO PONCE

(1608–after 1662)

Antonio Ponce began his professional life in the shadow of Van der Hamen. Over the thirty-year course of his career, he eventually developed a distinctive style of his own which, if it did not place him among the best still-life painters of his time or merit him a mention by Palomino or Ceán Bermúdez, nevertheless enabled him to leave his mark for later art historians to find.

Most of what we know about Ponce is based on recent archival research that has revealed important biographical information. In a witnessed instrument Ponce signed on September 10, 1642, he made a declaration of his personal history in connection with his application for one of the offices of Inspector of Weights and Measures offered by the City of Madrid.[1] In this document, he declares himself to be thirty-four years of age, born in Valladolid and brought to Madrid at the age of one month by his parents. He says that since 1628, when he was twenty, he has lived in the parish of San Ginés, where he married Francisca de Alfaro, the daughter of Diego de Alfaro [a tailor][2] and Juana de Herrera. As it happens, Juana de Herrera was the sister of Eugenia de Herrera Barnuevo, the wife of Van der Hamen.[3] Thus the older artist was the young man's uncle by marriage.

The families remained close even after Van der Hamen's death in 1631. When Van der Hamen's daughter María married in 1639, she was living in the house of Ponce's mother. Antonio Ponce, together with Francisco López, was called to appraise the paintings in her dowry, which were mostly those she had inherited from her father.[4] As we shall see, one hardly needs the benefit of documents to link the two artists.

Fig. IX.1   Antonio Ponce. MONTH OF MAY.
103 × 161.3 cm. Private collection.

Fig. IX.1, detail   MONTH OF MAY.

The earliest known document signed by Ponce is dated April 30, 1634, when he was one of thirty-six members of the Guild of Painters and Gilders to join the painter Francisco Barrera in a lawsuit that lasted for many years against the Royal Brotherhood of Our Lady of the Seven Sorrows involving the artists' obligation to carry an image of the Virgin through the streets during Holy Week.[5]

Like many artists of his time, Ponce appears to have occasionally painted portraits of the king and queen or other members of the royal family on a speculative basis, for sale. In an early reference to him (*Varia velazqueña* 1960), he and Francisco Barrera were among six painters whose commercial portraits of royal persons were collected by city officials and subjected to a critical review on October 3, 1633. A two-man committee, composed of Vincencio Carducho and Diego Velázquez, had been appointed for the purpose of curbing the spread of badly painted, improper or otherwise "unofficial" likenesses of the royal family. The report of the committee did not specify who had painted the few portraits that were allowed to pass without revision or, indeed, destruction. The percentage of works censured for one breach or another was very high.

In 1638, Ponce was among several artists working under the direction of Francisco Barrera on certain unspecified decorations at the Buen Retiro Palace (see Chapter X). This sort of decoration, no doubt much of it uncreative by its nature, seems to have been something he was prepared to do, for again in 1649 he was part of a team of artists and craftsmen, most of them unrecognized today, who were engaged to create the setting for the festive entry into Madrid of Philip IV's new consort, Queen Mariana of Austria.[6]

In 1657, Ponce and his wife wrote a joint testament, even though they declared themselves to be in good health.[7] The executor was Diego de Herrera, Francisca's uncle and Van der Hamen's brother-in-law. From this document we learn nothing new of interest, except that the artist was the legal guardian of his niece, María Álvarez, and that the couple lived in a house on Hortaleza Street which was rented

Fig. IX.2 Antonio Ponce. MONTH OF
SEPTEMBER. 104 × 163 cm. Formerly art market, Madrid.

Fig. IX.3 Antonio Ponce. BASKET OF
BISCUITS. Signed. 37 × 58 cm. Art market,
London.

in María Álvarez's name. Five years later, on May 28, 1662, Ponce was still living in, and paid part of a year's rent on, this house in his capacity as guardian of María Álvarez.[8] The date of his death is unknown.

Ponce's flowerpiece in the Museum of Fine Arts, Strasbourg (Plate 29), which has been variously dated 1630 and 1650, reveals very clearly that the origins of his style lie in his association with Van der Hamen. Although it and others like it have been known since 1935, its significance within Ponce's development has not been adequately assessed. The painting's rather dry naturalism is technically close to the way Van der Hamen painted flowers, but the picture fails to attain the same level of quality as his (see figs. VI.11, 12 and Plates 21, 22). Whether painted before Van der Hamen's death or not, it strongly suggests that Ponce, who had lived in the same parish as Van der Hamen since 1628, must at one time have been a member of the older artist's workshop. On the basis of this signed work, a connection can be made to several other paintings which, though not signed, must certainly have been painted by Ponce as well. This link represents a first step toward bringing some order to the confusion of anonymous paintings that somewhat resemble Van der Hamen's yet have a distinct style of their own.

In 1966 I saw on the art market in Madrid a pair of large still lifes representing the months of May and September which looked curiously like paintings by Van der Hamen. Unable to obtain photographs of them, I made sketches of the compositions. Several years afterward, the one representing the month of May (fig. IX.1) appeared on the London art market attributed to Van der Hamen.[9] The one representing the month of September (fig. IX.2) was sold to another dealer in Madrid who completely overpainted the background, obliterating the window with a landscape view which was an essential feature of the original composition. The MONTH OF MAY depicts a table spread with a red cloth at the right. On the table is an elaborate green and gold vase similar to those painted by Van der Hamen (figs. VI.11, 12) and filled with lilies, tulips, irises, peonies and other flowers painted in a

Fig. IX.4 Antonio Ponce. POMEGRANATES
AND BASKET OF FRUIT. Signed, 1642. 45×61
cm. Private collection, Madrid.

Fig. IX.5 Antonio Ponce. BASKET OF FRUIT
AND GLASSWARE. 45×61 cm. Private collection, Madrid.

manner identical to that in the Strasbourg canvas. Flanking the vase, are a plate of
figs and a basket of pea pods and cherries—two motifs also familiar from Van der
Hamen's still lifes (see Plate 21). The basket of flowers at the left (fig. IX.1, detail) is
also painted with the same rather dry naturalism and vivid colors as the Strasbourg
picture. The stone shelf on which the basket rests recalls the stepped still lifes of Van
der Hamen, but its form is rather vague and the perspective of its right edge is
frustratingly at odds with that of the left edge of the table. All things considered, we
can be reasonably certain that this is a painting by Antonio Ponce, although his
chronology is still too vague to be able to assign it a firm date.

The MONTH OF SEPTEMBER (fig. IX.2) was composed in a stepped format that
recalls Van der Hamen's late still lifes but which resembles even more the elaborate
paintings of the Seasons executed by Ponce's colleague Francisco Barrera in the late
1630s (figs. X.3–6, 8). As indicated above, the background of this painting was
completely overpainted before the photograph reproduced here was made, so that a
landscape that once was seen through a window at the upper left no longer gives
light and airiness to the composition. The hanging melon and peppers were also
recent additions. Unfortunately, the same dealer who overpainted the background
has since cut the painting into pieces and sold them as separate still lifes, which I
have seen in a private collection. Even though there were no flowers in this painting, we can assume that it was by the same hand as the MONTH OF MAY because of
the provenance, the identical execution of the baskets and the similarity between the
plate of figs in the one and the plate of peaches in the other.[10]

A signed painting by Ponce depicting a plaited basket of biscuits on a stone
ledge covered with a red cloth napkin (fig. IX.3) was also recently on the art market
in London.[11] In all likelihood, it too is a fragment cut from a larger composition. In
fact, a beautiful stepped still life with a similar motif was photographed during the
Spanish Civil War in 1937 by the Service for the Recovery of Works of Art. It

Fig. IX.6 Antonio Ponce. STILL LIFE WITH GRAPES AND PEACHES. 45 × 64.5 cm. Private collection, Madrid.

Fig. IX.7 Antonio Ponce. BASKET OF FRUIT. 45 × 64.5 cm. Private collection, Madrid.

suggests that Ponce continued the three-plane, stepped compositional format of Van der Hamen and that such paintings may still exist in private collections.

In a pair of small paintings signed and dated 1642 which were exhibited in Madrid in 1983–84 (figs. IX.4, 5),[12] Ponce continues to adhere to certain guidelines of still-life painting established by Van der Hamen, but at the same time he has developed some of the individual traits that will characterize his later works. In the STILL LIFE WITH POMEGRANATES AND BASKET OF FRUIT (fig. IX.4), the artist has arranged the objects on a stone plinth abbutting a wall at the right but unattached at the left. This is a variation of Van der Hamen's architectural devices that would become common in Ponce's works. As in the older artist's still lifes, the basket and the open pomegranate in Ponce's composition overhang the edge of the ledge, enhancing the sense of space. His background, however, is light instead of dark; the large grape leaves are back-lit and sharply silhouetted against the luminous background. In this respect, Ponce reveals the indirect influence of Caravaggio's BASKET OF FRUIT in the Ambrosiana (fig. 6) almost fifty years after it was painted. This can be seen even more dramatically in an unsigned still life, also exhibited in Madrid in 1983–84 (fig. IX.6), in which a luscious bunch of grapes dramatically fills the picture space and creates a monumental silhouette. These same qualities are also evident in the important STILL LIFE WITH GRAPES AND POMEGRANATES, 1651 (Plate 31).

In the small BASKET OF FRUIT in a private collection in Madrid (fig. IX.7), Ponce employs the same kind of plaited basket so often used by Van der Hamen, allowing the pile of fruit and dark leaves to stand out against the light background. But, unlike Van der Hamen, who created such a compelling sense of plasticity through his precise drawing and vigorous modeling of forms, Ponce has modeled his fruit in a softer and weaker way. The monumentality of the conception is not sustained by the execution. In this fundamental respect, Ponce remained an artist of the second rank who could not hold his own with the best of his generation.

NOTES

1. Agulló 1978, p. 130 (AHP M P#6447, fols. 703–05): *"Antonio Ponçe, pintor. veçino desta Villa = Digo que para poder oponerme a vna de las baras de Fiel que probé esta Uilla de Madrid, tengo necesidad de aberigüar con testigos de cómo ha que estoy biuo en esta Villa desde que tube hedad de vn mes y bine de la Çiudad de Valladolid, que ha más de treynta y quatro años, y de cómo más de catorze he estado continuamente en la parrochia de San Xinés, donde me cassé don doña Francisca de Alfaro, hija de Diego de Alfaro y de Juana de Herrera, la qual está bautiçada en la dicha parrochia y los dichos sus padres son naturales desta Villa..."* Signed: "Antº Ponce." As witnesses appeared Matías de Santos, Royal Notary; Francisco de Manzanares, Constable of the City of Madrid, and Diego de Herrera [uncle of Francisca de Alfaro], "Servant of His Majesty."

2. The information that Diego de Alfaro was a tailor comes from the artist's testament of 1657. See note 7 below.

3. Saltillo 1947b, p. 376, cites the testament of Juana de Herrera of October 22, 1652, in which she identifies her full name as Herrera Barnuevo.

4. Jordan 1967, pp. 212, 283, 292.

5. Lafuente Ferrari 1944, p. 92.

6. Agulló 1978, pp. 130–31 (AHP M P#8655, fols. 226v–27).

7. Agulló 1978, pp. 131–32 (AHP M P#9144, fols. 781–83).

8. Agulló 1978, p. 132 (AHP M P#9762, fol. 14). Ponce had been living in this house since at least September 4, 1653, when he was cited as executor of the estate of one Martín de Pablos: Agulló 1981, p. 164 (Book of Enterrments, San Ginés, 1653).

9. In a certificate of expertise dated July 24, 1970, Ingvar Bergström attributed the painting to Van der Hamen.

10. A variation of this composition containing large bouquets of flowers is known to me from a photograph made in 1937 during the Spanish Civil War by the Service for the Recovery of Works of Art.

11. The painting is signed on the front of the ledge at the right: *Antº Ponze fa.*

12. The painting represented in fig. IX.5 is signed *Antº Ponze/fe año 1642.* Its pendant is unsigned. Despite the poor condition and heavy repainting of the pendant, the identical basket and similar compositions reassure one that they are by the same hand.

BIBLIOGRAPHY

Poleró 1886, p. 39; Cavestany 1936–40, p. 81; Lafuente Ferrari 1944, p. 92, note 1; Oña Iribarren 1944, pp. 33, 93; Saltillo 1947b, pp. 365–93; *Varia velazqueña* 1960, pp. 236–37; Angulo 1971, p. 319; Mitchell 1973, p. 204; Agulló 1978, pp. 28, 130–32; Bergström et al. 1979, p. 207; Agulló 1981, p. 164; Madrid 1983, pp. 45–46, 216.

PLATE 29

VASE OF FLOWERS

Signed above table at right: *Fa Ant Ponze/16[?]0*

Oil on canvas

30¾ × 23 in. (78 × 58.5 cm.)

Musée des Beaux-Arts de la Ville de Strasbourg

THIS PAINTING IS THE ONE MENTIONED BY Cavestany (1936–40) as having recently been on the art market in Paris at the time of his writing. According to him, it was dated 1630. In clear contradistinction to the style of a painting (Plate 31) whose signature and date of 1651 he reproduced in facsimile, he wrote that this painting required advancing the date of the artist's birth earlier than had been thought prior to knowledge of its signature. Haug (1954), however, gave the date as 1650, which has been followed by Gaya Nuño (1958), Mitchell (1972) and others since then. The reason for the discrepancy is that the third digit of the date is fragmentary, with only the lower portion of the cipher still visible.[1] With the aid of imagination, it is possible to read it either way.[2]

If this painting was indeed painted during Van der Hamen's lifetime in 1630, then it antedates by at least five years the first flower paintings by Labrador (see discussion accompanying Plate 24). If it was painted in 1650, then it demonstrates a complete indifference to the chiaroscuro of Labrador's flowerpieces and is remarkably in retard of its date. Its rather dry naturalism follows instead the style of Van der Hamen that had prevailed in Madrid during Ponce's youth.

Cavestany related the Paris flowerpiece to others which had been sold in Madrid and to a pair of signed but undated ones which were loaned to the 1935 exhibition in Madrid from a private collection but not reproduced in the catalogue (figs. IX.8, 9).[3] Very similar in type, all of them depict glass vases on draped tabletops with bouquets of tulips, irises, peonies and other flowers, This general type of flower painting was first practiced in northern Europe at the turn of the seventeenth century and quickly spread throughout the continent. Although no flowerpiece signed by Van der Hamen has yet come to light in modern times, it is known from frequent references in contemporary inventories that he painted them. To judge from the vases of flowers that appear in the more complex still lifes by Van der Hamen (Plate 21), we have every reason to believe that they looked very much like Ponce's.

PROVENANCE
Art market, Paris, 1930s; acquired by the Musées Nacionaux in 1950; deposited in the Musée des Beaux-Arts, Strasbourg, 1951.

EXHIBITION
Paris, 1963, no. 67.

BIBLIOGRAPHY
Cavestany 1936–40, p. 81; Haug 1954, no. 54; Gaya Nuño 1958, p. 271, no. 2209; Paris 1963, pp. 183–85, no. 67, ill.; Mitchell 1973, p. 204, fig. 289; Bergström et al. 1979, p. 207, ill.; Pérez Sánchez 1983, p. 46.

NOTES
1. I am indebted to M. Jean Favière, Conservateur-en-chef of the Musée des Beaux-Arts, Strasbourg, for examining the painting's inscription closely and informing me that the third digit of the date is illegible.
2. We hope that examining the inscription with infra-red light at the time of the exhibition will resolve the issue objectively.
3. Cavestany 1936–40, p. 156, nos. 42 and 44.

Fig. IX.8 Antonio Ponce. VASE OF FLOWERS. 75 × 57 cm. Signed. Location unknown.

Fig. IX.9 Antonio Ponce. VASE OF FLOWERS. 75 × 57 cm. Signed. Location unknown.

30. KITCHEN STILL LIFE

Signed on right: *Ant° Ponze/feci*

Oil on canvas

22 × 37 in. (56 × 94 cm.)

Lafora Collection, Segovia

IN THIS WORK PONCE DEMONSTRATES HIS independence from the manner of still-life compositions he had learned from Van der Hamen and begins to show instead the influence of other compositional trends that began to appear in both Naples and Madrid around 1650. Pérez Sánchez (1983) has noted that Ponce relies in this composition on crossing diagonals and on a certain mounting up and overlapping of forms to achieve a cohesiveness of design. This compositional approach, seen in the still lifes of Giuseppe Recco and G. B. Ruoppolo in Naples from about 1650 onwards, appears in Madrid in the work of Antonio de Pereda (Plate 42) at about the same time, indicating that interchanges between the two capitals of Spain's vanishing dominion in Europe were frequent.

Ponce has set out in this work to define the textures of a wide variety of materials. He has arranged his objects on a simple stone slab the same color as the background. At the left of the composition is a coarsely woven basket containing fish and some quinces. The basket is cut off by the edge of the picture, as is the slab of stone on which it rests, creating a kind of stepped effect. The form of the basket and a sprig of foliage from the quince tree are silhouetted against the bright background. Next to the basket is an overturned copper canteen placed on a diagonal to the picture plane; its cap rests at a ninety degree angle to that diagonal between a sprig of white jasmine, two red carnations and a lemon. A large brass tankard and a copper pot complete the intricate balance of forces at the right, with a pink slab of raw fish providing a subtle chromatic touch near the corner of the stone ledge. The contours of the canteen, the tankard and the pot are sharply defined by the back-lighting reflected from the light background. Ponce has made an effort to particularize the surface of each of those objects by using shadow to define the various dints and peculiarities and highlights to suggest light glinting off the shiny metal. But, in the end, his efforts were only partially successful. All the forms—whether a lemon, a piece of metal or a fish—have much the same surface quality. This rather monotonous brushwork, quite unlike either Van der Hamen's or Pereda's, is also noticeable in the flowerpiece (Plate 29) and seems to be a constant characteristic of his hand.

PROVENANCE
Unknown.

EXHIBITIONS
Madrid 1966, no. 326; Madrid 1967, no. 14; Madrid 1983–84, no. 40.

BIBLIOGRAPHY
Torres Martín 1971, pl. 66; Madrid 1983, p. 62, no. 40, ill.

PLATE 30

KITCHEN STILL LIFE

PLATE 31

STILL LIFE WITH GRAPES AND POMEGRANATES

31. STILL LIFE WITH GRAPES AND POMEGRANATES

Signed and dated lower left: *Ant° Ponze/fa^t. 1651*

Oil on canvas

24⅜ × 32¹¹/₁₆ in. (62 × 83 cm.)

Private Collection, Barcelona

CAVESTANY (1936–40) ASSUMED THAT THIS was the painting by Ponce dated 1651 which was seen by Poleró in 1886 and described as being "painted from nature, of good color, and recalling the Flemish masters," although he took exception with "the claimed Flemish influence." Pérez Sánchez (1983), calling it one of the artist's most beautiful works, noted the somewhat dry technique and minuteness of detail which, in his opinion, must have prompted Poleró's observation.

Probably painted at more or less the same time as the masterly still life of grapes by Juan de Espinosa in the Prado (Plate 27) or that in the Louvre (Plate 28), this work and others like it (fig. IX.6) must be seen in relation to an evident fashion for still lifes of this fruit. Ponce developed a distinctive style and a particular flair in compositions of this type. Hence, he has arranged his still life within a niche of the sort used by Van der Hamen, but he shows only one corner of the opening and has discarded the black background that characterized the works of the earlier painter. Instead, the luminous background provides an additional source of light which dramatizes the contours of the forms silhouetted against it. This device originated in one of the earliest still lifes, Caravaggio's BASKET OF FRUIT, painted some fifty-five years earlier (fig.6).

Ponce has suspended the large branch of a grapevine by a single cord from a point above the picture space. The weight of the bunch of grapes hanging from it is underscored as it lies limply upon a white napkin loosely arranged on the ledge. A ripe pomegranate and some peaches are placed with the grapes to create a rich harmony of reds, golds and greens against the pure white of the napkin and the neutral tone of the niche. The effect is monumental. An evenness of texture in the paint surface and a blandness of modeling, also seen in Ponce's KITCHEN STILL LIFE (Plate 30), renders all forms much the same and does not achieve the degree of vigor seen in the works of Espinosa or Labrador.

PROVENANCE
Private collection, Spain, 1886; art market, London, 1979; art market, Barcelona, 1983.

EXHIBITION
Madrid 1983–84, no. 41.

BIBLIOGRAPHY
Poleró 1886, p. 39; Cavestany 1936–40, p. 81; Oña Iribarren 1944, pp. 33, 93, no. 22; Pérez Sánchez 1983, p. 63, no. 41, ill.

X. *FRANCISCO BARRERA*

(Documented in Madrid between 1632 and 1657)

Francisco Barrera, like Antonio Ponce, must have received his artistic training in Madrid in the 1620s when Van der Hamen was the dominant still-life
painter, for his works are occasionally reminiscent of the famous artist's style.
As in the case of Ponce's works, however, Barrera's still lifes have distinctive qualities which cannot be confused with anyone else's. Although he achieved some
degree of success in his career and was evidently a well-respected member of the
artistic community of Madrid, he was all but forgotten within a few decades of his
death. Palomino (1724) did not include his life among his biographies of painters;
therefore, very little knowledge of him passed down to the twentieth century.
Cavestany (1936–40) assumed that he was a Sevillian artist because his four most
important paintings happened to be in a Sevillian collection in modern times.
Lafuente Ferrari (1944) refuted this claim with documentary evidence, but in much
of the literature after Cavestany, Barrera is still erroneously called a Sevillian.

Although Palomino did not mention Barrera in his *Lifes of the Painters,* he did
make reference to him in another context, based on documents that were in his
possession. The reference occurs in Chapter III of his theoretical treatise *El museo
pictórico y escala óptica* (1715), which discusses the nobility of the art of painting as
proved by a series of successful lawsuits concerning the taxation of painters that
began with El Greco's famous litigation over his commission at Illescas and lasted
until Palomino's own lifetime. The fifth case that he cites was one brought before
the Royal Council of the Treasury by Francisco Barrera on behalf of all the painters
of Madrid on June 9, 1639.[1] At issue was a new tax of one percent that had been
levied on painters' earnings and which they were unwilling to pay. On July 3, 1640,

Fig. X.1   Francisco Barrera. STILL LIFE. 60 × 92 cm. Signed, 1642. Galleria degli Uffizi, Florence.

Fig. X.2   Pietro Paolo Bonzi. KITCHEN SCENE. 260 × 296 cm. Palacio de los Águila, Ávila.

a ruling was handed down in favor of the painters. As Pérez Sánchez (1983) observes, Barrera's position as "first signatory" in this proceeding leaves no doubt that he held a certain position of professional and moral authority in the eyes of his colleagues. Barrera's stance as a leader of his colleagues, however, goes back several years before that.

On April 30, 1634, the painter Francisco Barrera, who identified himself as *Hermano Mayor* of the Royal Brotherhood of Our Lady of the Seven Sorrows, a confraternity whose membership included at least thirty-six other members of the Guild of Painters and Gilders, represented his artist colleagues in a lengthy lawsuit over their obligation to march through the streets of Madrid during Holy Week with the image of the Virgin.[2]

Barrera's activity is also documented several times in the 1630s when he served as an appraiser of paintings.[3] At that time he lived in rented quarters facing the church of Saint Philip. On October 3, 1633, some portraits of royal persons which he had painted for commercial purposes were critically reviewed by Velázquez and Carducho.[4] In a document of 1638, he seems to be directing a small team of painters working on the decoration of the new Buen Retiro Palace.[5] On September 7 of that year, Antonio Ponce, Lorenzo Sánchez and Domingo de Yanguas declare that they have received payment from Barrera for work they did in the palace. Documents of 1645, 1653 and 1657 reveal that Barrera now owned property on which he collected rent.[6] He would, therefore, seem to have become a man of certain means. Angulo (1971) said that Barrera bought several prints from the estate sale of Antonio Puga in 1648, but this is not so. The artist who did that was a Jusepe Barrera, perhaps a relative of Francisco.[7] The date of Francisco's death is not known.

A certain similarity of Barrera's style to Van der Hamen's and Ponce's can be seen in the signed still life of 1642 in the Uffizi (fig. X.1). Here he makes use of the niche setting that became common in Madrilenian still lifes in the 1620s and adds in front of it a stone plinth. The sense of spatial clarity which Van der Hamen achieved by such means, however, is lacking, and the lack of a clear definition of space carries over to the objects that occupy it. The modeling of the fruit and clay pitcher, for example, have the same sort of blandness and uniformity that can be observed in many of Ponce's still lifes.

Barrera's most impressive works are four large still lifes painted in 1638 that form a series of the Four Seasons (figs. X.3–6). Sometimes compared to the works of Vincenzo Campi (fig. 4), they actually resemble more closely the large pantry scene by Pietro Paolo Bonzi (fig. X.2), whose stepped format they share. In addition to an elaborate still life, each painting features a landscape appropriate to the season represented and a figure who symbolizes it. The canvas representing Spring (fig. X.3) depicts a seated female figure crowned with an enormous wreath of flowers and holding in each hand a small floral spray. The landscape in the background shows part of a palace and formal gardens which, as Pérez Sánchez (1983) has noted, may represent the Buen Retiro Palace, which was being completed around the time of the picture's execution and in which Barrera had worked. The game fowl, fruits, vegetables and fish are those associated with the months of March, April and May, and, as Pérez Sánchez also noted, the bound lamb at the right was surely understood to be the paschal Lamb identified with the spring season.

The canvas representing Summer (fig. X.4) depicts a young man carrying a sheaf of wheat and the scythe with which it was harvested. The landscape, which recalls the Flemish-inspired vistas painted by other artists who worked at the Buen Retiro, depicts the scene of harvest in the middle distance, with a bathing scene beyond. The shelves on which the foodstuffs are placed tilt sharply toward the viewer. Among the articles represented is a flask of *aloja,* an aromatic infusion of honied water with spices sometimes scented with floral essences. Toward the left, near the watchful cat, is a wooden pail in which a long-necked flask of liquid is being chilled with snow from the nearby Guardarrama mountains. The drinking of chilled beverages in summer had become a fashionable practice in the early years of the seventeenth century in Madrid.

Autumn (fig. X.5) is represented as the time of grape harvest, both by the young man gathering grapes from a vine with his donkey in the foreground and by the harvest scene in the background. The leaves of the vine are shown in sharp silhouette against the bright sky. The scene of Winter (fig. X.6), perhaps the most successful of all, is mostly a representation of various meats and game fowl with winter greens, a basket of apples and mounds and boxes of sweets and preserves. The snow-covered tree and wintry sky in the background suggest the harsh climate against which an old man warms himself over a brazier at the left. This particular motif was a standard emblem of winter widely broadcast through the engravings of Antonio Tempesta (fig. X.7) and Jan Sadeler.

Cavestany cited two signed and dated still lifes of 1635 in private collections and exhibited an attributed one belonging at the time to Gelasio Oña Iribarren, which, judging from the reproduction, appears to be consistent with the signed canvases.[8] According to Lafuente Ferrari (1944), Ceán Bermúdez, in the manu-

Fig. X.7 Antonio Tempesta. WINTER. Engraving, 1592. Biblioteca Nacional, Madrid.

Fig. X.3 Francisco Barrera. Spring.
166 × 250 cm. 1638. Private collection, Seville.

Fig. X. 4 Francisco Barrera. Summer.
166 × 250 cm. Signed, 1638. Private collection,
Seville.

script for a history of painting that was never published, cited a canvas which he did not know when he published his *Diccionario* in 1800. He related it in a humorous way to the only other fact he knew about the artist:

> In the year 1639 he was a resident of Madrid, where he painted flowers and fruit with thinness, lightness and truth to life. Admirable is a canvas signed by his hand in that year, which represents some artichokes and other greens that appear natural. On July 3, 1640 he won a decision in a lawsuit he had with the Royal Treasury over the payment of *alcabala* [a tax] on the fruits, flowers and greens that he painted, as though they were edible.[9]

NOTES

1. Palomino 1715, ed. 1947, pp. 161–62; *"La quinta fué, por demanda, que pusieron a los profesores de la Pintura, en 9 de junio de 1639, los diputados de Rentas, y del Servicio de uno por ciento de esta villa de Madrid, sobre que pagasen los pintores el derecho nuevo impuesto; y se ejecutorió a favor de la Pintura, por el Real Consejo de Hacienda, en 3 de julio de 1640 años, a pedimento de Francisco Barrera, y demás pintores de esta Corte."*

2. Lafuente Ferrari 1944, pp. 91–92. See Saltillo 1947a, p. 664 for evidence that the suit was still being pursued in 1677 by a younger generation of artists.

3. On July 5, 1632, Barrera appraised the collection of Daniel Sabola, merchant. Jordan 1967, p. 78 (AHP M P#5876, fols. 184v–186); see Agulló 1978, pp. 26–28 for complete document. On July 16, 1632, he appraised the paintings left on the death of Matheo de la Cana," *"Alguacil que fue de la cassa y corte de Su Magd."* Jordan 1967, pp. 78–79 (AHP M P#5010). On September 28, 1634, Barrera, acting as one of the executors of an estate, names someone else to appraise the paintings in it. Agulló 1981, p. 26 (AHP M P#3643).

4. *Varia velazqueña* 1960, pp. 236–37; See also Ponce essay above.

5. Agulló 1978, p. 28 (AHP M P#7383, fol. 48).

6. Agulló 1978, p. 28, cites the following documents: Book of Enterrments, Parish of Saint Justus, March 25, 645 (someone dies who lives in a house he owns on the Calle de Carretas); AHP M P#8058, fol. 257, March 20, 1653 (collects rent on same house); AHP M P#8062, fol. 724, September 11, 1657 (collects rent again on same property).

7. María Luisa Caturla, "Un pintor gallego en la corte de Felipe IV, Antonio Puga," *Cuadernos de estudios gallegos,* Anejo VI (1952), p. 63. That Jusepe Barrera was a separate person than Francisco, and a painter, is confirmed by a document of 1640 concerning the indentured servitude of his eight-year-old daughter, published by Agulló 1981, p. 26. Joseph [sic] Barrera was also a signatory with Francisco of the 1634 document concerning the Holy Week march (see note 2 above).

8. Cavestany 1936–40, pp. 73–74; pp. 153–54, no. 23, pl. 28.

9. Lafuente Ferrari 1944, p. 92: *"Era vecino de Madrid el año de 1639, donde pintaba flores y frutas con delgadez, verdad y ligereza. Es admirable un lienzo firmado de su mano en aquel año, que figura unas alcachofas y otras verduras, que parecen naturales. En 3 de julio de 1640 ganó una executoria en el pleyto que sostuvo con la Real Hacienda sobre pagar alcabala de los frutos, flores y hortalizas que pintaba, como si fueran comestibles."* Viñaza (1889, vol. 2, p. 49) refers to the same picture, citing Valentín Carderera's annotated copy of Ceán Bermúdez's *Diccionario.*

Fig. X.5 Francisco Barrera. AUTUMN. 166 × 250 cm. Signed, 1638. Private collection, Seville.

Fig. X.6 Francisco Barrera. WINTER. 166 × 250 cm. 1638. Private collection, Seville.

BIBLIOGRAPHY

Palomino 1715, p. 162; Ceán Bermúdez 1800, vol. 1, p. 93; Quilliet 1816, p. 18; Viñaza 1889, vol. 2, p. 49; Mayer 1910; von Spielberg 1910, pp. 316–19; Cavestany 1936–40, pp. 34, 73, 153; Lafuente Ferrari 1935, p. 180; Lafuente Ferrari 1944, pp. 91–92; Oña Iribarren 1944, p. 92; Kubler and Soria 1959, p. 235; Jordan 1967, vol. 1, pp. 77–78; Bergström 1970, p. 59; Torres Martín 1971, p. 48; Angulo 1971, p. 263; Agulló 1978, pp. 26–28, 80; Bergström et al. 1979, p. 175; Florence, Uffizi, 1979 cat., p. 145; Agulló 1981, pp. 26, 164; Valdivieso and Serrera 1982, pp. 78–85; Harastzi 1983, pp. 163–64; Madrid 1983, pp. 46, 64–66, 201.

PLATE 32

FEBRUARY

PLATE 33

STILL LIFE WITH NAUTILUS CUP

Signed lower right (fragmentary signature since painting has been cut down)
Oil on canvas
39¾ × 61 in. (101 × 156 cm.)
Plácido Arango Collection, Madrid

THIS LARGE STILL LIFE IS A GOOD AND representative example of Barrera's style in the 1630s. Its abundant display of edibles and utensils on several planes is similar to the four large canvases of the Seasons which the artist painted in 1638 (figs. X.3–6), except that no large-scale, symbolic human figures are depicted. The wintry landscape seen through the window at the left, which depicts strolling minstrels approaching a house and yard, provides a foil for the colorful spread of apples, preserves, sweets, game fowl and the furry kid strung up by its foot. At the heart of everything is a brazier filled with glowing coals heating a copper chocolate pot. To the left, three red-and-white porcelain cups on a footed metal tray are prepared for the popular treat.

The gold letters denoting the month of February on the front of the principal stone ledge indicate that this still life was part of a series representing the months of the year. Likely to have been part of the same series is a work in similar format in the Stredoceska Galerie, Prague (fig. X.8), which bears an inscription with the same style of letters denoting the month of July. Its lush summer landscape supports the air of abundance suggested by the mound of game, squashes, cabbage, cucumbers, eggplants, grapes, berries and figs. On the upper level a live fish swims in a kettle of water; dead trout are piled at the right; in between is a pail for chilling a beverage.

While the canvases for February and July suggest that there may have been twelve canvases in the suite, this is not necessarily so. Some seventeenth-century inventories list only six or nine paintings signifying the months, which suggests that they served a decorative as well as a symbolic function and were sometimes limited in number to the spaces available where their presence was deemed appropriate.

PROVENANCE
Trafalgar Galleries, London, 1983.

EXHIBITION
London 1983, no. 11

BIBLIOGRAPHY
London 1983, p. 30.

Fig. X.8   Francisco Barrera. JULY. Stredoceska Galerie, Prague.

Signed on the meat pie: *Barrera*
Signed again and dated lower right:
Fran^{co} Barr… f./1642
Oil on canvas
25⅝ × 39⅜ in. (65 × 100 cm.)
Private Collection

THIS STILL LIFE IS UNIQUE AMONG THOSE BY Barrera currently known and shows us a more intimate and charming side of his personality. The picture lacks the formal rigor of Toledan and Madrilenian still lifes of the 1620s and is organized more intuitively. Its comparatively simple composition shows the artist's talents to better advantage than do some of his more complicated schemes.

The niche in the background seems in this case to be a kind of light well, admitting light into the depths of the composition but not illuminating the wall just behind the gilded spice cellar and lidded pitcher at the left. The meat pie placed on the napkin at the left is such a tour de force that the artist signed his name on it. The warm tonality of its baked crust is complemented on the right side of the composition by the golden apples with touches of red. The branch of white apple blossoms creates a sensitive echo of the white napkin and asserts a gentle diagonal that relieves the rectilinear pattern of the architecture. The nautilus cup in the center is the sort of object that is seldom seen in Spanish still lifes, although it is common in Dutch ones. The pitcher would also seem to be of Dutch origin.

PROVENANCE
Arthur de Heuvel, Brussels, March 1962; Dr. Curt Benedict, Paris, July 1962.

EXHIBITIONS
Brussels 1962; Bergamo 1971, no. 42.

BIBLIOGRAPHY
Bergström 1971, no. 42.

XI. CRISTÓBAL RAMÍREZ DE ARELLANO

Active in Toledo in the 1630s and 1640s)

T he still lifes of Cristóbal Ramírez de Arellano have been completely unknown until now. In fact, very little is known about either the man or his works. He must be the same painter who signed *Cristóbal Ramírez* on a full-length painting of Christ the Savior in the Prado Museum (fig. XI.1) to which Viñaza (1889) first called attention, reading its fragmentary date as "1678." The style of the painting, however, suggests a much earlier date.

Gómez Menor (1966) discovered in Toledo a document of 1631 listing "Christobal Ramirez Pintor" among those owing money to the silk merchant Agustín Tolentino. Even though the name is a fairly common one, this document and the style of THE SAVIOR strongly support a Toledan origin for the painter. Angulo and Pérez Sánchez believe that he may have been related to the Valencian manuscript illuminator who died at El Escorial in 1577. They also suggest that a "Xristofol Ramires" who was recorded in the *colegio de pintores* in Valencia in 1616 may be the same artist who later moved to Toledo. This cannot be considered certain, however.

Angulo and Pérez Sánchez (1972) make a convincing comparison of THE SAVIOR to a GUARDIAN ANGEL in the Museo de Santa Cruz in Toledo, which has a fragmentary signature: *...Ramírez,* and is clearly dated 1638. THE SAVIOR by Ramírez is a fairly conventional composition, but it does have one remarkable quality: the velvety modeling of the face and hands of the figure. Christ's right hand, in particular, is a beautiful study in chiaroscuro. The transparent crystal orb in his left hand is painted with delicacy, and the fingers, which are lightly reflected in the glass, are modeled with a very skilled transition from light to dark. Without know-

191

ing the artist's still lifes, Angulo and Pérez Sánchez astutely called attention to these painterly qualities that betray an eye trained to observe nature "in the manner of a still-life painter." This close study of nature, also evident in Ramírez's still lifes (Plates 34, 35), but here applied to a devotional image, suggests the important influence of still-life painting on rank-and-file Spanish painters.

BIBLIOGRAPHY
Viñaza 1889, vol. 3, pp. 283–84; Gómez Menor 1966, p. 89; Angulo 1971, p. 225; Angulo and Pérez Sánchez 1972, pp. 103–06.

Fig. XI.1   Cristóbal Ramírez. THE SAVIOR.
207 × 129 cm. Signed, 1638. Museo del Prado, Madrid.

34. STILL LIFE WITH GRAPES, MELON AND APRICOTS

Signed and dated right corner of stone plinth:
Christobal Ramirez de Arellano/fac. 1644
Oil on canvas
19½ × 41¾ in. (49.4 × 106 cm.)
Dumbarton Oaks, Washington

IN THIS PAINTING AND ITS PENDANT (PLATE 35) which are unknown to specialists of Spanish still life, we discover a unique and attractive personality by whom, it is to be hoped, other works will one day be identified. Although Ramírez de Arellano uses such Castilian still-life conventions as the hanging grapes, his warm, painterly style and mode of composition are quite distinct from those of any artist who preceded him.

He has placed a slice of melon and a shiny silver plate of apricots on a free-standing stone plinth which is off-center to the left. The edge of the stone is nicked and cracked and the objects cast soft shadows on its flat top. The background is especially dark, yet the colors of the fruit are clear and vivid. Alternating with the melon and the plate are two bunches of grapes which hang by cords from above, silhouetted along with their leaves against the darkness of the background. Particular skill has gone into the painting of the slice of melon, with the undulating edge of its rind and the sensitive observation of its seeds. The apricots are modeled with the soft edges and velvety quality that resemble especially the GUARDIAN ANGEL by Ramírez in the Museo de Santa Cruz in Toledo (see Angulo and Pérez Sánchez 1972, pl. 79). The high polish of the metal plate reflecting the fruit gives a sharpness to the image, as do the melon seeds, and this provides an interesting foil to the essentially coloristic image.

PROVENANCE
Mrs. Robert Woods Bliss, 1955; donated to Dumbarton Oaks from her Estate in 1969.

EXHIBITIONS
None.

BIBLIOGRAPHY
Unpublished.

35. STILL LIFE WITH CARDOON, POMEGRANATES AND GRAPES

Oil on canvas
19½ × 42 in. (49.5 × 106.7 cm.)
Dumbarton Oaks, Washington

IN APPROACHING THE TRADITIONAL SUBJECT of this painting, Ramírez de Arellano has not relied on some traditional formulas that he might have used. In not using a symmetrical format, for example, he has departed from the tradition of those still-life painters who were active in Toledo in the 1620s, such as Alejandro de Loarte (Plate 10) and Juan Bautista de Espinosa (Plate 9). He has arranged his still life on a stone shelf that extends across the entire width of the picture. The character of the composition is dominated by an unruly cardoon that arches upward at the right, filling almost the entire height of the picture. With a creamy impasto and delicate coloration, he has modeled the vegetable more sensitively than Loarte had done. There is just enough room at the left for the pomegranates on a silver plate. The mirror finish of the metal provides a sharp contrast to the earthy vegetal forms. Hanging grapes fill the remaining space.

In contrast to the rather dry manner of his Madrilenian contemporaries, Barrera and Ponce, Ramírez de Arellano's style seems to have been touched by the neo-Venetian taste emerging among some young painters in the 1630s. Although Angulo and Pérez Sánchez (1972) have noted that Ramírez de Arellano's figurative style is reminiscent of Sánchez Cotán, it is also not without parallels to such Madrilenian artists as Bartolomé Román.

PROVENANCE
Mrs. Robert Woods Bliss, 1955; donated to Dumbarton Oaks from her Estate in 1969.

EXHIBITIONS
None.

BIBLIOGRAPHY
Unpublished.

PLATE 34

Still Life with Grapes, Melon and Apricots

PLATE 35

STILL LIFE WITH CARDOON, POMEGRANATES AND GRAPES

XII. FRANCISCO DE BURGOS MANTILLA

(1609–1672)

*f*⁹ *Burgensis Mantilla f* 1631

Only one painting by Francisco de Burgos Mantilla is known today, a small still life of dried fruit (Plate 36) that was discovered around 1970. Before that time, his name was sometimes mentioned among the followers of Velázquez, a reliable bit of information contained in a brief sketch of his life written in 1658 by Lázaro Díaz del Valle. In a document that the artist himself signed in the same year, which came to light in 1960, he gave testimony on behalf of Velázquez's qualifications for membership in the noble Order of Santiago. He included therein a few crucial biographical details about himself, which have been overlooked until now in the scant literature on his still lifes.[1] In 1947 Saltillo published the artist's testament, dated March 28, 1672, without annotation of any kind. More recently, we have learned a good deal about the life and career of Burgos Mantilla through the archival research of Mercedes Agulló who published a series of documents in 1978. In 1981, in an article signed with Alfonso Pérez Sánchez, Agulló published an inventory of Burgos Mantilla's studio taken on the occasion of his third marriage in 1648. Pérez Sánchez's detailed analysis of the document discovered and transcribed by Agulló will remain the fundamental study of the painter until other signed paintings come to light which add substance to the relative abstraction of his personality.

In Burgos Mantilla's own account of December 24, 1658, he gave his age as forty-nine, and said that he was born in the city of Burgos in 1609. In his testament of 1672, he said that he was the son of Francisco de Burgos Mantilla and Ana Cuende de la Antadilla, natives of that city. Díaz del Valle tells us that his father was a lawyer in the royal courts in Burgos. The boy was brought to Madrid at the age of nine, according to his own testimony. At the appropriate age, perhaps a few years later, he was placed under the tutelage of Pedro de las Cuevas (c. 1583–1644), who, Díaz del Valle says, was his instructor of drawing. He may have coincided in the studio of de las Cuevas with Antonio de Pereda, who was about the same age and had come from Valladolid to study with the famous teacher. Thereafter, Díaz del Valle says, he became the disciple of Velázquez, "whom he has always tried to imitate in his admirable style."[2] In his 1658 affidavit on behalf of Velázquez, Burgos Mantilla says he had known him for thirty-four years, or since 1624. By 1658 Díaz del Valle said that Burgos Mantilla was "famous for making portraits from life, as shown by the many which he has made of various gentlemen in this city of Madrid which have gained him a great reputation."[3] Although no portraits by Burgos Mantilla are recognized today, doubtless some of those which have been attributed to Velázquez in the past are actually by his hand.

The inventory of Burgos Mantilla's studio taken in 1648 provides important insight into the kind of career he had. First, confirming what Díaz del Valle wrote, there were several signs of a link to Velázquez. Two original paintings by the master were listed: "A Cleopatra by the hand of Diego Velázquez, three-quarters (vara),"[4] and "head of a youth with a collar, original of Velázquez."[5] There were also four copies of paintings by Velázquez: "A portrait of the King on horseback, small,"[6] which was most likely a copy of the equestrian portrait made for the Buen Retiro Palace, now in the Prado; and a "white horse, small, copy of Velázquez,"[7] surely a copy of the work now in the Royal Palace, Madrid. Two "Heads" were also called copies of Velázquez. One of them was a portrait of the Count of Siruela, Bernardino López de Ayala, father of Isabel de Velasco, one of the maids of honor in Velázquez's famous masterpiece LAS MENINAS.[8] Such a portrait by Velázquez was not previously known to exist.

In addition to copies after Velázquez, Burgos Mantilla owned, and may have painted, copies of works by other famous artists of his time or earlier: Titian, Correggio, Raphael, Bassano, El Mudo (Juan Fernández de Navarrete), El Greco, Luca Cambiaso, Carducho, Ribera, Annibale Carracci, Guido Reni. Very likely, he made a large part of his living by copying the works of the masters. Although there were a number of religious paintings in the inventory that were probably of his own invention, they were far outnumbered by those which were acknowledged copies. He also owned a large collection of prints by a wide variety of Italian, Dutch and Flemish artists.

There is also some evidence of his work as a portraitist in Burgos Mantilla's 1648 inventory, although, as one would expect, most commissioned works probably left the studio soon after they were painted. Apart from the several portraits that were there, the inventory contains significant traces of his activity as a painter of miniature portraits: several dozen small copper plaques "for portraits."[9]

Surprisingly few still lifes were itemized in Burgos Mantilla's inventory. Of the five such paintings listed, two were small flower paintings;[10] one depicted figures and flowers but was only about three feet in size;[11] one was described as "a bunch of black grapes with their leaves";[12] and one with flowers and pomegranates was a copy of Van der Hamen.[13] Pérez Sánchez (1981, 1983) sees a close relationship between the signed still life by Burgos Mantilla and the works of Van der Hamen. To this observer, however, the style of that work seems to owe little to Van der Hamen.

It seems that Burgos Mantilla was not an artist who specialized to any considerable extent in still lifes. Like most adventuresome artists of his time, however, he occasionally tried his hand at that most determined form of imitating nature. By chance, his only recognized work that has come down to us is one that may not at all represent the majority of his oeuvre.

NOTES

1. *Varia velazqueña* 1960, vol. 2, p. 330: *"Testigo 87.—En la villa de Madrid, en veinte y quatro dias de el mes de diçiembre de el año de mil y seiscientos y çinquenta y ocho, para esta ynformaçion recibimos por testigo a Francisco de Burgos Mantilla, natural de la çiudad de Burgos y residente en esta Corte desde que tubo nuebe años de edad hasta oy; juro en forma de deçir verdad y..., dijo que conoçe a Diego de Silba Velazquez, pretendiente, desde que vino a esta Corte, que abra casi treinta y quatro años, aunque abia mas tiempo, que el pretendiente residia ya en ella y siempre le oyo llamar el sebillano y asi le tiene por natural de la çiudad de Sibilla..."* [the rest of the document deals with his knowledge of Velázquez's qualifications; he then states his own age] *"y que es de edad de quarenta y nuebe años."*

2. *"...al cual siempre ha procurado imitar en la admirable manera."*

3. *"...famoso en hacer retratos por el natural como lo manifiestan muchos qᵉ ha hecho en esta villa de Madrid de diferentes señores con que ha ganado grande opinión."*

4. Agulló and Pérez Sánchez 1981, p. 373: *"Vna Cleopatra de mano de Diego Belázquez, de tres quartas."*

5. *Ibid.*: *"Vna caueça de vn moço con cuello, original de Velázquez."*

6. Agulló and Pérez Sánchez 1981, p. 371: *"Vn retrato del Rey a cauallo, pequeño, copia de Velázquez."*

7. *Op. cit.*, p. 372: *"Vn cauallo blanco pequeño, copia de Velázquez."*

8. *Op. cit.*, p. 375: *"Dos caueças copias de Diego Velázquez, que vna es el conde de Siruela."*

9. Agulló and Pérez Sánchez 1981, pp. 362, 382: *"Otras tres doçenas de láminas para retratos."*

10. *Op. cit.*, p. 374: *"Vn ramilletero y vn Espíritu Santo,"* and p. 375: *"Otro ramilletero de açuçenas y rosas, pequeño."*

11. *Op. cit.*, p. 373: *"Vn lienço de bara de figuras y flores, orixinal."*

12. *Op. cit.*, p. 374: *"Vn raçimo de vbas negras con sus ojas, orijinal."* Pérez Sánchez (1983, p. 47) notes that Juan de Espinosa, who witnessed Burgos Mantilla's second marriage contract in 1645 (Agulló 1978, pp. 183–84) and was evidently his friend, was well-known for his paintings of grapes and speculates that this picture might have been by Espinosa, or a copy of one of his. However, in the context of this inventory, the use of the word *"orijinal"* with no other attribution given would imply that the painting was by Burgos Mantilla himself.

13. *Op. cit.*, p. 374: *"Vn lienço de tres quartas de flores y granadas, copia de Balderamen."*

BIBLIOGRAPHY

Díaz del Valle 1658, p. 372; Palomino 1724, p. 850; Ceán Bermúdez 1800, vol. 1, p. 181; Beruete 1906, p. 136, no. 1; Mayer 1922, p. 427; Saltillo 1947a, pp. 642–46; *Varia velazqueña* 1960, p. 330; López-Rey 1968, p. 122; Young 1976, p. 211; Agulló 1978, pp. 35, 183–85; López-Rey 1979, pp. 123, 169, no. 191; Agulló and Pérez Sánchez 1981, pp. 359–82; Madrid 1983, pp. 46–47.

PLATE 36

STILL LIFE WITH DRIED FRUIT

Signed and dated lower right: *fr°. Burgensis Mantilla f ¹ 1631*

Oil on canvas

11⁷/₁₆ × 23³/₁₆ in. (29.1 × 58.9 cm.)

Yale University Art Gallery, Stephen C. Clark Fund, New Haven, Connecticut

IN THE PRESENT STATE OF OUR KNOWLEDGE of the development of Spanish still-life painting, this little picture must be assigned a place of importance. Not only is it the only signed work by Burgos Mantilla that is known, but, dated in the year of Van der Hamen's death, it reveals that the young artist was already following a completely different approach to the grouping of objects and to their description with the brush than had been followed by the Madrilenian artist during the 1620s.

The composition is organized on a very narrow stone ledge that spans the width of the picture. The point of view is very close, and the ledge is sharply tilted forward. Several paper cones of dried fruits are placed diagonally upon the ledge; spilling from them and grouped randomly around them are various kinds of nuts. There is no geometrical or symmetrical organizing principal at work here, as there would have been in a still life by Van der Hamen. The artist has intuitively balanced the forms in a way that, as Volpe (1974) remarked, more closely resembles the still lifes of certain followers of Caravaggio in the 1620s, such as Cecco de Caravaggio. How such interchanges took place is not now known, but the date of this picture is the year of Velázquez's return from Italy. As Young (1976) suggested, it may have been Velázquez who encouraged the young artist to try his hand at the still life. It might also have been Velázquez who guided him toward a new approach he had seen on his recent journey.

The painterly approach to this picture would be hard to imagine without the example of the looser brushwork and controlled palette of silvery grays, blacks and earth tones noticeable in Velázquez's works around this time. The way the light falls on the irregular forms of the paper cones and the way the brush lightly and spontaneously creates highlights on creases and edges have nothing to do with Van der Hamen and everything to do with Velázquez's rediscovery of the Venetian masters. The skillful rendition of the raisins and dried apples at the right is an unmistakable sign of Velázquez's influence. The accomplishment of the artist makes us wish that we might one day discover a signed portrait by his hand and encourages us to credit Díaz del Valle in his observation made during the artist's lifetime that he skillfully imitated Velázquez's "admirable style."

PROVENANCE
Frederick Mont, Inc., New York, c. 1970; acquired from Mont by Yale University Art Gallery in 1972.

EXHIBITIONS
New Haven, 1972; Madrid, 1983–84, no. 46.

BIBLIOGRAPHY
Art Journal 1972, pp. 42–43, ill.; Shestack 1973, pp. 3, 54, ill. p. 34; Volpe 1974, p. 34, fig. 20; Young 1976, p. 211, fig. 18; López-Rey 1979, p. 123, pl. 35; Agulló and Pérez Sánchez 1981, pp. 359, 361, 368, ill.; Sterling 1981, p. 19; Pérez Sánchez 1983, pp. 46–47, 66, no. 46, ill.; Cherry 1984, p. 60.

XIII. *FRANCISCO DE PALACIOS*

(c. 1615–before 1652)

The painter Francisco de Palacios is first mentioned in art historical literature by Palomino (1724), who says in his very brief biography that he was a disciple of Velázquez and among those who most closely imitated his style *("de los que más imitaron su manera")*. Palomino acknowledged that he did not know of a single work of his in a public place but that there existed, and he had seen, excellent pictures by him in private houses—"especially portraits, which he made excellently, and in which one recognizes the good school in which he was formed, and how far he advanced in it."[1] He added only that he died in Madrid at the age of thirty-six in 1676.

In 1922 Mayer was the first to publish a pair of still lifes signed by Palacios in 1648, which had belonged to the Harrach family collection in Vienna since the seventeenth century (Plates 37 and 38). Mayer followed Palomino and Ceán Bermúdez in giving the artist's dates as 1640–1676 and let pass without comment the implication that the still lifes would have been painted when the artist was eight years old if those dates were correct. In publishing a catalogue of the Harrach collection in 1926, Hermann Ritschl recognized Palomino's apparent error and suggested that the artist's birth date was "before 1630," which would allow him to have been at least eighteen at the time he painted the still lifes. Also in 1926, the Sociedad de Amigos del Arte exhibited in the *Exposición del antiguo Madrid* a signed oval canvas representing Saint Onuphrius, which had been seen by Ponz (1776) and Ceán Bermúdez (1800) in the old Convent of the Magdalen, and its pendant representing Saint Francis, which had oddly been attributed to El Greco by Ponz. Although the signature on the painting of Saint Onuphrius is clearly legible, the date is fragmentary. The authors of the catalogue decided to insert a question mark after the artist's supposed birth date of 1640. To this day, the pair of still lifes and the SAINT ONUPHRIUS are the only known signed paintings by Palacios. In 1935 Xavier de

Salas published an article on the two still lifes in which he underscored the necessity of advancing the date of the artist's birth.

The vexing discrepancy of dates was finally resolved in 1978 when Agulló published the testament of Francisco Bergés, a painter and art dealer, dated September 25, 1652. Bergés, as it turns out, was Palacios's father-in-law and refers in the document to his daughter as "Jusepa, who is the widow of Francisco de Palacios, painter."[2] In the same document, reference is made to "the Estate of Francisco de Palacios." Therefore, September 1652 has become the new *terminus post quem* for the death of Palacios. Angulo and Pérez Sánchez (1983), assuming that Palomino may have been well-informed at least about Palacios's age at the time of his death, hypothesize a birth date of c. 1614–15. He might, of course, have been born even slightly later.

Conceivably part of the reason for Palomino's confusion over the date of Palacios's death is the fact, brought to light by another document published by Agulló in 1981, that the painter had a son of the same name. On January 14, 1674, the young man signed an official claim for the inheritance left him by his grandfather, Francisco Bergés. As Angulo and Pérez Sánchez (1983) suggest, the claimant had probably just reached his twenty-fifth birthday, which would place the date of his birth around 1649, a date compatible with what we now know about his father. We do not know if the young Palacios was a painter or when he died.

The only other facts we know about Palacios are that in 1647 he attempted to collect money owed him for a painting of Saint John which he had made on commission for one Gerónimo González of Madrid,[3] and that in 1648 he bought several prints and drawings from the estate sale of the painter Antonio Puga.[4]

Most likely Palomino was correct in saying that Palacios was primarily a portrait painter. We know that he also painted religious works, but there is no reason to believe that he painted many still lifes. In 1976 Eric Young attributed to him a pair of Vanitas still lifes on which he thought he could read a partial signature and which he dated in the 1660s. Sterling (1981) accepted both the attribution and the dating. Angulo and Pérez Sánchez (1983) reject the attribution. Young has since (by letter) renounced the attribution of these works to Palacios, a position that seems correct.

NOTES
1. Palomino, ed. 1947, p. 984: *...especialmente retratos, que los hizo con excelencia; y en que se conoce la buena escuela en que se crió, y lo mucho que adelantó en ella."*
2. Agulló 1978, p. 31 (AHP M P#9139, fols. 767–74): *"...doña jusepa bergés, biuda que es de Francisco de Palaçios, pintor...."*
3. Agulló 1978, p. 125 (AHP M P#8655, fol. 78).
4. Caturla 1952, p. 60.

BIBLIOGRAPHY
Palomino 1724, p. 984; Ponz 1776, vol. 5, p. 233; Ceán Bermúdez 1800, vol. 4, p. 23; Beruete 1906, p. 131, no. 1; Mayer 1922, pp. 427–28; Ritschl 1926, p. 106; Madrid 1926, p. 312, nos. 884 and 885; Salas 1935, pp. 276–77; Cavestany 1936–40, p. 80; Caturla 1952, pp. 60–66; Kubler and Soria 1959, p. 236; Kirstel 1962, pp. 31ff.; López-Rey 1968, p. 123; Bergström 1970, p. 68; Young 1976, p. 212; Agulló 1978, pp. 30, 124–25; López-Rey 1979, p. 123; Bergström et al. 1979, p. 206; Sterling 1981, p. 19; Agulló 1981, p. 154; Angulo and Pérez Sánchez 1983, pp. 133–37; Madrid 1983, p. 47.

PLATE 37

STILL LIFE WITH FRUIT

Signed and dated lower right: *F^co DE PALACIOS. F.!/1648*

Oil on canvas

23¼ × 30¹¹/₁₆ in. (59 × 78 cm.)

Schloss Rohrau, Graf Harrach'sche Familiensammlung, Austria

ALTHOUGH VELÁZQUEZ DID NOT PAINT pure still lifes himself, it is generally agreed that the painter of this picture and its pendant (Plate 38) was very much under the influence of the master's mature painting style, thus confirming Palomino's account of his training. Palacios's compositions have also been said to place him in the tradition of Van der Hamen—and, in a sense, that is true—but, in a profounder sense, his painterly vision with its atmospheric emphasis is radically different from Van der Hamen's.

Palacios has depicted metal plates of figs and peaches; a single peach on the ledge, as though it has fallen off the plate; a knife; another plate with a pie, a bun and a folded napkin; a small silver vessel for drinking wine; a wood and cork beverage cooler; and a simple pottery wine pitcher. These objects on a gray stone shelf are suffused with a soft light that enters from the left, casting no harsh shadows, and creating a sense of atmosphere quite different from the dramatic tenebrism of Van der Hamen's still lifes. This sense of ambient air is augmented by the diagonal shaft of light that falls from the upper left. The objects are arranged randomly, free of the imposed order characteristic of the earlier generation of still lifes. The plate with the pie and the napkin at the left is partially cut off by the edge of the picture, a device often used by Velázquez to create the feeling of casual observation. This is mirrored on the opposite side of the pendant composition, suggesting that this was meant to be the lefthand picture of the pair.

PROVENANCE

Count Ferdinand Bonaventura Harrach, Austrian Ambassador to the Spanish court in the reigns of Philip IV and Charles II.

EXHIBITIONS

Madrid, 1981–82b, no. 32; Munich/Vienna, 1982, no. 60.

BIBLIOGRAPHY

Mayer 1922, pp. 427–28; Vienna, Harrach, 1926 cat., p. 106, no. 428; Salas 1935, pp. 275–77, pl. 1; Cavestany 1936–40, pp. 39, 80; Mayer 1947, p. 451; Gaya Nuño 1958, p. 262, no. 2098; Kubler and Soria 1959, p. 236; Vienna, Harrach, 1960 cat., pp. 55–56, no. 152; Heinz, 1960a, pp. 3–4; Kirstel 1962, p. 31ff, ill.; López-Rey 1968, p. 122; Bergström 1970, p. 68; Young 1976, p. 212; Bergström et al. 1979, p. 206; Madrid 1981b, p. 92, no. 32, ill.; Vienna 1982, p. 216, no. 60, ill.; Angulo and Pérez Sánchez 1983, p. 136, no. 4, pl. 144; Pérez Sánchez 1983, p. 47, ill.

Signed and dated lower left: *F^co DE PALACIOS. F.!/1648*

Oil on canvas

23¼ × 31½ in. (60 × 80 cm.)

Schloss Rohrau, Graf Harrach'sche Familiensammlung, Austria

THE EMPHASIS OF FRUIT IN THE PENDANT TO this still life (Plate 37) is replaced in this painting by one of baked goods and sweets. A plate of sugared almonds, candied fruit and pine nut paste appears at the left. Next to it are two loaves of braided bread and a bun, or tart. At the right are a silver pitcher, a red ceramic jar and a long-necked, glass wine decanter partially cut off by the edge of the composition. Toward the back of the shelf are another red ceramic vase with two handles, a watermelon and a copper pitcher. Although Van der Hamen often arranged his still lifes along a narrow ledge, Palacios does not employ the distinct zig-zag pattern that the earlier artist used to bring order to his compositions. Instead, his unifying factor is an optical one that defines a whole field of vision. The sensitive, interlaced brushwork closely approximates Velázquez's in the decade of the 1640s—especially in the definition of the loaves of bread and the silver pitcher. The pitcher is a tour de force whose surface seems to have depth like a mirror and to reflect flashes of light at the same time.

PROVENANCE

See no. 37.

EXHIBITIONS

See no. 37.

BIBLIOGRAPHY

Mayer 1922, pp. 427–28; Vienna, Harrach, 1926 cat., p. 106, no. 432; Salas 1935, pp. 275–77, pl. 2; Cavestany 1936–40, pp. 39, 80, fig. 20; Oña Iribarren 1944, pp. 31, 93, no. 18; Mayer 1947, p. 451; Gaya Nuño 1958, p. 262, no. 2099; Kubler and Soria 1959, p. 236; Vienna, Harrach, 1960 cat., p. 56, no. 150, pl. 6; Heinz, 1960a, pp. 3–4, fig. 10; Kirstel 1962, pp. 31ff. ill.; López-Rey 1968, p. 122; Bergström 1970, p. 68, fig. 49; Angulo 1971, p. 213, fig. 196; Young 1976, p. 212; Bergström et al. 1979, p. 206, pl. 145; Madrid 1981b, p. 92, no. 33, ill.; Vienna 1982, p. 218, no. 61, ill.; Angulo and Pérez Sánchez 1983, p. 137, no. 5, pl. 145; Madrid 1983, p. 47, ill.

PLATE 38

STILL LIFE WITH BRAIDED BREAD

XIV. Antonio de Pereda
(1611–1678)

pereda.f 165c

I n the generation of painters born around 1610, Antonio de Pereda stands out as the one truly great painter of still lifes. Far from being a specialist in the genre, he created a thriving practice as a painter of traditional subjects. But to the modern eye, at least, his still lifes represent the high point of his career. A painter of extraordinary technical facility, he represents at once the culmination of a development begun half a century before him and the beginning of an approach to the still life that was wholly new in Spain.

Pereda was the eldest son of a family of artists and was baptized on March 20, 1611 in the city of Valladolid.[1] For a few years, following the death of Philip II, Valladolid had enjoyed a period of efflorescence when the young King Philip III established his court there, but that was before Pereda was born; by 1606 the court had returned to Madrid, leaving the old Castilian city a fairly dispirited and inactive place as far as painting was concerned. The young Pereda was evidently a precocious boy whose potential as an artist could not be realized in such an environment, and he did not long remain there. We are lucky to be rather well informed about him by his friend from childhood, Lázaro Díaz del Valle, who wrote (though he did not publish) the first biographies of the Spanish painters. Díaz del Valle's life of Pereda, written in 1657, more than twenty years before the artist's death, has served as the basis for all subsequent accounts of the early part of his career. Considerable archival research conducted since the late nineteenth century has also provided a large body of facts about his life.

Fig. XIV.1   Antonio de Pereda. RELIEF OF
GENOA BY THE MARQUIS OF SANTA CRUZ.
290 × 370 cm. Signed, 1634. Museo del Prado,
Madrid.

Fig. XIV.1, detail   RELIEF OF GENOA.

Pereda probably began to learn the rudiments of his profession from his father, who died when the boy was eleven years old.[2] Two of his six siblings were painters, and even his mother once described herself as *"pintora."*[3] It has been assumed that much of his early training in Valladolid, however, was received from Andrés Carreño, executor of his father's will, a painter, and the uncle of Juan Carreño de Miranda (1614–1685), one of the most talented of Pereda's contemporaries. According to Díaz del Valle, after his father died the young boy was taken to Madrid "where he learned the principles of art" from Pedro de las Cuevas (c. 1583–1644). De las Cuevas, by whom not a single painting is known today, was the most influential teacher of painting in Madrid at the time, running an academy which included among its students some of the most gifted painters of the day—Francisco Camilo, his stepson; Juan Carreño de Miranda; and José Leonardo.

While a pupil in the studio of de las Cuevas, Pereda had the luck, Díaz del Valle tells us, to be noticed by Francisco Tejada, Justice of the Royal Council, whose house, according to Vincencio Carducho, contained a "discreet museum."[4] Tejada took young Pereda into his household and, "desirous of helping him to learn," allowed him to copy the works of the great masters that he owned. While he was there, some of his paintings came to the attention of Giovanni Battista Crescenzi, Marquis of La Torre, a connoisseur of great credit with Philip IV and of powerful influence in the court. Pereda finished his education under the patronage and protection of Crescenzi, and when he had reached the age of eighteen, Díaz del Valle tells us, his paintings "seemed as though by a very experienced artist." According to the biographer, a painting of the Immaculate Conception of the Virgin executed around this time created quite a stir in the court and awakened much envy before the marquis sent it to his brother, Pietro Paolo Cardinal Crescenzi, in Rome.[5]

Fig. XIV.2 Antonio de Pereda. THE CHRIST CHILD TRIUMPHANT OVER DEATH. 195 × 140 cm. Signed. Church of Las Maravillas, Madrid.

The protection and encouragement of Crescenzi not only contributed to Pereda's development as an artist, it also opened the doors of royal patronage to the younger painter. In 1634, at the age of twenty-three and doubtless through the influence of the marquis, he received the most important opportunity of his career. He was selected along with two other young painters (José Leonardo and Félix Castelo) to represent the younger generation of artists in the decoration of the Hall of Realms in the new Buen Retiro Palace. The paintings of these young men were to be hung alongside those commissioned from the older generation of artists at the court—Vincencio Carducho, Eugenio Caxés and Juan Bautista Maino—and those of Zurbarán, who had been called from Seville expressly for the purpose, and, of course, Velázquez. This cycle of paintings was the brainchild of the Count-Duke of Olivares, and its object was to glorify the monarchy and its military victories during the Count-Duke's ascendancy as the king's favorite. Pereda's contribution to the scheme was the large RELIEF OF GENOA BY THE MARQUIS OF SANTA CRUZ (fig. XIV.1), which, with its neo-Venetian warmth and striking naturalism, stands out as one of the best of the twelve canvases in the series.

Among the few of Pereda's paintings specifically mentioned by Díaz del Valle was one which he called "*El desengaño del mundo*," (The Undeceiving of the World), which he understood was painted prior to the RELIEF OF GENOA and which he said was "everything which the art of painting can achieve." He probably referred to the painting preserved today in Vienna (Plate 40), a representation of the theme of the vanity of life. Its composition must have been an innovation in Spanish art if it, like the Vienna canvas, contained a prominent still-life element with symbolic content. Because of Crescenzi's well-known commitment to still-life painting, we can safely assume that he encouraged Pereda to develop his skill in the depiction of inanimate objects. Indeed, the artist's earliest signed still life is dated 1634 (Plate 39), during the height of their relationship as patron and painter. Known to have encouraged still-life painting since his early days in Rome—and to have practiced it himself—Crescenzi must have taken pride in the achievement of the young artist. Of such quality are his first such works that, indeed, Crescenzi might easily have seen them as the fulfillment of a lifelong ideal.

Just on the threshold of a brilliant career, however, fate "cut the thread of his hopes," as Díaz del Valle phrased it, when in March of 1635, Crescenzi died. This must have been a tremendous blow or the biographer would not have mentioned it among the few facts of the artist's life which he chose to relate twenty-two years after Crescenzi's death. Indeed, the closeness of the men is even underscored in Pereda's last will and testament dated January 11, 1678, when he expressed his wish to endow a memorial for the souls of his wives, his son, his parents and grandparents, "and that of the Marquis, my lord."[6] The hopes Pereda might have entertained of royal patronage as a result of his commission for the Buen Retiro came to nothing, some think because of the enmity between Olivares and Crescenzi. Whatever the reason, without the marquis behind him, Pereda was never to work again for the royal household.[7] He had instead to build his career primarily on his work for religious institutions.

Pereda's career as a religious painter, however, was relieved by his continued

practice of still-life painting, for which there was always a market. The talent for keen observation of detail revealed in his youthful works continued to develop as he matured and, as his command of his medium became more fluent with the years, the brilliance of his still lifes became truly spectacular. This flair for description of objects also carried over into his religious paintings, giving him the ability to heighten the emphasis of certain attributes of the saints or of the Passion to very dramatic effect (fig. XIV.2). Availing himself of the rich collections of Madrid, Pereda obviously knew and assimilated the best of still-life painting from Holland, Flanders and Italy. But, imitating no one, he created a style of his own that expressed the opulence, the ripeness and the abundance of the baroque as completely as they were ever expressed in still lifes.

With a pair of still lifes dated 1652, formerly in the Russian Imperial Collection (figs. XIV.3,4), Pereda reached one of the peaks of his career. In composing them, he rejected the austere formalism of the previous generation in favor of a certain nonchalance. Nevertheless, he followed in the same tradition of celebrating the painter's ability to feign the appearances of reality. In the Leningrad STILL LIFE WITH AN EBONY CHEST (fig. XIV.3), Pereda contrasts an impressive variety of textures and materials in one picture; in the end, however, he emphasizes with his sensuous brushwork that the image is only an illusion made with paint (fig. XIV.3, detail).

The beautiful STILL LIFE WITH A CLOCK in the Pushkin Museum (fig. XIV.4) brings up a problematical aspect of the artist's biography as recounted by Palomino in 1724. The painting is signed at the lower right in a trompe l'oeil imitation of Roman letters chiselled in stone: *D. ATONIO / PEREDA F. / 1652* [sic]. The "N" in Antonio is omitted. According to Palomino, who moved to Madrid from Córdoba in the year of Pereda's death, the artist, although he was well-to-do and of

Fig. XIV.4   Antonio de Pereda. Still Life
with a Clock. 80 × 94 cm. Signed, 1652.
Puskin Museum, Moscow.

rather high social status, could neither read nor write. Yet, Palomino says, he had a
great library of books in several languages. He would have his disciples read to him
aloud and, to sign his pictures, would have them write his name on a piece of paper,
which he would then copy as if he were drawing. The biographer concludes by
saying that Pereda possessed such discretion and cleverness that he was able to
dissemble this defect. While many scholars have argued that Palomino's story must
be a total fabrication, Pérez Sánchez (1978) is inclined to accept it as substantially
true. Pereda was too well known a figure in Madrid, he argues, and Palomino's
sources who knew him too reliable for there not to have been some truth to it.
There is no question, however, that Pereda could sign his name. His testament and
other legal documents were signed by him in the presence of witnesses.[8] Nevertheless, the signatures on his paintings are extremely variable and sometimes clumsy.
The omission of the "N" in Antonio in the Pushkin signature does not seem so
much a sign of not knowing how to write, as it may be one of severe dyslexia, a
phenomenon that was certainly not understood in Palomino's time. If that was
Pereda's problem, it no doubt made his life more difficult but did not prevent him

from becoming an educated man. Those who have denounced Palomino's account of this matter have merely been defending the obvious fact that Pereda was a man of subtle mind and refined sensibilities. If there is even some truth to Palomino's story, then it makes even more remarkable the great sophistication of the artist's paintings.

NOTES
1. Urrea 1976.

2. García Chico 1946.

3. Urrea 1976, pp. 337–38. In 1627 Pereda's mother was still living in Valladolid. Urrea understands the usage of the word "*pintora*" in this context to mean "merchant of pictures."

4. *Diálogos de la pintura* (1633), ed. 1979, p. 446.

5. Angulo and Pérez Sánchez 1983, no. 41, pl. 147, make a convincing case for the identification of this painting with the IMMACULATE in the Musée des Beaux Arts, Lyon, which Martin Soria had earlier attributed to Pereda.

6. Viñaza 1889, p. 243.

7. Viñaza 1889, p. 248, notes that in 1636 the Count of Castrillo paid Pereda for two landscapes that were to adorn the Buen Retiro Palace.

8. Viñaza 1889, pp. 235, 245.

BIBLIOGRAPHY
Díaz del Valle 1656–59, pp. 374–76; Palomino 1724, pp. 957–60; Ceán Bermúdez 1800, vol. 4, pp. 62–68, vol. 6, pp. 377–78; Viñaza 1889, vol. 3, pp. 233–48; Martí Monsó 1898–1901, pp. 512, 571; Pérez Pastor 1914, p. 174; Cavestany 1936–40, pp. 77–78; García Chico 1940–46, vol. 3, pt. 2 (1946), pp. 117–23; Saltillo 1944, pp. 43ff.; Saltillo 1951, p. 47; Sterling 1959, pp. 76–77; Caturla 1960, pp. 333–55; Bergamo 1971, nos. 52, 53; Torres Martín 1971, pp. 77–80; Young 1976, p. 212; Urrea 1976, pp. 336–38; Pérez Sánchez 1977, pp. 417–59; Valderde Madrid 1978; Agulló 1978, pp. 127–28, 205, 215; Madrid 1978; Angulo 1978, pp. 271–74; Urrea 1979; Agulló 1981, pp. 14, 73, 142, 158–60, 223, 229; Angulo and Pérez Sánchez 1983, pp. 138–239; Madrid 1983, pp. 94–96, 215.

39. WALNUTS

Signed and dated lower right: *AP 1634*
Oil on panel
8¼ in. (20.7 cm.)
Private Collection, Spain

ALTHOUGH PEREDA DID NOT SIGN WITH initials on any other still life, there can be no doubt that the initials on this small panel are his. Angulo and Pérez Sánchez (1983) observe that the walnuts are painted with a technique and a minute observation of detail similar to the painting of walnuts in the Moscow STILL LIFE WITH A CLOCK of 1652 (fig. XIV.4). The circular format of the panel is somewhat unusual, but in the 1630s El Labrador also occasionally worked in a circular format (Plate 24). The challenge of designing a stable composition within the circle was probably immediately recognized, but the principal effect of the continuous perimeter surrounding the still life is to focus our scrutiny, almost like a magnifying glass, upon the subject matter.

The few walnuts resting on the narrow horizontal shelf are somewhat larger than life-size and, because they are the sole focus of the composition, they assume a certain monumentality. The artist, determined to show us every aspect of the nut, has disected them with the care of a surgeon. At the right is a whole, uncracked walnut; the strong light falling from the upper left turns imperceptibly into velvety shadow on its wrinkled shell. The tightly sealed shell conveys a hermetic sense of mystery. To the left of it are two other walnuts whose shells have been cracked and partially peeled away. With breathtaking skill, the artist begins to reveal the anatomy of his subject. He shows us a cross-section of the shell, with its microscopically thin outer and inner layers and its woody interior. He shows us the membranes and fibrous dividers of the internal architecture. And finally, in the fragments toward the front, he shows us the treasure, the meat, held like a gemstone in a setting. In contrast to the brittle quality of the shells, he has managed to convey the moist and oily quality of the nut meat. In fact, almost every aspect of the nature of a nut has been addressed in this tiny picture, whose naturalism would seem to be a culmination of the tradition begun over three decades earlier by Sánchez Cotán.

We can see in this small tour de force by the twenty-three-year-old Pereda the signs of genius that must have attracted the Marquis of La Torre. The panel, painted when the young artist had already lived for several years under his guidance and protection, is dated in the same year that Crescenzi's influence helped him win the commission to paint the RELIEF OF GENOA by the MARQUIS OF SANTA CRUZ for the Buen Retiro Palace (fig. XIV.1). Certainly in 1634, no artist in Madrid was painting still lifes so brilliantly.

PROVENANCE
Unknown.

EXHIBITION
Madrid 1983–84, no. 66.

BIBLIOGRAPHY
Angulo and Pérez Sánchez 1983, pp. 152, 223, no. 148, pl. 146; Madrid 1983, p. 107, ill.

PLATE 39

WALNUTS

40. VANITAS

Oil on canvas

54⅞ × 68½ in. (139.5 × 174 cm.)

Kunsthistorisches Museum, Gemäldegalerie, Vienna

DIEGO ANGULO (1978) HAS CALLED Pereda's VANITAS in Vienna "without doubt one of the greatest paintings of the Madrilenian School," an opinion that can hardly be disputed. Although it makes use of universally understood symbols that had become common properties in Dutch still lifes of the first third of the seventeenth century, such imagery was new in Spanish painting when Pereda painted the picture.

Long attributed to the Flemish artist Frans Luyck, Mayer (1911) was the first to recognize the painting as the work of Pereda. The attribution has been universally accepted since and was reaffirmed recently through direct comparisons in the important exhibition of the artist's works held in Madrid in 1978–79, the tricentennary of his death. Traditionally, the painting has been dated by scholars in the 1650s on the basis of the artist's known dated still lifes in the Soviet Union (figs. XIV.3,4) and Portugal (Plate 42). Pérez Sánchez (1978), however, recognized a similarity in the style of the angel and its drapery to the IMMACULATES that Pereda painted in the mid-1630s and convincingly demonstrated that the painting dates from the artist's youth.

In view of the painting's early date, we must consider seriously that it might be the work which Díaz del Valle (1657) said was painted just prior to the RELIEF OF GENOA—that is to say, about 1634 or before—and described as the "canvas of the Undeceiving of the World (El desengaño del mundo), with some skulls and other spoils of death, which is everything that the art of painting can achieve, painted with naturalism, tenderness and freshness; its drawing, composition and brushwork of the Venetian School."[1] Palomino referred to the same picture in

1724, saying that, because it was such a famous work, the hereditary Admiral of Castile placed it in a special hall of his palace designated for paintings by eminent Spaniards. Palomino made clear that he was referring to the tenth Admiral of Castile, Juan Gaspar Alonso Enríquez de Cabrera, VI Duke of Medina de Rioseco (1625–1691), who was the patron and protector of Juan de Alfaro, Velázquez's disciple and close friend of Palomino. It was Alfaro who helped to arrange and care for the Admiral's extraordinary collection of paintings, so Palomino should have been well informed. He does not tell us whether the Admiral had purchased the Pereda or whether he had inherited it from his father, Juan Alfonso Enríquez de Cabrera (1600–1647), ninth Admiral and the principal majordomo of Philip IV. The ninth Admiral's activity as a collector, mentioned by Carducho in 1633,[2] had reached such a pitch by 1638 that it attracted the notice of Sir Arthur Hopton (fig. VII.1), British Ambassador at the court, who wrote on August 5th to Lord Cottington in London:

> They are now become more judicious in and more affectioned unto the Art of Painting, than they have been, or than the world imagines. And the king within this 12 month, had gotten an incredible number of ancient and of the best modern hands, and over with the Conde de Monte Rey came the best of Italy, particularly the Baccanalian of Titian and in this town is not a piece worth any thing but the king takes and pays very well for them, and in his imitation the Admirante [the Duke of Medina de Rioseco, Admiral of Castile], don Lewis de Haro [the Marquis of El Carpio] and many others are making collections.[3]

On June 19, 1647, following the Admiral's death, an inventory and appraisal of his collection was ordered to be made by the painter Antonio Arias. That inventory, published in 1903 by Fernández Duro, shows the contents of the collection to be truly staggering, not only in terms of

number—there were 938 paintings—but also in terms of the percentage of works by the great masters of the past (Dürer, Raphael, Leonardo, Titian, Sebastiano del Piombo, Giovanni Bellini, etc.) and of the great masters of that time (Rubens, Van Dyck, Caravaggio, Ribera, Guido Reni, Guercino, Domenichino, etc.). Listed as number 391, with the very high valuation of 4000 *reales*, was probably Pereda's "*El desengaño del mundo*", although Fernández Duro appears to have made an error in transcribing the artist's name, arriving at a meaningless attribution: "A canvas of *un respice finem* [a last reproof], with four death's heads, by the hand of the Esparido [sic]."[4] The last six letters of that name are so close to Pereda as to suggest that the modern paleographer misunderstood the handwriting. Elsewhere in the same inventory, a small still life of fruit by Pereda was recorded: "515. *Un fruterico pequeño del maestro Perea* [sic]."[5] Therefore, it seems likely that the painting mentioned by Díaz del Valle was acquired by the ninth Admiral of Castile and was inherited by his son, in whose collection Palomino described it.

If the Vienna canvas is "*El desengaño del mundo*" described by Díaz del Valle, then its strong Habsburg symbolism may be seen as a prelude to Pereda's good fortune to be chosen as a young man of twenty-three to paint one of the scenes of victory for the Hall of Realms in the Buen Retiro Palace.

Pereda's composition is presided over by a magnificent angel, or genius, with pale skin, languid eyes and aristocratic features. The angel holds an elegant cameo of the Emperor Charles V and points to the globe of the world which he dominated. Resting against the base of the gilded astrological clock is an antique gold medal of Caesar Augustus, making the obvious point of the continuum of the empire. The gold chain hanging over the edge of the red velvet buffet is the type worn across the chest that had become extremely fash-

Fig. XIV.5 Francisco Velázquez Vaca. VANITAS. 94 × 131 cm. Signed, 1639. Convent of San Quirce, Valladolid.

Fig. XIV.6 Attributed to Antonio de Pereda. DREAM OF THE KNIGHT. 152 × 217 cm. Real Academia de Bellas Artes de San Fernando, Madrid.

ionable in the royal family and among gentlemen of the highest rank at the Spanish court in the 1620s, as can be seen in Velázquez's portraits of the king and his brother—the Infante Don Carlos—and the Count-Duke of Olivares.[6] At the right are several miniature portraits of ladies. The largest one represents the style of dress current in the reign of Philip II. The sitter of the small portrait appears to

be a widow from more or less the same time. The small portrait at the right, however, depicts a lady dressed in the style of the early 1630s. All of the portraits must have had very personal significance and allude to the sentiment of love. Among the miniatures are a strand of pearls, a bottle of perfume and an embroidered purse from which spills a quantity of gold and silver coins. All of these things are symbols of the riches and vanity of earthly life.

At the left is a lower table of rough wood. Near its splintered front edge are inscribed the Latin words "NIL [sic] OMNE" ("Everything is Nothing"). Visually the two tables are connected by the fall of the golden chain, the lines of which exactly coincide with the elaborately inlaid stock of the musket pointing obliquely into the midst of spoils of death. Gállego (1972) has observed that the two tables are also connected visually by the presence of playing cards near the edge of each one. He sees these as a sign of "the permanent passage from life into death." Pérez Sánchez (1978) notes that the higher table has only cards from the suit of Spades, whereas the lower one has only Clubs, which surely conveys some specific emblematic message. Near the inscription on the table is an hourglass with the sand run out and a human skull whose snaggled teeth add import to the meaning of the words. Behind it, other skulls are piled atop two large tomes signifying science and learning. The light, which is strongest at the left, plays upon the surface of the parchment and gives almost surreal presence to the leather thongs attached to the upper book. The skulls, creating a macabre mound, are in some cases turned so that the light and shadow can define the porous underside of the craniums. In examining so minutely the objective reality of these forms, the artist underscores their power as symbols of death. At the back of the table, on the other side of the musket barrel, is a pile of richly wrought armor and a general's baton, symbols of

power and command. Rising from their midst is a brass candelabrum with a spent candle. The light reflects brightly from this object, which, having ceased to perform its intended function, has become a symbol of the instantaneous advent of death. In the same way that the artist has used light glinting off the steely halberds in the RELIEF OF GENOA (fig. XIV.1, detail) to bring a heightened presence and special significance to the instruments of war, so Pereda, the still-life painter, emphasizes the physical reality of a significant object.

Unlike earlier Spanish still-life painters, Pereda in this work has used his formidable skill in the service of a moral message that was fundamental to the ethos of his century. He has done so with elegance, grace and restraint, but at the same time with a grandeur that exceeds that of most Dutch and Flemish examples of the theme he might have known.[7] A few years later, in 1639, a minor, provincial artist named Francisco Velázquez Vaca (d. 1661) painted a poor and very literal version of the same subject (fig. XIV.5). It is known that Francisco Collantes (1599–1656), recognized mostly for his landscapes and a few religious works, painted Vanitas still lifes.[8] In the second half of the seventeenth century, Juan de Valdés Leal (1622–1690), Andrés Deleito and others made the theme more common in Spain.

We cannot now be sure what happened to "El desengaño del mundo" that Díaz del Valle described in 1657, but following the few clues we have may lead us closer to the answer. The eleventh and last Admiral of Castile, Juan Tomás Enríquez de Cabrera, who inherited his father's collection in 1691, came to a sad end. In the wrenching apart of Spanish society that accompanied the change of dynasty from Habsburg to Bourbon in 1701 and in the ensuing War of the Spanish Succession, his sympathies were not with the French. He fled to Lisbon and publicly denounced the government of Madrid. In turn, he was declared a traitor and his

PLATE 40

VANITAS

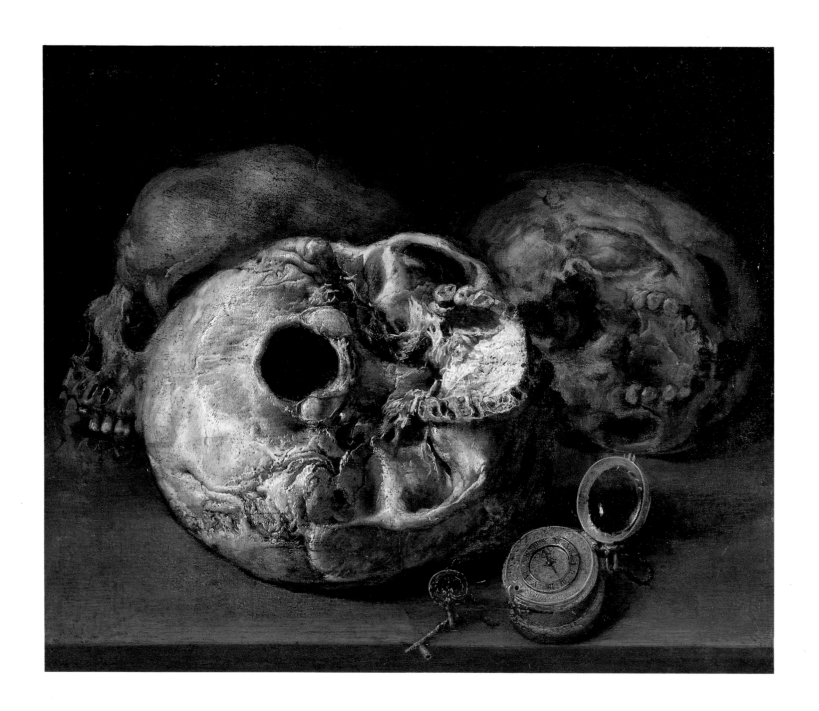

PLATE 41

Vanitas

property was confiscated in 1703. In the following years of war, anything might have happened to the picture—the collection is now widely dispersed. But it may not be just a coincidence that during that time the Archduke Charles of Austria, later Emperor Charles VI, was leading an allied army on Spanish soil in defense of his claim to the throne, a claim which the Admiral of Castile supported. The painting now in Vienna was first inventoried in the Austrian Imperial Collection in 1733, the name of its artist forgotten.

According to Palomino, there was in 1724 another version of this subject by Pereda still in the possession of the artist's heirs in Madrid. This might have been the version now in the Uffizi, which Pérez Sánchez attributes to Pereda[9] and Duncan Kinkead to Valdés Leal.[10] In any case, it cannot have been the famous DREAM OF THE KNIGHT (*Sueño del caballero*) (fig. XIV.6) which has traditionally been attributed to Pereda on the strength of Díaz del Valle's description of the painting belonging to the Admiral of Castile. Soria, who doubted the attribution to Pereda, first pointed out (1959) the Velázquezlike qualities of this masterpiece that place its date definitely closer to the 1650s than the 1630s and seem to indicate that it was painted by an artist in the orbit of Velázquez (Soria thought unconvincingly of Carreño) who was familiar with Pereda's earlier composition. Although the DREAM OF THE KNIGHT should not be retained as a work within Pereda's oeuvre, we cannot yet give it an alternative attribution.[11]

PROVENANCE
Probably Juan Alfonso Enríquez de Cabrera, IX Admiral of Castile, V Duke of Medina de Rioseco, until 1647 (see discussion above); Juan Gaspar Alonso Enríquez de Cabrera, X Admiral of Castile, VI Duke of Medina de Rioseco, until 1691; Juan Tomás Enríquez de Cabrera, XI Admiral of Castile, VII Duke of Medina de Rioseco, until 1703; Austrian Imperial Collection since before 1733 (when recorded in Stallburg).

EXHIBITION
Madrid 1978–79, no. 7.

BIBLIOGRAPHY
Díaz del Valle 1656–59, p. 375; Palomino 1724, p. 958; Fernández Duro 1903, p. 203; Mayer 1911, p. 199; Lafuente Ferrari 1935, p. 178; Cavestany 1936–40, p. 78; Lafuente Ferrari and Friedlander 1935, pp. 620, 700; Mayer 1947, p. 457; Trapier 1956, pp. 18, 22; Montañés Fontela 1957, p. 186ff.; Hernández Perera 1958, p. 30; Gaya Nuño 1958, p. 269, no. 2191; Kubler and Soria 1959, pp. 281–82; Bergström 1962, p. 30; Bergström 1970, p. 75, fig. 55; Angulo 1971, p. 216; Gállego 1972, p. 246; Vienna, Kunsthistorisches Museum, 1973 cat., p. 133, pl. 137; Kinkead 1974, pp. 155–63; Kinkead 1976, p. 80, pl. 39; Klauner 1978, p. 421, fig. 230; Madrid 1978, no. 7; Angulo 1978, p. 273; Bergström et al. 1979, pl. 142; Angulo and Pérez Sánchez 1983, pp. 235–36, no. 160, pl. 149; Madrid 1983, p. 94, ill.

NOTES
1. *"Tambien pinto (entiendo q^e antes deste) un lienzo del desengaño del mundo, con unas calaveras y otros despojos de la muerte, que son todo a lo que puede llegar el arte de la pintura, por q^e este artifice pinta muy al natural, tierno y fresco; su dibujo disposicion y pincel es de la escuela veneciana...."*

2. *Diálogos de la pintura,* 1979 ed., p. 417.

3. Quote from Brown and Elliott 1980, p. 115.

4. Fernández Duro 1903, p. 203, no. 391: *"Un lienzo de 'un respice finem,' con cuatro cabezas de muertes, de mano del Esparido...4.000 Reales."* (AHN M Confiscos y secuestros, Legajo 4, pieza 3.ª) Tormo (1916, 1949 ed., p. 294), who seems not to have known the Vienna canvas and who believed that the DREAM OF THE KNIGHT (fig. XIV.6) was the painting mentioned by Díaz del Valle and Palomino, looked for the painting in this inventory but did not recognize it.

5. *Op. cit.,* p. 206. Pereda's name was often written without the "d". The use of "maestro" here suggests the possibility that Fernández Duro misread an abbreviation of that word in entry number 391 as the "Es" [sic] joined to "parido" [sic]. I have been unable to check the original manuscript of the inventory in order to clarify this before going to press.

6. Harris 1970, p. 371.

7. Soria 1959, p. 281, suggested that Pereda might have been inspired by such a Dutch engraving as H. Hondius's FINIS CORONAT OPUS of 1626.

8. Agulló 1981, p. 214.

9. Madrid 1978, (no pagination) discussed in cat. no. 7. See also Angulo and Pérez Sánchez 1983, p. 224, no. 149.

10. Kinkead 1974, pp. 153–55; Kinkead 1978, p. 352, no. 39

11. Pérez Sánchez 1978, no. 39, and Angulo and Pérez Sánchez 1983, p. 228, discuss the problems of fitting the painting into Pereda's chronological development but believe that the traditional attribution should be maintained.

Oil on canvas
12¼ × 14⅝ in. (31 × 37 cm.)
Museo Provincial de Bellas Artes, Zaragoza

THE TRADITIONAL ATTRIBUTION OF THIS small painting to Pereda was confirmed beyond doubt in the Madrid exhibition of 1978–79. Pérez Sánchez speculated on that occasion that the picture might be a fragment of a larger, more complex one. Since then, Díaz Padrón (Madrid 1981a) has speculated that the composition may have been inspired by the *memento mori* engravings of Barthel Beham (1502–1540). Although it has suffered extensive damage and restoration in places, the painting is a powerful and eloquent invention that still demonstrates Pereda's phenomenal control of his medium.

The three skulls and the gold-and-silver watch on a red tabletop create a trenchant emblem of the certainty of death. Pereda has arranged the skulls so that they can be seen from several angles. His favorite angle for studying the skull—used in many of his paintings where a single skull symbolizes death or the Passion of Christ—is the view from underneath, where the configuration is extremely complex and challenging from the painterly point of view. The middle skull in this composition is seen from below. As Pérez Sánchez observed, the same skull seen from almost the identical angle is depicted both in Pereda's INFANT CHRIST TRIUMPHANT OVER DEATH in the Parish of Arc-Senans in France, painted about 1640, and in the similar composition of the same subject in the church of Las Maravillas in Madrid (fig. XIV.2) said to date from 1644. This particular skull, in fact, seems to have been a favorite studio prop. Its unique fissures and concavities can be recognized in several of Pereda's major compositions, including the VANITAS in Vienna from around 1634 (Plate 40) and the PENITENT MAGDALEN dated in 1640 which is in the Pushkin Museum in Moscow. Unlike artists of an earlier generation, such as Sánchez Cotán or Van der Hamen, who repeated a single image of a given object in several paintings, Pereda returned time and again to the thing itself, painting it from a slightly different angle and rendering afresh its individual features. With uncanny skill, he manipulates the creamy impasto until its texture as well as its hue imitates the object under scrutiny. In this way he was able to make this tiny painting, which might so easily have been dry sermon in lesser hands, a sensuous image whose moral weight is carried by its physical presence. Even the image of the watch, which conveys so much of the object's rich detail, is executed with a painterly breadth that reveals the artist's roots in the Venetian tradition favored at the Spanish court.

Pérez Sánchez has pointed out that the watch in this painting is similar to one depicted in the large VANITAS in the Uffizi which he attributes to Pereda and assigns a date in the late 1660s. The presence of the watch serves as no more compelling a means of dating this picture, however, than that of the skull, which appears frequently in works of the 1640s. Although it is impossible to be precise, a date in the 1640s would seem to be more appropriate for the Zaragoza VANITAS than one in the 1660s.

PROVENANCE
Don Luis Betegón de la Portilla; donated to the museum in 1908.

EXHIBITIONS
Madrid 1978–79, no. 38; Valladolid 1979, no. 42; Caracas 1981, no. 51; Madrid 1981–82a, no. 47; Madrid 1983–84, no. 67.

BIBLIOGRAPHY
Zaragoza, Museo Provincial, 1929 cat., p. 90, no. 247; Gaya Nuño 1955, p. 791; Montañés Fontela 1957, p. 186 ff.; Hernández Perera 1958, p. 31, pl. 7; Zaragoza, Museo Provincial, 1964 cat., p. 66, no. 43; Gállego 1972, p. 247; Pérez Sánchez 1978, no. 38, ill.; Madrid 1981a, pp. 77–78, no. 47, ill.; Pérez Sánchez 1983, p. 107, no. 67, ill. (image reversed); Angulo and Pérez Sánchez 1983, p. 236–37, no. 161, pl. 210.

Signed and dated on the cask at right; *pereda f. 1650*
Oil on canvas
29½ × 56¼ in. (75 × 143 cm.)
Museu Nacional d'Arte Antiga, Lisbon

PEREDA'S TWO MONUMENTAL STILL LIFES AT Lisbon represent a significant departure from the tradition of still-life painting that existed in Spain in his youth. Developing the brilliant promise of his own youthful works and assimilating the richness and diversity of the European still lifes collected by the aristocracy in Madrid, Pereda brought a new flair and robust spirit to the genre. Although he obviously learned by looking at the art around him, to see the Lisbon paintings merely in terms of their resemblances to others would be a disservice to them and to the history of art, for in their inventiveness and the brilliance of their technique they are unsurpassed.

One of the pair (Plate 42) depicts mostly fruits; the other shows garden vegetables and cooking utensils (fig. XIV.7). Both paintings are characterized by a series of parallel diagonals receding into the depth from right to left. But the compositions are knit together by an overlapping and piling up of forms. The many lines of force suggested by jutting vegetables or shafts of wheat and straw infuse a sense of movement or unrest into each painting. This energetic pulse replaces the noble stasis of the works of Sánchez Cotán and Van der Hamen. That motionless quality of earlier naturalism lent a feeling of certainty to the artists' observations. Indeed, in Van der Hamen's case, the emphatic plasticity of a particular form seemed to endow it with an almost Platonic primacy. Pereda's idea of naturalism is more theatrical. He seeks to flood our senses with tactile allusions and contrasts, but never for a moment do we forget that we are looking at a painting. So vigorously has he worked the surface of the canvas with his brush—that is to say, so much has he drawn attention to himself as virtuoso—that the supremacy of the work

Fig. XIV.8 Antonio de Pereda. STILL LIFE WITH VEGETABLES. Signed, 1651. 108 × 166 cm. Private collection, Finland.

PLATE 42

STILL LIFE WITH FRUITS

Fig. XIV.7   Antonio de Pereda. STILL LIFE WITH VEGETABLES. 74 × 143 cm. Signed, 1651 [?]. Museu Nacional d'Arte Antiga, Lisbon.

of art over the thing it represents is stressed. His technique asserts a baroque *maniera,* or beautiful facture, that has nothing to do with the striving for objectivity of a Sánchez Cotán or a Labrador. It has more in common with a conception of art deriving from Rubens or Pietro da Cortona—a purposeful artificiality that would characterize much painting from the second half of the seventeenth century in Spain.

There has been some confusion in the literature concerning the date of the Lisbon paintings. Cavestany (1936–40) read the date of the painting of fruit (Plate 42) as "1650," even though the upper part of the zero is not completely closed. Pérez Sánchez (1978) read it as "1651." To my way of seeing, the last digit of the date is clearly a zero, since it resembles in no way the "1" with which it begins. The date on the pendant still life has also been read as "1651," though that too is unclear and may also really be "1650."

In 1651 Pereda did another, larger version of the Lisbon STILL LIFE WITH VEGETABLES that is in a private collection in Finland (fig. XIV.8)[1] Although he used many of the same elements and groupings of objects, he freely changed the relative proportions of things and added other objects, such as the painted jar at the right that he used again in the Leningrad still life (fig. XIV.3) in the following year.

PROVENANCE
Queen Carlota Joaquina of Portugal; donated to the museum in 1859.

EXHIBITIONS
Madrid 1978–79, no. 16; Madrid 1983–84, no. 68.

BIBLIOGRAPHY
Cavestany 1936–40, p. 178; Oña Iribarren 1944, p. 92, no. 14; Mayer 1947, p. 457; Lafuente Ferrari 1953, p. 361; Gaya Nuño 1958, p. 268, no. 2181; Kubler and Soria 1959, p. 282; Lisbon, Museu Nacional d'Arte Antiga, 1966 cat., p. 67, no. 273; Bergström 1970, p. 69, fig. 50; Torres Martín 1971, p. 78–79, pl. 64; Angulo 1971, p. 223; Camón Aznar 1978, p. 404; Madrid 1978, no. 16, ill.; Bergström et al. 1979, p. 206, ill.; Angulo and Pérez Sánchez 1983, p. 225, no. 152, pl. 178; Pérez Sánchez 1983, p. 108, no. 68, ill.

NOTE
1. See Stockholm, Nationalmuseum. *Stora Spanska Mästare.* 1959, p. 68, no. 80.

XV. JUAN DE ZURBARÁN

(1620–1649)

Juan de Zurbaran fatic
1640

Some months before Francisco de Zurbarán left Seville in June 1634 to assist in the decoration of the new Buen Retiro Palace in Madrid, he signed his name and the date 1633 on the only still life he is known for certain to have painted.[1] The publication by Mayer in 1924 of that now-famous STILL LIFE WITH LEMONS, ORANGES AND A CUP OF WATER (fig. 24) was the first indication in art historical literature that the great master of the Andalusian Baroque had attempted the lowly genre of the independent still life which his older colleague Francisco Pacheco considered a pastime occasionally indulged in as a tour de force by great painters. Pacheco, who finished writing his *Arte de la pintura* in 1638 although it was not published until 1649, made a point of naming those artists of his time who had excelled at this kind of picture. The only painters he mentioned were from the areas of Toledo and Madrid (Blas de Prado, Juan Sánchez Cotán—before he became a Carthusian—and Juan van der Hamen). He included no painters from his native Seville who were known as specialists in independent still lifes, because, it appears from all the evidence, the new genre was not yet common there.

Because Francisco de Zurbarán's only signed still life is also one of his most powerful works of art, scholars and art lovers have since its discovery tried to attribute to him other still lifes that more or less resemble it. However, almost all of those who have made the effort have underscored the unavoidable fact that none of the still lifes attributed to Zurbarán, such as the STILL LIFE WITH POTTERY JARS (fig. XV.1), quite reaches the level of his performance in the famous work of 1633. STILL LIFE WITH POTTERY JARS in the Prado Museum is the better of two versions of this composition once owned by Francisco Cambó in Barcelona.[2] While the Prado painting presents certain similarities of composition and lighting to the STILL LIFE WITH LEMONS, ORANGES AND A CUP OF WATER, the sense of space is not as lucid and the objects—particularly the metal plates—are not as precisely drawn, nor as subtly and firmly modeled. These differences have led most scholars to a justifiable degree of equivocation regarding the attribution, especially in view of the fact, learned only in 1938, that Zurbarán's son Juan also painted still lifes. In that year a brief notice appeared in *The Burlington Magazine* stating that the recent cleaning of a still life attributed to Francisco de Zurbarán in the Museum of Western Art in Kiev (fig. XV.3) had revealed a signature with the first name of Juan. Since that discovery, several rather speculative studies have been made of the still lifes of Francisco and Juan de Zurbarán,[3] but that body of literature is not a high moment in the history of art. While Juan's personality remains somewhat nebulous on the basis of present knowledge, considerable progress can be made simply by reexamining the documents relating to his life, published in an excellent article by María Luisa Caturla (1957), and by studying the few signed paintings that have been discovered, one of which had not been recognized until now. The personality that emerges is surprisingly rich and deserves to be reconsidered independent of his father and of the interpretive clichés that have prevented many critics from looking afresh at the still lifes of either man.

Juan was Zurbarán's son by his first marriage, to María Páez, and was born on June 23, 1620 in the city of Llerena.[4] In 1623 or 1624, the boy's mother died, and in 1625 his father married Doña Beatriz de Morales, a well-to-do widow thirteen years his senior. The family lived in her large townhouse in the same city. In 1629, at the invitation of the City Council of Seville, Zurbarán moved to the cosmopolitan capital of Andalucía with his wife and three children by his first marriage. The family lived in fairly affluent circumstances, employing eight servants to run their household. With his career thriving, the elder Zurbarán was a respected member of the community. Juan was instructed in the art of painting by his father and by 1639, the year of his stepmother's death, he had become an accomplished painter. On August 18, 1641, the young artist married Mariana de Quadros, a native of Seville and the daughter of Jorge de Quadros, who appears to have been a wealthy money lender who provided his daughter with a handsome dowry valued at 50,000 *reales*.[5] The dowry contract is signed by both Juan and his father, who served as a witness. It is interesting to note that the son signed the document "Don Juan de Zurbaran Salazar," while underneath his father signed simply "Francisco de Zurbaran Salazar."[6] Juan's consistent use of the aristocratic "Don" in referring to himself was a pretention of high social standing completely uncharacteristic of his father, and may have been encouraged by the example of Doña Beatriz de Morales. In September 1642, Juan's first child was born and was baptized with the grand name of Francisco Máximo.[7] In January 1644, a daughter, Antonia, was born.[8]

Juan obviously moved in fairly elegant circles. A curious insight into his personality is provided by a sonnet he wrote and dedicated to Juan de Esquivel Navarro. The poem precedes the published text of Navarro's *Discursos sobre el arte del danzado,* a small treatise published in Seville in 1642 dealing with the courtly art

Fig. XV.1 Francisco de Zurbarán. STILL LIFE WITH POTTERY JARS. 46 × 84 cm. Museo del Prado, Madrid.

Fig. XV.2 Juan de Zurbarán. PLATE OF GRAPES. 28 × 36 cm. Signed, 1639. Lung Collection, Bordeaux.

of the dance. Printed at the end of the book is a list of nine disciples of José Rodríguez Tirado, *"maestro de Dançar";* among them is "Don Juan de Zurbarán, son of Francisco Zurbarán the great painter."[9] Juan's poem is faddishly elegant and rather bad. As Caturla has noted, these clues lead to the inevitable conclusion that the young man was what might have been called a dandy in another age.

In January 1644, Juan served as a witness to his father's third marriage.[10] In the document, he states that he is a painter and lives in the parish of Santa Cruz. According to Caturla, he had moved into his father-in-law's house upon marrying. On April 2nd of the same year, Juan signed a contract for two paintings depicting miracles of Our Lady of the Rosary for the Brotherhood of the Rosary in the town of Carmona.[11] No doubt given a traditional education in painting by his father, his practice must have been predicated to a great extent on painting traditional kinds of pictures. Nevertheless, there is reason to believe that he was one of the first Sevillian painters to specialize to some extent in the painting of still lifes. Since his father was still the dominant painter with ecclesiastical clients, perhaps the still life, which may have just been becoming fashionable among collectors in Seville, was one area in which he could achieve professional independence.

At the age of twenty-nine, after a career that had lasted for only a decade, Juan de Zurbarán succumbed on June 8, 1649 to the catastrophic epidemic of bubonic plague that exterminated two-thirds of the population of Seville. His death certificate gives his name and describes him merely as "the son-in-law of Jorge de Quadros."[12] Caturla searched in vain for his testament and inventory in the notarial archives, but such customary legal details were often disregarded in times of crisis.

Only three signed paintings by Juan de Zurbarán, all of them still lifes, are known today. Despite what one often reads in the literature, they are quite unlike the still life his father signed in 1633. The exhibition in Bordeaux in 1955 of a small copper panel depicting a silver plate of grapes, signed and dated 1639, was a revela-

Fig. XV.3   Juan de Zurbarán. STILL LIFE WITH CHOCOLATE SERVICE. 48 × 75 cm. Signed, 1640. Museum of Western and Oriental Art, Kiev.

Fig. XV.3, detail   STILL LIFE WITH CHOCOLATE SERVICE

tion (fig. XV.2). Although Juan van der Hamen had painted single plates of fruit in the 1620s, Juan's technique in this small painting is as different from his as it is from his own father's. Pérez Sánchez (1983) remarked that to his eye, the earthy, sensuous character of the subject matter is underscored in the manner of the Dutch painters. This particular work, however, also resembles in a general way such Italian still lifes as the COMPOTE OF GRAPES AND PEACHES signed by the Cremonese artist Panfilo Nuvolone in 1620.[13] In young Zurbarán's painting, the attentive observation of detail in the fruit and its reflection in the flange of the silver plate is paralleled by the great pains the artist took to particularize the cracks and chips in the edge of the stone ledge on which the plate rests. This focus on accidental details was quite alien to his father's sensibility.

The following year, at the age of twenty, he painted the remarkable Kiev still life depicting a chocolate service (fig. XV.3, detail) which bears no resemblance in its subject matter, composition or execution to the signed still life by the artist's father. The setting is exceedingly dark. The bright light that gives relief to the forms neither penetrates the shadows nor defines a lucid space, as in Francisco's STILL LIFE WITH LEMONS, ORANGES AND A CUP OF WATER. The objects in the Kiev still life emerge from the darkness in a grouping that seems intuitively balanced. The forms overlap one another, achieving a cohesive overall design that gives the artist an opportunity to study the reflections and sensuous surface characteristics of a variety of patterns and materials. He does so with short, decisive strokes of a rather stiff brush that leave the surface of the pigment richly textured. Highlights on the porcelain cups and the pitchers are indicated by single, bold strokes of heavy, white impasto. This is the work of a thoroughly accomplished and original artist.

Other still lifes of this type have been attributed to Juan de Zurbarán, but most are merely imitations of his style. A painting in the Bertrán y Güell Collection, Barcelona (formerly that of José Bertrán y Musitu), repeats most of the same ob-

Fig. XV.4   Imitator of Juan de Zurbarán.
STILL LIFE WITH CHOCOLATE MILL. 46 × 84 cm.
Bertrán y Güell Collection, Barcelona.

Fig. XV.5   Imitator of Juan de Zurbarán.
STILL LIFE WITH CHOCOLATE SERVICE. 51 × 74
cm. Musée des Beaux-Arts, Besançon.

jects—the chocolate mill, the silver pitcher, the wooden box and spoon, the silver plate and inlaid egg, the colorful napkin (fig. XV.4).[14] While the composition is conceived in a similar fashion, the execution of the painting is dry and poor by comparison to the Kiev canvas. The explanation of these differences cannot be found in a different date of execution, but only in a different hand. That Juan de Zurbarán could have had imitators (even some in his own employ) so early in his career is not at all inconsistent with what we know of him. The STILL LIFE WITH CHOCOLATE SERVICE in the Musée des Beaux-Arts, Besançon (fig. XV.5) has long been attributed tentatively to Juan de Zurbarán. Its quality, though, on a par with the Barcelona painting, is far below the level achieved by the artist in the Kiev still life.

A beautiful still life depicting a meat pie and a white napkin (fig. XV.6, detail) in the collection of Javier Serra in Madrid was attributed to Francisco de Zurbarán by Soria (1955), but to his son by Pemán (1958). The extremely dramatic chiaroscuro and the sensuous detail of the pastry and glassware strongly support the attribution to Juan.

The well-known still life in the Thyssen-Bornemisza Collection in Lugano-Castagnola (fig. XV.7, detail) has been wrongly attributed to Van der Hamen by Sterling (1952) and Soria (1959). Pemán, pointing out that the composition somewhat resembles that of the Kiev still life, tentatively attributed the painting to Juan de Zurbarán. While certain similarities do exist, the execution of the painting is completely different from Juan's style as seen in the Kiev painting. The unknown hand that painted the Thyssen still life had a much lighter touch; its definition of forms lies very much on the surface. Both the Thyssen painting and the Serra one, for example, depict glass bowls, but the glass seems much denser in the latter, and the highlights more decisively indicated.

Having now achieved some small sense that we can differentiate the styles of

Fig. XV.6 Attributed to Juan de Zurbarán. STILL LIFE WITH NAPKIN AND MEATPIE. 60×79 cm. Javier Serra Collection, Madrid.

Fig. XV. 6, detail STILL LIFE WITH NAPKIN AND MEATPIE

Francisco and Juan de Zurbarán, we return to the perplexing STILL LIFE WITH POTTERY JARS in the Prado (fig. XV.1) to see if any of the features we have come to recognize in Juan's style are present in it. Certainly the composition, reminiscent of Van der Hamen (fig. VI. 13), has no parallel among the signed works of Juan. The weakness in the realization of the metal plates also remains a problem, as these are inferior to the plate in either the Bordeaux PLATE OF GRAPES or in the Kiev work. In 1955 Soria adopted the position that both the Prado and the Barcelona versions of this composition could be copies of a lost original by Francisco. In the present state of our knowledge that theory remains a possibility. Nevertheless, one should also hold open the more likely possibility that the Prado still life is a late painting by Francisco dating from after his move to Madrid in 1658, a period when his drawing of such still-life details and his sense of space definitely lacked the precision of the 1630s.[15]

A related problem is presented by a still life depicting a basket of fruit, some peppers, a cucumber, a silver gilt cup and salver and a red pottery jar, which appeared on the London art market in 1976 with an attribution to Francisco de Zurbarán (fig. XV.8).[16] This painting lacks the quality and purity of design of the elder Zurbarán's signed still life of 1633, but it reveals certain parallels of composition and execution to the Prado painting. Perhaps the resolution of its attribution to Zurbarán also hinges upon its date which may be later by far than previously thought.

The two signed paintings by Juan de Zurbarán that have been known until now probably date from the very beginning of his career. Here, for the first time, we are able to study another signed canvas (Plate 43), dated 1645. This surprising and important painting considerably enlarges our view of the artist's style and allows us to attribute to him with more or less certainty two famous still lifes that have long been associated with the Sevillian School (Plates 44 and 46). On the basis of the

Fig. XV.7 Unknown artist. STILL LIFE WITH SWEETS AND POTTERY. 77 × 100 cm. Thyssen-Bornemisza Collection, Lugano-Castagnola.

Fig. XV 7, detail STILL LIFE WITH SWEETS AND POTTERY

works that can now be identified as his, Juan emerges as a major still-life painter who practiced a style totally distinct from his father's. If we assume that his father tried his hand at the still life in the same spirit that Pacheco described—as a challenge to his ability and as an exception to his accustomed practice—then it appears that Juan was among the first Sevillian artists to make a specialty of the genre. His untimely death cut short what definitely promised to be a career of major import in the history of still-life painting in Spain.

NOTES

1. See Introduction for further discussion of this painting and its place in Zurbarán's oeuvre.

2. Sr. Cambó gave one of the paintings to the Museo del Prado. The other, now belonging to the Museo de Barcelona, is exhibited with the Cambó Collection in the Palau de la Virreina in Barcelona.

3. Seckel 1946; Pemán 1958; Soria 1959.

4. Caturla 1947.

5. Caturla 1957, pp. 271–80.

6. Caturla 1957, pp. 280–81. The name Salazar from the family's past was occasionally used by Francisco from 1622 and was adopted by both Juan and his sister Paula.

7. Caturla 1957, pp. 282–83.

8. *Ibid*.

Fig. XV.8   Attributed to Francisco de Zurbarán. FRUIT IN A BASKET, VEGETABLES AND UTENSILS ON A TABLE. 47×74.3 cm. Kredisin Foundation, Vaduz.

9. Caturla 1957, p. 270: *"Don Juan de çurbaran, hijo de Francisco çurbaran el gran pintor."*

10. Montoto 1920.

11. Unpublished document discovered by Celestino López Martínez, cited by Caturla, *op. cit.,* pp. 280–81.

12. Caturla 1957, p. 283. Pemán interprets this, without sufficient grounds, to mean that Juan was estranged from his father at the time of his death, and his unsubstantiated claim has been repeated by others.

13. See Spike 1983, p. 33, fig. 7. That such paintings were sent to Spain is documented by the presence of one in the collection of the Marquis of Leganés in Madrid in 1655. See López Navio 1962, p. 315, no. 1115.

14. I am grateful to the owner for permitting me to study the painting.

15. An ANNUNCIATION TO THE VIRGIN, plausibly attributed to this period of Zurbarán's activity by Gudiol (Gállego and Gudiol 1977, cat. no. 530, fig. 470), depicts exactly the same white vase.

16. Eric Young, *In the Light of Caravaggio,* Trafalgar Galleries, London, 1976, no. 10; *Trafalgar Galleries at The Royal Academy II,* 1979, pp. 62–67, no. 27.

BIBLIOGRAPHY
Montoto 1920, p. 400; Cavestany 1936–40, p. 77; Ghilarov 1938, p. 190; Seckel 1946, pp. 289–91, and appendix 1947, p. 62, nos. 8–10; Caturla 1947, p. 280; Soria 1955, pp. 25–26; Bordeaux 1955, p. 54, no. 93 bis; Ainaud 1955, p. 116; Caturla 1957, pp. 270–86; Pemán 1958, pp. 193–211; Soria 1959, pp. 273–80; Pemán 1959, pp. 319–20; Guinard 1960, p. 282; Madrid 1964, pp. 83–91; Gállego and Gudiol 1977, pp. 16–19, 50, 68–69, 127, 294; Madrid 1983, p. 77.

43. STILL LIFE WITH BASKET OF FRUIT AND CARDOON

Signed and dated lower left (the first two letters are interlaced): *DJuan de Zurbaran, faciebat / 1645* (last digit indistinct)

Oil on canvas

29 5/16 × 41 3/4 in. (74.5 × 106 cm.)

The Gösta Serlachius Fine Arts Foundation, Mänttä, Finland

RECOGNITION OF THIS PAINTING AS A WORK by Juan de Zurbarán is an overdue and important step in the advancement of knowledge about Spanish still-life painting. Due to the Italianate qualities of the painting, the few scholars who were aware of its existence ignored its perfectly genuine signature. When STILL LIFE WITH BASKET OF FRUIT AND CARDOON was purchased in Stockholm in 1938, its signature was legible. In that same year, the Kiev STILL LIFE WITH CHOCOLATE SERVICE (fig. XV.3) was discovered to be signed by Juan de Zurbarán and for the first time it was learned that the artist had painted still lifes. A facsimile of the signature on the Russian canvas was not published, however, until twenty years later by César Pemán. While the signature on the STILL LIFE WITH BASKET OF FRUIT AND CARDOON (fig. XV.9) shares many features in common with those on the Kiev picture and the PLATE OF GRAPES in Bordeaux (fig. XV.2), which was not published until 1955, it is not imitative of either one and could not possibly have been concocted by a forger in 1938.

Because the painting does not conform to the prevailing idea of how Juan de Zurbarán painted, the signature was assumed to be false and the painting was attributed by members of the staff of the Nationalmuseum in Stockholm to the Neapolitan painter Giovanni Battista Ruoppolo (1629–1693). In an exchange of letters between the owner of the painting and the late Raffaello Causa in 1958, the noted Neapolitan art historian expressed the view that the painting was by Luca Forte (active c. 1625–1655). In 1964 Causa included the still life in the exhibition *La*

natura morta italiana, which he organized at the Palazzo Reale in Naples and which also traveled to Zurich and Rotterdam. By that point, he had rejected the attribution to Luca Forte and proposed that it had been painted by Michelangelo da Campidoglio (1610–1670), by whom no signed still lifes are known to have survived. Causa failed to mention in his catalogue entry, if only to dispute it, that the painting bears an inscription with the name of Juan de Zurbarán and a date in the 1640s.

Recognition of Neapolitan qualities in this still life is not only understandable but necessary. The extremely dark shadows from which the sensuous forms emerge could only have been inspired by the followers of Caravaggio. Causa's analogy to the works of Luca Forte is understandable in terms of this use of light and shadow.[1] But the technique with which the painting is executed is quite different from Forte's polished surfaces (fig. XV. 10). The pigment is rather thickly applied and bears the marks of repeated, tiny brush strokes with which the artist had worked the surface. Highlights, such as those on the apple and the pomegranate in the basket, are indicated by thick strokes of white impasto, in the same manner as in the Kiev painting (fig. XV.3, detail). In the BASKET OF APPLES AND QUINCES (Plate 44), the identical way of painting fruit and the same use of light and shadow is found in a painting whose national origin has never been questioned.

In view of two incontrovertible facts about this picture—that its signature is genuine and that it is strongly influenced by Neapolitan painting—we must be willing to revise the traditional way of thinking about Juan de Zurbarán. It is evident in examining his other signed still lifes that he was not a servile follower of his father's style. His interest in modish or fashionable things may have attracted him to a more "modern" style than his father's. Trade and cultural ties between Seville and Naples—two major cities of the

Oil on canvas

28⅜ × 41⅜ in. (72 × 105 cm.)

Museo de Arte de Cataluña, Barcelona

This monumental composition has puzzled scholars for years and has been attributed to various artists who worked in Andalucía. None of the attributions given it, however, has been convincing, and it was exhibited as by an anonymous Sevillian artist in the still-life exhibition in Madrid during 1983–84.

Soria (1959) related the painting to the work of Pedro de Camprobín because of the painting's resemblance to Pears in a China Bowl (Plate 46) in the Art Institute of Chicago, which at the time he believed was by Camprobín. While the observation that the two paintings are quite similar was a valid one, the style of Camprobín as we now understand it shares none of the dramatic naturalism of either picture.

Soria also suggested that the painting might be by the Sevillian artist Pedro de Medina (c. 1620–after 1682). This hypothesis was based on comparison to a large, signed still life dated in 1682 containing a great china fruit bowl surrounded by plates of other fruits, with a landscape vista in the background. That painting, whose whereabouts have been unknown for years, was reproduced in a bad photograph by Cavestany (1936–40). Judging from the reproduction, there is nothing about its complex composition that bears any relation to the simple grandeur of Basket of Apples and Quinces. I have recently seen a signed painting by Pedro de Medina in a private collection in Madrid and can attest that its much looser execution shares little in common with the intense naturalism of this painting.

The breakthrough in attributing Basket of Apples and Quinces comes in the discovery of the signed Still Life with

Fig. XV.9 Detail of signature, Still Life with Basket of Fruit and Cardoon

Spanish Empire—were not uncommon or difficult. This painting shows the broadening influence of such cross-cultural exchange.

Provenance
Purchased by Mr. Gösta Serlachius from the dealer Louis Richter, Stockholm, in 1938.

Exhibitions
Naples 1964, no. 132; Mänttä 1984, no. 169.

Bibliography
Naples 1964, pp. 67–68, pl. 59b.

Note
1. It is important to note that still lifes by the Neapolitan artist Luca Forte were already in at least one important Madrilenian collection by the 1640s. Upon the death in 1647 of Juan Alfonso Enríquez de Cabrera, IX Admiral of Castile and V Duke of Medina de Rioseco, two still lifes by Forte were recorded in his collection as follows: *"65. Un cuadro de cestas de ubas, y otras, sin marco, de mano de Lucas Fuerte . . .220 reales;"* and *"142. Un cuadro de zidras, naranjas y flores, de mano de Lucas Fuerte, con marco dorado . . . 600 reales."* See Fernández Duro 1903, pp. 191, 193. The Admiral of Castile had been Viceroy of Naples from 1644 to 1646. That such paintings were also in the collections of noble Sevillians is not unlikely.

PLATE 43

STILL LIFE WITH BASKET OF FRUIT AND CARDOON

PLATE 44

BASKET OF APPLES AND QUINCES

Fig. XV. 10   Luca Forte. STILL LIFE WITH BIRD. 79 × 104.5 cm. Ringling Museum of Art, Sarasota.

BASKET OF FRUIT AND CARDOON by Juan de Zurbarán (Plate 43). Although the compositions of the two paintings differ in details, they are similarly conceived in the broadest terms and are executed with an identical technique. The strong light and very dark shadows in both paintings lend an emphatic plasticity to the fruit. The modeling of the quinces at the lower left of each composition could not be more similar. There is a striking congruity in the definition of the pomegranates and in the way the light reflects off the surface of the leaves. Finally, the ledges and the backgrounds are treated in a very similar way that has none of the geometric clarity one would expect from Francisco de Zurbarán or from Van der Hamen. Over-all, both paintings share an earthy vision of reality that relates to other signed paintings by Juan de Zurbarán and gives us a new insight into the art of Seville in the 1640s.

PROVENANCE
Colección Gil, Barcelona; donated to the Museo de Arte de Cataluña in 1944.

EXHIBITION
Madrid 1983–84, no. 65.

BIBLIOGRAPHY
Soria 1959, p. 279, pl. 4; Torres Martín 1971, p. 99, ill. 12; Madrid 1983, p. 91, ill.

XVI. PERSISTENT PROBLEMS OF ATTRIBUTION

Fifty years after the historic exhibition of still lifes held in Madrid in 1935, we can look back at five decades of steady progress in coming to understand the role of still-life painting in Spanish art and in recognizing the styles of individual artists. Despite that progress, however, several great paintings remain misattributed or have completely eluded convincing attribution. Two of those—the beautiful PEARS IN A CHINA BOWL from Chicago and the powerful BODEGÓN KEEPER from Amsterdam—are discussed in the following pages. Recognizing the pitfalls which these two works have historically presented those seeking to attribute them, I do not pretend to have found the ultimate solution to the problems. Nevertheless, I have put forth some new approaches in the interest of advancing the discussion.

Oil on canvas
39⅜ × 48¹⁄₁₆ in. (100 × 122 cm.)
The Rijksmuseum, Amsterdam

THE ATTRIBUTION OF THIS EXTRAORDINARY *bodegón* has been one of the most persistent problems of connoisseurship in the field of Spanish painting. During the nineteenth century, it was considered to be a work by Velázquez, but in his monograph on that master (1908), Walter Gensel rejected the traditional attribution without suggesting an alternative. August L. Mayer (1915, 1922) regarded the painting as a work by Sánchez Cotán. In his 1925 monograph on Velázquez, Allende-Salazar rejected Mayer's attribution but underscored the painting's "Castilian" qualities. He was the first to perceive a resemblance to THE POULTRY VENDOR (Plate 11) painted by Alejandro de Loarte in 1626. In his 1934 article on Loarte, Méndez Casal took up Allende-Salazar's idea and attributed the painting to Loarte, but used the attribution to argue his theory that the artist had been trained alongside Velázquez in the studio of Pacheco in Seville. In 1935 the painting was exhibited as a work by Loarte in the Madrid exhibition *Floreros y bodegones en la pintura española*. Later that year Lafuente Ferrari, who had had the opportunity to compare the picture in the exhibition directly to the signed Loarte of 1626, concluded that the Amsterdam painting is by an artist superior to Loarte. He noted in particular the rich and skillful handling of impasto. In the definitive catalogue of the Madrid exhibition (1936–40), Cavestany reviewed the various attributions but maintained "without reservation" the one to Loarte. Since then, that attribution has largely prevailed, although not without reservations. In 1971, however, Angulo rejected the attribution to Loarte, and in 1972 he and Pérez Sánchez did not even mention the painting in their thorough study of the artist.

In 1959 Martin Soria attributed the painting, which he called THE COOK, to Juan van der Hamen. The work's exceptional sensuality and disorderly composition, however, are completely alien to what we know of Van der Hamen's style (see Chapter VI). A photograph of a lost *bodegón* with two figures signed by Van der Hamen (fig. VI.15) proves that he did paint such pictures, but that painting's composition is quite different from this one. If the Van der Hamen painting is located one day, perhaps a more meaningful comparison can be made, but the indications at present do not at all favor Soria's attribution. A few scholars, such as Haraszti (1983), continue to ascribe the painting to Loarte, but Bergström et al. (1979) caption it simply "Unknown Seventeenth-Century Painter."

As we have seen in examining Loarte's THE POULTRY VENDOR (Plate 11), which was painted in the year of his death and must therefore represent his most mature development, his manner of painting human figures and drapery was rather dry. Completely absent was the kind of rich modeling with light and shadow that we see in the animated face of the *bodegón* keeper in this painting. Loarte's crowded composition with its outdoor setting also seems more old fashioned and derivative of Italian models than the intimate presence of this man and the objects around him in THE BODEGÓN KEEPER. The objects are simply laid out on the countertop so that each one can be studied by the painter individually, instead of being arranged with the kind of studied artifice that one would expect to find in a composition by Van der Hamen. Uncommon skill is shown in the definition of a variety of textures—feathers, fish scales, meat, pottery, cheese, pastry, melon, coins, playing cards, human flesh, hair and cloth. The artist has not spared paint in his effort to define those textures. Especially in the light areas—the scales of the fish and the joint of meat—the impasto is heavy. In his definition of form, he has also achieved a remarkable sense of the solidity of matter, as in the two fish near the center, whose very weight we can almost gauge in our minds. The painter has turned the large ham hanging from overhead at the right, so that the visually more interesting, inner side of the joint shows. This calls to mind Pereda's way of turning a human skull upside down to emphasize the sensuous nature of the object and to confront the more difficult painterly challenge (Plate 41).

Obviously, the reason that the painter has been so difficult to identify is that he must not have painted many pictures like this one. Indeed, no one has ever been able to point to another picture that is truly comparable. We must assume that the painter was somewhat younger than Loarte, because his painterly style is much more advanced. From the style of the *bodegón* keeper's costume, the painting seems to date from around 1630, a date also compatible with the picture's naturalism. From the painting's extremely high level of quality, we can assume that its maker was among the most gifted painters of his generation.

On the basis of these qualifications, I do not think it unreasonable to suggest, though tentatively, that the young Antonio de Pereda is its author. We recall that Díaz del Valle (1657) wrote that, by the time Pereda had reached the age of eighteen (1629), his paintings "seemed as though by a very experienced artist" (see Chapter XIV). His skill at painting objects was demonstrated to be exceptional by 1634 or thereabouts, when he painted WALNUTS (Plate 39) and the VANITAS in Vienna (Plate 40). His later still lifes, such as those in Lisbon (Plate 42) display the virtuosic command of impasto technique that had always characterized his work. Although no signed paintings of exactly comparable subject matter are known, a signed still life in the collection of the Dukes of Sueca (exhibited in Madrid in 1935 as cat. no. 22), which I know only from a reproduction, depicts a melon

PLATE 45

THE BODEGÓN KEEPER

similarly tied with a cord and some game birds.

This painting also presents certain elements similar to the Vienna VANITAS. In the midst of a profusion of objects and symbols, such as the coins and playing cards which may allude to the theme of Gluttony,[1] the central figure holds a bowl of wine with both hands and confronts the viewer directly. In this way, he seems to be calling attention to the moral content of the painting. Similarly, the angel in the Vienna VANITAS points to the globe, holds the cameo of the Emperor Charles V and gazes out at us, thereby endowing every object in the picture with a sense of moral significance. The coins and playing cards in the two paintings offer a striking parallel, as do the foreshortened hands in both pictures. The right hand of the *bodegón* keeper holding the bowl shows the artist's willingness to tackle a rather difficult drawing problem, as does the depiction of the angel's left hand holding the cameo. Thus it seems possible that THE BODEGÓN KEEPER could be an early work of Pereda, one which predates the VANITAS in Vienna and reflects the artist's early interest in still-life painting and its potential as a moral force. We cannot prove that at present, so it is probably best to present the suggestion as a tentative one in the long tradition of dispute that has been associated with this great painting.

PROVENANCE
Sir J. C. Robinson Collection, London; Charles Newton Robinson Collection, London; Robinson Sale, Berlin (Lepke), March 31, 1914, no. 23; Charles Sedelmeyer, Paris, 1922; donated to the Rijksmuseum by members of the Rembrandt Society, 1922.

EXHIBITIONS
Madrid 1935, no. 15; Bordeaux 1955, no. 33; Rome 1956–57, no. 188.

BIBLIOGRAPHY
Robinson 1906, pp. 178–83, ill.; Gensel 1908, p. 168, ill.; Calvert 1908, p. 182, pl. 6; Mayer 1915, p. 124, ill.; Mayer 1922, p. 362, fig. 268; Allende-Salazar 1925, p. 287, pl. 255; Méndez Casal 1934, p. 194, pl. 8; Lafuente Ferrari 1935, p. 175; Cavestany 1936–40, pp. 151–52, no. 15, pl. 25; Grassi 1942, pp. 180–81; Mayer 1947, pp. 246, 298; Amsterdam, Rijksmuseum 1951 cat., p. 105, no. 1478; Bordeaux 1955, p. 22, no. 33; Ainaud 1955, p. 116, fig. 8; Rome 1956, p. 171, no. 188; Gaya Nuño 1958, p. 219, no. 1574; Kubler and Soria 1959, p. 235, pl. 122B; Camón Aznar 1963, p. 285; Camón Aznar 1964, p. 322; Jordan 1967, vol. 1, pp. 77, fig. 44; Vliegenthart 1968, no. 25, ill.; Angulo 1971, p. 24; Torres Martín 1971, p. 50; Amsterdam, Rijksmuseum 1976 cat., p. 351; Camón Aznar 1978, p. 208; Bergström et al. 1979, p. 141, pl. 132; Haraszti 1983, pp. 91–92, 175, no. 49, ill.

NOTES
1. Barry Wind (in press) has suggested that the painting represents the theme of Gluttony.

Oil on canvas
33½ × 42¾ in. (82.6 × 108.6 cm.)
The Art Institute of Chicago, Wirt D. Walker Fund

THIS NOBLE STILL LIFE IS ONE OF THE MOST beautiful executed in Spain during the seventeenth century. Throughout much of its recorded history it was attributed to Francisco de Zurbarán, but in the 1950s, general acceptance of that traditional attribution began to dissipate. For the last thirty years the painting has represented a perplexing problem to students of the subject. While we cannot definitively solve the problem here, reconsideration of this great still life in the light of a fuller understanding of Juan de Zurbarán and the exhibition of it side by side with his signed STILL LIFE WITH BASKET OF FRUIT AND CARDOON (Plate 43) may lead to the comfortable acceptance that he was probably its author.

The first doubt about the attribution of this painting came as a result of Sterling's assertion (1952) that he failed to see in it the monumentality of Francisco de Zurbarán's signed STILL LIFE WITH LEMONS, ORANGES AND A CUP OF WATER (fig. 24). In 1958 Pemán unconvincingly speculated that the painting was possibly a joint effort by both Francisco and Juan de Zurbarán, with the father responsible for the best features of the painting. In 1959 Soria reprinted in the article cited below a brief discussion of the Chicago picture that he had published on July 15, 1958 in the *Christian Science Monitor,* in which he abandoned his attribution of the painting to Francisco de Zurbarán (1944, 1955) and laid out his reasons for reattributing it to Pedro de Camprobín. In so doing, he noted the similarity of the picture to the Barcelona BASKET OF APPLES AND QUINCES (Plate 44). While that observation is quite valid, neither picture shares the delicate, airy style of Camprobín as we now understand it.

The Chicago still life resembles the

Barcelona BASKET OF APPLES AND QUINCES inasmuch as both depict large containers of fruit in a very naturalistic manner. The more central placement of the bowl in the Chicago painting is further accentuated by the objects being raised on a low block of the same gray material as the main shelf. The treatment of the light falling on the gray shelf is somewhat different from that in either the signed still life by Juan de Zurbarán (Plate 43) or the Barcelona example (Plate 44). In the Chicago picture, the light illuminates most brightly the horizontal planes of the supports, while the vertical planes remain in shadow.

The most striking similarity between the Chicago painting and the others attributed to Juan de Zurbarán is the way in which the richly colored fruit is modeled with tiny, concentrated brush strokes. The branch of quinces stuck into the arrangement of pears at the upper left is especially close in its almost Neapolitan chiaroscuro to the way in which that fruit and its foliage are painted in both the Barcelona and Finnish paintings. The radial effect of the composition, a quality noticed by Sterling (1952), with elements thrusting away from the center, is a feature that all three paintings have in common.

In 1977 a smaller version of this composition was called to my attention (fig. XVI. 1). It repeats fairly closely the design of the larger version, but it is painted on a copper plate. Juan de Zurbarán's earliest dated painting, PLATE OF GRAPES (fig. XV.2), was likewise painted on this support, one uncommon among Spanish still-life painters. While this may be of only coincidental interest, it nevertheless tightens the web of suspicion that this enigmatic Sevillian master may have been responsible for the splendid PEARS IN A CHINA BOWL.

Fig. XVI.1 Juan de Zurbarán. (?) PEARS IN A CHINA BOWL (replica). Copper, 60 × 43 cm. Private collection.

PROVENANCE
José de Madrazo, Madrid, 1856; Marquis of Salamanca, Madrid, 1883; Countess of Montarco, Madrid, 1905; Knoedler and Co., New York, 1935; Joseph Brummer, New York, 1944–46; acquired by The Art Institute of Chicago in 1947.

EXHIBITIONS
Madrid 1905, no. 48; New York 1955, no. 21; Milwaukee/Cincinnati 1956, no. 59; Baltimore 1961; Philadelphia 1963; Newark 1964–65, no. 39.

BIBLIOGRAPHY
Blas de la Vega 1905, p. 302; Cascales 1911, p. 93; Kehrer 1918, p. 147; Soria 1944a, p. 129, fig. 2; Soria 1944b, p. 164; Seckel 1946, pp. 288–89, fig. 8; Malone 1948, p. 17, ill.; Soria 1955, pp. 19, 24, 177, 191, no. 178, fig. 124; Pemán 1958, pp. 201–02, pl. 4; Gaya Nuño 1958, p. 343, no. 3102; Soria 1959, pp. 278–79, pl. 1; Sterling 1959, p. 143, note 154; Guinard 1960, p. 281, no. 602; Chicago, Art Institute, 1961 cat., p. 490, ill. p. 97; Torres Martín 1963, p. 86, no. 114; Torres Martín 1971, p. 69; Gregori and Frati 1973, p. 117, no. 567.

PLATE 46

PEARS IN A CHINA BOWL

BIBLIOGRAPHY

AEA	Archivo Español de Arte
AEAyA	Archivo Español de Arte y Arqueología
AGS	Archivo General de Simancas
AGS TMC	Tribunal Mayor de Cuentas
AHN	Archivo Histórico Nacional, Madrid
AHP M	Archivo Histórico de Protocolos, Madrid
AHP T	Archivo Histórico de Protocolos, Toledo
BM	Burlington Magazine
BSEE	Boletín de la Sociedad Española de Excursiones
GBA	Gazette des Beaux-Arts
leg.	legato
P#	protocolo number

Agueda 1982
Mercedes Agueda. "La colección de pinturas del Infante Don Sebastián Gabriel." *Boletín del Museo del Prado*, vol. 3, no. 8 (1982), pp. 102–17.

Agulló 1978
Mercedes Agulló y Cobo. *Noticias sobre pintores madrileños de los siglos XVI y XVII.* Granada, 1978.

Agulló 1981
_____ . *Mas noticias sobre pintores madrileños de los siglos XVI al XVIII.* Madrid, 1981.

Agulló and Péréz Sánchez 1981
_____ and Péréz Sánchez. "Francisco de Burgos Mantilla." *Boletín Seminario de Estudios de Arte y Arqueología: Universidad de Valladolid* (1981), pp. 359–82.

Ainaud 1955
Juan Ainaud de Lasarte. "Pintura española del siglo de oro, en Burdeos." *Goya*, no. 8 (1955), pp. 115–19.

Allende-Salazar 1925
Juan Allende-Salazar. *Velázquez.* Stuttgart, 1925.

Álvarez y Baena 1789–91
J. A. Álvarez y Baena. *Hijos de Madrid, ilustres en santidad, dignidades, armas, ciencias y artes.* 4 vols. Madrid, 1789–91.

Amsterdam, Rijksmuseum, 1951 cat.
Amsterdam, Rijksmuseum. *Catalogus van de Tentoongestelde.* 1951.

Amsterdam, Rijksmuseum, 1976 cat.
_____ . *All the Paintings of the Rijksmuseum in Amsterdam.* 1976. Catalogue by Pieter van Thiel et al.

Andrews 1947
See San Diego, Fine Arts Gallery, 1947 cat.

Angulo 1947
Diego Angulo Iñiguez. "Obras juveniles de Sánchez Cotán." *AEA*, no. 77 (1947), p. 146–47.

Angulo 1948
_____ . "Las Hilanderas: Sobre la iconografía de Aragne." *AEA*, vol. 21 (1948), pp. 1–19.

Angulo 1971
_____ . *Pintura del siglo XVII.* Ars Hispaniae, vol. 15. Madrid, 1971.

Angulo 1978
_____ . "La exposición del centenario de D. Antonio de Pereda (1611–1678)." *AEA*, vol. 51 (1978), pp. 271–74.

Angulo and Pérez Sánchez 1972
_____ and Pérez Sánchez. *Historia de la pintura española: Escuela toledana de la primera mitad del siglo XVII.* Madrid, 1972.

Angulo and Pérez Sánchez 1983
_____ . *Historia de la pintura española: Escuela madrileña del segundo tercio del siglo XVII.* Madrid, 1983.

Armstrong 1896
Walter Armstrong. *The Life of Velázquez.* London, 1896.

Art Journal 1972
"College Museum Notes: Acquisitions." *Art Journal*, vol. 32 (1972), pp. 42–43.

Art Quarterly 1956
"Accessions of American and Canadian Museums." *Art Quarterly*, vol. 19 (1956), p. 73.

Asturias and Bardi 1969
Miguel Angel Asturias and P. M. Bardi. *L'opera completa di Velázquez.* Milan, 1969.

Azcárate 1970
José María Azcárate. "Algunas noticias sobre pintores cortesanos del siglo XVII." *Anales del Instituto de Estudios Madrileños*, vol. 6 (1970), pp. 43–61.

Baglione 1642
G. Baglione. *Le vite de' pittori, scultori, architetti ed intagliatori, dal pontificato di Gregorio XIII dal 1572, fino a' tempi di Papa Urbano VIII nel 1642.* Rome, 1642.

Baldinucci 1681–1728
Filippo Baldinucci. *Notizie de' professori del disegno.* Florence, 1681–1728.

Bank of Spain 1970
Una visita de la planta noble. Bank of Spain, Madrid, 1970.

Barcelona 1947
Barcelona, Sala Parés. *Exposición de floreros y bodegones de colecciones barcelonesas.* 1947.

Barnard Castle, The Bowes Museum, 1967 cat.
Barnard Castle, The Bowes Museum. *Four Centuries of Spanish Painting.* 1967. Catalogue by Eric Young.

Barnard Castle, The Bowes Museum, 1970 cat.
_____ . *Catalogue of Spanish and Italian Paintings.* 1970. Catalogue by Eric Young.

Barrio Moya 1979
José Luis Barrio Moya. "La colección de pinturas de don Francisco de Oviedo, secretario del Rey Felipe IV." *AEA*, vol. 82 (1979), pp. 163–71.

Baticle 1978
See Bordeaux 1978.

Bayón 1971
Damián Bayón. "Originalidad y significado de las primeras naturalezas muertas españolas." *Revista de Ideas Estéticas*, no. 109 (1970), pp. 15–41.

Bénézit 1911–23
E. Bénézit. *Dictionnaire critique et documentaire des peintres, sculpteurs, dessinateurs et graveurs.* Paris, 1911–23. New edition, 7 vols. Paris, 1966.

Bergamo, 1971
Bergamo, Galleria Lorenzelli. *La natura in posa.* 1971. Catalogue by Ingvar Bergström.

Bergamo 1981
_____ . *Vanitas.* 1981. Catalogue by Alberto Veca.

Bergström 1956
Ingvar Bergström. *Dutch Still-Life Painting.* New York, 1956.

Bergström 1962
_____ . "L'égalité suprême." *L'Oeil*, vol. 95 (1962), p. 30.

Bergström 1970
_____ . *Maestros españoles de bodegones y floreros del siglo XVII.* Madrid, 1970.

Bergström 1971
See Bergamo 1971.

Bergström 1973
_____ . "Flower-pieces of Radical Composition in European 16th and 17th Century Art." In *Album Amicorum J. G. Van Gelder.* The Hague, 1973, pp. 22–26.

Bergström 1978

_____ . "A Flowerpiece by Juan van der Hamen." *Apollo*, vol. 103 (1978), pp. 238–41.

Bergström 1979
_____ . "Juan Sánchez Cotán et l'art de la nature morte italienne en marqueterie Renaissance." In: *Estudios sobre literatura y arte, dedicados al profesor Emilio Orozco Díaz*. Granada, 1979, pp. 137–42.

Bergström et al. 1979
_____ , Guinn, Rosci, Faré and Gaya Nuño. *Stilleben*. Zurich, 1979.

Bermejo 1960
Elisa Bermejo. "Exposición: Grandes maestros españoles en el Museo Nacional de Estocolmo." *AEA*, nos. 129–32 (1960), pp. 328–30.

Beruete 1906
Aureliano de Beruete. *Velázquez*. London, 1906.

Birkmeyer 1958
Karl Martin Birkmeyer. "Realism and Realities in the Paintings of Velázquez." *GBA*, vol. 52 (1958), pp. 63–80.

Bordeaux 1955
Bordeaux, Galerie des Beaux-Arts. *L'age d'or espagnol*. 1955. Catalogue by Gilberte Martin-Méry.

Bordeaux 1978
_____ . *La nature morte de Brueghel à Soutine*. 1978. Catalogue by Gilberte Martin-Méry and Jeannine Baticle.

Bottineau 1975
Yves Bottineau. "Nouveaux regards sur la peinture espagnole du XVIᵉ et du XVIIᵉ siècle." *GBA*, vol. 25 (1975), pp. 312–22.

Braham 1965
Allan Braham. "A Second Dated Bodegón by Velázquez." *BM*, vol. 107 (1965), pp. 362–65.

Braham 1970
See London, National Gallery, 1970 cat.

Braham 1972
_____ . *Velázquez*. Themes and Painters in the National Gallery, no. 3. London, 1972.

Braham 1981
See London 1981.

Briganti 1954
Giuliano Briganti. "Michelangelo Cerquozzi pittore di nature morte." *Paragone*, vol. 4 (1954), pp. 47–52.

Brigstocke 1978
Hugh Brigstocke. *Italian and Spanish Paintings in National Gallery of Scotland*. Glasgow, 1978.

Brown 1973
Jonathan Brown. *Francisco de Zurbarán*. New York, 1973.

Brown 1982a
See Toledo, Ohio 1982.

Brown 1982b
Jonathan Brown, ed. *Figures of Thought: El Greco as Interpreter of History, Tradition and Ideas*. Washington, D.C., 1982.

Brown and Elliott 1980
_____ and J. H. Elliott. *A Palace for a King: The Buen Retiro and the Court of Philip IV*. New Haven, 1980.

Buchanan 1824
W. Buchanan. *Memoirs of Paintings, with Chronological History of the Importation of Pictures by Great Masters into England since the French Revolution*. 2 vols. London, 1824.

Bulletin of the Cleveland Museum of Art 1981
Sherman E. Lee. "The Year in Review for 1980." *The Bulletin of the Cleveland Museum of Art*, June 1981, pp. 164, 186, 211.

Bürger 1865
See Stirling-Maxwell 1865.

Burke 1984
Marcus B. Burke. "Private Collections of Italian Art in Seventeenth-Century Spain." Diss., 2 vols., New York University, 1984.

Calandre 1953
Luis Calandre. *El Palacio del Pardo*. Madrid, 1953.

Calvert 1908
A. F. Calvert. *Velázquez: An Account of His Life and Works*. London, 1908.

Camón Aznar 1964
José Camón Aznar. *Velázquez*. Madrid, 1964.

Camón Aznar 1978
_____ . *La pintura española del siglo XVII*. Summa Artis, vol. 25. Madrid, 1978.

Caracas 1981
Caracas, Museo de Bellas Artes. *400 años de pintura española*. 1981.

Carderera y Solano 1866
Valentín Carderera y Solano. *Notas a los discursos practicables del nobilísimo arte de la pintura por Jusepe Martínez*. Madrid, 1866.

Carducho 1633
Vicente Carducho. *Diálogos de la pintura*. Madrid, 1633. Francisco Calvo Serraller, ed. Madrid, 1979.

Cascales 1911
José Cascales y Muñoz. *Francisco de Zurbarán*. Madrid, 1911.

Caturla 1947
María Luisa Caturla. "Zurbarán en Llerena." *AEA*, vol. 20 (1947), pp. 265–84.

Caturla 1952
_____ . *Un pintor gallego en la corte de Felipe IV: Antonio Puga*. Santiago de Compostela, 1952.

Caturla 1953
_____ . *Zurbarán, estudio y catálogo de la exposición celebrada en Granada en junio de 1953*. Madrid, 1953.

Caturla 1957
_____ . "Juan de Zurbarán." *Boletín de la Real Academia de la Historia*. (1957), pp. 265–87.

Caturla 1960
_____ . "Cartas de pago de los doce cuadros de batallas para el Salón de Reinos del Buen Retiro." *AEA*, vol. 33 (1960), pp. 333–55.

Cavestany 1935
See Madrid 1935.

Cavestany 1936–40
Julio Cavestany. *Floreros y bodegones en la pintura española*. Madrid, 1936–40.

Cavestany 1942
_____ . "Tres bodegones firmados, inéditos." *AEA* (1942), pp. 97–102.

Cavestany 1943
_____ . "Blas de Ledesma, pintor de fruteros." *Arte Español*, vol. 14, (1943), pp. 16–18.

Ceán Bermúdez 1800
Juan Agustín Ceán Bermúdez. *Diccionario histórico de los más ilustres profesores de las bellas artes en España*. 6 vols. Madrid, 1800. Reprint, Madrid, 1965.

Cervera Vera 1967a
Luis Cervera Vera. *El conjunto palacial de la villa de Lerma*. Valencia, 1967.

Cervera Vera 1967b
_____ . *Bienes muebles en el Palacio Ducal de Lerma*. Valencia, 1967.

Cherry 1984
Peter Cherry. Review of the exhibition, *Pintura española de bodegones y floreros de 1600 a Goya*. BM, vol. 126 (1984), p. 60.

Chicago, The Art Institute, 1961 cat.
Chicago, The Art Institute of Chicago. *Paintings in The Art Institute of Chicago: A Catalogue of the Picture Collection*. 1961.

Clemen 1930
Paul Clemen. *Die Kunstdenkmäler der Stadt Köln*. Düsseldorf, 1930.

Collins-Baker 1926
See London, Hampton Court, 1926 cat.

Craig 1983
Kenneth M. Craig. "Pars Ergo Marthae Transit: Pieter Aertsen's 'Inverted' Paintings of Christ in the House of Martha and Mary." *Oud Holland*, vol. 97 (1983), pp. 25–39.

Crombie 1973
Theodore Crombie. "The Legacy of Vitoria: Spanish Paintings at Apsley House." *Apollo*, vol. 98 (1973), pp. 210–15.

Cruz y Bahamonde 1812
Nicolás de la Cruz y Bahamonde, Count of Maule. *Viaje de España, Francia e Italia*. 11 vols. Cadíz, 1812.

Cruzada Villaamil 1885
Gregorio Cruzada Villaamil. *Anales de la vida y de las obras de Diego de Silva Velázquez*. Madrid, 1885.

Cumberland 1787
Richard Cumberland. *An Accurate and Descriptive Catalogue of the Several Paintings in the King of Spain's Palace at Madrid: With Some Account of the Pictures in the Buen Retiro*. London, 1787.

Curtis 1883
Charles B. Curtis. *Velázquez and Murillo*. London, 1883.

Deleito y Piñuela 1954
José Deleito y Piñuela. *La mujer, la casa y la moda en la España del rey poeta*. Madrid, 1954.

Denny 1972
Don Denny. "Sánchez Cotán, 'Still Life with Carrots and Cardoon.'" *Pantheon*, vol. 30 (1972), pp. 48–53.

Díaz del Valle 1656–59
Lázaro Díaz del Valle. "Epílogo y nomenclatura de algunos artífices." In *Fuentes literarias para la historia del arte español* by Sánchez Cantón. Madrid, 1933, vol. 2, pp. 323–93.

Díaz Padrón et al. 1981
See Madrid 1981a

Díaz Pérez 1884
Nicolás Díaz Pérez. *Diccionario de extremeños ilustres*. 1884

Di Stefano 1954
Ada di Stefano. "Un boceto de Velázquez en Roma." *AEA*, vol. 27 (1954), pp. 257–59.

Eisler 1977
Colin Eisler. *Paintings from the Samuel H. Kress Collection: European Schools Excluding Italian*. London, 1977.

Enggass and Brown 1970
Robert Enggass and Jonathan Brown. *Sources and Documents in the History of Art: Italy and Spain, 1600–1750*. Englewood Cliffs, 1970.

Entrambasaguas 1941
Joaquín de Entrambasaguas. "Para la biografía de los Van der Hamen." *Arte Español*, vol. 12 (1941), pp. 1–4.

Evans 1959
Grose Evans. *Spanish Paintings in the National Gallery of Art*. Washington, D.C., 1959.

Fayard 1979
Janine Fayard. "Les membres du conseil de Castile a l'époque moderne." *Memoires et documents publiés par la Société de l'Ecole de Chartres* (1979), pp. 458–67.

Félibien 1666–85
André Félibien. *Entretiens sur les vies et sur les ouvrages des plus excellens peintres anciens et modernes*. Paris, 1725. Reprint, Farnborough, Hants, 1967.

Fernández Duro 1903
Cesáreo Fernández Duro. *El Último Almirante de Castilla Don Juan Tomás Enríquez de Cabrera*. Madrid, 1903.

Florence, Uffizi, 1979 cat.
Florence, Galleria degli Uffizi. *Catalogo generale*. Florence, 1979.

Florit 1906
José M. Florit. "Inventario de los cuadros y otros objetos de arte en la quinta real llamada 'La Ribera' en Valladolid." *BSEE*, vol. 14 (1906), pp. 153–60.

Gállego 1968
Julián Gállego. *Vision et symboles dans la peinture espagnole du siècle d'or*. Paris, 1968.

Gállego 1972
_____ . *Visión y símbolos en la pintura española del siglo de oro*. Madrid, 1972.

Gállego 1974
_____ . *Velázquez en Sevilla*. Seville, 1974.

Gállego and Gudiol 1977
_____ and José Gudiol. *Zurbarán 1598–1664*. London, 1977.

Gallego Burín 1946
Antonio Gallego Burín. *Guía de Granada*. Madrid, 1946.

García Chico 1940–46
Esteban García Chico. *Documentos para el estudio del arte en Castilla*. 3 vols. Valladolid, 1940–46.

Gaya Nuño 1948
Juan Antonio Gaya Nuño. *Zurbarán*. Barcelona, 1948.

Gaya Nuño 1953
_____ . "Después de Justi. Medio siglo de estudios velazquistas." Appendix to Spanish edition of *Velázquez y su siglo* by Carl Justi. Madrid, 1953.

Gaya Nuño 1955
_____ . *Historia y guía de los museos de España*, Madrid, 1955.

Gaya Nuño 1956
_____ . "En el centenario de Collantes: escenarios barrocos y paisajes disimulados." *Goya*, no. 10 (1956), pp. 222–27.

Gaya Nuño 1958
_____ . *La pintura española fuera de España*. Madrid, 1958.

Gaya Nuño 1964
_____ . *La pintura española en los museos provinciales*. Madrid, 1964.

Gazette des Beaux-Arts 1974
"Chronique des Arts." *Gazette des Beaux-Arts*, vol. 83 (1974), p. 9.

Gensel 1908
Walter Gensel. *Velázquez*. Klassiker der Kunst. Stuttgart, 1908.

Gerstenberg 1957
Kurt Gerstenberg. *Diego Velázquez*. Munich, 1957.

Ghilarov 1938
S. A. Ghilarov. "Juan de Zurbarán." *BM*, vol. 72 (1938), p. 190.

Gómez Menor 1966
José C. Gómez Menor. "Un dato sobre el pintor Cristóbal Ramírez." *Boletín de arte toledano*, no. 2 (1966), p. 89.

Gómez Moreno 1892
Manuel Gómez Moreno y Martínez. *Guía de Granada*. Granada, 1892.

Gómez Moreno 1919
_____ . "Los pintores Julio y Alejandro." *BSEE*, p. 20.

Granada 1953
See Caturla 1953.

Grassi 1942
Luigi Grassi. "Incontro con il giovane Velázquez." *L'Arte*, vol. 13 (1942), pp. 180–81.

Grate 1960
Pontus Grate. "Sánchez Cotán och bodegonmålerlets guldålder." *Spanske Mästare: En Konstbok från Nationalmuseum*. Stockholm, 1960.

Gregori 1973
Mina Gregori. "Notizie su Agostino Verrocchie e un ipotesi per Crescenzi." *Paragone*, vol. 24 (1973), pp. 36–56.

Gregori and Frati 1973
_____ and Tiziana Frati. *L'opera completa de Zurbarán*. Milan, 1973.

Gudiol 1941
See Toledo, Ohio 1941.

Gudiol 1974
José Gudiol Ricart. *Velázquez*. London, 1974.

Guidol 1977
_____ . "Natures mortes de Sánchez Cotán (1561–1627)." *Pantheon*, vol. 35 (1977), pp. 311–18.

Guinard 1960
Paul Guinard. *Zurbarán et les peintres espagnols de la vie monastique*. Paris, 1960.

Haraszti 1973
Marianna Haraszti-Takács. "Quelques problèmes des bodegones de Velázquez." *Bulletin du Musée Hongrois des Beaux-Arts*, vol. 41 (1973), pp. 21–48.

Haraszti 1983
_____ . *Spanish Genre Painting in the Seventeenth Century*. Budapest, 1983.

Harris 1935
Enriqueta Harris. "Obras españolas de pintores desconocidos." *Revista Española de Arte*, vol. 12 (1935), pp. 258–59.

Harris 1967a
_____ . "Escritura de contrato para realizar varias obras de pintura entre la Santa Hermandad Vieja de Toledo y el pintor Juan Bautista de Espinosa." *Boletín de arte toledano*, vol. 1, no. 3 (1967), pp. 154–55.

Harris 1967b
_____ . "Spanish Painting at the Bowes Museum." *BM*, vol. 109 (1967), pp. 483–84.

Harris 1970
_____ . "Cassiano dal Pozzo on Diego Velázquez." *BM*, vol. 112 (1970), pp. 364–73.

Harris 1974a
_____ . "Caravaggio e il naturalismo spagnolo." *Arte Illustrata*, no. 58 (1974), pp. 235–45.

Harris 1974b
_____ . "Las flores de El Labrador Juan Fernández." *AEA*, vol. 47 (1974), pp. 162–64.

Harris 1982
_____ . *Velázquez*. Oxford, 1982.

Harris and Troutman 1981
See Nottingham 1981.

Haug 1954
H. Haug. *Catalogue des natures mortes du Musée de Strasbourg*. Strasbourg, 1954.

Heinz 1960a
Günter Heinz. "Die Galerie Harrach." *Alte und Moderne Kunst*, no. 4 (1960), pp. 3–4.

Heinz 1960b
See Vienna, Harrach, 1960 cat.

Held 1979
See Münster / Baden-Baden 1979.

Hernández Díaz 1978
José Hernández Díaz. Review of *Blas de Ledesma y el bodegón español* by Torres Martín. *AEA*, vol. 51, no. 204 (1978), pp. 449–51.

Hernández Perera 1958
Jesús Hernández Perera. *La pintura española y el reloj*. Madrid, 1958.

Hibbard 1983
Howard Hibbard. *Caravaggio*. New York, 1983.

Indianapolis 1963
Indianapolis, John Herron Museum of Art. *El Greco to Goya*. 1963.

Iñiguez Almech 1952
Francisco Iñiguez Almech. *Casas reales y jardines de Felipe II*. Madrid, 1952.

Jordan 1965
William B. Jordan. "Juan van der Hamen y León: A Madrilenian Still-Life Painter." *Marsyas*, vol. 12 (1964–65), pp. 52–69.

Jordan 1967
_____ . "Juan van der Hamen y León." Diss., 2 vols., New York University, 1967.

Jordan 1974
_____ . *The Meadows Museum: A Visitor's Guide to the Collection*. Dallas, 1974.

Junquera 1966
Paulina Junquera. "El museo del Monasterio de la Encarnación." *Anales del Instituto de Estudios Madrileños*, vol. 1 (1966), pp. 385–90.

Justi 1889
Carl Justi. *Diego Velázquez and His Times*. London, 1889.

Justi 1933
_____ . *Diego Velázquez und sein Jahrhundert*. Zurich, 1933.

Kagan 1982
See Toledo, Ohio 1982.

Kagan 1984
Richard L. Kagan. "Pedro de Salazar de Mendoza as Collector, Scholar and Patron of El Greco." In *El Greco: Italy and Spain*. Jonathan Brown and J. M. Pita Andrade, eds. Washington, D.C., 1984, pp. 85–92.

Kahr 1976
Madlyn Millner Kahr. *Velázquez: The Art of Painting*. New York, 1976.

Kauffmann 1982
See London, Apsley House, 1982 cat.

Kehrer 1918
Hugo Kehrer. *Francisco de Zurbarán*. Munich, 1918.

Kemenov 1977
Vladimir S. Kemenov. *Velázquez in Soviet Museums*. Leningrad, 1977.

Kinkead 1974
Duncan T. Kinkead. "An Important Vanitas by Juan de Valdés Leal." In *Hortus Imaginum*. Robert Enggass and Marilyn Stokstad, eds. Lawrence, Kansas, 1974, pp. 155–63.

Kinkead 1976
_____ . *Juan de Valdés Leal (1622–1690): His Life and Work*. Diss., University of Michigan, 1976. Reprint, New York, 1978.

Kinkead 1980
_____ . "Tres bodegones de Diego Velázquez en una colección sevillana del siglo XVII." *AEA*, vol. 52 (1980), pp. 185–86.

Kirstel 1962
Harvey E. Kirstel. "The Still Lifes of Francisco de Palacios within the Development of the School of Madrid." M.A. thesis, New York University, 1962.

Klauner 1978
Friderike Klauner. *Die Gemäldegalerie des Kunsthistorischen Museums in Wien*. Salzburg, 1978.

Klemm 1979
See Münster / Baden-Baden 1979.

Kubler and Soria 1959
George Kubler and Martin Soria. *Art and Architecture in Spain and Portugal*. Baltimore, 1959.

Lafuente Ferrari 1935
Enrique Lafuente Ferrari. "La peinture de bodegones en Espagne." *GBA*, ser. 6, vol. 14 (1935), pp. 169–83.

Lafuente Ferrari 1943
_____ . *Velázquez*. London, 1943.

Lafuente Ferrari 1944
_____ . "Borrascas de la pintura." *AEA*, no. 62 (1944), pp. 91–92.

Lafuente Ferrari 1953
_____ . *Breve historia de la pintura española*. Second edition. Madrid, 1953.

Lafuente Ferrari and Friedlander 1935
_____ and Max J. Friedlander. "El realismo en la pintura del siglo XVII." *Historia del Arte Labor*, vol. 12 (1935).

Law 1898
See London, Hampton Court, 1898 cat.

Lehmann 1974
Jürgen M. Lehmann. Review of exhibition, "Caravaggio y el naturalismo español." *Kunstchronik*, (1974), pp. 348–50.

Lisbon, Museu Nacional d'Arte Antiga, 1966 cat.
Lisbon, Museu Nacional d'Arte Antiga. Catalogue. 1966.

Llordén 1959
P. Andrés Llordén. *Pintores y doradores malagueños*. Ávila, 1959.

von Loga 1914
Valerian von Loga. *Velázquez des meisters gemälde*. Stuttgart, 1914.

London 1920
London, The Royal Academy of Art. *Exhibition of Spanish Painting*. 1920.

London 1946
London, The Arts Council of Great Britain. *An Exhibition of Spanish Paintings*. 1946. Catalogue by Neil MacLaren.

London 1947
_____ . *An Exhibition of Spanish Paintings*. 1947. Catalogue by Neil MacLaren.

London 1976
London, Trafalgar Galleries. *In the Light of Caravaggio*. 1976.

London 1979
_____ . *Trafalgar Galleries at The Royal Academy II*. 1979. Entries on Spanish paintings by Eric Young.

London 1981
London, The National Gallery. *El Greco to Goya: The Taste for Spanish Paintings in Britain and Ireland*. 1981. Catalogue by Allan Braham.

London 1983
London, Trafalgar Galleries. *Trafalgar Galleries at The Royal Academy III*. 1983.

London / Paris 1976
London, The Royal Academy of Art. *The Golden Age of Spanish Painting*. 1976. Catalogue entries by Pérez Sánchez. French edition: Paris, Musée du Petit Palais, 1976.

London, Apsley House, 1982 cat.
London, Wellington Museum, Apsley House. *Catalogue of Paintings in the Wellington Museum*. 1982. Catalogue by C. M. Kauffmann.

London, Hampton Court, 1898 cat.
London, Hampton Court Palace. *The Royal Gallery of Hampton Court*. 1898. Catalogue by Ernest Law.

London, Hampton Court, 1926 cat.
_____ . *Catalogue of the Pictures at Hampton Court*. 1926. Catalogue by C. H. Collins-Baker.

London, National Gallery, 1952 cat.
London, National Gallery. *The Spanish School*. 1952. Catalogue by Neil MacLaren.

London, National Gallery, 1970 cat.
_____ . *The Spanish School*. 1970. Catalogue by Neil MacLaren, revised by Allan Braham.

Longhi 1950
Roberto Longhi. "Un momento importante nella storia della 'Natura Morta.'" *Paragone*, vol. 1, no. 1 (1950), pp. 34–39.

Longhi 1967
_____ . "Anche Ambrogio Figino sulla soglia della 'Natura Morta.'" *Paragone*, vol. 18, no. 209 (1967), pp. 18–22.

López Navio 1961
José López Navio. "Velázquez tasa los cuadros de su protector Juan de Fonseca." *AEA*, vol. 34 (1961), pp. 53–84.

López Navio 1962
_____ . "La gran colección de pinturas del Marqués de Leganés." *Analecta Calasanctiana*, no. 8 (1962), pp. 260–330.

López-Rey 1963a
José López-Rey. "The Variety of Spanish Painting." *Apollo*, (1963), pp. 511–14.

López-Rey 1963b
_____ . "Del Greco a Goya: Exposición de pintura española en los Estados Unidos." *Goya*, vol. 54 (1963), pp. 420–23.

López-Rey 1963c
_____ . *Velázquez*. London, 1963.

López-Rey 1964
See Newark 1964.

López-Rey 1968
_____ . *Velázquez' Work and World*. London, 1968.

López-Rey 1979
_____ . *Velázquez: The Artist as Maker*. Lausanne, 1979.

López Serrano 1965
Matilde López Serrano. "Nuevo museo de Madrid: El Monasterio de la Encarnación." *Reales Sitios*, vol. 2 (1965), pp. 12–30.

Lozoya 1965
El Marqués de Lozoya. "El Monasterio de la Encarnación: Un nuevo museo en Madrid." *Goya*, no. 66 (1965), pp. 376–83.

Lurie 1983
Ann Tzeutschler Lurie. "Un nuevo cuadro de Juan van der Hamen." *AEA*, vol. 56 (1983), pp. 115–22.

Lyversberg 1837
Sammlung der Gemälde J. Lyversberg im Köln. Köln, 1837.

MacLaren 1946
See London 1946.

MacLaren 1947
See London 1947.

MacLaren 1952
See London, National Gallery, 1952 cat.

MacLaren 1970
See London, National Gallery, 1970 cat.

Madrid 1905
Madrid, Museo Nacional de Pintura y Escultura. *Catálogo oficial ilustrado de la exposición de obras de Francisco de Zurbarán*. 1905. Catalogue by Salvador Viniegra.

Madrid 1926
Madrid, Sociedad Española de Amigos del Arte.

Exposición del antiguo Madrid. 1926.

Madrid 1935
Madrid, Sociedad Española de Amigos del Arte. *Floreros y bodegones en la pintura española*. 1935. Exhibition-guide by J. Cavestany.

Madrid 1960
Madrid, Casón del Buen Retiro. *Velázquez y lo velazqueño*. 1960.

Madrid 1964
Madrid, Casón del Buen Retiro. *Exposición Zurbarán en el III centenario de su muerte*. 1964.

Madrid 1966
Madrid, Casón del Buen Retiro. *1.ª exposición de anticuarios*. 1966.

Madrid 1967
Madrid, Club Urbis. *Maestros del tenebrismo español*. 1967. Catalogue by Ramón Torres Martín.

Madrid 1978
Madrid, Palacio de Bibliotecas y Museos. *Antonio de Pereda y la pintura madrileña de su tiempo*. 1978. Catalogue by Pérez Sánchez.

Madrid 1981a
Madrid, Palacio de Velázquez, Parque del Retiro. *El arte en la época de Calderón*. 1981. Catalogue by Matías Díaz Padrón et al.

Madrid 1981b
Madrid, Museo del Prado. *Pintura española de los siglos XVI al XVII en colecciones centroeuropeas*. 1981.

Madrid 1983
Madrid, Museo del Prado. *Pintura española de bodegones y floreros de 1600 a Goya*. 1983. Catalogue by Alfonso Pérez Sánchez.

Madrid, Prado, 1963 cat.
Madrid, Museo del Prado. *Catálogo de las pinturas*. 1963.

Málaga, Museo Provincial de Bellas Artes, 1933 cat.
Málaga, Museo Provincial de Bellas Artes. *Extracto del catálogo*. 1933. Catalogue by Rafael Murillo Carreras.

Malone, 1948
P. T. Malone. "A Spanish Still Life." *Chicago Art Institute Bulletin*, vol. 42, no. 2 (1948), p. 17.

Marías 1978
Fernando Marías. "Nuevos documentos de pintura toledana de la primera mitad del siglo XVII." *AEA*, vol. 51, no. 204 (1978), pp. 409–26.

Martí Monsó 1898–1901
José Martí Monsó. *Estudios histórico-artísticos relativos principalmente a Valladolid*. Valladolid, 1898–1901.

Martín González 1958
J. J. Martín González. "Sobre las relaciones entre Nardi, Carducho y Velázquez." *AEA*, vol. 31 (1958), p. 59.

Martin-Méry 1955
See Bordeaux 1955.

Martin-Méry 1978
See Bordeaux 1978.

Matsui 1980
Michiko Matsui. "El papel del toledano Sánchez Cotán: Reexamen de su ambiente artístico y el origen del naturalismo español." *Art History*, Tohoku University, no. 3 (1980), pp. 123–33.

Mayer 1910
August L. Mayer. "Francisco Barrera." *Monatshefte für Kunstwissenschaft*, vol. 3 (1910).

Mayer 1911
_____ . *Die Sevillaner Malerschule*. Leipzig, 1911.

Mayer 1915
_____ . "Uber einige Velázquez zu Unrecht zugeschriebene Stilleben und Genrebilder." *Monatshefte für Kunstwissenschaft*, vol. 8 (1915), pp. 124–27.

Mayer 1918–19
_____ . "Velázquez und die niederländischen Küchenstücke." *Kunstchronik und Kunstmarkt*, vol. 30 (1918–19), pp. 236–37.

Mayer 1922
_____ . *Geschichte der Spanischen Malerei*. Leipzig, 1922.

Mayer 1924
_____ . "Zurbarán's 'Education of the Virgin.'" *BM*, vol. 44 (1924), p. 212.

Mayer 1926
_____ . "A Still-Life by Zurbarán." *BM*, vol. 49 (1926), p. 55.

Mayer 1927a
_____ . "Still-Lifes by Zurbarán and Van der Hamen." *BM*, vol. 51 (1927), pp. 230ff.

Mayer 1927b
_____ . "Das original der 'Küchenmagd' von Velázquez." *Der Cicerone*, vol. 19 (1927), p. 562.

Mayer 1936
_____ . *Velázquez*. London, 1936.

Mayer 1947
_____ . *Historia de la pintura española*. Madrid, 1947.

Méndez Casal 1934
Antonio Méndez Casal. "El pintor Alejandro de Loarte." *Revista Española de Arte*, (1934), pp. 187–202.

Méndez Casal 1936
_____ . "La pintura antigua española en Escandinavia." *Revista Española de Arte*, (1936), pp. 2–11.

Mesonero Romanos 1899
Manuel Mesonero Romanos. *Velázquez fuera del Museo del Prado*. Madrid, 1899.

Mestre Fiol 1973
Bartolomé Mestre Fiol. "El espejo referencial en la pintura de Velázquez: Jesús en casa de Marta y María." *Traza y Baza*, vol. 2 (1973), pp. 15–36.

Mitchell 1973
Peter Mitchell. *European Flower Painters*. London, 1973.

Moffitt 1978
John F. Moffitt. "Image and Meaning in Velázquez's Water-Carrier of Seville." *Traza y Baza*, vol. 7 (1978), pp. 5–23.

Moffitt 1979
_____ . Review of *Velázquez: The Art of Painting* by Madlyn Kahr. *Art Journal*, vol. 38 (1979), pp. 213–16.

Moffitt 1980
_____ . "Observations on Symbolic Content in Two Early Bodegones by Diego Velázquez." *Boletín del Museo Instituto Camón Aznar*, vol. 1 (1980), pp. 82–95.

Moffitt 1984
_____ . "Terebat in mortario: Symbolism in Velázquez's Christ in the House of Martha and Mary." *Arte Cristiana*, vol. 72, (1984), pp. 13–24.

Montañés Fontela 1957
L. Montañes Fontela. "Bodegones y vanidades del barroco español." *Cuadernos de Relojería*, no. 13 (1957), p. 186ff.

Montoto 1920
Santiago Montoto. "Zurbarán: Nuevos documentos para ilustrar su biografía." *Arte Español*, vol. 5 (1920–21), pp. 400–04.

Munich 1984
Munich, Bayerische Staatsgemäldesammlungen Alte Pinakothek. *Italian Still Life Painting from Three Centuries: The Silvano Lodi Collection*. 1984. Catalogue by Luigi Salerno.

Munich / Vienna 1982
Munich, Haus der Kunst. *Von Greco bis Goya*. 1982.

Munich, Alte Pinakothek, 1963 cat.
Munich, Alte Pinakothek. *Bayerische Staatsgemäldesammlungen Alte Pinakothek Munchen; Spanische Meister*. 1963. Catalogue by Halldor Soehner.

Münster / Baden-Baden 1979
Münster, Westfälisches Landesmuseum für Kunst und Kulturgeschichte. *Stilleben in Europa*. Catalogue essays by Jutta Held, Christian Klemm et al. 1979.

Murrillo Carreras 1933
See Málaga, Museo Provincial de Bellas Artes, 1933 cat.

Naples 1964
Naples, Palazzo Reale. *La natura morta italiana*. 1964.

Newark 1964
Newark, New Jersey, The Newark Museum. *The Golden Age of Spanish Still Life Painting*. 1964. Catalogue essay by José López-Rey.

New York 1983
New York, National Academy of Design. *Italian Still Life Paintings from Three Centuries*. 1983. Catalogue by John T. Spike.

New York 1985
New York, The Metropolitan Museum of Art. *The Age of Caravaggio*. 1985. Catalogue by Mina Gregori et al.

Nottingham 1981
Nottingham University Gallery. *The Golden Age of Spanish Art*. 1981. Catalogue by Enriqueta Harris and Philip Troutman.

Oña Iribarren 1944
Gelasio Oña Iribarren. *165 firmas de pintores tomadas de cuadros de flores y bodegones*. Madrid, 1944.

Orihuela Maeso 1982
Mercedes Orihuela Maeso. "Dos obras inéditas de Van der Hamen depositadas en la Embajada de Buenos Aires." *Boletín del Museo del Prado*, vol. 3 (1982), pp. 11–14.

Orozco Díaz 1946
Emilio Orozco Díaz. "Sobre la época toledana de Sánchez Cotán." *Boletín de la Universidad de Granada*,

vol. 18 (1946), pp. 159–64.

Orozco Díaz 1947
———. *Temas del barroco*. Granada, 1947.

Orozco Díaz 1952a
———. "El pintor cartujo Sánchez Cotán y el realismo español." *Clavileño*, no. 16 (1952), pp. 18–28.

Orozco Díaz 1952b
———. "Un importante antecedente de los nocturnos de Georges de la Tour." *Arte Español*, vol. 19 (1952), pp. 69–74.

Orozco Díaz 1954a
———. "Realismo y religiosidad en la pintura de Sánchez Cotán." *Goya*, no. 1 (1954), pp. 19–29.

Orozco Díaz 1954b
———. "Sobre las citas de pintores españoles en los tratadistas de arte franceses." *Clavileño*, vol. 5, no. 25 (1954), pp. 28–31.

Orozco Díaz 1954c
———. *Las Vírgenes de Sánchez Cotán*. Granada, 1954.

Orozco Díaz 1965
———. "Cotán y Zurbarán." *Goya*, no. 64–65 (1965), pp. 224–31.

Orozco Díaz 1966a
———. "La partida de bautismo de Sánchez Cotán." *Cuadernos de arte y literatura de la facultad de la Universidad de Granada*, vol. 1 (1966), pp. 133–38.

Orozco Díaz 1966b
———. *Guía del Museo Provincial de Bellas Artes, Granada, Palacio de Carlos V*. Madrid, 1966.

Orozco Díaz 1967
———. "Algunos cuadros desconocidos de Sánchez Cotán." *Cuadernos de arte de la facultad de la Universidad de Granada*, vol. 2 (1967), pp. 111–20.

Orozco Díaz 1984
———. "Cotán y la tradición artística toledana." *Studies in the History of Art*, vol. 13 (1984), pp. 125–30.

Ortega y Gasset 1943
José Ortega y Gasset. *Velázquez*. Bern, 1943.

Pacheco 1649
Francisco Pacheco. *Arte de la pintura*. 2 vols. Seville, 1649. Francisco Sánchez Cantón, ed. Madrid, 1956.

Palomino 1715
Antonio Palomino de Castro y Velasco. *El museo pictórico y escala óptica*. Madrid, 1715. Madrid, 1947 ed.

Palomino 1724
———. *El Parnaso español pintoresco laureado*. Madrid, 1724. Madrid, 1947 ed.

Pantorba 1955
Bernardino de Pantorba. *La vida y la obra de Velázquez*. Madrid, 1955.

Paris 1952
Paris, Musée de l'Orangerie. *La nature morte de l'antiquité à nos jours*. 1952. Catalogue by Charles Sterling.

Paris 1963
Paris, Musée du Louvre. *Trésors de la peinture espagnole: Églises et musées de France*. 1963.

Paris, Louvre, 1981 cat.
Paris, Musée du Louvre. *Italie, Espagne, Allemagne, Grande-Bretagne et divers*. Catalogue sommaire illustré des peintures du Musée du Louvre, vol. 2. Paris, 1981. Spanish School sections by Jeannine Baticle, Geneviève Lacambre and Claudie Ressort.

Parro 1857
Sisto Ramón Parro. *Toledo en la mano*. 2 vols. Toledo, 1857.

Pau 1876
Catalogue abregé des Tableaux exposés dans les Salons de l'ancien Asile de Pau appartenant aux heritiers du feu Msr. l'Infant don Sebastian de Bourbon et Bragance. Pau, 1876.

Pemán 1958
César Pemán. "Juan de Zurbarán." *AEA*, vol. 31 (1958), pp. 193–211.

Pemán 1959
———. "Un nuevo Juan de Zurbarán." *AEA*, vol. 32 (1959), pp. 319–20.

Pérez de Montalván 1633
Juan Pérez de Montalván. "Índice de los ingenios de Madrid," Appended to *Para todos, exemplos morales, humanos y divinos*. Huesca, 1633.

Pérez Pastor 1910
Cristóbal Pérez Pastor. *Noticias y documentos relativos á la historia y literatura española*. Memorias de la Real Academia Española, vol. 10. Madrid, 1910.

Pérez Pastor 1914
———. *Noticias y documentos relativos a la historia y la literatura española*. Memorias de la Real Academia Española, vol. 11. Madrid, 1914.

Pérez Sánchez 1967
Alfonso E. Pérez Sánchez. "Sobre bodegones italianos, napolitanos especialmente." *AEA* (1967), pp. 311ff.

Pérez Sánchez 1968
———. "La crisis de la pintura española en torno a 1600." In *España en las crisis del arte europeo*. Madrid, 1968.

Pérez Sánchez 1972
———. Review of *Maestros españoles de bodegones y floreros* by I. Bergström. *AEA*, vol. 45, no. 177 (1972), pp. 74–76.

Pérez Sánchez 1973
See Seville 1973.

Pérez Sánchez 1974
———. "Caravaggio y los Caravaggistas en la pintura española." In *Caravaggio e i Caravaggeschi*. Rome, 1974, pp. 57–85.

Pérez Sánchez 1976
See London / Paris 1976.

Pérez Sánchez 1977
———. "Las colecciones de pintura del Conde de Monterrey (1653)." *Boletín de la Real Academia de la Historia*, vol. 174 (1977), pp. 417–59.

Pérez Sánchez 1978
See Madrid 1978.

Pérez Sánchez 1983
See Madrid 1983.

Philadelphia 1818
The Pennsylvania Academy of the Fine Arts. *Catalogue of the Paintings, Statues, Prints, etc. Exhibiting at The Pennsylvania Academy of the Fine Arts*. Philadelphia, 1818.

Philadelphia 1847
The Pennsylvania Academy of the Fine Arts. *List of Paintings, Busts, etc. Received at the Academy of the Fine Arts for the Exhibition of May 1847*. Philadelphia, 1847.

Picón 1899
Jacinto Octavio Picón. *Vida y obras de don Diego Velázquez*. Madrid, 1899.

Pita Andrade 1962
J. M. Pita Andrade. "Un informe de Francisco de Moro sobre el incendio del Palacio del Pardo." *AEA*, vol. 35 (1962), pp. 265–70.

Poland 1958
Reginald Poland. "Cherries, Iris and Lupin [sic] by Blas de Ledesma." Pamphlet published by the Atlanta Art Association, 1958.

Poleró 1857
Vicente Poleró. *Catálogo de la colección de cuadros del Excmo. Sr. Marqués de Santa Marca*. Madrid, 1857.

Poleró 1898
———. "Firmas de pintores españoles." *BSEE*, vol. 5 (1897/98), pp. 21–23.

Ponz 1776
Antonio Ponz. *Viaje de España*. 18 vols. Madrid, 1772–94. Reprint, Madrid, 1972.

Quilliet 1816
Frédéric Quilliet. *Dictionnaire des peintres espagnols*. Paris, 1816.

Revue du Louvre 1973
"Les récentes acquisitions des musées nationaux." *Revue du Louvre*, vol. 23, no. 2 (1973), p. 135.

Ritschl 1926
See Vienna, Harrach, 1926 cat.

Robinson 1906
Sir Charles Robinson. "The Bodegones of Early Works of Velázquez." *BM*, vol. 10 (1906), pp. 172–83.

Rome 1956
Rome, Palazzo delle Esposizioni. *Il Seicento Europeo*. 1956. Catalogue by L. Salerno and A. Marabottini.

Ruiz Alcón 1973
María Teresa Ruiz Alcón. "Dos cuadros del Patrimonio Nacional identificados: Son dos bodegones pintados por Juan van der Hamen en 1621 y 1623." *Reales Sitios*, no. 35 (1973), pp. 71–73.

Ruiz Alcón 1977
———. "Colecciones del Patrimonio Nacional. Pintura XXVII. J. Van der Hamen." *Reales Sitios*, no. 52 (1977), pp. 29–36.

Rutledge 1955
Anna Wells Rutledge. *The Pennsylvania Academy of Fine Arts 1807–1870*. Philadelphia, 1955.

Sainsbury 1859
W. N. Sainsbury. *Original Unpublished Papers Illustrative of the Life of Peter Paul Rubens*. London, 1859.

Salas 1773
Francisco Gregorio de Salas. *Elogios poéticos, dirigidos a varios héroes, y personas de distinguido mérito*. Madrid, 1773.

Salas 1935
Xavier de Salas Bosch. "Sobre dos bodegones de Francisco de Palacios." *AEA*, vol. 2 (1935), pp. 275–77.

Salas 1965
    _____ . "Inventario de las pinturas de la colección de don Valentín Carderera." *AEA*, nos. 151–52 (1965), pp. 205–07.
Salas 1966
    _____ . "Noticias de Granada reunidas por Ceán Bermúdez." *Cuadernos de arte y literatura de la facultad de la Universidad de Granada*, vol. 1 (1966), pp. 133–38, 198–201.
Salerno 1984
    See Munich 1984.
Saltillo 1933
    Marqués del Saltillo. *Mr. Frédéric Quilliet, comisario de Bellas Artes del gobierno intruso en Sevilla el año 1810.* Madrid, 1933.
Saltillo 1944
    _____ . "Un pintor desconocido del siglo XVII: Domingo Guerra Coronel." *Arte Español* (1944), pp. 43ff.
Saltillo 1947a
    _____ . "Efemérides artísticas madrileñas del siglo XVII." *Boletín de la Real Academia de la Historia*, vol. 120 (1947), I, pp. 605–85.
Saltillo 1947b
    _____ . "Prevenciones artísticas para acontecimientos regios en el Madrid sexcentista (1646–1680)." *Boletín de la Real Academia de la Historia*, vol. 120 (1947), II, pp. 365–93.
Saltillo 1951
    _____ . "Iniciadores de ferrocarriles y empresas industriales (1845–46)." *Boletín de la Real Academia de la Historia*, vol. 129 (1951), pp. 39–72.
Saltillo 1953
    _____ . "Artistas madrileños." *BSEE* (1953), pp. 137–243.
Sánchez Cantón 1915
    Francisco Javier Sánchez Cantón. "Los pintores de los Austrias." *BSEE* (1915), p. 61.
Sánchez Cantón 1916
    _____ . *Los pintores de cámara de los reyes de España.* Madrid, 1916.
Sánchez Cantón 1923–41
    _____ . *Fuentes literarias para la historia del arte español.* 5 vols. Madrid, 1923–41.
Sánchez Cantón 1947
    _____ . "Sobre la vida y las obras de Juan Pantoja de la Cruz." *AEA*, no. 78 (1947), pp. 95–120.
Sánchez Cantón 1955
    _____ . *La Colección Cambó.* Barcelona, 1955.
Sánchez Cantón 1956–59
    _____ . *Inventarios reales, bienes muebles que pertenecieron a Felipe II.* Madrid, 1956–59.
San Diego, The Fine Arts Gallery, 1947 cat.
    San Diego, The Fine Arts Gallery. *Catalogue of European Paintings 1300–1870.* 1947. Catalogue by J. G. Andrews.
San Diego, The Fine Arts Gallery, 1968 cat.
    San Diego, The Fine Arts Gallery. *Master Works from the Collection of The Fine Arts Gallery of San Diego.* 1968.
Santos Torroella 1962
    Rafael Santos Torroella. "Sánchez Cotán en la pintura de bodegones." *Enguera*, no. 14 (1962), pp. 62–63.
Seckel 1946
    Helmut P. G. Seckel. "Francisco de Zurbarán as a Painter of Still Life." *GBA*, vol. 30 (1946), pp. 277–300; Appendix, vol. 31 (1947), pp. 61–62.
Serrera (in press)
    Juan Miguel Serrera. "El viaje a Marruecos de Blas de Prado. Constatación documental." *Actas del Congreso de Historia del Arte celebrado en Zaragoza en 1982.* In press.
Seville 1970
    Seville, Reales Alcázares. *Exposición de las últimas adquisiciones del Museo de Bellas Artes de Sevilla.* 1970.
Seville 1973
    Seville, Reales Alcázares. *Caravaggio y el naturalismo español.* 1973. Catalogue by Pérez Sánchez.
Shestack 1973
    Alan Shestack. "Director's Report." *Yale University Art Gallery Bulletin*, vol. 34, no. 2 (1973), pp. 3, 54.
Soehner 1955
    Halldor Soehner. "Velázquez und Italien." *Zeitschrift für Kunstgeschichte*, vol. 18 (1955), pp. 1–39.
Soehner 1960
    _____ . "Die Herkunft der Bodegones de Velázquez." In *Varia velazqueña*, vol. 1, pp. 233–44.
Soehner 1963
    See Munich, Alte Pinakothek, 1963 cat.
Soria 1944a
    Martin S. Soria. "Zubarán, Right and Wrong." *Art in America*, vol. 32 (1944), pp. 126–41.
Soria 1944b
    _____ . "Francisco de Zurbarán: A Study of His Style." *GBA*, ser. 6, vol. 25 (1944), pp. 33–48, 153–74.
Soria 1945
    _____ . "Sánchez Cotán's 'Quince, Cabbage, Melon and Cucumber.'" *Art Quarterly*, (1945), pp. 225–30.
Soria 1949
    _____ . "An Unknown Early Painting by Velázquez." *BM*, vol. 91 (1949), pp. 123–28.
Soria 1955
    _____ . *The Paintings of Zurbarán.* London, 1955.
Soria 1959
    _____ . "Notas sobre algunos bodegones españoles del siglo XVII." *AEA*, vol. 32 (1959), pp. 273–80.
Soto de Rojas 1652
    Pedro Soto de Rojas. *Paraíso cerrado para muchos, jardines abiertos para pocos.* Granada, 1652.
von Spielberg 1910
    H. von Spielberg. "Francisco Barrera." *Velhagen und Klasings Monatshefte*, vol. 25 (1910), pp. 316–19.
Spike 1983
    See New York 1983.
Steinberg 1965
    Leo Steinberg. Review of *Velázquez: A Catalogue Raisonné of His Oeuvre* by José López-Rey. *Art Bulletin*, vol. 47 (1965), pp. 274–94.
Steinberg 1971
    _____ . "The Water Carrier of Velázquez." *Art News*, vol. 70 (1971), p. 54.
Steingräber 1974
    Erich Steingräber. Review of exhibition, "Caravaggio y el naturalismo español." *Pantheon*, vol. 32, no. 1 (1974), pp. 103–05.
Sterling 1952a
    See Paris 1952.
Sterling 1952b
    Charles Sterling. *La nature morte de l'antiquité à nos jours.* Paris, 1952.
Sterling 1959
    _____ . *Still Life Painting from Antiquity to the Present Time.* Paris, 1959.
Sterling 1981
    _____ . *Still Life Painting from Antiquity to the Twentieth Century.* New York, 1981.
Stirling-Maxwell 1848
    Sir William Stirling-Maxwell. *Annals of the Artists of Spain.* 4 vols. London, 1848.
Stirling-Maxwell 1865
    _____ . *Velázquez and His Works.* New edition, with catalogue by W. Bürger. Paris, 1865.
Stockholm 1959
    Stockholm, Nationalmuseum. *Stora Spanska Mästare.* 1959.
Suida and Shapley 1956
    William E. Suida and Fern Rusk Shapley. *Paintings and Sculpture from the Kress Collection.* Washington, D.C., 1956.
Sutton 1984
    Denys Sutton. "Bodegones y Floreros: An Exhibition of Spanish Still Life." *Apollo*, vol. 119 (1984), pp. 185–94.
Talley 1982–83
    M. Kirby Talley. "Small, Unusual, and Vulgar Things: Still-Life Painting in England 1635–1760." *The Walpole Society*, vol. 49 (1982–83), pp. 133–223.
Taylor 1979
    Réné Taylor. "Juan Bautista Crescencio y la arquitectura cortesana española." *Boletín de la Real Academia de Bellas Artes de San Fernando*, no. 48 (1979), pp. 63–126.
van Thiel et al. 1976
    See Amsterdam, Rijksmuseum, 1976 cat.
Thieme Becker 1907–50
    Ulrich Thieme and Felix Becker, eds. *Allgemeines Lexikon der bildenden Künstler von der Antike bis zur Gegenwart.* 37 vols. Leipzig, 1907–50.
Toledo, Ohio 1941
    Toledo, The Toledo Museum of Art. *Spanish Painting.* 1941. Catalogue by José Gudiol.
Toledo, Ohio 1982
    Toledo, The Toledo Museum of Art. *El Greco of Toledo.* 1982. Catalogue by Jonathan Brown, William B. Jordan, Richard L. Kagan and Alfonso E. Pérez Sánchez.
Toledo, Spain 1982
    Toledo, Hospital de Tavera and San Pedro Mártir. *El Toledo de El Greco.* 1982.
de Tolnay 1961
    Charles de Tolnay. "Las pinturas mitológicas de Velázquez." *AEA*, vol. 34 (1961), pp. 31–45.
Tormo 1916

Elías Tormo y Monzó. *Un gran pintor vallisoletano: Antonio de Pereda.* Valladolid, 1916. Reprinted in *Pintura, escultura y arquitectura en España: Estudios dispersos de Elías Tormo y Monzó.* Instituto Diego Velázquez. Madrid, 1949, pp. 247–336.

Tormo 1917
_____ . "La clausura de la Encarnación en Madrid." *BSEE,* (1917), pp. 131–34.

Torres Martín 1963
Ramón Torres Martín. *Zurbarán: el pintor gótico del siglo XVII.* Seville, 1963.

Torres Martín 1967
_____ . "Blas de Ledesma, un pintor recién descubierto." Diputación Provincial de Badajoz, 1967.

Torres Martín 1971
_____ . *La naturaleza muerta en la pintura española.* Barcelona, 1971.

Torres Martín 1974
_____ . "Blas de Ledesma y el origen del bodegonismo español." *Goya,* vol. 118 (1974), pp. 217–23.

Torres Martín 1976
_____ . *Los bodegones de Blas de Ledesma.* Catalogue. Seville, 1976.

Torres Martín 1978
_____ . *Blas de Ledesma y el bodegón español.* Madrid, 1978.

Trapier 1948
Elizabeth Du Gué Trapier. *Velázquez.* New York, 1948.

Trapier 1956
_____ . *Valdés Leal: Baroque Concept of Death and Suffering in His Paintings.* New York, 1956.

Trapier 1967
_____ . "Sir Arthur Hopton and the Interchange of Paintings between Spain and England in the Seventeenth Century." *Connoisseur,* vol. 164 (1967), pp. 239–43; vol. 165 (1967), pp. 60–73.

Triadó 1975
Joan-Ramón Triadó. "Juan van der Hamen, bodegonista." *Estudios Pro-Arte,* no. 1 (1975), pp. 31–76.

Urrea 1976
Jesús Urrea. "Antonio de Pereda nació en 1611." *AEA,* vol. 49 (1976), pp. 336–38.

Urrea 1979
_____ . "Notas a la exposición vallisoletana 'Antonio de Pereda.'" *Boletín Seminario de Estudios de Arte y Arqueología de la Universidad de Valladolid* (1979).

Valverde Madrid 1978
José Valverde Madrid. "En el centenario del pintor Antonio de Pereda." *Boletín de Bellas Artes Academia de Santa Isabel de Hungría, Sevilla.* 2ª época, no. 6 (1978).

Valdivieso 1972
Enrique Valdivieso González. "Un florero firmado por Juan Fernández 'El Labrador.'" *AEA,* vol. 45 (1972), pp. 323–24.

Valdivieso 1975
_____ . "Un bodegón inédito de Juan van der Hamen." *AEA,* vol. 48 (1975), pp. 402–03.

Valdivieso 1983

_____ . "Nuevos datos y obras de Pedro Camprobín." *Revista de Arte Sevillano,* no. 3 (1983), pp. 72–75.

Valdivieso and Serrera 1979
_____ and J. M. Serrera. *Catálogo de pinturas del Palacio Arzobispal de Sevilla.* Seville, 1979.

Valdivieso and Serrera 1982
_____ . *La época de Murillo: Antecedentes y consecuentes de su pintura.* Seville, 1982.

Valentiner 1950
W. R. Valentiner. "Meat, Saints and Poetry." *Art News,* vol. 49 (1950), pp. 34–37.

Valladolid 1979
Valladolid. *Exposición conmemorativa del III centenario de la muerte del pintor Antonio de Pereda (1611–1678).* 1979.

Van der Doort 1639
Abraham van der Doort. *A catalogue and description of King Charles the First's capital collection of pictures . . . now first published from the original manuscript in the Ashmolean Museum at Oxford.* London, 1757 ed.

Varia velazqueña 1960
Varia velazqueña; homenaje a Velázquez en el III centenario de su muerte, 1660–1960. 2 vols. Madrid, 1960.

Veca 1981
See Bergamo 1981.

Vienna, Harrach, 1926 cat.
Vienna, Gräflich Harrach'schen Gemälde-Galerie. Catalogue by H. Ritschl. 1926.

Vienna, Harrach, 1960 cat.
_____ . Catalogue by Günter Heinz. 1960.

Vienna, Kunsthistoriches Museum, 1973 cat.
Vienna, Kunsthistoriches Museum. Gemäldegalerie. *Verzeichnis der Gemälde.* 1973.

Vienna 1982
See Munich / Vienna 1982.

Viñaza 1889
El Conde de la Viñaza. *Adiciones al diccionario histórico de los más ilustres profesores de las Bellas Artes en España de D. Juan Agustín Ceán Bermúdez.* 4 vols. Madrid, 1889. Reprint, Madrid, 1972.

Viniegra 1905
See Madrid 1905.

Víu 1852
José Víu. *Antigüedades de Extremadura.* 1852.

Vliegenthart 1968
Adriaan Willem Vliegenthart. *Openbaar Kunstbezit,* vol. 12 (1968), nr. 25.

Volk 1980
Mary Crawford Volk. "New Light on a Seventeenth-Century Collector: The Marquis of Leganés." *Art Bulletin,* vol. 62 (1980), pp. 256–68.

Volpe 1973
Carlo Volpe. "Una proposta per Giovanni Battista Crescenzi." *Paragone,* vol. 24 (1973), pp. 25–36.

Volpe 1974
_____ . "I Caravaggeschi Francesi alla Mostra di Roma." *Paragone,* vol. 25, no. 287 (1974), pp. 29–44.

Vroom 1943
N. R. A. Vroom. "Fra Juan Sánchez Cotán, een spaansch Stillevenschilder." *Oud Holland,* vol. 60

(1943), pp. 151–57.

Wind (in press)
Barry Wind. *Velázquez's Bodegones: A Study in Seventeenth-Century Genre Painting.* In press.

Young 1967
See Barnard Castle, The Bowes Museum, 1967 cat.

Young 1970
See Barnard Castle, The Bowes Museum, 1970 cat.

Young 1976
Eric Young. "New Perspectives on Spanish Still-Life Painting of the Golden Age." *BM,* vol. 118 (1976), pp. 203–14.

Young 1979
See London 1979.

Zaragoza, Museo Provincial, 1929 cat.
Zaragoza, Museo Provincial de Bellas Artes. *Catálogo del Museo Provincial de Bellas Artes de Zaragoza.* 1929.

Zaragoza, Museo Provincial, 1964 cat.
Zaragoza, Museo Provincial de Bellas Artes. Catalogue by Antonio Beltrán Martínez. 1964.

EXHIBITIONS

Amsterdam 1970
  Amsterdam, Historich Museum. *Art Dealer and Collector.* 1970.
Atlanta 1958
  Atlanta, Atlanta Art Association. *Still Life Exhibition.* 1958.
Atlanta 1966
  Atlanta, High Museum of Art. *Masterpieces in the High Museum of Art.* 1966.
Baltimore 1961
  Baltimore, Baltimore Museum of Art. *Still Life: Fruits and Flowers.* March 7–April 4, 1961.
Barcelona 1947
  Barcelona, Sala Parés. *Exposición de floreros y bodegones de colecciones barcelonesas.* May 1947.
Barnard Castle, The Bowes Museum 1967
  Barnard Castle, The Bowes Museum. *Four Centuries of Spanish Painting.* 1967.
Bergamo 1971
  Bergamo, Galleria Lorenzelli. *La natura in posa.* 1971.
Bergamo 1981
  _____ . *Vanitas.* 1981.
Bordeaux 1955
  Bordeaux, Musée et Galerie des Beaux-Arts. *L'age d'or espagnol.* May 15–July 31, 1955.
Bordeaux 1978
  _____ . *La nature morte de Brueghel à Soutine.* May 5–September 1, 1978.
Brussels 1962
  Brussels. *7e Kunstbeurs.* March 1962.
Caracas 1967
  Caracas, Museo de Bellas Artes. *Grandes maestros, siglos XV, XVI, XVII y XVIII.* November 5–December 17, 1967.
Caracas 1981
  _____ . *400 años de pintura española.* February 19–April 19, 1981.
Cleveland 1981
  Cleveland, The Cleveland Museum of Art. *Year in Review for 1980.* 1981.
Granada 1953
  Granada, Palacio de Carlos V. *Zurbarán.* 1953.
Indianapolis/Providence 1963
  Indianapolis, John Herron Museum of Art. *El Greco to Goya.* February 10–March 24, 1963. Travelled to Providence, Museum of Art, Rhode Island School of Design. April 19–May 26, 1963.
London, 1888
  London, The Royal Academy of Art. *Old Masters.* 1888.
London 1895–96
  London, New Gallery. *Spanish Art.* 1895–96.
London 1901
  London, Guildhall. *Spanish Painters.* 1901.
London 1913–14
  London, Grafton Galleries. *Spanish Old Masters.* 1913–14.
London 1920
  London, The Royal Academy. *Exhibition of Spanish Painting.* 1920.
London 1946
  London, The Arts Council of Great Britain. *An Exhibition of Spanish Paintings.* 1946.

London 1947
  _____ . *An Exhibition of Spanish Paintings.* 1947.
London 1976
  London, Trafalgar Galleries. *In the Light of Caravaggio.* 1976.
London 1979
  _____ . *Trafalgar Galleries at The Royal Academy II.* 1979.
London 1981
  London, The National Gallery. *El Greco to Goya: The Taste for Spanish Paintings in Britain and Ireland.* September 16–November 29, 1981.
London 1983
  London, Trafalgar Galleries. *Trafalgar Galleries at The Royal Academy III.* 1983.
London/Paris 1976
  London, The Royal Academy of Art. *The Golden Age of Spanish Painting.* January 10–March 14, 1976. Travelled to Paris, Musée du Petit Palais. 1976.
London, Western Ontario 1955
  London, Canada, McIntosh Memorial Gallery, University of Western Ontario. *Spanish Masters.* February 19–March 19, 1955.
Los Angeles/San Diego 1960
  Los Angeles, University of California Art Galleries. *Spanish Masters.* January 24–March 6, 1960. Travelled to San Diego, Fine Arts Gallery. March 25–May 1, 1960.
Madrid 1905
  Madrid, Museo Nacional de Pintura y Escultura. *La exposición de obras de Francisco de Zurbarán.* 1905.
Madrid 1935
  Madrid, Sociedad Española de Amigos del Arte. *Floreros y bodegones en la pintura española.* May 1935.
Madrid 1960–61
  Madrid, Casón del Buen Retiro. *Velázquez y lo velazqueño.* December 10, 1960–February 23, 1961.
Madrid 1964–65
  _____ . *Exposición Zurbarán en el III centenario de su muerte.* November 1964–February 1965.
Madrid 1966
  _____ . *1a exposición de anticuarios.* June–July 1966.
Madrid 1967
  Madrid, Club Urbis. *Maestros del tenebrismo español.* February 2–March 15, 1967.
Madrid 1978–79
  Madrid, Palacio de Bibliotecas y Museos. *Antonio de Pereda y la pintura madrileña de su tiempo.* December 1978–January 1979.
Madrid 1981–82a
  Madrid, Palacio de Velázquez, Parque del Retiro. *El arte en la época de Calderón.* December 1981–January 1982.
Madrid 1981–82b
  Madrid, Museo del Prado. *Pintura española de los siglos XVI al XVII en colecciones centroeuropeas.* December 1981–January 1982.
Madrid 1983–84
  _____ . *Pintura española de bodegones y floreros de 1600 a Goya.* November 1983–January 1984.
Mänttä 1984

Mänttä, Finland, Gösta Serlachius Konstmuseum. *50-Års Jublileumsutställning.* June 2–December 31, 1984.
Milwaukee/Cincinnati 1956
  Milwaukee, Milwaukee Art Institute. *Still Life Exhibition of Early European Paintings.* 1956. Travelled to Cincinnati, Cincinnati Art Museum. 1956.
Munich 1984–85
  Munich, Bayerische Staatsgemäldesammlungen Alte Pinakothek. *Italian Still Life Painting from Three Centuries: The Silvano Lodi Collection.* November 27, 1984–February 22, 1985.
Munich/Vienna 1982
  Munich, Haus der Kunst. *Von Greco bis Goya.* February 28–April 25, 1982. Travelled to Vienna, Künstlerhaus. May 14–July 11, 1982.
Münster/Baden-Baden 1979–80
  Münster, Westfälisches Landesmuseum für Kunst und Kulturgeschichte. *Stilleben in Europa.* November 25, 1979–February 24, 1980. Travelled to Baden-Baden, Staatliche Kunsthalle. March 15–June 15, 1980.
Naples 1964
  Naples, Palazzo Reale. *La natura morta italiana.* October–November 1964.
Newark 1964–65
  Newark, The Newark Museum. *The Golden Age of Spanish Still Life Painting.* December 10, 1964–January 26, 1965.
New Haven 1972
  New Haven, Yale Art Gallery. *Summer Exhibition: 100 Acquisitions since 1971.* 1972.
New Orleans 1962–63
  New Orleans, Isaac Delgado Museum of Art. *Fêtes de la palette.* 1962–63.
New York 1955
  New York, E. and A. Silberman Galleries. *An Exhibition of Paintings for the Benefit of the Research Fund of Art and Archaeology, The Spanish Institute.* October 12–November 1, 1955.
New York 1983
  New York, National Academy of Design. *Italian Still Life Painting from Three Centuries.* February 2–March 13, 1983.
Nottingham 1981
  Nottingham, Nottingham University Gallery. *The Golden Age of Spanish Art.* 1981.
Paris 1952
  Paris, Musée de l'Orangerie. *La nature morte de l'antiquité à nos jours.* April–September 1952.
Paris 1963
  Paris, Musée du Louvre. *Trésors de la peinture espagnole: églises et musées de France.* January–April 1963.
Pau 1876
  Les Tableaux exposés dans les Salons de l'ancien Asile de Pau appartenant aux héritiers du feu Msr. l'Infant don Sebastian de Bourbon et Bragance. 1876.
Philadelphia 1818
  Philadelphia, The Pennsylvania Academy of the Fine Arts. *Exhibition of Paintings, Statues, Prints, etc.* 1818.
Philadelphia 1847
  _____ . *Exhibition of May 1847.*
Philadelphia 1963

INDEX